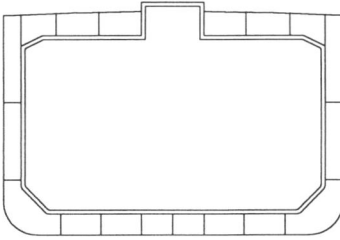

Bridgestone Maru
JAPAN

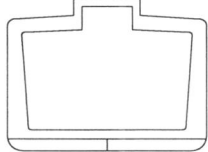

Esso Centro America
GERMANY

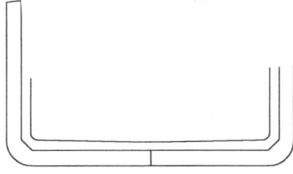

William R Grace
NETHERLANDS

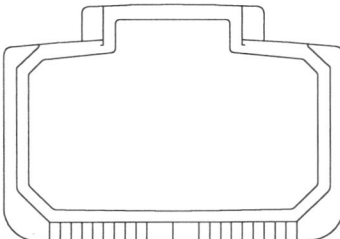

Paul Endacott
SWEDEN

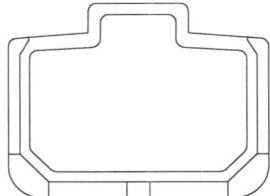

Havgas
NORWAY

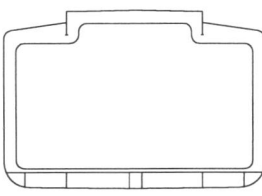

Clerk-Maxwell
UNITED KINGDOM

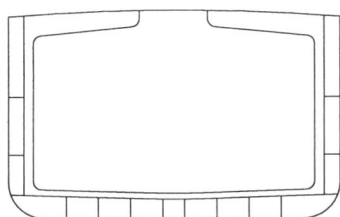

Kristian Birkeland
FRANCE

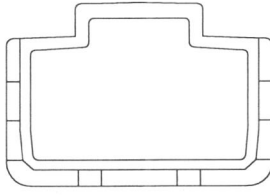

Alexander Hamilton
SPAIN

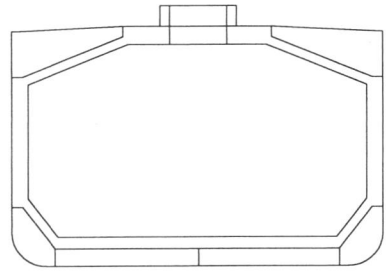

Jane Maersk
SOUTH KOREA

Cover photograph: Nanga Parbat

Fully Refrigerated LPG Carriers

FIRST EDITION

Syd Harris

First Edition 2004
© Syd Harris

ISBN 1 85609 266 6

WITHERBYS
PUBLISHING

All rights reserved

Published by
Witherby & Company Limited
32–36 Aylesbury Street, London EC1R 0ET
Tel No. 020 7251 5341   Fax No. 020 7251 1296
International Tel No. +44 20 7251 5341   Fax No. +44 20 7251 1296
E-mail: books@witherbys.co.uk   Website: www.witherbys.com

British Library Cataloguing in Publication Data

Fully Refrigerated LPG Carriers
    Harris, Syd
    1. Title

ISBN 1 85609 266 6

Dedication

This book is dedicated to all the shipyard designers, engineers, draughtsmen and craftsmen who built and remember with affection their first born, i.e. Hulls; 845 (Mitsubishi), 486 (Kockums), 676 (Verolme), 226 (IHI), 150 (Moss), 759 (Hawthorn Leslie), 1375 (CNIM), 235 (La Ciotat), 203 (Eskalduña), 1191 (HDW), 1366 (A G Weser), 111 (Cadiz), 1130 (Kawasaki) and 4633 (Bethlehem Steel).

Preface

The evolution of *Clerk-Maxwell* and the music of John, Paul, George and Ringo made for exciting times for me as a young naval architect at the Tyneside shipyard of Hawthorn Leslie during the swinging sixties. Looking back, it was a time of change and a time of progress in many areas, and the field of gas ship design was no exception. Designers and engineers from across the world independently began to address the challenge of transporting liquefied gases in bulk at close to atmospheric pressure. I had the good fortune to be a member of the small design team, in the appropriately named Prospect Work Department (PWD), who were preparing designs, estimates and bids to win the first United Kingdom order for a fully refrigerated Liquefied Petroleum Gas (LPG) carrier. Perfectly named for a gas carrier, the ship was delivered as *Clerk-Maxwell*. Great days, great memories.

I have always felt that this fascinating and challenging period of gas ship design should be recorded. The chapters of this book are loosely arranged around each ship building yard, as each made a significant contribution to making the safe sea transport of liquefied gases in bulk the success it is today. This progress was generally made independently by the yards and as such, each has a story in its own right. Many yards had unique and distinctive characteristics which were built into the designs and were often repeated and improved on later ships, as experience was gained and capacities increased.

The chapters begin with each yard's first FRLPGC and continue to the present day, or to the last built before a yard closed. To identify the various historical milestones and to settle any arguments and claims, I would refer you to Appendix 1 and the chronological listing. The scale of each of the drawings has been chosen to fit the pages and as such each drawing is small and each scale is large. The drawings are intended to give a general indication of the overall design of the ships and few details have been included. Rest assured that all of these ships have lifeboats, guard rails, winches, derricks, windows etc, but these items are not shown for the sake of clarity.

Throughout the text, the original name of each gas ship has been used to identify the design. The Appendices show listings of the original and current names as well as name changes for all of the ships featured.

My task has not been easy with so many of the shipyards experienced in building gas ships now long gone. This includes such famous names as Boelwerf SA, Temse, Belgium, Chantiers Navals de la Ciotat, La Ciotat, France, Constructions Navales & Industrielles de la Méditerranée (CNIM), La Seyne, France, Euskalduña, Bilbao, Spain, R & W Hawthorn Leslie & Company, Hebburn-upon-Tyne, United Kingdom and Kockums Mekaniska Verkstads AB, Malmö, Sweden. Key pioneering manufacturers of equipment and components have also vanished.

In addition, in my early stages of research I discovered, that the notorious fire in Le Havre in August 1997 did not just destroy files from French state owned bank Credit Lyonnais, which was being investigated in a financial scandal. Also stored in the same building, and also destroyed, were many drawings and documents covering the early days of the LPG vessels belonging to Gazocéan.

The high cost of storage, the takeover of smaller companies by disinterested major companies and the closure of key shipyards have meant that many useful documents have been shredded, destroyed or discarded as being of no value. There was also great secrecy in the early days of gas ship design and construction. I heard of one shipyard, where workers' personal notebooks used during the construction of the gas ships were destroyed when the ship was delivered.

Fortunately in my foraging for useful information I have been able to call on many friends and colleagues in the gas shipping business who have kept priceless material in their personal archives. I would particularly like to thank; LNG expert and author Roger Ffooks for his help and encouragement; Johannes Paulsen, retired naval architect with Marine Service GmbH., Hamburg, for his extensive knowledge and tuneful assistance when identifying useful old drawings; Kay Kitahara Anderson of the Japan Ship Centre in London for her attention to detail and friendly enthusiasm, Jan Flatseth for his warm welcome to Bergehus in Oslo, Pieter Van Robaeys of Viamar NV, Temse, William O. Gray of Gray Maritime Company for his archive material on Esso, Bruno Dabouis of Bureau Veritas in Paris for finding dusty boxes from the fifties and librarians David Bartle and Nuala Briody of the Institute of Marine Engineering in London.

Many others have provided invaluable information from photographs to launch programmes to contact details of the old guys. Thank you to everyone who responded to my visits, e-mails, faxes, letters and telephone calls. Sometimes I have received a solitary delivery date, a hint of an interesting feature or a shared moment of enthusiasm, which have all helped me in my task. For this much appreciated help my thanks go to; ex Gazocéan chief engineer Jean-Ives Coffineau, P&O historian and archivist Stephen Rabson, Gasper Villasenor, Marine Surveyor and Consultant, Tampico, Mexico, D2M's co-founder Jean-François Desplat, Hideo Uetani of Mitsui Engineering & Shipbuilding, Moss Maritime's Lars Sannes, Alex Pastahov of AVP Corp, Shin-ichi Nagahama of Hitachi Zosen, Kåre Tandstad of the Havinvest Group, ex *Havgas* captain Leif Emblemsvåg, *la Forge* captain Thierry le Hors, *Methania* captain Jean Ducarme, Bureau Veritas host Yves Le Gal, Roger Grahn of York Refrigeration, Sven Erik Elstad of Hamworthy KSE, Per-Christian Willoch Fett of Fernleys, Pat Craig, Marco Montorsi and Benedetto Agnello of EGM Genoa Srl Shipmanagement, David Cullen with Ebara, Tryggve Tobiesen of Det Norske Veritas, artist Georg Holm, Neil Currie of Thistle Associates, Dr. Christian Ostersehlte HDW historian, Wolfram Wöber of Marine Services GmbH, Hamburg, Ron Brand and Kees van Putten of the Maritiem Museum, Rotterdam, Nick Orfanidis of Marine Transport Lines, Giorgio Liubicich retired surveyor with ABS Genoa, Wojciech Kusinski of Centromor, Masanori Sumitani of Cryopump, Henry Smith of Carter Cryogenic Services, Elizabeth Kovach of Bethlehem Steel, Bill Haesloop of Nikkiso Cryo, Kiyotaka Takeda of NKK Corporation, Lucy Heller of Burckhardt Compression, Ranjit Singh of Qatar Shipping, Marian Bala of Klub Wysokogórski-Kraków, Haye Hinrichsen of Thyssen Nordseewerke GmbH, editor Dan Thisdell from The Motor Ship, Keith Hutchinson of Armstrong Technology, Soichi Kawai from Kawasaki Shipbuilding Corporation, Nobuhiko Hirakata, Tatsuo Koniwa and Kazuaki Yuasa from Mitsubishi Heavy Industries, Horio Hanaki of Universal Shipbuilding Corporation, Dorchester Maritime's Chris Clucas, SIGTTO's Roger Roue, Jim MacDonald of Lloyd's Register of Shipping, Class NK helpers Tetsushi Agata in London, Masaki Matsunaga in Tokyo and Yosei Usami in Ulsan, pioneers René Boudet, John Houlder and Jim Whyte, and ex Hawthorn Leslie PWD friends Dave Catchpole, Michael Corkhill, Robin Grey, Ken Lorrison, Gordon Mackey and Paul Winch.

I have tried to include in this publication as much of the information as I was able to find, but there will undoubtedly be some gaps. If you think I have missed an important piece of the jigsaw, please let me know, so that it can be used in any future editions. With regard to the photographs in the book every attempt has been made to identify the original source of the pictures and I acknowledge with thanks the permission given for their use.

Syd Harris
Spring 2004

Contents

Introduction

Sophisticated ships they may be, but the designs of gas carriers are based on the simple parameters of the ideal gas laws governing the relationships between pressure, temperature and volume. In addition, the materials in direct contact with the liquid cargo must be matched with the properties and characteristics of the cargo. The key to the designs is the atmospheric boiling temperature of the liquid cargo, i.e. ambient for fully pressurised LPG, -33°C for anhydrous ammonia, -48°C for propane, -104°C for ethylene and -163°C for LNG.

LPG carriers can be grouped into three categories; fully pressurised, pressurised and refrigerated and fully refrigerated. The first ships designed to carry LPG were fully pressurised and today there are many trading routes where butane and propane are still transported under pressure at ambient temperature. Almost half of the total number of LPG carriers in service are small fully pressurised ships, with most operating coastal or island services in Japanese, Korean, Chinese and Caribbean waters.

The most versatile LPG carriers are the small to medium sized pressurised and refrigerated vessels, with capacities up to 30,000 m³, capable of loading and discharging a wide range of LPG and chemical gases. Modern gas carriers of this type are generally designed for a minimum temperature of -48°C, a maximum pressure of 5 to 8 kg/cm² and a maximum specific gravity of 0.97 for vinyl chloride monomer (VCM).

The design of fully refrigerated LPG carriers has evolved over the years from other types of LPG carriers, to make the most efficient use of the on board cubic space available. The minimum design cargo temperature is generally -48°C for propane, with the maximum design pressure 0.25 kg/cm² greater than atmospheric pressure.

Fully refrigerated LPG carriers have been built with capacities up to 100,988 m³. Apart from the cargo temperature, the FRLPG carrier has more in common with the LNG carrier than the smaller pressurised LPG carriers. Much of the extensive research and development of the late nineteen fifties and early nineteen sixties on LNG carriers also resulted in the first designs for fully refrigerated LPG carriers.[1] There is a considerable overlap of the techniques which have gone into both the LNG carrier and the FRLPG carrier, each with many similar design features. Throughout the gas ship building industry the learning curve has been gradual with yards progressing to larger vessels after cutting their teeth on smaller ships. Most yards with fully refrigerated LPG ship building experience moved on into the LNG market. A notable few exceptions were; Harland and Wolff, Chantiers de France Dunkerque, Boelwerf and Daewoo, who took the reverse approach and started with LNG carrier construction.

When comparing the construction of the first purpose built fully refrigerated LPG carrier, *Bridgestone Maru*, delivered from MHI in 1961, with a typical modern FRLPG carrier, the differences in general appear to be slight rather than radical. This was not so in the decade following the delivery of *Bridgestone Maru*, particularly in Europe, where ships were delivered with a selection of tank shapes and insulation arrangements. A popular arrangement on many earlier ships included above deck trunks, allowing an increase in cargo capacity without any increase in hull dimensions. With experience, the shipbuilders found that the tanks with trunks were not so easy or cheap to construct, particularly with the increased number of the tanks' radius edges and part spherical shaped corners.

Naval architects quickly realised the advantages of constructing FRLPG carriers with a flush deck, with longitudinally framed sloping upper and lower wing ballast tanks at the sides and a transversely framed side hull forming the secondary barrier. This arrangement, which first appeared on 25,540 m³ *Antilla Cape*, delivered from A. G. Weser in 1968, has now become almost the standard configuration for the modern FRLPG carrier. In fact, every fully refrigerated LPG carrier delivered since 39,113 m³ *Kelvin*, from IHI in 1990, has had this arrangement for cargo tanks and water ballast tanks. The IHI ship had a slight variation on the standard arrangement by having the inner bottom extending to the side hull to form the lower water ballast tanks.

In 1976, the *Code for the Construction and Equipment of Ships Carrying Liquefied Gases in Bulk* was first published by the then Inter-Governmental Maritime Consultative Organization (IMCO). For the first time, the Code set out international standards for the safe carriage of liquefied gases in bulk.

From the time of the first meeting, in September 1971, of an *Ad Hoc* Working Group within IMCO [2], until the Code was published in 1976, shipbuilders were well aware that the pending Code would require changes to the design of FRLPG carriers. As it turned out, wholesale changes were not required to existing practices, rather a fine tuning of layouts and tank locations within the ship, with extra safety, fire-fighting and monitoring equipment added. The main areas requiring changes were; damaged stability requirements, cargo tank and ballast tank locations, segregation of the cargo area, openings in accommodation spaces and fire protection systems.

The new Code had more radical effects on the design of smaller LPG carriers than on larger LPG carriers. In the intervening years the Code has been reviewed, revised and amended. The 1993 edition published by the International Maritime Organization (IMO), became the *International Code for the Construction and Equipment of Ships Carrying Liquefied Gases in Bulk (IGC Code)*.

A number of the earlier built LNG carriers were designed to carry both LNG and LPG, as no long term LNG trading had yet been fixed at the time of ordering, and the spot LPG market offered opportunities for employment of the ships. Some of the smaller LNG/LPG carriers were also able to load ethylene. Few traded with LPG cargoes and detailed descriptions of these ships have not been included in this book, as the ships are primarily LNG carriers. One technical point, which may have contributed to the remarkable life span of these vessels is that the carriers were designed for a propane specific gravity of 0.58. This represents a considerable margin of safety when loading LNG with a specific gravity of 0.44.

The following is a brief summary of the combined LNG/LPG and LNG/LPG/ethylene carriers built:

- *Esso Brega* now *LNG Palmaria* – 41,000 m³ with Esso prismatic tanks built at Italcantieri, Genoa, Italy in 1969 and modified to carry LPG at Moss Rosenburg, Stavanger, in 1976.

- *Descartes* – 50,000 m³ with Technigaz membrane tanks built at l'Atlantique, St. Nazaire, France in 1971.

- *Euclides* – 4,000 m³ including ethylene, with Technigaz spherical tanks built at Le Havre in 1971 and broken up as *Chem Unity* in 2002.

- *Norman Lady* and *LNG Challenger* now *Hoegh Galleon* – 88,000 m³ with Moss spherical tanks built at Moss Rosenburg, Stavanger, Norway, in 1973 and 1974.

- *Venator* now *Havfru* and *Lucian* now *Century* – 29,000 m³ including ethylene, with Moss spherical tanks built at Moss Værft, Norway, in 1973 and 1975.

- *Ben Franklin* – 120,000 m³ with Technigaz membrane tanks built at La Ciotat, France, in 1975.

- *Kentown* now *Isabella* and *Montana* now *Annabella* – 35,400 m³ with Gaz Transport membrane tanks built at CNIM, La Seyne, France, in 1975.

- *Hilli*, *Gimi* and *Khannur* – 126,000 m³ with Moss spherical tanks built at Moss Rosenburg, Stavanger, Norway, between 1975 and 1977.

- *Mostefa Ben Boulaid* – 125,000 m³ with Gaz Transport membrane tanks built at La Ciotat, France, in 1976.

- *Sant Jordi* – 5,000 m³ including ethylene, with Sener spherical tanks built at Tomas Ruiz, Spain, in 1976 and sunk as *Red Star* on 6 January 1994.

- *Gastor* now *LNG Lagos* and *Nestor* now *LNG Port Harcourt* – 122,200 m³ with Gaz Transport membrane tanks built at l'Atlantique, St. Nazaire, France, in 1976 and 1977.

- *Golar Freeze* and *Hoegh Gandria* – 125,000 m³ with Moss spherical tanks built at HDW, Kiel, Germany, in 1977.

- *Mourad Didouche* and *Ramdane Abane* – 126,000 m³ with Gaz Transport membrane tanks built at l'Atlantique, St. Nazaire, France, in 1980 and 1981.

As an introduction to the construction and layout of a typical fully refrigerated LPG carrier, the next chapter will take you on board such a ship.

[1] Ffooks, Roger, *Gas Carriers*, Fairplay Publications, 1974.
[2] Ffooks, Roger, *Natural Gas by Sea,* Witherby & Co. Ltd., 1993.

List of Figures

List of Plates

The photographs with no original source indicated were taken by the Author.

Glossary

A G Weser Aktien-Gesellschaft Weser.

ACSM Ateliers et Chantiers de la Seine Maritime.

Aft At or towards the stern of a ship.

Airlock A small compartment with two steel doors providing access between a gas-dangerous space on the open deck and a gas-safe space.

American Bureau of Shipping International classification society with its headquarters in the United States of America.

AMPEC Arab Maritime Petroleum Transport Company.

Anhydrous ammonia An alkali gas (NH_3), which is toxic, colourless as a liquid, has a dense white vapour, is pungent and suffocating. Used as a fertiliser and in commercial cooling operations.

Anhydrous Without water.

Anti-collision key A steel and timber key fitted between the cargo tank and the ship's structure designed to withstand the forces acting on the cargo tank from a collision.

Anti-floatation chock A steel and timber chock fitted between the cargo tank and the ship's structure designed to prevent the cargo tank, when empty, from lifting in the event of the adjacent spaces being flooded.

Anti-rolling key A steel and timber key fitted between the cargo tanks and the ship's structure and designed to prevent movement of the tank from ship rolling.

Arctic D A niobium treated, control rolled, carbon manganese steel for low temperature applications.

ASTANO Astilleros y Talleres del Nordeste SA.

Azobé African hardwood used for cargo tank chocks, keys and supports. Also known as ekki or bongossi.

B&W Burmeister & Wain.

BIS Boelwerf Insulation System.

Booster pump A pump used when cargo discharge is through a cargo heater to pressurised shore storage.

Bottom support A steel and timber support fitted between the cargo tank and the ship's inner bottom and designed to support the weight of tank and also to allow the tank to contract and expand from cargo temperature variations and hull deflections.

Bow The forward end of a ship.

Breakwater An inclined steel structure on the weather deck to deflect overboard water coming over the bow of a ship.

Bulbous bow A bow with a bulb shape below the waterline which offers less resistance when a ship is underway.

Bulkhead A vertical partition which subdivides the interior of a ship into various compartments, tanks or spaces.

Bulwark Plating above the edge of the deck providing protection from adverse weather and green seas.

Bureau Veritas International classification society with its headquarters in France.

Butadiene A hydrocarbon gas (C_4H_6), which is flammable, colourless with a mild aromatic odour. Used in the manufacture of synthetic rubbers.

Butane A hydrocarbon gas (C_4H_{10}), which is flammable, colourless and odourless. Used as a fuel and in the manufacture of synthetic rubber.

Butylene A hydrocarbon gas (C_4H_8), which is flammable, colourless and virtually odourless. Used for many industrial synthetics.

C1 dry cargo ship Standard design of dry cargo ship mass produced in the United States during the Second World War.

Camber The rise of a deck across a ship which allows any rain or sea water on the deck to drain overboard.

Capacity co-efficient Gas ship design co-efficient based on the total cargo capacity in cubic metres divided by the product of the ship's length between perpendiculars, breadth and depth with the ship's dimensions in metres.

Carbon dioxide A carbonic acid gas (CO_2), which is colourless, odourless and slightly pungent with an acid taste. Used as a refrigerant gas and for fire extinguishing.

Cargo control room A room where all controls for monitoring the cargo handling systems are installed.

Cargo heater Shell and tube heat exchanger with sea water generally used in the tubes to heat the cargo which passes around the tubes.

Cargo manifold The valves, connections and pipework through which the cargo is loaded and discharged.

Cargo tank dome Structure at the top of a cargo tank providing access to the cargo tank and the point through which cargo pipework and other cargo handling systems can pass.

Cargo tank trunk The top of a cargo tank, generally for the full length of the cargo tank, which is arranged above the ship's main deck.

Cascade reliquefaction The process of using a refrigerant to condense cargo vapours from the cargo tank and return them to the cargo tank as a liquid.

Caustic soda A white deliquesacent solid that dissolves in water to give an alkaline solution. Used in the manufacture of soap, rayon and other chemicals.

Cc Capacity co-efficient.

CFC Chlorofluorocarbons.

CFD Chantiers de France Dunkerque.

Chlorine A halogen gas (Cl_2), which is toxic, has a green colour as a gas and amber as a liquid and has a pungent and irritating odour. Used in the manufacture of bleaching powder, disinfectants, hydrochloric acid and many organic compounds.

Classification society An independent authority which sets the standards to which a ship must be built and maintained.

CMB Compagnie Maritime Belge.

CMR Compagnie Marseillaise de Réparations.

CNC Chantiers Navals de la Ciotat.

CNIM Constructions Navales & Industrielles de la Méditerranée.

CO_2 Carbon dioxide.

Cofferdam A narrow space between two bulkheads on a ship.

Compressor A machine used to increase the pressure of a gas.

Condensation The change from vapour to liquid.

Condenser A shell and tube heat exchanger.

Cruiser stern A spoon-shaped stern.

Deep-well pump A pump which can be electrically or hydraulically driven by a motor on the cargo tank dome and has a long shaft to the pump assembly located at the bottom of the cargo tank.

Det Norske Veritas International classification society with its headquarters in Norway.

Direct cycle reliquefaction The process to compress and condense the cargo vapours and return them to the cargo tank as a liquid.

Double bottom A compartment at the bottom of a ship between the inner bottom and the shell plating.

DSME Daewoo Shipbuilding & Marine Engineering.

Eductor A pumping device used to remove liquid or gas from a space or tank.

Ekki African hardwood used for cargo tank chocks, keys and supports. Also known as azobé or bongossi.

ESD Emergency shutdown.

Ethyl chloride A halogenated hydrocarbon gas (C_2H_5Cl), which is toxic and flammable, is colourless with an ether-like pungent odour. Used as an industrial refrigerant, an intermediate in organic synthesis, a solvent and for the manufacture of tetraethyllead and ethylcellulose.

Ethylene A hydrocarbon gas (C_2H_4), which is flammable and colourless with a faintly sweet odour. Used in the manufacture of ethanol and many other organic chemicals. It polymerizes to polythene.

Ethylene oxide An oxirane gas (C_2H_4O), which is flammable, toxic and colourless with an ether-like odour. Used to make glycol, ethanolamines, etc.

FCM Forges et Chantiers de la Méditeeranée.

Forecastle deck A superstructure fitted at the forward end of a ship's upper deck.

Freeboard Distance from the waterline to the freeboard deck at side.

Freon 22 A refrigerant gas. Also known as R22. (See R22)

FSO Floating Storage & Offloading.

Gas-freeing Process of removing toxic or flammable vapours from a tank or enclosed space followed by the introduction of fresh air.

HDW Howaldswerke-Deutsche Werft.

ICI Imperial Chemical Industries.

IGC Code International Gas Carrier Code.

IHI Ishikawajima-Harima Heavy Industries.

IMCO Original Inter-Governmental Maritime Consultative Organization, now IMO.

IMO International Maritime Organization.

IMO type 2G ship Is a gas carrier intended to transport products which require significant preventive measures relating to the ship survival capability and the location of the cargo tanks.

IMO type A cargo tank Is an independent cargo tank with scantlings taking into account the internal pressure and based on recognised standards. A type A cargo tank requires a secondary barrier.

IMO type B cargo tank Is an independent cargo tank with scantlings based on comprehensive analysis taking into account all dynamic and static loads, plastic deformation, buckling, fatigue failure, crack propagation, wave loads and stress levels. A type B cargo tank requires a partial secondary barrier.

Inert gas A gas with insufficient oxygen to support combustion.

Inert gas plant On board plant producing inert gas for use in the cargo tanks and cargo piping systems for gas freeing.

Inner bottom Plating on a ship forming the top of the double bottom.

Integral tank A tank which is part of the structure of a ship. Generally used for cargo with a boiling point above -10°C.

Intrinsically safe A term relating to electric equipment and wiring installed in gas dangerous spaces ensuring that electrical or thermal energy levels present are too low to cause gas ignition.

Invar An alloy with 63.8% iron, 36% nickel and 0.2% carbon which has a very low coefficient of expansion.

KASMET Kawasaki Semi-Membrane Tank.

Lee Sheltered side of a ship.

Length b.p. The length of the ship between the aft and forward perpendiculars.

Length o.a. The length overall of a ship measured from the aft point of the stern to the forward point of the stem.

LGA Liquid-Gas Anlagen.

LGE Liquid Gas Equipment.

Liquefied Natural Gas A natural gas, principally methane, which has been liquefied for convenience of shipping.

Liquefied Petroleum Gas A mixture of petroleum gases, usually butane and propane which can be stored under pressure or refrigeration as a liquid. LPG can be a refinery by-product or may be produced from natural gas or associated gas.

Lloyd's Register of Shipping International classification society with its headquarters in the United Kingdom.

LNG Liquefied Natural Gas.

LPG Liquefied Petroleum Gas.

MAN Maschinenfabrik Augsburg-Nurnberg.

Manhole A hole cut in decks, bulkheads and tanks for access.

Membrane A thin liquid-tight metal lining used as part of some cargo tank containment systems.

Methanol A toxic and colourless liquid (CH_3OH) which was formerly obtained as wood naphtha and is now made by catalytic oxidation of methane. Used to denature methylated spirit, as a solvent and in the chemical industry.

MHI Mitsubishi Heavy Industries Ltd.

Mineral wool Hard man-made non-flammable thermal insulating material comprising natural minerals like basalt or diabase.

Naphtha A mixture of hydrocarbons in various proportions obtained from paraffin oil or coal tar.

Neoprene A synthetic rubber having a high tensile strength and better heat and ozone resistance than natural rubber.

NH$_3$ Anhydrous ammonia.

Nippon Kaiji Kyokai International classification society with its headquarters in Japan.

Nitrogen An odourless, colourless, chemically inactive gas. Used as an inert gas for gas freeing.

NKK Nippon Kokan K.K.

NORMED Chantiers du Nord et de la Méditerrenée.

N-TUF 33 Steel produced by Nippon Steel Corporation with low-temperature toughness and a minimum yield point of 33 kg/mm^2.

NYK Nippon Yusen Kaisha.

P&O Peninsular & Oriental Steam Navigation Company.

P&S Port and starboard.

PEMEX Petroleos Mexicanos.

Perlite A type of volcanic rock. When the ore particles are heated rapidly to around 1,000°C they melt and expand to between 4% and 40% of their original volume. The resulting white granules are lightweight with good thermal insulation properties.

Polyester A polymer used in the manufacture of synthetic resins, fibres and plastics.

Polyurethane foam A closed cell rigid foam made from polyol and isocyanate. Used as an insulating material for cargo tanks and pipework.

Poop deck A superstructure fitted at the aft end of a ship's upper deck.

Port Left hand side of a ship looking forward.

PPG Pittsburgh Plate Glass Company.

Pressure relief valve A safety valve fitted in the cargo handling system, designed to open and release cargo when the design pressure of the system has been reached.

Pressure vessel A cargo tank or storage tank with scantlings based on the internal pressure and based on pressure vessel design theory.

Primary barrier The boundary of a tank designed to contain cargo.

Prismatic cargo tank A cargo tank with a rectangular or trapezoidal cross-section.

Propane A hydrocarbon gas (C_4H_8), which is flammable, colourless and odourless. Used as a fuel.

Propylene A hydrocarbon gas (C_4H_6), which is flammable, colourless with a slight characteristic odour. Used to make polypropane, a flexible plastic material.

Purge To introduce vapour to the top or bottom of a space to replace the atmosphere in the space by displacement.

R12 A refrigerant gas dichlorodifluromethane (CCl_2F_2).

R22 A refrigerant gas monochlorodifluromethane ($CHClF_2$).

Reducer Tapered piping piece with flanged ends to enable connections to be made between pipework with a different diameter.

Registro Italiano Navale International classification society with its headquarters in Italy.

Reliquefaction The process of taking vapours from the cargo tank and by compression and refrigeration returning the product to the tank as a liquid.

Rolled section General term used for steel shipbuilding sections, such as flat bars, angle bars, channel bars or offset bulb plates, which have been produced in a steel mill by rolling.

Scantlings The term used to denote the dimensions of structural elements of a ship i.e. the thickness of plating or the cross-section of a stiffener.

Seam Fore and aft edge joint of shell or deck plating.

Secondary barrier Structure surrounding the cargo tank designed to retain any leaking cargo for up to fifteen days.

Semi-membrane A liquid-tight steel lining used as the primary barrier of some containment systems shaped like a cube with all the edges rounded. The semi-membrane has a greater thickness than a membrane.

Sheer strake The side shell plating next to the strength deck of a ship.

Sheer The longitudinal curve of the deck of a ship.

SIGTTO Society of International Gas Tanker and Terminal Operators.

Skeg A vertical fin at the stern of a ship to prevent erratic steering when underway.

Spool piece Piping piece with flanged ends to enable connections to be made between pipework with the same diameter.

Starboard Right hand side of a ship looking forward.

Stern Aft end of a ship.

Stringer A horizontal girder on a ship.

Stripping pump A pump, generally of smaller capacity than a cargo pump, which is used to remove cargo left in the tank which the cargo pump was unable to discharge.

Submerged electric cargo pump An electrically driven pump with the pump motor, impeller and bearing totally submerged at the bottom of a cargo tank.

Svenska Sjöfartsstyrelsen Swedish national shipping administration.

Swash bulkhead A longitudinal or transverse bulkhead fitted in a tank with large holes in the plating. The swash bulkhead decreases the movement of the surface of the liquid in a partially filled tank when the ship is rolling or pitching.

T1 tanker Standard design of oil tanker mass produced in the United States during the Second World War.

T2 tanker Standard design of oil tanker mass produced in the United States during the Second World War.

Transom stern A square-ended stern.

Tripping bracket Steel plates or flat bars fitted at frames, stiffeners or beams which keep the angle of the stiffener constant.

Trunk A vertical or inclined boxed-in space providing access between spaces or tanks.

Turn of the bilge The radiused part of the bottom shell plating at each side of a ship.

Ullage gauge An instrument used to measure the distance from the top of the tank to the surface of the cargo in order to determine the amount of cargo remaining in the tank.

USCG United States Coast Guard.

Vaporiser A heat exchanger used to change liquid gas into a vapour.

VCM Vinyl chloride monomer.

Vinyl chloride monomer A halogenated hydrocarbon gas (C_2H_3Cl), which is flammable, toxic and colourless with a sweet odour. Used to make polyvinylchloride (PVC).

Void space The enclosed space around a self-supporting cargo tank.

Web A built-up frame on a ship with a plate web and flanged or flat bar edge stiffening fitted to provide support for smaller regular frames, beams or stiffeners.

Bibliography

America Bureau of Shipping, *The Record,* New York, Annual publication.

Baroutakis, M. A., *LPG/LNG Handling,* Piraeus, 1971.

Boudet, René, avec la collaboration de Paulette Boudet, *La Joie D'Entreprendre,* June 1999.

Bruggen, van Coosje, *Frank O. Gehry: Guggenheim Museum Bilbao,* Guggenheim Museum Publications.

Bureau Veritas, *The Register of Ships,* Paris, Annual publication.

Clarke, J. F., *Power on Land & Sea, A History of R & W Hawthorn Leslie,* 1977.

Clarkson Research Studies, *The Liquid Gas Carrier Register,* London, Annual publication.

Corkhill, Michael, *LPG and Chemical Gas Carriers,* Fairplay Publications, London, 1975.

Det Norske Veritas, *Register of Ships,* Oslo, Annual publication.

Dougan, David, *The History of North East Shipbuilding,* George Allen & Unwin, 1968.

Drewry Shipping Consultants, *The Market for LPG Carriers in the 1980s,* Survey No. 26, London, 1982.

Drewry Shipping Consultants, *LPG Carriers: Market Prospects to 2000,* London, 1994.

Drewry Shipping Consultants, *Drewry Annual LPG Market Review and Forecast,* London, Annual publication.

Ffooks, Roger, *Gas Carriers,* Fairplay Publications, 1974.

Ffooks, Roger, *Natural Gas by Sea, The Development of a New Technology,* Second Edition, Witherby & Company Ltd., London, 1993.

Hautefeuille, Roland, with Clayton, Richard, *Gas Pioneers,* Paris, 1998.

International Chamber of Shipping (ICS), *Safety in Liquefied Gas Tankers,* Witherby & Company Ltd., London, 1980.

International Chamber of Shipping (ICS), *Tanker Safety Guide (Liquefied Gas),* Second Edition, Witherby & Company Ltd., London, 1996.

International Maritime Organization, *International Code for the Construction and Equipment of Ships Carrying Liquefied Gases in Bulk (IGC Code),* London, 1993.

Japan Ship Exporters' Association (JSEA), *Shipbuilding and Marine Engineering in Japan,* Tokyo, Bi-annual publication, 1970 - 1993.

Jean, Pierre, and Petit, Henri, *Quand le Méthane prend la mer,* Gaz Transport & Technigaz, 1998.

Kläy, Hans, R., *Schweizer Pioniere der Wirtschaft und Technik, Franz Burckhardt 1809-1882, August Burckhardt 1851-1919, ckdt Maschinenbauer aus Basel,* Verein für wirtschaftshistorische Studien, 1994.

Lloyd's Register of Shipping, *Register of Ships,* London, Annual publication.

McGuire, Graham, and White, Barry, *Liquefied Gas Handling Principles on Ships and in Terminals,* Third Edition, SIGTTO, Witherby & Company Ltd., London, 2000.

Nippon Kaiji Kyokai, *Register of Ships,* Tokyo, Annual publication.

Priestley, J. B., *English Journey,* Mandarin, 1994.

Rabson, Stephen, and O'Donoghue, Kevin, *P&O, A Fleet History,* World Ship Society, January 1989.

Society of International Gas Tanker and Terminal Operators (SIGTTO), *Glossary of Terms Used in Liquefied Gas Shipping,* Witherby & Company Ltd., London, 1998.

Society of International Gas Tanker and Terminal Operators (SIGTTO), *Liquefied Gas Carrier, Your Personal Safety Guide,* Witherby & Company Ltd., London, 2002.

Somner, Graeme, *George Gibson & Company,* World Ship Society, May 1988.

Vaudolon, Alain, *Liquefied Gases: Marine Transportation and Storage,* Witherby & Company Ltd., London, 2000.

Watson, Nigel, *The Bibby Line 1807-1990, Story of Wars, Booms and Slumps,* James & James 1990.

Woolcott, T. W. V., *Liquefied Petroleum Gas Tanker Practice,* Brown, Son & Ferguson Ltd., Glasgow, 1977.

About the Author

In 2003, Syd Harris reached the milestone of 25 years as an independent consultant with a world-wide involvement in the fascinating, challenging and richly rewarding gas shipping business. Back in the sixties his career began as young naval architect at the Tyneside shipyard of Hawthorn Leslie. He was a member of the small design team working on the historically significant 757 m³ *Abbas* and 11,750 m³ *Clerk-Maxwell*. *Abbas* was a converted general cargo vessel which became the first gas ship from a United Kingdom shipyard to be fitted with a reliquefaction plant and *Clerk-Maxwell* was the first purpose built fully refrigerated LPG carrier to be constructed in the United Kingdom.

He recalls leaving his home town Hebburn as a young man, for the bright lights of London, with good wishes from the company naval architect Julian Eckhard whose parting words questioned whether it would be possible to find more interesting and satisfying work than what he was leaving behind. In the capital, his gas ship career moved forward when he became a technical surveyor with the American Bureau of Shipping reviewing hull and containment systems for LPG and LNG carriers being built in Europe, for compliance with ABS Rules for Classification. Some of the newbuildings reviewed were; the largest fully refrigerated LPG carrier ever built, 101,988 m³ *Esso Westernport*, the 50,240 m³ LNG/LPG carrier *Descartes*, the 135,000 m³ *El Paso Paul Kayser* series of LNG carriers and other LPG and LNG carriers being built in France, Sweden and Poland during the seventies.

Syd formed his own consultancy firm in 1978 and his work has covered a wide range of gas ship projects which have taken him to many destinations across the globe. He has inspected LPG carriers in Alaska, Chile, Singapore, mainland China and across Europe and the Middle East, maintained extensive records of gas carrier designs and incidents, assessed potential collision damage, offered advice in legal disputes, presented technical papers at the Gastech conferences, as well as completing many design and feasibility studies. All of the drawings in the book have been produced by Syd in his own style and he also took many of the unique and previously unpublished photographs.

He is a Fellow of the Royal Institution of Naval Architects, a Chartered Engineer and a Member of the Society of Consulting Marine Engineers & Ship Surveyors. A further insight into his involvement in the world of gas shipping can be found on his web pages at www.fsharris.co.uk.

Chapter 1

Virtual On Board Inspections

In this chapter, you will be taken on two virtual on board inspections, where you will be able to share the unusual experience of exploring an LPG ship and observing the workings of these vessels at close range. In reality, the object of these surveys would be to assess the condition for further trading and to consider the life expectancy of the ship. The vessel will be an older, medium size, fully refrigerated LPG/anhydrous ammonia carrier with four cargo tanks, typical of many of the vessels described in this book and each inspection will take around one week. The first will be on a loaded passage with a propane cargo and the second in dry dock with the ship in a gas free condition.

FIRST INSPECTION ON LOADED PASSAGE

The loaded ship is trading in the warm waters of the Arabian Gulf, from where large quantities of LPG are transported to Europe or the Far East every day. The vessel is waiting at the roads, so a motor launch is taken from the port to board the ship. The LPG carrier can generally by spotted easily amongst the other ships at the roads; the large deck vents, deck storage tanks and reliquefaction house are distinguishing features. A circuit around the vessel in the launch is always a good chance to take photographs and get a first impression of the general condition of the ship.

Boarding the vessel from the small launch can be a precarious operation which needs to be undertaken with care and patience, especially if there is a heavy swell running. The launch draws up along the lee side of the ship, and bags are hauled on board by a helpful crew member. Access to the main deck is by a rope ladder hanging below the hinged aluminium accommodation ladder. Timing is crucial, as the step on to the rope ladder is best taken when the launch is relatively still on the crest of a wave. Many mariners believe that boarding, and particularly leaving the vessel in this way is the most dangerous moment of all during the time on board and around the gas ship.

Once on board, introductions are made to the captain, and the nature and time scale of the inspection is explained and discussed, along with any relevant shipboard safety procedures. It should always be remembered that the propane cargo is flammable. Because of this, personal mobile telephones, which are not intrinsically safe, should not be used forward of the living quarters and smoking is only permitted in designated areas. Much of the inspection on passage will be in the ballast tanks, some of which may require to be pumped out. The water ballast tanks also need to be ventilated and made safe for entry. A suitable order of inspecting the tanks can be planned, taking into account the ship's longitudinal strength, trim and stability, and the availability of officers and crew.

FIRST IMPRESSIONS

With most of the gas handling equipment arranged on the main deck, forward of the accommodation, the first impression can be overwhelming, as at first there appears to be no obvious order to the complex arrangement of pipework, vents and deck houses in view. The way to make any sense of the purpose and location of all this equipment is to consider each area separately.

At least LPG carriers are relatively clean ships when compared, for example, to oil tankers, chemical carriers, bulk carriers or general cargo ships. On these vessels, the cargo itself can make working conditions difficult and cause problems with inspections.

The inspection begins at the bow of the ship and then moving aft takes in the forward most cargo dome and the deck storage tanks. Aft of the deck storage tanks on both sides of the ship there are cargo manifolds through which the cargo is loaded or discharged. While moving aft each of the four cargo domes can be inspected in turn. On the main deck between cargo tank Nos. 2 and 3 there is a deckhouse for the reliquefaction plants and cargo pumps motors with a cargo control room over. Throughout the whole cargo area, the above deck pipework and equipment can be observed for cargo handling, gas freeing, fire protection and the ship's general services.

At the bow of the ship, the first thing to notice is that there is no forecastle fitted. This is because the cargo carried is comparatively light, so the freeboard is considered high enough to eliminate the need for a forecastle. Instead, a bulwark at the forward main deck protects the conventional anchor handling and mooring equipment. A centreline breakwater just forward of No. 1 cargo dome provides additional protection of deck equipment from green seas.

CARGO TANK DOMES

Aft from the bow on the main deck is the forward cargo tank dome, which can be seen clearly as there is less pipework here than around the other three domes. Each cargo tank dome has the same equipment for cargo handling and provides the only access into the below deck cargo tanks. The cargo dome is positioned at approximately the mid-length of the cargo tank. The dome is not rigidly fixed to the main deck, as vertical and horizontal movement must be allowed for, due to the thermal expansion or contraction of the cargo tanks. This is achieved with the use of a flexible weather tight seal placed around the dome. A pair of large pressure relief valves are positioned either side of the centreline and will lift and release cargo vapours to the vents in the unlikely event of a build-up of pressure in the cargo tanks which exceeds design limits. Cargo liquid, condensate and vapour piping pass through the cargo dome. Liquid and vapour flow valves can be opened or closed either manually on the dome, or by remote control from the control room.

Plate 1-1   Cargo tank domes

Plate 1-2   Iced-up condensate line on a cargo tank dome

The most important design feature of the cargo handling systems which should always be borne in mind, is that under normal operating conditions, the cargo system is totally enclosed. On this ship it is not possible to see any liquid cargo. The whole system is held at just above atmospheric pressure and the ship is designed to transport LPG or ammonia without any cargo loss from vaporisation.

Throughout the system, most of the cargo in the cargo tanks will be carried as a liquid but due to ambient sea and air temperatures, ship movements and heat loss, the liquid cargo will invariably warm up and partially vaporise. This is dealt with on board by taking the vapours from the cargo tanks and pipework and, by compression and refrigeration, the cargo is returned to the tanks as liquid. For this reason every part of the cargo handling system must be monitored continuously.

Another control on the dome opens and closes the valve in the cargo tanks liquid tight centreline bulkhead. This centreline valve is open during loading and discharge and closed when on passage. The temperature and pressure of the cargo is monitored at the cargo dome with thermometers and gauges. Sampling points are provided for monitoring the progress of purging and gas-freeing and for cargo surveyors. Ullage measuring equipment with local and remote readings is fitted at the tank dome. Also on the dome will be a fusible element which is designed, in the event of fire, to melt at temperatures between 98°C and 104°C and automatically bring into action the emergency shut-down (ESD) system. On all sides above the tank dome, there is a framework of small bore pipes with nozzles to spray water onto the dome in case of fire.

Plate 1-3   Ullage gauge

Plate 1-4   Fusible element

Plate 1-5   Water spray system under test at the cargo tank dome

Similar water spray protection is provided at each cargo dome, at the cargo manifolds, at the deck storage tanks, at the aft accommodation front and around the perimeter of any deck houses normally manned, i.e. cargo control, reliquefaction plant and cargo pump motor rooms.

Plate 1-6   Water spray system on the accommodation front

Other types of fire protection equipment are provided on the open deck within the cargo area. The fire water main, fire hydrants and hoses are arranged to reach any part of the deck in the cargo area and the above deck gas handling equipment. In addition, a dry chemical powder system is also fitted, to cover a similar area as the fire main, and clearly marked hose storage lockers are located throughout the cargo area.

This ship is designed for the carriage of both LPG and ammonia cargoes and deep-well pumps are used for cargo discharge. Two deep-well pumps are located on a small dome on the main deck at the aft end of each cargo tank. For ships with submerged electric cargo pumps, cable junction boxes and piping connections would be fitted on the tank domes.

Plate 1-7   Deep-well pumps

DECK STORAGE TANKS

On the open deck above the forward cargo tanks there are two cylindrical pressurised storage tanks of about 150 m³ capacity for LPG or anhydrous ammonia. These deck tanks are used when changing the type of cargo carried. The advantage of having these deck tanks is that with LPG or anhydrous ammonia stored on board, the ship's cargo tanks can be prepared at sea for the next voyage, which reduces the time spent at the loading port. The deck tanks are not insulated and are designed for a maximum pressure of 18 kg/cm² at ambient temperature. The deck tanks and associated equipment are designed in a similar way to cargo tanks and require saddle supports, pressure relief valves, loading and discharge lines, a water spray system, thermometers and pressure gauges.

Rising above the main deck are the tall centreline cargo vents, which have large diameter pipe work connections at the base, from the inert gas and ventilation lines and relief valves. The open ends of the vents are located well above the main deck in order to expel, for example, inert gas, air, or in an emergency, cargo vapours, safely and effectively, clear of the deck and accommodation spaces. The distinctive wider upper ends of the vents are arranged to discharge the vapours upwards, and at the same time, a cover prevents water, rain or snow from entering the vent system.

CARGO MANIFOLDS

Aft of the deck storage tanks there are the cargo crossover pipework and the manifolds, through which the cargo is loaded and discharged. In order to be able to load and discharge from either side of the ship, identical manifolds are located at each side of the vessel, close to amidships. Each manifold has two liquid lines and two vapour lines. On passage, blank plates are fitted over the ends of the manifolds. Steel trays are fitted under the manifolds to protect the ship's deck from possible leakage of liquid cargo when ship/shore connections are being disconnected.

On this ship, the cargo handling system can be segregated to carry two different compatible cargoes simultaneously, where cargo tanks Nos. 1 and 4 can be used for one product and cargo tanks Nos. 2 and 3 can be used for the other. The separation is achieved by the removal of built-in bolted spool pieces in the pipework between the pairs of tanks or by the use of hinged piping blanks.

Emergency Shutdown (ESD) valves are arranged at the cargo manifolds. The valves can be closed in an emergency from stop buttons or levers in the cargo control room, at the accommodation house front, at the fore and aft walkway and at the compressor rooms. The valves can also be closed manually at the manifolds. They are designed with pressure surge in mind not to close suddenly, but to fully close smoothly within 30 seconds of being activated. When the emergency stop buttons are operated, the cargo pumps and cargo compressors are also automatically shut down. This emergency system also shuts down automatically if electric control power is lost, if a fire at a cargo dome melts the fusible elements or if liquid levels in the cargo tanks reach the high level alarms.

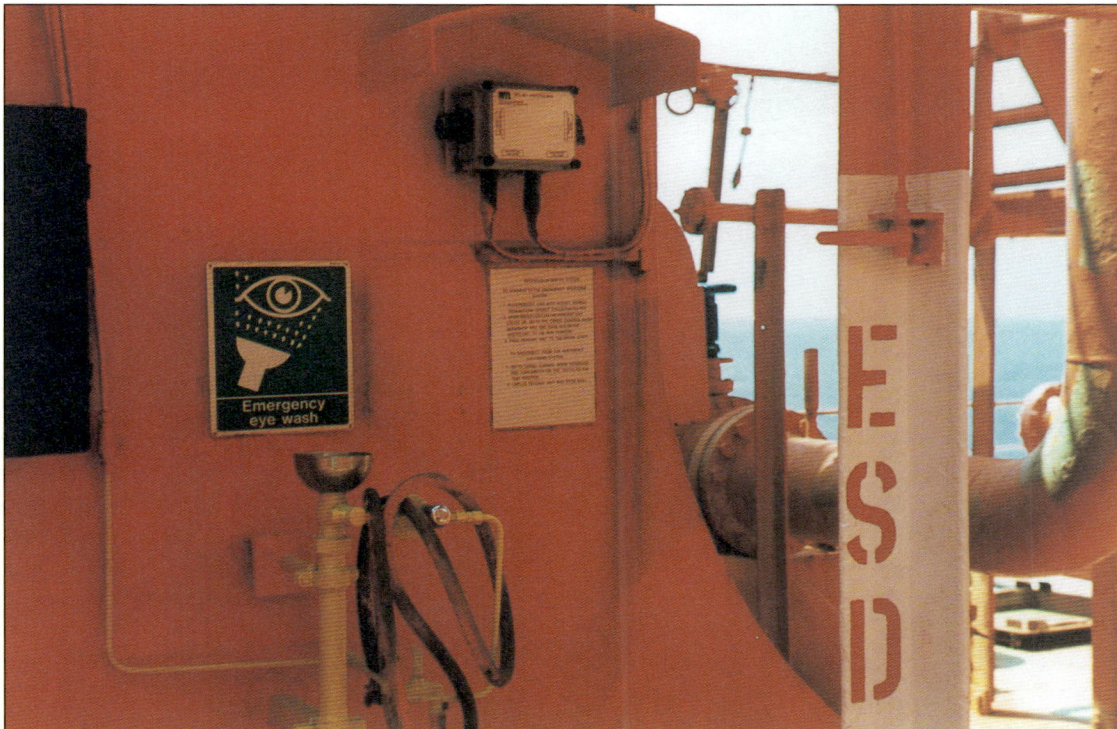

Plate 1-8   Eye wash, ship shore link box and ESD stop lever

Near the manifolds on the main deck there are two horizontally mounted centrifugal booster pumps, which can be operated in series with the main cargo pumps, if an increased discharge head is required for the terminal storage tanks. The electric motors for the booster pumps are intrinsically safe and flame and weather proof. The cylindrically shaped unit next to the booster pumps is a shell and tube heat exchanger which is used for cargo heating. Sea-water is pumped through the unit's tubes, and cargo flows around the tubes within the shell. The heat exchanger is used when shore storage tank design temperatures are higher than the temperature of the refrigerated cargo on board the ship.

CARGO CONTROL ROOM

Aft of the manifolds on the main deck, and located above No. 3 cargo tank there is a deckhouse for the reliquefaction plants room and a cargo control room. Entry to the air conditioned cargo control room above the reliquefaction plants offers cool relief from the daytime heat on the open deck. Windows in the control room give a good view of the cargo area and manifolds.

On this ship the cargo control room is in the cargo area. On other fully refrigerated LPG carriers, the owners or shipbuilders may choose to locate the cargo control room in the forward part of the aft accommodation spaces, at either the main deck level or under the bridge deck. There are pros and cons for all locations concerning safety, practicality and cost. Cargo engineers, designers, chief mates, crew and shipbuilders will all have their preferences, and a consensus is hardly ever reached as to the perfect location.

A large central console dominates the cargo control room. The console incorporates schematic diagrams and remote controls for both the cargo handling systems valves and pumps, and the water ballast tanks valves and pumps. Ullage readings from each of the cargo tanks are displayed, as are pressure and temperature readings, taken from locations throughout the cargo systems. A comprehensive alarm panel covers the operational functions of the cargo handling systems, and alerts officers or crew if any design limits are exceeded. Alarms are triggered, for example, if maximum and minimum operating pressures and temperatures are reached, if high liquid levels are indicated in the cargo tanks, if low liquid levels are indicated at the cargo pumps, if equipment malfunctions in a reliquefaction plant or if a gas leak is detected. Bright visual alarms and powerful audible alarms are set off by the monitoring systems.

Plate 1-9   Central console in the
                   cargo control room

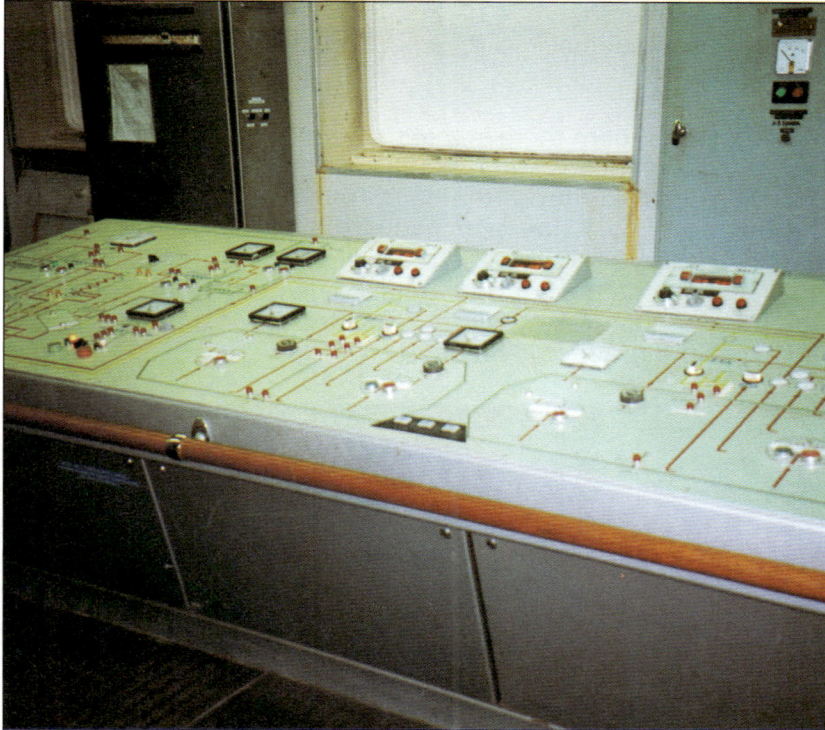

Plate 1-10 Schematic diagrams and remote controls

CARGO LOG BOOKS

The condition of the cargo is monitored and recorded in various cargo log books. A daily log records events as they happen and typical timed entries include; completed cargo survey, hoses connected, commenced discharge, commenced receiving vapour, stop ballast forepeak tank, completed discharge and hoses disconnected.

During cargo loading and discharge, hourly readings are taken to monitor the cargo tanks and manifolds. Cargo liquid and vapour temperatures and pressures are recorded for each cargo tank. Temperatures and pressures are recorded at each manifold. A glance at the resulting hourly tabulation can identify whether or not the loading or discharge is progressing satisfactorily. Potential problems can be pinpointed if temperatures are not constant or if pressures are rising or falling uncharacteristically.

During cargo discharge, hourly records are kept of the performance of the cargo pumps, with the pressures and amperage noted. Also recorded, are cargo quantities discharged per hour from each tank, the total cargo on board and the total cargo discharged. If the booster pumps and the cargo heater are used during discharge, the performance of both are recorded hourly. The cargo heater's inlet and outlet temperatures and pressures are recorded for both sea water and cargo. The pressure of the booster pumps suction, discharge and seal, and the amperage are recorded, as well as the pressure and temperature at the cargo manifold.

A log is also kept of the performance of the cargo reliquefaction plants, which includes extensive monitoring of the cargo compressors and Freon compressors. This essential log includes ambient air and sea temperatures, compressor suction, internal and discharge temperatures and pressures, lubricating oil pressures, amperage, running hours, cargo tank liquid and vapour temperatures and cargo tank pressures.

This extensive monitoring and recording of all parts of the cargo handling system contributes greatly to the safe operation of the fully refrigerated LPG carrier. The condition of the ship and cargo are continually checked by many different types of monitoring equipment. Any potential problem can be identified at an early stage, double checked by a secondary method, and if necessary, action taken to keep the ship operating safely.

On one side of the cargo control room there is a gas detection unit, which continually takes samples of air from some twenty eight locations throughout the cargo handling and machinery spaces and living quarters. Air samples are taken from the cargo tank void spaces, the compressor room, the cargo electric motor room, the air lock, the main machinery spaces, the inert gas generator room and the accommodation. Air samples are taken and analysed from each location at least once every 30 minutes. Audible and visual alarms are set off if gas is detected. When flammable cargoes, such as propane or butane are carried, the system will be activated when a vapour concentration of 30% of the lower flammable limit of the product is reached.

Plate 1-11   Gas detection unit

RELIQUEFACTION PLANTS

The next areas to be inspected are the spaces below the cargo control room, housing the reliquefaction plants and the cargo electric motors. The ventilation system must be in operation before these enclosed spaces are entered. The fixed mechanical ventilation system, which is controlled from outside the spaces, is designed to provide at least 30 changes of air per hour to prevent the accumulation of flammable or toxic vapours.

The reliquefaction plant room is a tightly packed space of noisy, heavy machinery which gives an awe inspiring impression of power and strength. The purpose of each plant is to take cargo vapour from the tanks, and by compression and refrigeration, return the product to the tanks as a liquid. The reliquefaction plants are used to cool down the cargo tanks and piping prior to loading, to deal with cargo vapour generated during loading and to control the cargo temperature and pressure to within the design limits of the cargo system during passage. On this ship there are four identical plants based on a cascade system of reliquefaction, and each plant is made up of the same components. Three plants have the capacity to cover all operational needs and the fourth plant is a stand-by unit. The system is totally enclosed with no viewing ports, so the progress from vapour to liquid can be monitored but not seen.

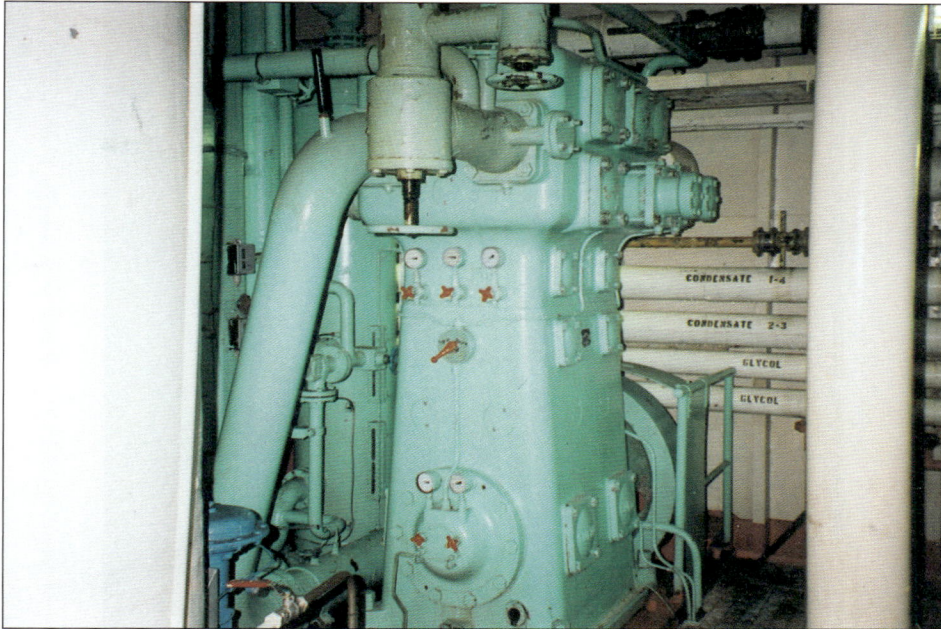

Plate 1-12   Sulzer oil-free labyrinth LPG compressor

Initially, cargo vapours are drawn from the cargo tank, pass through an oil-free labyrinth compressor and are discharged under pressure into a R22 cooled shell and tube condenser. R22 used as the refrigerant is a colourless and non-flammable gas, also known as Freon 22. It has been the most commonly used refrigerant gas for fully refrigerated LPG carriers, but is now being phased out, and more environmentally friendly refrigerants, such as propane are being introduced.

R22 is pumped through the condenser tubes and cargo flows around the tubes, within the shell, where it is condensed and then returned to the cargo tank. R22 is stored in a receiver tank from where it is pumped through the cargo condenser tubes where the cargo, when being condensed, evaporates the R22. The R22 vapour then passes through a R22 compressor and a sea water cooled shell and tube condenser. This completes the full refrigeration cycle as the R22 is returned to the receiver tank as a liquid. The flow of the cargo and the flow of the refrigerant are totally separate. A major advantage of this cascade system is that a single refrigerant can be used for all cargoes.

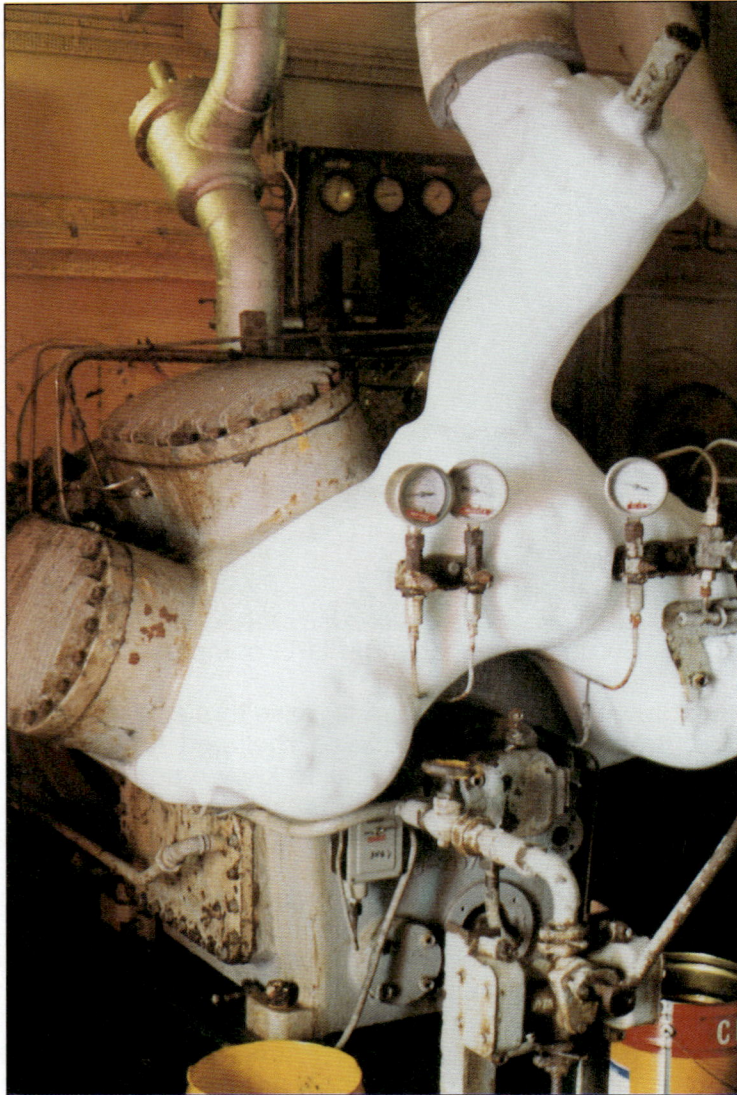

Plate 1-13   Iced-up R22 compressor

The pipework and nozzles which can be seen above the equipment, are part of the carbon dioxide (CO_2) fire extinguishing system. Also overhead and around the perimeter of the space are the rectangular ducts and the circular inlets and outlets for the mechanical ventilation system. On this ship, which can carry LPG with vapours heavier than air, or ammonia with vapours lighter than air, the ducts are arranged to extract vapours from both the upper and lower parts of the space. Circular closing plates can be seen when looking upwards from directly under the ventilator inlets.

Plate 1-14   Circular closing plate under the ventilator inlets

The cargo and R22 compressors are shaft driven by electric motors which are housed in a separate space from the reliquefaction plants. There is no direct access between the two compartments as they are separated by a gas tight steel bulkhead.

Most of the newer vessels have direct condensation type reliquefaction gas plants fitted, rather than cascade type. The refrigeration cycle is eliminated by using larger capacity 3-stage LPG compressors and sea-water cooled condensers.

ELECTRIC MOTOR ROOM

The electric motor room is a gas-safe space and therefore entry from the open deck has to be via an airlock. Once in the airlock the external door must be closed before opening the internal door. If both doors are open at the same time, audible and visual alarms will be set off. The doors are about two metres apart. The airlock is monitored for cargo vapours, is mechanically ventilated and any electrical lights and fittings are designed to be intrinsically safe. Once through into the electric motor room, the internal airlock door needs to be closed, in case others want to enter the airlock from outside.

The motor room is a clean and bright space with a switchboard, control panel and related monitoring equipment for the motors. The eight electric motors, each driving a separate horizontal shaft to the four cargo and four R22 compressors, are fitted perpendicular to the gas tight bulkhead, which separates the motor room from the reliquefaction plants space. Gas tight seals are fitted in the bulkhead around each of the compressor shafts. Gas tight view ports are also fitted in the bulkhead.

Back on the main deck around the reliquefaction house there are storage lockers and other rooms. A vaporiser room is fitted next to the electric motor room, with two shell and tube vaporisers. Steam is passed through the tubes to vaporise the cargo, for example when gassing up cargo or to control cargo tank pressure during discharge when no vapour return line to the shore is fitted. Steam is supplied through deck lines from the machinery spaces. Another room is used to store cylinders for the foam fire protection system, and a third contains spool pieces and reducers for the cargo manifolds. On the forward side of the reliquefaction house, there is an emergency decontamination shower and eye wash. A second similar shower and eye wash is located on the main deck at the accommodation house front.

Plate 1-15   Spool pieces and reducers

DECK CARGO PIPEWORK

The fore and aft walkway running between the cargo control room and the aft accommodation is a good vantage point to take in many of the onboard safety features. The external mechanical ventilators on the top of the reliquefaction house have enclosed, intrinsically safe electric motors, and the location of the vent discharges is at least ten metres from the intakes and openings to safe spaces.

Plate 1-16   Mechanical ventilators

The aft sections of the cargo pipework and Nos. 3 and 4 cargo tank domes can be seen from the walkway. The run of each pipeline can be followed from the reliquefaction house to the cargo domes.

The liquid, condensate and vapour lines are clearly marked. The liquid and condensate lines are insulated.

The design of the cargo pipework must take into account possible movement from thermal contraction and expansion of the cargo, from movement of the cargo tanks and from the ship's motions. There are no long straight runs of cargo piping, but bends, loops, expansion joints and bellows are built into the system. The piping supports not only need to be designed to take the weight of the pipes, but also to allow for horizontal movement and the contraction and expansion of the pipes. For the liquid and condensate lines, the supports are insulated to prevent any heat loss. Like the cargo tanks, the cargo piping systems are protected by pressure relief valves.

Access hatches to the void spaces can be seen from the walkway as well as pressure relief valves for the void spaces. Also seen at deck level are the many control valves for the fire protection systems, and the inert gas piping connections from the machinery spaces. The underside of the walkway is used to support cable runs extending from the machinery spaces to the reliquefaction house and cargo tank domes. All electrical equipment, lights, fittings and wiring in the cargo area must be intrinsically safe.

Plate 1-17   Void space relief valve

ACCOMMODATION SPACES

The fore and aft walkway leads to the accommodation spaces, located in the aft part of the ship, clear of the cargo area. On the accommodation front, there are no windows or doors which open on to the cargo area. Similarly, the forward parts of the house sides have no entrances or windows which can be opened. As part of the fire protection systems, water spray pipework and nozzles are arranged to cover the full height and width of the accommodation front.

The side doors of the wheelhouse, which need to be opened regularly for navigation and operational reasons, can quickly be made gas and vapour tight in an emergency situation. Other openings and air intakes into the accommodation have closing covers or closing plates fitted. On this ship, as ammonia cargo is toxic, the openings must be able to be closed from inside the various spaces.

The external aft part of the ship is arranged for non-gas related equipment such as mooring winches, bollards and fairleads, port and starboard lifeboats and derricks, machinery casings and uptakes. At the main deck level, there are well marked fire and safety stations, where fire fighting outfits, gas protective clothing, breathing apparatus and related safety equipment are stored.

MACHINERY SPACES

Below the accommodation spaces and the main deck there are the machinery spaces. Much of the equipment here is not specifically gas related, but without the services provided, the ship, gas handling and safety systems could not function. The main diesel engine provides the ship's propulsion through a single shaft. Electrical power for the ship's systems, including cargo compressors and pumps, is supplied by diesel auxiliary engines and generators, located in the machinery spaces.

Day to day workings of the equipment in the machinery spaces and important functions performed by the engineering staff will not be dwelt upon here. However, the inert gas generating plant at the upper forward part of the machinery spaces is an important gas related component. Inert gas is produced for use in the cargo tanks and cargo piping systems for gas freeing purposes. It is also used to ensure that no flammable mixture exists at any time in the void spaces. The plant consists of a horizontally mounted combustion chamber burning marine diesel or heavy fuel oil, a vertically mounted scrubber unit and control panels. The inert gas main is directly connected to the above deck cargo area, without passing through any accommodation spaces. Two non-return valves are fitted in the main in the cargo area, to prevent any back flow of cargo gas.

Plate 1-18   Inert gas plant

WATER BALLAST TANKS

The next task will be the lengthy inspection of the water ballast tanks. Entry to the tanks in the cargo area is from the main deck. Early morning is the best time of the day to inspect the upper wing tanks, before the heat of the sun in the Gulf makes the wet spaces unbearably hot and humid. Like all below deck spaces, the tanks must be well ventilated, with the atmosphere tested as safe by a responsible officer, and permission to enter has to be obtained before passing through the manhole.

There are four tanks on each side of the ship, each approximately thirty five metres long, extending between the transverse bulkheads at the ends of each cargo tank space. No. 3 port water ballast tank is a good place to start as it is worth finishing first, because it can be the most uncomfortable tank to be in, due to the noise of the working compressors above in the reliquefaction house. The upper wing tanks are also good places to judge the condition of the steel work and coatings of the ballast tanks in general, as they are often in the worst condition, being more susceptible to corrosion than the lower tanks. This is because the tops of the tanks are not always full of water, so they can be exposed to both air and moisture.

Manholes are located near the aft and forward ends of the tank, with a vertical ladder providing access to the bottom. Standing at the base of the ladder, the construction of the tank can be taken in. The depth is approximately five metres at the side hull. The bottom of the tank slopes upwards at an angle of about 30° from the vertical side hull, parallel to the upper slope of the cargo tank underneath. The main deck is overhead with a radius gunwale at the side. The tank is longitudinally framed with transverse webs. Climbing up and down the slope, over each transverse web in this hot and wet space can be a tiring exercise.

The upper wing ballast tanks are common with the lower wing ballast tanks and double bottom, and access to the lower tanks is via vertical trunks at each end of the space. Access is relatively comfortable to the amidships spaces but can be more difficult at the forward ends of No. 1 tank and the aft ends of No. 4 tank, where the trunks follow the curved shape of the ship's hull. Designers often seem to fail to take into consideration the practicalities of actually using these narrow end access trunks. On the descent, for example, the person on the ladder has to follow the curve of the hull, arching their back outwards in the tight space between the ladder and the inboard side of the trunk to reach the lower tank.

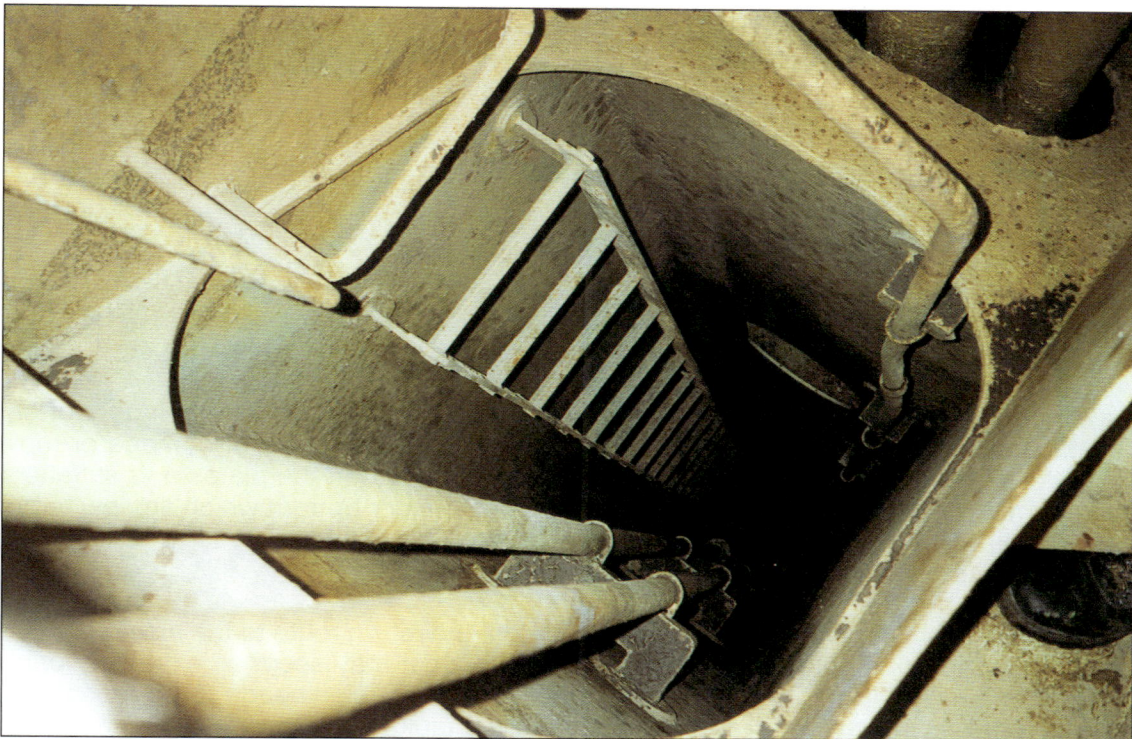

Plate 1-19 Vertical access trunk between upper and lower wing ballast tanks

The lower ballast tank is the same length as the upper ballast tank and has approximately the same depth, but a smaller cross section. The inboard side slopes at an angle of about 60° from the inner bottom. The curve of the bilge hull, side hull and inner slope have longitudinal stiffeners supported by transverse open plate webs. It is possible to stand upright in the lower wing tanks and by stepping through the transverse openings the full length of the tank can be examined.

The final section of the ballast tank to be inspected is the double bottom, which extends to the centreline of the ship. It is some time since the ship's last dry docking and the remains of sand, mud and ballast water which could not be pumped out, lie in the bottom of the tank. The height of the double bottom on this ship is 1600 mm, which means that this can be an uncomfortable space to work in, being too low for some people to stand fully upright.

The double bottom is constructed with longitudinal bottom and inner bottom stiffeners, supported by a criss-cross of transverse plate floors and longitudinal plate girders. Access to all the separate parts of the tank is through 600 x 400 mm manholes in the floors and girders. Crawling on all fours is therefore necessary to reach each part of the double bottom. The time taken to complete the zigzag course through each of the bays is greatly reduced if the need to backtrack is eliminated, by a well designed layout of access openings, particularly at the ends and sides of the tank.

Plate 1-20   Double bottom manholes

While crawling through the tank, the additional stiffeners on the underside of the inner bottom, fitted in way of the cargo tank supports and keys are examined for any signs of damage or movement. Sometimes there are differences in the condition of the coatings on the plates and stiffeners of the hull which are mild steel, and the plates and stiffeners of the inner bottom which are low temperature tank quality steel. The condition of the water ballast pipework, flanges and valve casings within the tanks is also checked.

Once the double bottom inspection has been completed, the return route to the main deck is through the access trunk and upper wing ballast tank and out to what may seem an extremely bright open deck after the darkness of the below deck tanks. The same exercise needs to be repeated another seven times in order to inspect the remaining water ballast tanks in the cargo area. Other below deck spaces to be inspected include the aftpeak, forepeak, aft and forward transverse cofferdams, forward pump room and stores.

This stage of the inspection has now been completed as far as possible. There is propane in the cargo tanks and the void spaces are filled with inert gas, so the secrets of these remaining tanks and spaces will have to wait until the ship has been gas freed. The ship is approaching the terminal and being prepared for discharge, which is a good time to see the cargo systems working. Rather than having to step backwards off a rope ladder into a small motor launch, disembarkation is by a solid gangway between the deck to the shore terminal. The surveyor then awaits news of where the ship is going to be placed for dry docking and gas freeing.

SECOND INSPECTION, IN DRY DOCK

The decision as to where the ship will be dry docked depends on the owner's and superintendent's past experiences, the trading pattern of the ship, the availability of dry docks, and the quotes received. Unfortunately this decision is totally out of the surveyor's control. If only all inspections could take place in southern Europe in late spring, like this one. With the ship in dry dock, in a gas free condition, the task ahead is to inspect each of the four cargo tanks and void spaces around the cargo tanks.

CARGO TANKS

At the repair shipyard, the dry docking programme is well underway, and the deck is bustling with activity. Most of the work is on the ship's external hull, ballast tanks and machinery spaces. Away from the crowded parts of the ship lies sanctuary in one of the cargo tanks. The tank is divided at the centreline by a liquid tight bulkhead, and the port side of No. 2 tank is the first part of the four cargo tanks to be visited. Gas-free certificates have been obtained, and permission to enter given. Entry to the tank is through the access hatch on the tank dome. The dome has an open centreline bulkhead forming a common vapour space. Below the dome, the seventeen metre descent to the bottom of the port side tank is relatively easy, as angled ladders with hand rails extend downwards between small gratings.

After becoming accustomed to the darkness of this cavernous space, the first impression, despite the ship's age, is that the condition of the tank's internal structure appears almost as new. The tank is thirty three metres long and fifteen metres across at the widest part. The top and bottom outboard corners of the tank are sloped, and large transverse webs at the bottom, side and top support longitudinal stiffeners. The ends of the tank has large vertical webs supporting horizontal stiffeners. To prevent excessive free surface movement of the liquid cargo, a transverse swash bulkhead is fitted at the mid-length of the tank. To reduce the possibility of thermal stresses, all edges of the tank have a radius of 600 mm and the corners of the tank are partially spherical in shape to match the radius of the edges. These complicated, partially spherical corner connections are worth special attention. They can be a good indication of the standard of the shipbuilder's workmanship, and the quality of the welding in the rest of the tank.

The aft end of the tank can be reached along a fore and aft walkway fitted on the web plates of the bottom transverse webs. The deep-well pump is in the aft section of the tank, close to the centreline bulkhead, with its lower suction bellmouth in a small sump in the bottom of the tank. The drive shaft for the pump's centrifugal impeller is inside the vertical cylindrical pump column and is driven by an electric motor fitted on the external pump dome. A low level alarm is fitted near the pump to indicate when the tank is almost empty during discharging. At the bottom of the tank around the pump, there are puddle heating coils used to remove any remaining liquid cargo. The puddle heating system is used to evaporate the residual liquid when gas-freeing or changing grades. Next to the pump and parallel to the pump column is the liquid cargo filling pipe line, which is connected to the deck liquid line.

Plate 1-21   Liquid cargo filling pipe line and deep-well pump

Looking forward from the pump column, pipework of varying sizes can be seen, which carry the liquid cargo, condensate and vapour. There are two horizontal grids of pipework, one at the upper and one at the lower level of the tank, with small holes spaced along the length of the pipes. These purge lines are used when gas-freeing the tank, to evenly spread the inert gas or vapour throughout. The reverse happens when gassing up the tank, when the inert gas or vapour is evenly drawn from the tank. There are also two spray lines with a much smaller diameter than the purge lines, located at the mid and upper levels of the tank, which are connected to the deck condensate line. The lines are used for cooling the tank, and run from one end to the other, releasing condensate from upward facing nozzles.

The fore and aft walkway leads to the bottom of the mid-length transverse swash bulkhead, below the cargo tank dome. An ullage float, with its vertical measuring tape and pair of guide wires extending from the dome can be seen near the centreline bulkhead. Also near the base of the centreline bulkhead is the valve connecting the port and starboard sides of the tank. The lower part of the tank, forward of the swash bulkhead is inspected before heading upwards on the ladder to the dome.

Plate 1-22   Ullage float

Plate 1-23   Centreline bulkhead valve

There is a certain beauty in the construction of the large transverse webs, and the cut outs in the swash bulkhead, especially when looking along a line of face flats or brackets, to appreciate the precision of the repeated structural details. The precision skills of the shipyard workers who built ships long before computers controlled accuracy of the construction are worthy of note.

Near the top of the tank, a number of safety features come into view. A high level float switch can be seen, which will set off audible and visual alarms in the cargo control room during loading when the cargo level reaches the filling limit of the tank. Various small vapour and liquid sampling lines can be seen in way of the tank dome. On each side of the underside of the dome are piping openings for the main cargo relief valves. The vapour piping connection can also be seen on the underside of the dome.

When the inspection of the port side of one cargo tank has been completed, the exercise is repeated on the starboard side, where the tank structure and cargo handling equipment are similar, but to the opposite hand. The construction of the other three cargo tanks is similar to No. 2 cargo tank, however, the geometry of No. 1 forward tank and No. 4 aft tank are different. No. 1 tank is narrower at its forward end, and No. 4 tank is narrower at its aft end, to fit within the hull lines.

VOID SPACES

The void spaces around the four cargo tanks are to be inspected next. On fully refrigerated LPG carriers, the arrangements within the void spaces have presented naval architects with numerous technical challenges. Construction materials, tank supports, thermal contraction and expansion, insulation, access, and the full range of motions of the ship, have all needed to be taken into consideration, yet many naval architects have reached the same conclusions about how to solve these complex problems. This vessel has the now almost standard configuration within the void space, with upper and lower sloping side ballast tanks, and the side hull constructed with cargo tank quality steel. This configuration first appeared on *Antilla Cape* which was delivered from the Bremen yard of A G Weser in 1968, and since the mid-eighties, almost all FRLPG carriers have adopted this arrangement.

It is a pity that the cargo tank cannot be lifted out of the ship temporarily, just to take in the clever construction and arrangements of the void space. If this was possible, what would be seen is that the side hull and side frames, and every panel of plating and stiffeners in view, form the secondary barrier. The secondary barrier, constructed with the same quality steel as the cargo tank, is a major safety feature on fully refrigerated LPG carriers. In the event of a liquid cargo leak from the cargo tanks, the surrounding structure is designed to retain the leaking cargo within the void space for up to fifteen days.

No. 3 void space is the first of the four to be inspected. Entry to the aft end of the space is through a hinged deck hatch near the ship's centreline, with a seventeen metre descent to the inner bottom on a series of vertical ladders on the transverse bulkhead. It is safer to wait until each person entering the void space has reached the bottom of a section of ladder and stepped aside, before setting off. This will prevent any possibility of the person on the ladder being showered with dirt, dislodged surface corrosion or worse, being struck by dropped tools or torches.

At the aft end of the space, there is a float alarm to detect any leakage from adjacent water ballast tanks, and a small eductor is provided to remove any liquid. However, insignificant amounts of water are sometimes found lying at the aft end of the space, from ice which may have formed on the tank supports and keys when the tanks were loaded with propane.

Plate 1-24   Float alarm

The external steel plating of the cargo tank can not be seen from inside the void space, as the tank is covered with insulation. The polyurethane foam insulation is 100 mm thick and covered with a vapour seal of glass fibre cloth and mastic. Underneath the cargo tank, the vertical distance from the ship's inner bottom to the insulation is only 625 mm, so it is necessary to crawl on all fours in order to view the tank bottom supports and keys. Occasionally, on some ships, a four wheeled bogie is available, which is small enough to pass through the access hatches. This makes the inspection of the area underneath the cargo tank much easier.

The supports and keys are symmetrical about the centreline. The bottom supports are arranged in line with the double bottom floors and girders, and also in line with the cargo tank transverse webs. Steel supports with side and end brackets are welded to the inner bottom, and similar supports are welded to the bottom of the cargo tank. Two layers of azobé hardwood are fitted between the two supports with one layer of wood fixed to the inner bottom supports and the other fixed to the cargo tank supports. This arrangement supports the weight of the tank and at the same time allows for horizontal movement due to thermal expansion and contraction.

Plate 1-25   Bottom support

The bottom anti-rolling keys which are located at the centreline, have a central steel foundation welded to the inner bottom, and side keys welded to the bottom of the cargo tank. Lengths of azobé hardwood are positioned between the steel foundations. During a ballast passage in stormy weather, noise from the movement of the cargo tanks is sometimes heard as far away as the living quarters. This can be very loud, and quite alarming to the unaccustomed, especially when the ship is rolling heavily and the cargo tanks are moving from side to side. Anti-collision keys, which have almost the same design as the anti-rolling keys, are fitted across the ship on the inner bottom. These keys are designed to prevent any forward movement of the cargo tank in the event of a collision.

Plate 1-26   Bottom anti-rolling key

Plate 1-27   Bottom anti-collision key

On either side of the inner bottom, running forward and aft under the cargo tank, there are pipes which are used when inerting the void space. When transporting flammable gases, the void spaces are filled with dry inert gas, supplied from an inert gas plant in the machinery spaces. The inert gas pipework can be identified by the small holes spaced along the horizontal parts of the pipes.

When the forward end of the void space is reached, the inspection in the space under the cargo tank is completed. The next task is to move upwards and begin to inspect the transverse bulkheads and inner hull side frames. Access around the void space is provided by horizontal walkways, which are spaced at various levels around the ends and sides of the cargo tank. The first end walkway on the forward transverse bulkhead, is in line with the top of the lower wing ballast tanks, which is a good place to inspect the lower ends of the side frames. At this level, there is no side walkway, so progress aft is made along the top of the port ballast tank by stepping over each of the bottom tripping brackets of the side frames. At the aft transverse bulkhead a walkway leads to the starboard side. The full circuit of the cargo tank at the first level is completed when the forward transverse bulkhead is reached, along the top of the starboard ballast tank.

Vertical ladders on the forward bulkhead provide access to each level of walkways, where further full circuits of the cargo tank can be made to continue the inspection. When the upper slope of the cargo tank is reached, there is a line of anti-lift or anti-floatation chocks to be inspected. The chocks run fore and aft, and are fitted in line with the cargo tank transverse webs and the ballast tank transverse webs. The steel foundations are welded to the underside of the ballast tank and azobé hardwood is secured to the cargo tank in line with the chock, with a small gap between the two. The purpose of the chocks, fitted on both upper slopes of the cargo tanks, is to prevent the tanks from lifting in the event of the void space flooding, which could damage the main deck and ballast tanks above. In the lifetime of most gas carriers, however, the design of these key elements of the cargo tank positioning arrangements are never put to the test.

Plate 1-28   Anti-floatation chock

Another circuit of the cargo tank is made at this level before moving on to the top of the tank at the centre, just under the main deck. Access to the top of the tank and the cargo tank dome is from the aft end. Care needs to be taken when stepping from the vertical ladder on the transverse bulkhead, on to the top of the tank, as the edge of the tank is curved. At the aft part of the cargo tank, the insulated pumps column and the underside of the deep-well pumps dome can be seen.

The span and depth of the transverse deck webs are important factors in ensuring a maximum possible capacity for the cargo tanks. This design consideration is one of the reasons for the adoption of the standard cross-section, with the inboard bulkhead of the ballast tanks providing support, and reducing the span of the transverse deck webs. If no wing tanks were fitted, the span of the deck transverses would be the full beam of the ship, the depth of the transverses would be greatly increased, and considerable cargo carrying capacity would be lost. The result of this decision by naval architects to provide the maximum cubic capacity for the cargo tanks, is that the gap between the deck transverse face flat and the cargo tank top is made as small as possible. To continue forward, the choice is to squeeze through a gap at the deck transverses of about 200 mm or to make use of the top slope of the tank at side, where there is slightly more room.

In a similar manner to the bottom anti-rolling keys, steel foundations with azobé hardwood form the top keys at the centreline. They are smaller than the bottom keys with each foundation welded to the top of the tank and the underside of the main deck, and azobé hardwood positioned between the foundations.

Plate 1-29　　　　　　　　　Top anti-rolling key

At the mid-length of the tank, the cargo tank dome trunk provides a welcome chance to stand upright in the space between the dome and the dome trunk. There is a flexible neoprene weather seal around all sides of the trunk. This seal allows the cargo tank to move in all directions and at the same time prevents any ingress of water. Switching off inspection lamps for a moment will, if the seal is tight and in good condition, produce pitch darkness in the trunk space.

There is one final tight space to negotiate, along the forward part of the top of the cargo tank, before climbing out of the void space and back onto the open deck. Three more similar void spaces would be inspected before finishing this virtual tour of a typical fully refrigerated LPG carrier.

This tour has illustrated the multitude of tried and tested design and safety features of this type of ship. How has this sophisticated level of marine engineering been reached? The following chapters trace the development of fully refrigerated LPG carriers, from the late nineteen fifties to the present day. This gradual evolution has challenged engineers, naval architects and shipbuilders all over the world, whose expertise and dedication have made the large scale sea transportation of liquefied petroleum gas the success it is today.

Chapter 2

French Refrigeration Breakthrough

The introduction of refrigeration to transport LPG developed rapidly in a relatively short space of time. An experiment on a shipboard tank of less than 40 m³ capacity in 1958 was the first practical beginning and within a few years, large purpose built fully refrigerated LPG carriers were being constructed in Europe and Japan. Étienne Schlumberger of Société Maritime Shell, René Boudet of Gazocéan and Chantiers Navals de la Ciotat (CNC), were together instrumental in moving from theory to practice the concept of cooling LPG cargo by introducing refrigeration.[1, 2, 3, 4] In his memoirs, *La Joie D'Entreprendre,* René Boudet recalls a dinner conversation with Étienne Schlumberger in May 1958 on the night train from La Spezia to Paris. The engineer and the entrepreneur had been attending 1,012 m³ LPG carrier *Löex,* which was in the final stages of a conversion and lengthening from general cargo ship *Haut-Brion* at the Industrie Navali Meccaniche Affini (INMA) yard. *Löex* was fitted with nine fully pressurised cylindrical horizontal cargo tanks. Suddenly in the middle of the pleasant dinner Étienne put his hand to his head and said to René:

> Mais c'est complètement idiot ce que nous avons fait avec le *Löex*. Pour transporter 500 tonnes de gaz, ce bateau va transporter toute sa vie le même poids de cuve, alors que si ce gaz était réfrigéré (le butane à -6 et le propane à -40) nous n'aurions besoin que de cuves rectangulaires légères, en acier à faible teneur en nickel. Pour la même taille de bateau, la capacité de transport de liquide serait pratiquement doublée et, de plus, la densité des produits serait augmentée d'environ 20%.[1]

> What we have done with *Löex* is absolutely foolish. To transport 500 tonnes of gas, this ship will always have to carry tanks weighing 500 tonnes, whereas if the gas were refrigerated (the butane at -6°C and the propane at -40°C) we would only need light rectangular tanks made of steel with a small percentage of nickel. The ship would be the same size but the liquid capacity of the cargo would practically double and what is more, the density of the products would increase by 20%.[5]

By the time the train reached the Gare de Lyon both men had convinced each other that refrigeration would open up immense possibilities for LPG trading and that an experimental ship would have to be built.

Plate 2-1   *Löex* after conversion at La Spezia   Gazocéan

Étienne Schlumberger started his experiments on a ship in service, the first CNC built gas carrier, 1,390 m³ *Butagaz*, with 36 vertically mounted cylindrical pressurised tanks, which had been delivered to Société Maritime Shell in 1955. Insulation was added to the forward tank on *Butagaz* and with the use of a gas compressor the cargo was cooled to check how the specific gravity of the cargo changed with the temperature. Resulting from this experimental work ,the first semi-refrigerated gas ship was ordered from CNC and delivered to Gazocéan in 1959 as 920 m³ *Descartes*.

Iridina

Principle Particulars	
Length o.a.	169.38 m
Length b.p.	161.55 m
Breadth	21.11 m
Depth	11.89 m
Draught	9.04 m
LPG Capacity	10,808 m³
Engine	Parsons turbine
Power	8,500 hp/6,251 kW
Service speed	15.6 knots

Étienne Schlumberger also headed the Société Maritime Shell team responsible for the challenge of converting the 18,000 tonnes deadweight products tanker *Iridina* into the first refrigerated gas carrier, designed to transport refrigerated butadiene or butane at near atmospheric pressure. The tanker was built by CNC in 1955 with eleven centre and wing cargo tanks. CNC also carried out the complex conversion. The theme of the original launch ceremony highlighted the co-operation between Metropolitan France and the North Africa Territories, as the tanker then was destined to supply finished products from the nearby Beere Refinery to Algeria, Morocco and Tunisia. The long-established Shell Group custom of naming the ship after a shell was followed, with *Iridina* appropriately named after a freshwater mussel found in Lake Tanganyika, Central Africa.

Iridina, classed with Bureau Veritas, was redelivered to the Société Maritime Shell in August 1961 with a refrigerated gas capacity of 10,808 m³ in the centre tanks. Bureau Veritas had published for the first time, in its 1958 Rules, special requirements for LPG carriers. The design of the centre tanks on *Iridina* were based on a minimum cargo temperature of -5°C, a specific gravity of 0.64 and a maximum pressure of 0.5 kg/cm³.

Each of the eleven centre tanks were internally insulated with 50 mm of mineral wool protected with a wire mesh. Azobé hardwood sections, spaced 768 mm apart, provided support for the 3 mm steel membrane. The tanks' deck and bottom shell longitudinals and the large centreline girders were boxed in. The square tank edges were internally insulated with quarter radius segments, covered with the 3 mm steel membrane. Quarter radius segments of insulation and membrane were fitted at each of the tank corners.

Two turbine driven vertical Guinard pumps were located in the aft pump room and discharged cargo through 300 mm diameter horizontal pipes running though each centre tank.

Iridina was broken up in 1969.

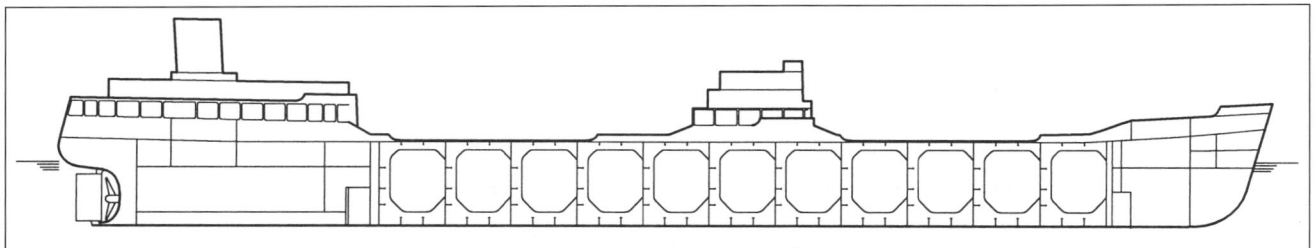

Figure 2-1 Profile of *Iridina*

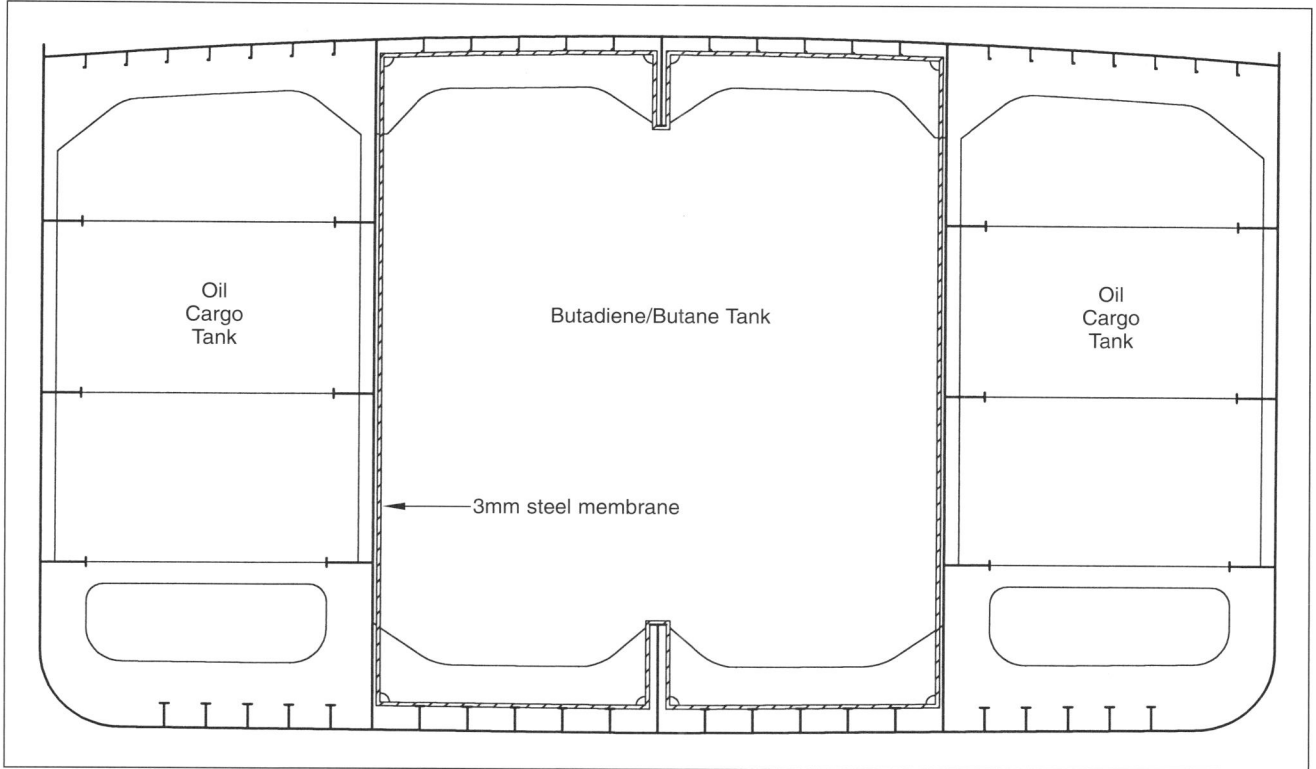

Figure 2-2 Midship Section of *Iridina* showing Centre Tank Membrane

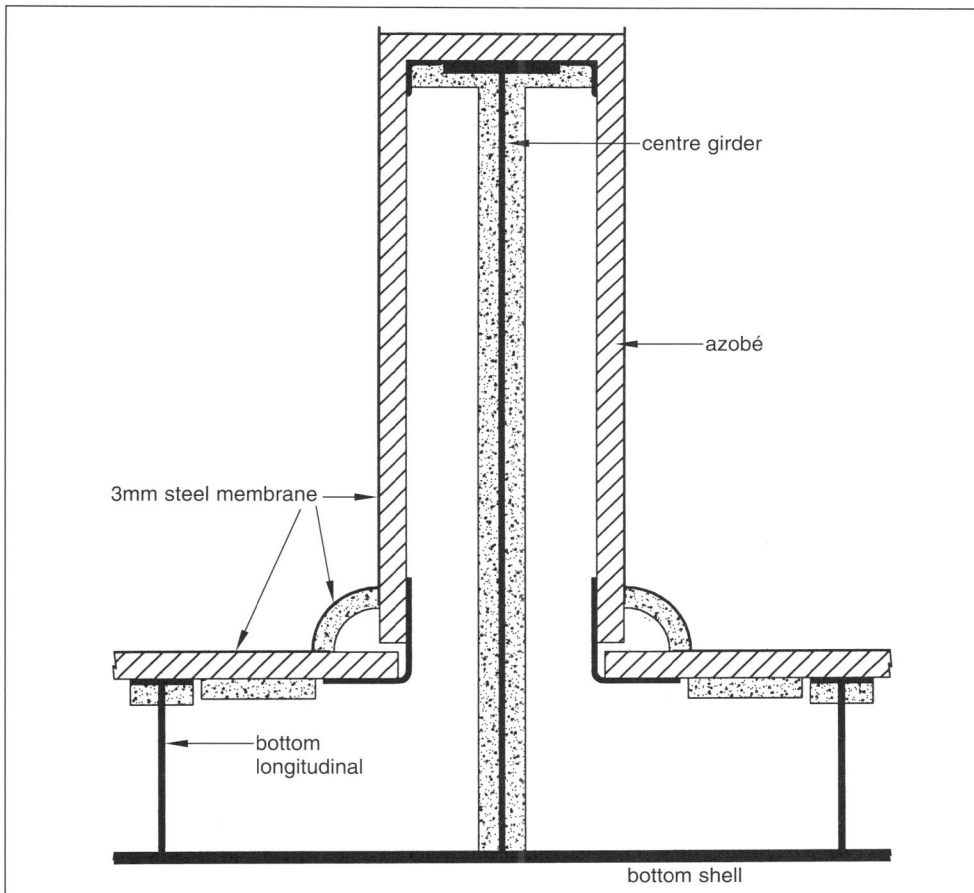

Figure 2-3 *Iridina* – Detail of Boxed-in Bottom Centre Girder

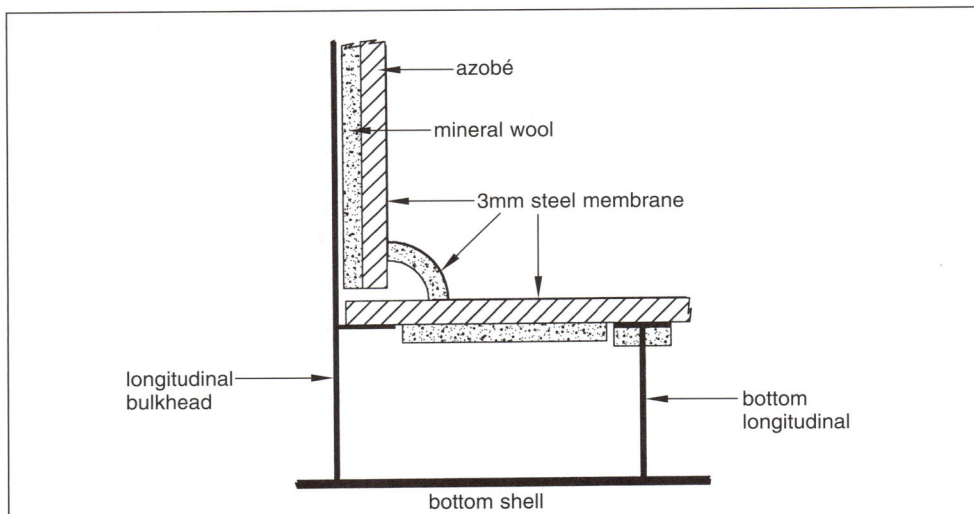

Figure 2-4 *Iridina* – Detail of Tank Corner

An engineering company, Technigaz, was set up in 1963, in order to develop new techniques for the LPG carriers being designed by Gazocéan. Technigaz was also to provide engineering services to shipyards.[6] Chantiers Navals de la Ciotat (CNC) had worked in close co-operation with the Gazocéan shipping company since 1958, and had built pressurised and semi-refrigerated LPG carriers for Gazocéan. A licence agreement was made with Technigaz regarding designs for fully refrigerated LPG carriers using a technique that was exclusively French. The distinctive feature of this Technigaz design was the use of loose silicon treated perlite granules for insulation, which were poured into the void space around the cargo tank.

Perlite is a type of volcanic rock. When the ore particles are heated rapidly to around 1,000°C they melt and expand to between 4% and 40% of their original volume. The resulting white granules are lightweight with good thermal insulation properties. From a shipbuilder's point of view, the advantages of using perlite are that the cost is relatively low, labour man hours are reduced, the void spaces can be filled after the cargo tanks are finished and the granules are not flammable.

Perlite insulation had been used for prototype and experimental LNG carrier studies in France. The 25,500 m³ LNG carrier *Jules Verne*, completed in March 1967, by Ateliers et Chantiers de la Seine Maritime (ACSM) of Le Trait, had perlite around the cargo tanks. The plywood boxes of the Gaz Transport LNG membrane system are also filled with perlite.

Isfonn

Principle Particulars	
Length o.a.	177.00 m
Length b.p.	165.00 m
Breadth	24.40 m
Depth	13.70 m
Draught	7.72 m
LPG Capacity	18,790 m³
Engine	Mantes-Sulzer 6RD68
Power	8,000 hp/5,884 kW
Service speed	15 knots

The first fully refrigerated LPG carrier to be constructed at La Ciotat was the 18,790 m³ *Isfonn*, which was delivered on 24 March 1967, to owners Sigval Bergesen, of Stavanger.[7] This newbuilding was the fourth LPG carrier for the Norwegian company from La Ciotat, who previously, between 1962 and 1965, had delivered three 4,100 m³ semi-refrigerated vessels *Nordfonn, Sydfonn* and *Frostfonn* to Sigval Bergesen.

Isfonn was built to Det Norske Veritas classification as a Tankskip for Kondensert Gass and to the requirements of the US Coast Guard, for a minimum cargo temperature of -48°C and a maximum pressure of 0.275 kg/cm². The vessel, built for the carriage of LPG, NH_3 and butadiene, had three prismatic cargo tanks, in three holds, with a double bottom, a double hull and transverse bulkheads between the cargo tanks. The vessel was delivered with cargo tank insulation fitted on the inner hull. After some time in service, when the compressors were unable to perform satisfactorily, due to the arrangement of the insulation, the void space between the cargo tank and the inner bottom, inner sides and transverse bulkheads were filled with loose perlite. Additional plywood divisions were fitted over the transverse bulkhead stiffeners.

Gas handling equipment fitted included six 300 m³/hr submerged electric cargo pumps, two 600 m³/hr booster pumps, six direct cycle reliquefaction units and an inert gas plant.

Isfonn was sold to Indian breakers as *Excel* in 1997.

Plate 2-2   *Isfonn* as *Sheldon Gas* in dry dock   Dubai Drydock

Capella

Principle Particulars

Length o.a.	150.61 m
Length b.p.	141.00 m
Breadth	21.70 m
Depth	13.30 m
Draught	7.88 m
LPG Capacity	14,268 m³
Engine	Mantes-Sulzer 6RD68
Power	8,000 hp/5,884 kW
Service speed	16 knots

In 1967, La Ciotat shipyard delivered two 14,268 m³ fully refrigerated LPG carriers, which were to provide the basis for future designs using perlite insulation. The first of the pair was ordered by Transocéangas Shipping, an affiliated company of Gazocéan. The ship was launched on 10 November 1966 as *Franklin*, but was delivered on 22 July 1967, as 14,268 m³ *Capella*, to Swedish owners Svea. The second ship, *Arquimédes,* was delivered on 29 September 1967 to International Gas Shipping, Naviera-Fierro SA, an affiliated company of Gazocéan.

The ships were classed with Bureau Veritas, and to obtain a US Coast Guard Letter of Compliance a plan review and inspection programme were followed. The cargo systems were designed for LPG, NH_3, and propylene, with a minimum cargo temperature of -48°C and a maximum pressure of 0.275 kg/cm². The arrangement of the ship was similar to *Isfonn*, with three cargo tanks, a single transverse bulkhead fitted between each tank and perlite insulation in the void spaces. The cargo tanks and secondary barrier were constructed with carbon manganese nickel silicon steel TGZ 201 bis 2.

Gas handling equipment fitted included six 250 m³/hr Guinard submerged electric cargo pumps, two 750 m³/hr Guinard booster pumps, direct cycle reliquefaction with five Loire compressors and an inert gas plant.

Capella was broken up as *Qeshm Gas* in 1998. *Arquimédes* was sold to Taiwan breakers in 1985, as *Pythagore*.

Kristian Birkeland

Principle Particulars

Length o.a.	171.00 m
Length b.p.	159.00 m
Breadth	24.40 m
Depth	15.50 m
Draught	8.75 m
LPG Capacity	22,246 m³
Engine	Fiat SGM 906 S
Power	13,800 hp/10,150 kW
Service speed	17 knots

Three 22,246 m³ LPG carriers were delivered from La Ciotat to Norwegian owners during 1968 and 1969.[8, 9] The first of the trio, *Kristian Birkeland*, was delivered on 8 August 1968 to the equally shared ownership of Fearnley & Eger, Norske Hydro and Gazocean Norsk. The second, *Cypress*, was delivered to A/S Rederiet Odfjell on 31 July 1969 and the third, *Gas Master*, was delivered to S/A Golden West on 22 December 1969.

The ice-strengthened ships were each classed with Det Norske Veritas as a Tanker for Liquefied Gas for a minimum temperature of -48°C and a maximum pressure of 0.275 kg/cm². The ships were arranged with a cruiser stern, an aft accommodation deck house, a flush main deck with forward sheer, a raked stem with a bulbous bow and three hold spaces with a prismatic cargo tank in each hold. The inner bottom and the inner hull formed the secondary barrier and the double bottom and double side were used as water ballast tanks. Transverse cofferdams were fitted between each cargo tank with perlite insulation in the hold spaces and mineral wool insulation on the top of the cargo tanks.

A compressor and pump room and an electric motor room were located on the main deck aft of the amidships manifolds and a cargo control room was located in the aft accommodation, overlooking the cargo area. Other features of the Technigaz design included a cargo tank dome located at the mid-length of each cargo tank, the cargo tank base and top were longitudinally parallel to the ship's base line and an inner bottom and cargo tank bottom, which sloped downwards to the centreline. This arrangement was to become the standard layout for future designs using perlite as insulation.

Two 400 m³/hr J C Carter submerged electric cargo pumps were located in wells at the aft part of each tank. Two 400 m³/hr Guinard electric booster pumps and a cargo heater were also fitted on the main deck. The direct cycle reliquefaction plant consisted of three Loire two piston compressors with heat exchangers. A nitrogen generator, a 70 m³ nitrogen deck storage tank and a vaporiser were installed.

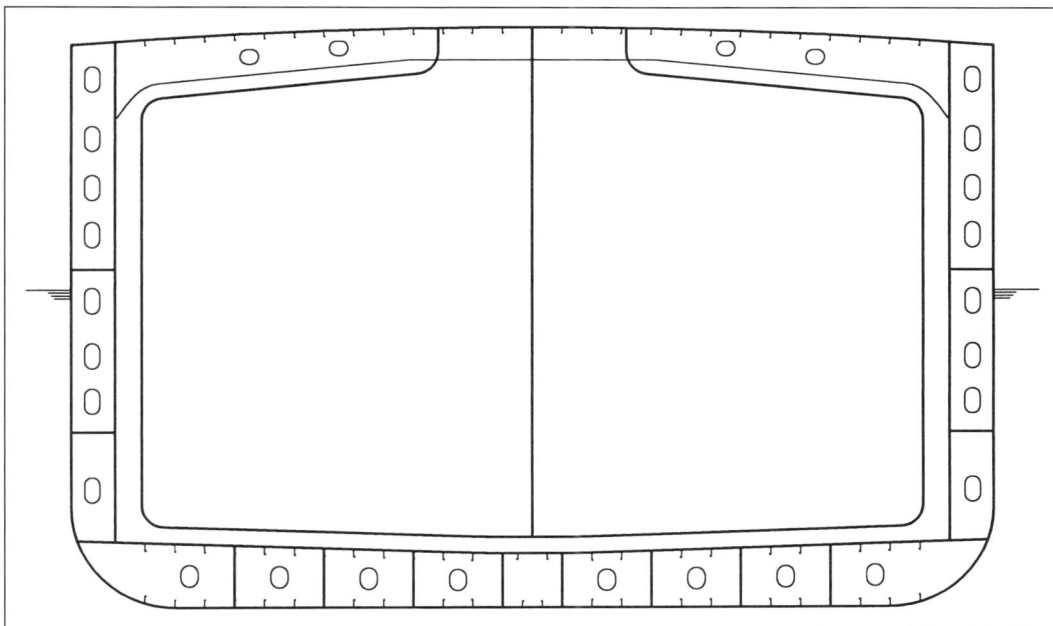

Figure 2-5 Midship Section of *Kristian Birkeland*

Cypress was broken up in 2001 as *Mundogas Atlantic* and *Gas Master* was scrapped as *Cronos* in 2002.

A fourth vessel, *Sydfonn*, with the same hull dimensions and cargo tank geometry was delivered from La Ciotat on 5 June 1978 to Sigval Bergesen. Some small changes to the design were necessary to satisfy the requirements of the IMCO Gas Code, first published in 1976. The profile appearance was changed with a refrigeration plant house and cargo control room on the main deck above the aft cargo tank, and a 150 m³ propane tank and a 60 m³ ammonia tank, for changing grades, were fitted on the main deck forward of the cargo manifolds. Deep-well cargo pumps were fitted in preference to the submerged pumps. Three oil-free LPG compressors were fitted. The main propulsion unit was a Sulzer 6RND76M diesel engine, rated at 14,400 hp/10,590 kW for a service speed of 17.75 knots.

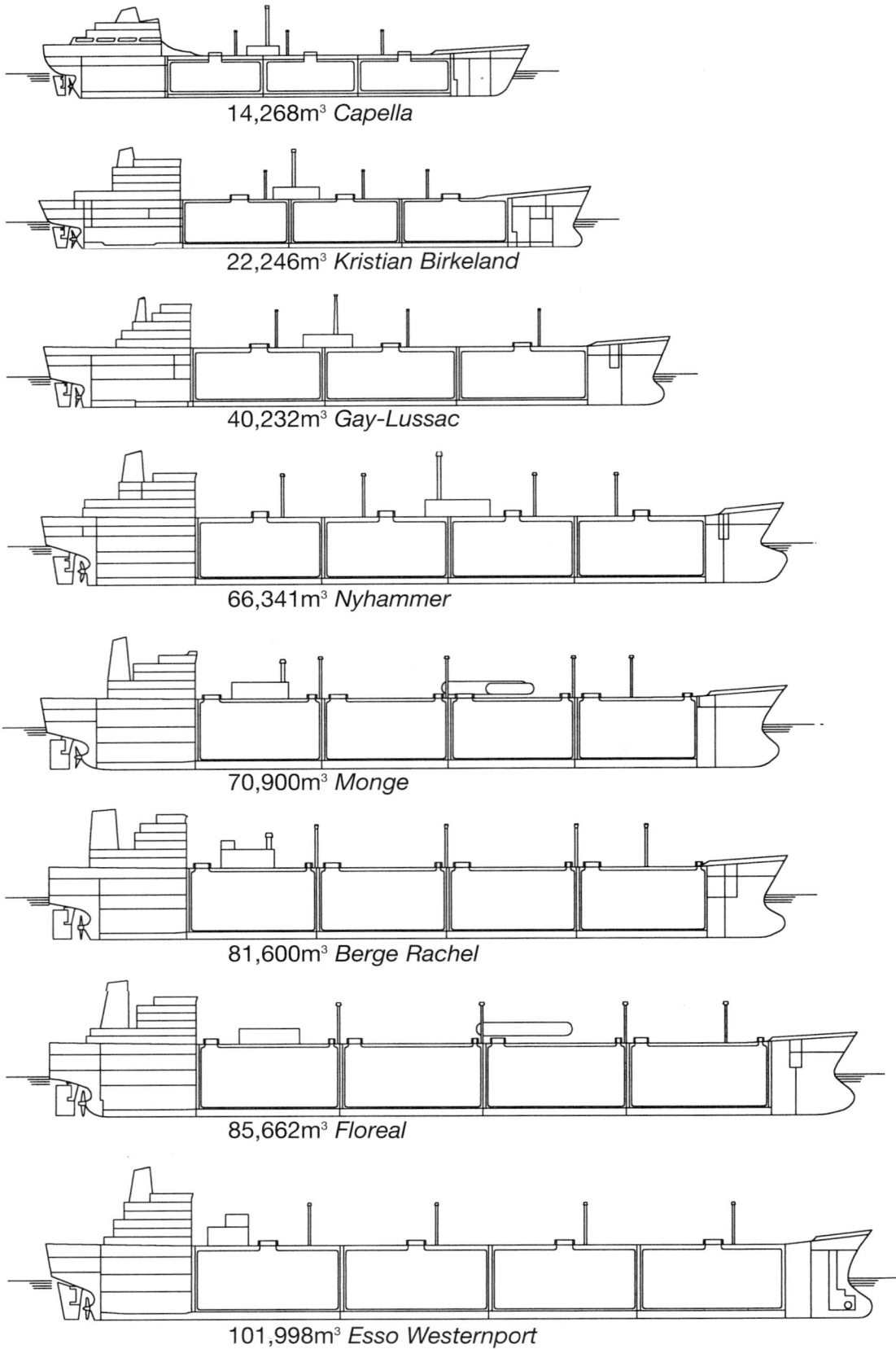

14,268m³ *Capella*

22,246m³ *Kristian Birkeland*

40,232m³ *Gay-Lussac*

66,341m³ *Nyhammer*

70,900m³ *Monge*

81,600m³ *Berge Rachel*

85,662m³ *Floreal*

101,998m³ *Esso Westernport*

Figure 2-6 Chantiers Navals de la Ciotat Perlite Series Profiles

Plate 2-3   Main deck looking aft of *Gas Master* as *Mundogas Pacific* at Kenai, Alaska in October 1987

Plate 2-4   Main deck looking forward of *Gas Master* as *Mundogas Pacific* at Kenai, Alaska in October 1987

4 October 1999 – From Dockyard to Scrap Yard

When in dry dock at Subic Shipyard on 4 October 1999 an explosion occurred on *Kristian Birkeland* as *Mundogas Europe*.[10] *Mundogas Europe* had been sold to Olympo of Chile in September 1999. The ship had been in the dry dock for nine days for bottom hull repairs and general refurbishing work. Five shipyard workers were killed, who at the time had been fitting a cargo heater on the side of the reliquefaction plants' deck house, and seven others were injured. The explosion was below the main deck in way of No. 2 void space, and caused extensive damage to the main deck. The damages to *Mundogas Europe* were not repaired and the ship was sold to Chinese breakers in 2000.

Gay-Lussac

Principle Particulars	
Length o.a.	194.13 m
Length b.p.	182.00 m
Breadth	29.00 m
Depth	18.90 m
Draught	9.91 m
LPG Capacity	40,232 m³
Engine	Fiat SGM 906 S
Power	15,000 hp/11,032 kW
Service speed	17.25 knots

Gay-Lussac, with a capacity of 40,232 m³, was a larger, improved version of *Kristian Birkeland*, fitted with three cargo tanks. Delivered from La Ciotat on 20 May 1969 to Transocéangas Shipping, an affiliated company of Gazocéan, the ship was classed with Bureau Veritas. A raked transom stern and twin funnels on the casing top were the distinctive external changes. Internally, a 45° chamfered corner was introduced in the perlite filled void spaces, at the connection between the inner bottom and the inner side longitudinal bulkhead.

Two 400 m³/hr J C Carter submerged electric cargo pumps were fitted in each tank. In addition a similar type and capacity portable emergency pump was available, which could be used in each tank, if the main pumps failed. A 400 m³/hr Guinard electric booster pump and a cargo heater were fitted. The direct cycle reliquefaction plant again consisted of three Loire two piston compressors with heat exchangers. *Gay-Lussac* was sold in 1981, to be operated by Naftomar Shipping & Trading of Athens, and renamed *Gaz Fountain*.

A second ship, *Cavendish*, with the same capacity was delivered on 10 August 1971 to another Gazocéan affiliated company, Ocean Gas Transport Ltd.[11] *Cavendish* as *Gaz Supplier* was sold for scrap in 2002.

Plate 2-5   *Gay-Lussac*   Chantiers Navals de la Ciotat

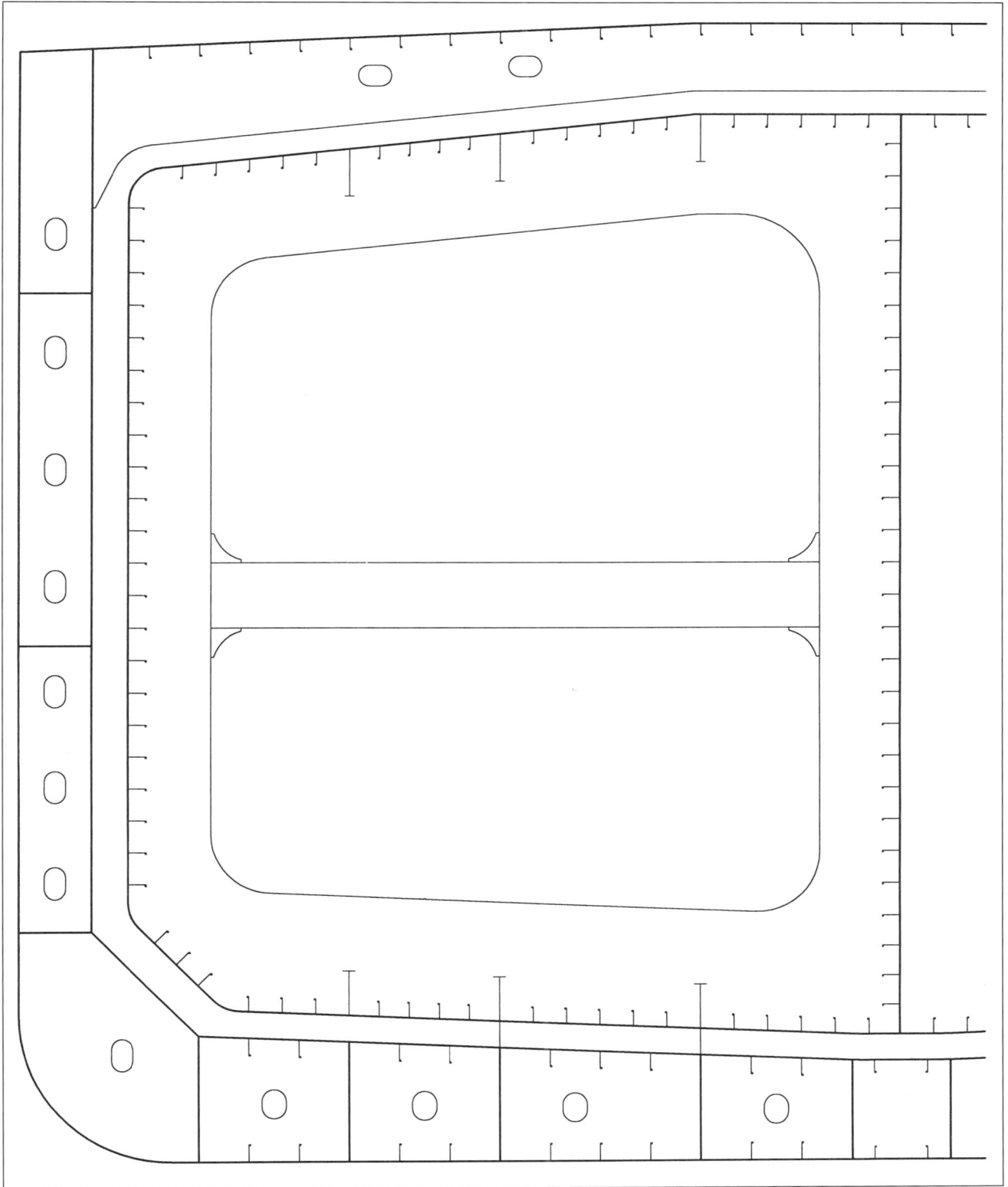

Figure 2-7 Midship Section of *Gay-Lussac*

12 October 1984 – Remarkable Salvage

Gaz Fountain was attacked on the morning of 12 October 1984, during the Iran/Iraq war, by an Iranian aircraft, which fired three rocket propelled missiles at the gas ship.[12] The vessel was on a loaded passage from Ras Tanura to Fujairah and was attacked about 145 miles north west of Dubai. No. 1 tank was fully loaded with 6,300 tonnes of propane, No. 2 tank was about half full with 4,460 tonnes of butane and No. 3 tank was fully loaded with 7,680 tones of butane. One missile exploded on the main deck above No. 2 tank causing extensive damage to the deck, cabling and pipework, but the cargo tank remained intact. The other two missiles struck the main deck in way of No. 3 tank, with one exploding above the deck and the other exploding on the cargo tank top and rupturing it. The release of butane from the tank caused a large fire on the main deck which spread to the accommodation house.

The 29 Spanish crew members, a Greek superintendent and three Greek technicians, safely abandoned ship in the lifeboats, and were soon rescued, without any injuries. Before leaving the ship the crew were able to shut down the cargo systems, stop the main engine and close doors between the lower accommodation and the engine room.

Selco Salvage tug *Salvanguard* arrived on the scene late on 13 October, equipped with mast water and foam cannons, and during the early hours of 14 October the fires were extinguished. The vessel was taken in tow towards Dubai. A salvage team boarded the vessel and set about assessing the damage, with the intention of safely patching up steel and pipework, restoring power, making the cargo pumps operable and preparing the ship in order that the cargo onboard could be discharged. Master Mariner John Carter who was involved as Tanker Safety Adviser to Selco Salvage gave a detailed account of this remarkable salvage operation at the Gastech 85 Conference in Nice.[13]

On the morning of 16 November, 27,546 m³ *Ribagorça, ex Bridgestone Maru No. 3,* berthed alongside *Gaz Fountain* and the ship to ship transfer of cargo commenced. Early on the morning of 20 November the transfer was completed, with the total amount of cargo saved being 17,204 tonnes of propane and butane. The ship was handed back to her owners on 12 December, following a lengthy period of gas freeing of the perlite insulation in No. 3 void space.

This safe and successful salvage, including the rescue of all the ship's crew, is a true reflection of both the sound overall structural design of this type of fully refrigerated LPG carrier, and the technical professionalism of the salvage team. The cargo tanks were protected with a double bottom and double side hull, the secondary barrier was exposed to cargo, and the robust ship's equipment could be repaired. The on board specialists had a working knowledge of the gas ship's design, construction, equipment and cargoes, and gradually and safely dealt with problems relating to fire, cargo venting, pressure build up, cold spots, structural damage and burnt out electrical equipment. The salvage team also had to perform these seemingly impossible tasks in a dangerous and hazardous environment.

Gaz Fountain was declared a constructive total loss and was broken up on Gadani Beach, Pakistan, in 1985.

Nyhammer

Principle Particulars	
Length o.a.	230.89 m
Length b.p.	215.00 m
Breadth	32.20 m
Depth	21.50 m
Draught	12.60 m
LPG Capacity	66,341 m³
Engine	Mantes-Sulzer 8RND90
Power	23,200 hp/17,064 kW
Service speed	18 knots

The first fully refrigerated LPG carrier from CNC with four prismatic cargo tanks, 66,341 m³ *Nyhammer*, was delivered to Norwegian owners Nygass & Company on 4 July 1975, under the management of Christian Haaland. The breadth of the ship was the maximum allowed for passage through the Panama Canal. This ice strengthened vessel was classed with Det Norske Veritas for LPG and ammonia cargoes, at a minimum temperature of -48°C and a maximum pressure of 0.275 kg/cm². The direct reliquefaction plant consisted of four Loire two piston compressors with heat exchangers. A fixed and a removable submerged electric cargo pump, each rated at 363 m³/hr, were fitted in each cargo tank.

Nyhammer was sold to breakers in Bangladesh in 2002 as *OGC Energy*.

29 November 1993 – Dockside Tragedy

An explosion occurred on 29 November 1993 on board *Nyhammer* while the ship was afloat alongside Hyundai Mipo Dockyard Ltd., Ulsan.[14] The master, chief officer, cargo engineer and three shipyard technicians were killed, who had been inspecting the vessel to agree a repair schedule. Ten other workers were injured. The main deck and upper side shell plating on both sides of the ship in way of the aft cargo tank were fractured and damaged, as well as the top of the aft cargo tank.

The insurance underwriters accepted the vessel as a constructive total loss and the damaged ship was sold and delivered to Arbross Ship Management of Hong Kong on 17 July 1994. After extensive repairs at Sembawang Dockyard, the vessel left Singapore on 16 January 1995 bound for Colombo, Sri Lanka, as *Mundogas Energy*.

Plate 2-6   *Nyhammer*   Chantiers Navals de la Ciotat

Monge

Principle Particulars	
Length o.a.	231.10 m
Length b.p.	216.18 m
Breadth	34.80 m
Depth	22.30 m
Draught	13.55 m
LPG Capacity	70,900 m³
Engines (2)	SEMT-Pielstick 10PC4 570
Power	30,000 hp/22,065 kW
Service speed	19 knots

Two 70,900 m³ LPG/NH$_3$ carriers were delivered in 1977 from La Ciotat, powered by twin Pielstick 10PC4 medium speed diesel engines through a single shaft. The twin engines were mounted close together each side of the ship's centreline, which left a spacious machinery arrangement. The first ship, Monge was delivered to Compagnie Générale Maritime (CGM) on 6 July 1977 and the second Razi was delivered to Iranocean on 16 December 1977. Both ships were to be operated by Gazocéan and classed with Bureau Veritas. The minimum cargo temperature was slightly increased to -46°C and cargoes carried were butane, propane and ammonia.

The cross section of the ship and the cargo tank domes were changed on Monge compared to previous CNC designs. The bottom of the cargo tanks still sloped towards the centreline but the inner bottom was now horizontal. The mid-length cargo tank dome was replaced with two domes, with a liquid dome at the aft part of the tank and a vapour dome at the forward part of the tank. Two 500 m³/hr Guinard deep-well cargo pumps, rather than submerged electric pumps, were fitted on the aft dome in each of the four cargo tanks. Two 500 m³/hr Guinard booster pumps and a cargo heater were fitted. Two pressurised tanks for cargo changes, 150 m³ for ammonia and 350 m³ for propane, were fitted on the main deck forward of the cargo manifolds.

Due to the increased capacity of the ships, the performance of the reliquefaction plant needed to be improved. For the first time, on a fully refrigerated LPG carrier built by La Ciotat, cascade cycle reliquefaction installations were fitted.[15, 16] A reason behind this change was that user's requirements were becoming stricter with regard to the contamination of cargo by lubrication oil from the compressors, and another factor was the known presence of ethane in commercial propane. Three reliquefaction plants were fitted, each with an oil free labyrinth two stage Sulzer compressor and a Sabroe R22 compressor, with each plant rated at 690,000 Fg/hr (Kcal/hr) in propane service. Other cargo handling equipment fitted included a Smit Ovens inert gas generator, a Hibon vapour blower and a vaporiser.

Plate 2-7   *Monge* in La Ciotat fitting out basin   Gazocéan

Plate 2-8   *Monge* after delivery   Gazocéan

Esso Westernport

Principle Particulars	
Length o.a.	255.45 m
Length b.p.	239.50 m
Breadth	35.50 m
Depth	23.45 m
Draught	12.60 m
LPG Capacity	100,988 m³
Engines	Mantes-Sulzer 7RND90M
Power	23,450 hp/17,247 kW
Service speed	16.75 knots

On 27 July 1977, CNC delivered to Esso Tankers Inc., the largest LPG carrier ever built, 100,988 m³ *Esso Westernport*.[17] The distinction of this ship being the largest LPG carrier still stands today, as in the intervening years no larger vessel has been constructed. The vessel was classed with the American Bureau of Shipping and complied with the requirements of the US Coast Guard. The ship was one of the first fully refrigerated LPG carrier to be issued with a IMCO (now IMO) Certificate of Fitness. Designed with four cargo tanks designated for the carriage of butane and propane, *Esso Westernport* traded initially from Ras Tanura, Saudi Arabia, to Japan, before switching to loading for Japan, at the Long Island Point Fractionation Plant, Westernport, Australia. A 1,200 hp (883 kW) bow thruster was fitted. The cargo handling equipment was similar to *Monge*, but as eight 500 m³/hr J C Carter electric submerged cargo pumps were fitted, the mid-length single tank dome arrangement was adopted. In addition 50 m³/hr J C Carter stripping pumps were fitted in each tank. An emergency portable 500 m³/hr J C Carter submerged pump was also available.

Plate 2-9   *Esso Westernport* alongside repair yard   Sembawang

Gas Al-Kuwait

Principle Particulars	
Length o.a.	231.10 m
Length b.p.	216.18 m
Breadth	34.80 m
Depth	22.30 m
Draught	12.71 m
LPG Capacity	72,121 m³
Engine	Mantes-Sulzer 8RND90M
Power	26,800 hp/19,711 kW
Service speed	19 knots

Between 1978 and 1980 La Ciotat delivered four 72,121 m³ LPG/NH$_3$ carriers to the Kuwait Oil Tanker Company. The ships, *Gaz Al-Kuwait, Gas Al-Burgan, Gas Al-Ahmadi* and *Gas Al-Minagish* had the same hull dimensions and cargo tanks' arrangement as the 1977 built *Monge*. The main propulsion unit on each ship was a single Sulzer 8RND90M diesel engine. *Gas Al-Kuwait* was delivered on 30 March 1978, *Gas Al-Burgan* was delivered on 2 April 1978, *Gas Al-Ahmadi* was delivered on 5 September 1979 and *Gas Al-Minagish* was delivered on 10 March 1980.

Al Berry

Principle Particulars	
Length o.a.	228.86 m
Length b.p.	216.00 m
Breadth	36.50 m
Depth	22.25 m
Draught	13.52 m
LPG Capacity	76,929 m³
Engines (2)	Atlantique-Pielstick 12PC 3V
Power	22,800 hp/16,769 kW
Service speed	18.5 knots

Two French built fully refrigerated LPG/NH$_3$ carriers, with perlite insulation, not constructed at La Ciotat were 76,929 m³ *Al Berry* and *Al Bida*.[18, 19] The Saint-Nazaire yard of Chantiers de l'Atlantique delivered the two ships in 1979, under a licence agreement with Technigaz. The owners were the Arab Maritime Petroleum Transport Company (AMPTC), an organisation of eight member countries; Saudi Arabia, Qatar, Abu Dhabi, Libya, Iraq, Algeria, Kuwait and Bahrain. AMPTC originally placed an order with Chantiers de l'Atlantique for two 278,100 deadweight crude oil carriers in 1974. After the oil crisis of the early seventies this order was changed in 1976, into the newbuilding of the two LPG/NH$_3$ carriers.

The ships were classed with Bureau Veritas. *Al Berry* sailed under the flag of Saudi Arabia and *Al Bida* was flagged with Kuwait. Like *Monge* the ships were powered by twin Pielstick medium speed diesel engines through a single shaft. Compared with *Monge*, some cargo handling changes were made; two 520 m³/hr J C Carter submerged electric cargo pumps were fitted in each cargo tank, the cargo piping was 18/8 stainless steel and a single 250 m³ pressurised deck tank was available for cargo changes.

Floreal

Principle Particulars

Length o.a.	249.80 m
Length b.p.	237.00 m
Breadth	35.50 m
Depth	22.90 m
Draught	12.85 m
LPG Capacity	85,662 m³
Engines	Mantes-Sulzer 6RLA90
Power	20,400 hp/15,004 kW
Service speed	17 knots

In 1983, the three French shipbuilders Chantiers Navals de la Ciotat (CNC), Constructions Navales et Industrielles de la Méditerranée (CNIM) and Chantiers de France Dunkerque (CFD) merged to form Chantiers du Nord et de la Méditerranée (NORMED).[7]

The first fully refrigerated LPG/NH_3 to be delivered under the NORMED name was 85,662 m³ *Floreal*. The ship's keel was laid on 25 May 1981 and launched on 7 May 1982. *Floreal* was handed over to Elf Ocean, a joint company of Elf-Aquitaine and Compagnie Nationale de Navigation, on 28 March 1983.

Designed with the same 35.50 m beam and similar draught to *Esso Westernport* the hull parameters were such that the vessel could pass through the Suez Canal fully loaded, and discharge at the major US Gulf Coast receiving terminals. Classed with Bureau Veritas, the ship had four cargo tanks designed for a minimum temperature of -48°C and a maximum pressure of 0.275 kg/cm².

Each tank was arranged with two domes to suit the eight 600 m³/hr deep-well pumps. Three reliquefaction plants with oil free compressors were fitted with each plant rated at 210,000 Fg/hr (Kcal/hr) for propane service. After delivery the ship traded on a 12 months time charter to Trammo.

Plate 2-10   *Floreal* under charter to Trammo   Elf Ocean

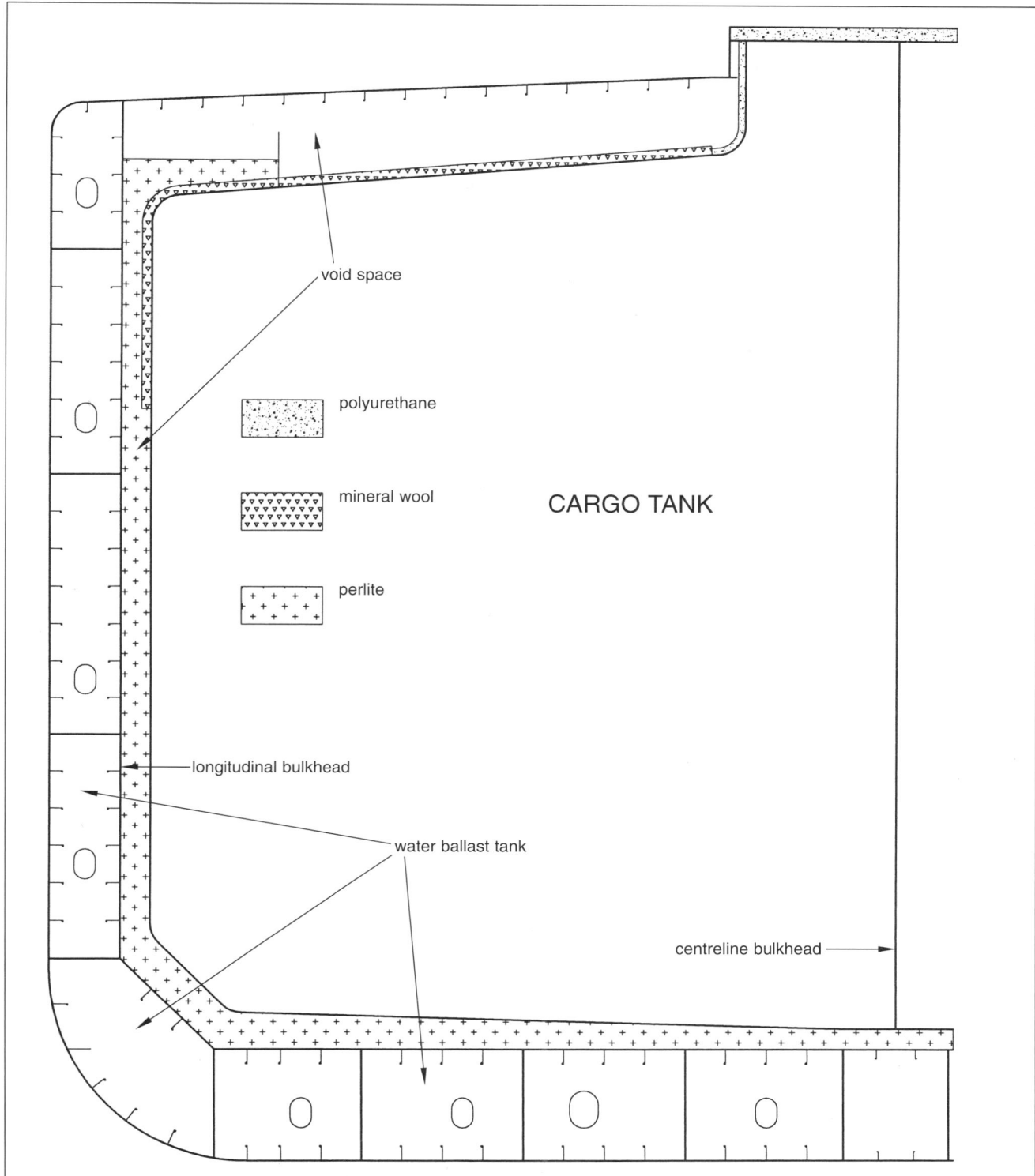

Figure 2-8 Midship Section of *Floreal* showing Perlite Insulation

void space

polyurethane

mineral wool

perlite

CARGO TANK

longitudinal bulkhead

water ballast tank

centreline bulkhead

DÉFENSE DE FUMER
NO SMOKING

Plate 2-11   *Floreal* main deck looking forward   NORMED

Berge Rachel

Principle Particulars	
Length o.a.	228.60 m
Length b.p.	216.00 m
Breadth	35.50 m
Depth	22.80 m
Draught	13.68 m
LPG Capacity	81,600 m^3
Engines	Mantes-Sulzer 5RLB90
Power	17,000 hp/12,503 kW
Service speed	15.5 knots

The final perlite trio of fully refrigerated LPG/NH$_3$ carriers to leave the La Ciotat yard were 81,600 m^3 *Berge Rachel* on 26 April 1984, *Berge Racine* on 18 March 1985 and *Berge Ragnhild* on 6 January 1986. Classed with Det Norske Veritas, the ships were 21 m shorter in length than *Floreal* with the same 35.50 m beam, but generally were of similar design to the Elf Ocean ship. Two 580 m^3/hr Thune Eureka deep-well pumps were fitted in each of the four cargo tanks.

[1] Boudet, René avec la collaboration de Paulette Boudet, *La Joie D'Entreprendre*, June 1999.
[2] Hautefeuille, Roland, with Clayton, Richard, *Gas Pioneers,* Paris, 1998.
[3] Buret, Jean, *Liquefied Gas Carrier Development and Specialisation at La Ciotat,* Shipbuilding & Shipping Record, 30 November 1967.
[4] Ffooks, R.C., *The Shipping of LNG and other Gases – Twenty Years of Steady Progress,* Proceedings of the Institution of Mechanical Engineers, Volume 193, 1979.
[5] English translation by Pauline Harris.
[6] Jean, Pierre, and Petit, Henri, *Quand le Méthane prend la mer,* Gaz Transport & Technigaz, 1998.
[7] Buret, J., and Heryo, Y., *LPG Carriers at Nord Méditerranée, Experience and New Trends,* Gastech 84, Amsterdam.
[8] Shipping World & Shipbuilder, *Kristian Birkeland, LPG Carrier for Norwegian Owners,* October 1968.
[9] Fearnley & Eger brochure, *The Handy-Size Carrier,* 1979.
[10] Lloyd's List Casualty Reports, *Mundogas Europe,* October 1999/July 2000.
[11] Shipping World & Shipbuilder, *Cavendish, Automated LPG Carrier for Ocean Gas Transport,* November 1971.
[12] Lloyd's List Casualty Reports, *Gaz Fountain,* October 1984/September 1985.
[13] Carter, J. A., *Salvage of Cargo from War-Damaged Gaz Fountain,* Gastech 85, Nice.
[14] Lloyd's List Casualty Reports, *Nyhammer,* November 1993/January 1995.
[15] Buret, J., and Bertrand J-P., *Chantiers Navals de La Ciotat and the LPG and Ammonia Carriers,* Gastech 78, Monaco.
[16] The Motor Ship, *First 10PC4 Engines Enter Service in the Monge,* July 1977.
[17] Exxon Marine, *The Largest LPG Carrier in the World,* Summer 1978.
[18] Shipping World & Shipbuilder, *Al Berry – First of Two LPG Carriers for AMPTC,* September 1979.
[19] Holland Shipbuilding, *Al Berry – 76,710 m^3 LPG/NH$_3$ Carrier Delivered by Navales de Alstom-Atlantique,* November 1979.

Chapter 3

Japanese Pioneers Bridgestone and Mitsubishi

The Bridgestone LPG Company Ltd, a subsidiary of the Bridgestone Tyre Co. Ltd., was a major player in the development of the LPG industry in Japan. The company became involved in the then new venture of importing refrigerated LPG into Japan in 1955. At that time, while Constock Liquid Methane Corporation were planning to develop the LNG business on a commercial scale in the USA, Bridgestone chose to follow the LPG route. The three main reasons behind this decision were that the liquefaction of LPG is easier and cheaper than that of LNG, the scope of LPG use is larger and marketing is also easier than that of LNG, and the LPG business can be started on a smaller scale. Later, Constock, with Shell involvement, was to become Conch International Methane Ltd. In May 1959, a Technical Assistance Agreement was made between Bridgestone and Conch International Methane Ltd., for the design and construction of LPG carriers, and in February 1960, Bridgestone agreed a contract with British Petroleum Co. Ltd., for the supply of LPG from Kuwait.[1]

The first purpose built fully refrigerated LPG carrier 28,837 m³ *Bridgestone Maru* was completed at the Yokohama yard of Mitsubishi Nippon Heavy Industries Ltd., (MHI) on 31 January 1962. From this momentous beginning, MHI have remained at the forefront of innovations in gas ship technology. Deliveries from the Yokohama and Nagasaki shipyards of MHI have including LPG carriers with prismatic tanks and internal insulated tanks, and LNG carriers with spherical and membrane tanks. They are also successful in building the unprecedented *V-Series* of 78,000 m³ LPG carriers.

Bridgestone Maru

Principle Particulars	
Length o.a.	183.71 m
Length b.p.	175.00 m
Breadth	25.00 m
Depth	16.70 m
Draught	9.30 m
LPG Capacity	28,837 m³
Engine	Mitsubishi-MAN K9Z 78/140C
Power	13,000 hp/9,561 kW
Service speed	16 knots

A warm memory expressed, some 20 years after the ship was delivered from Yokohama, by a senior Mitsubishi engineer to a British friend and colleague, who also worked on *Bridgestone Maru,* could well echo the thoughts of many others from that time; *"Bridgestone Maru* is so dear a name to my heart and reminds me of the hardest works in my youth."

Naval architects J J Henry Company Inc., of New York, were the designers of *Bridgestone Maru,* which was based on Conch International Methane Ltd. technology.[2, 3] The two companies were involved with extensive research and development for early LNG carrier designs and this Japanese LPG newbuilding was closely related to the Conch LNG work.

Jointly owned by Bridgestone Liquefied Petroleum Gas Co. Ltd., and Nippon Yusen Kaisha (NYK), the ship was operated by NYK on a long term contract from the British Petroleum Co. Ltd., to transport propane and butane from Kuwait to the Bridgestone LPG import terminal at Kawasaki, Japan.[4, 5] The first LPG cargo to be imported by *Bridgestone Maru* was delivered to the Kawasaki terminal in March 1962.

Bridgestone reported the building cost of *Bridgestone Maru* as US $ 9.5 million. Classed with the American Bureau of Shipping, the keel was laid on 23 February 1961 and the ship was launched on 7th November 1961.

The caution of the designers was evident in the steel used for the cargo tanks and ship's inner hull. By today's standards the choice of steel grades on *Bridgestone Maru* was conservative. The four independent prismatic cargo tanks were constructed with 3½% nickel steel and the inner hull with 2¼% nickel steel. The two grades of nickel steel formed respectively the primary container and the secondary barrier.

The cargo tanks were supported on load bearing insulation on the ship's double bottom and were anchored by keys at the top and bottom to prevent movement from rolling and pitching. The glass fibre insulation was protected with aluminium foil. Transverse cofferdams were fitted between each cargo tank. The double bottom and double hull wing tanks were used for water ballast.

The tanks, with the insulation work completed, were positioned in the holds when the ship was on the building slip. The slip was inclined and by an ingenious system of lifts, trolleys, pulleys and wires, each cargo tank was rolled into position, beginning with the aft tank No 4.

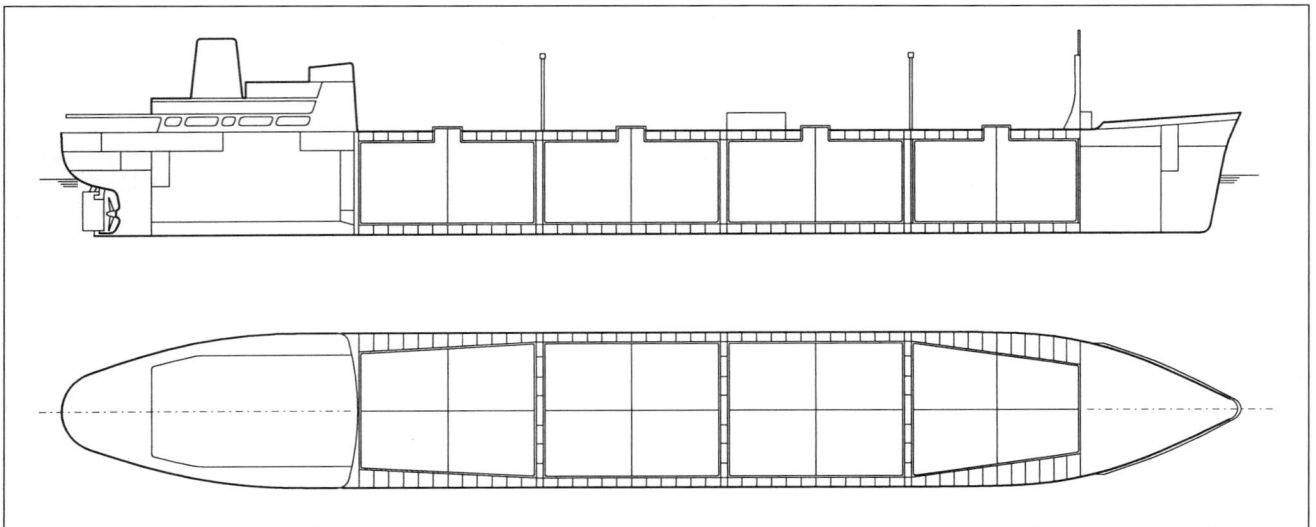

Figure 3-1 Outline Arrangement of *Bridgestone Maru*

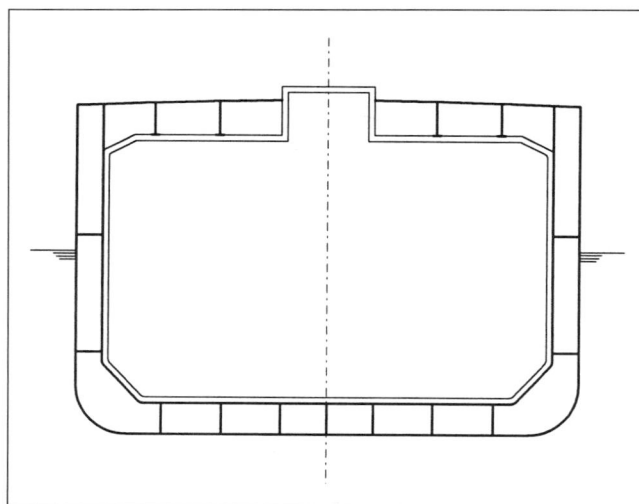

Figure 3-2 Midship Section of *Bridgestone Maru*

Plates 3-1 a-f   *Bridgestone Maru* – Positioning of cargo tanks   MHI

During the first three years in service *Bridgestone Maru* performed well, but also in that time experienced some teething problems with the eight deep-well centrifugal cargo pumps. No consensus was reached regarding the reasons for the pumps' malfunctioning. It was in turn blamed on excessive water content in the cargo, dirt in the cargo, incorrect pump clearances or incorrect pump bearing material. At the third annual survey the pumps' bearing material was changed, which was to eliminate the problems and from then on the pumps operated satisfactorily.

Bridgestone Maru was broken up in 1987, as *Sea Petro*, after a quarter of a century of successful LPG trading.

Plate 3-2   *Bridgestone Maru*   MHI

Bridgestone Maru II

Principle Particulars	
Length o.a.	187.49 m
Length b.p.	178.00 m
Breadth	27.50 m
Depth	18.30 m
Draught	10.50 m
LPG Capacity	36,007 m³
Engine	Mitsubishi-MAN K8Z 78/140C
Power	11,600 hp/8,532 kW
Service speed	15 knots

Japan Line Ltd., who had been trading with pressurised LPG carriers since 1960, took delivery of 36,007 m³ *Bridgestone Maru II* from the Yokohama yard of Mitsubishi Heavy Industries Ltd., on 5 November 1964. The keel was laid on 11 February 1964 and the ship was launched on 30th July 1964. The ship was to operate on charter from the Bridgestone Liquefied Petroleum Co. Ltd., to transport propane and butane from the Middle East to Japan.[6]

Bridgestone Maru II was completed three years after the delivery of *Bridgestone Maru,* and according to Bridgestone's Managing Director Katsuro Yamamoto, savings in construction costs, at U.S. $7.1 million, were in part due to more realistic safety standards by the regulatory authorities, less labour man hours, domestic rather than imported materials, cheaper prices from equipment suppliers and simplified pipework.[1] Conch acted as consultants for the design.

The ship was classed with Nippon Kaiji Kyokai and like *Bridgestone Maru* was constructed with four prismatic cargo tanks. The cross section in way of the cargo tanks was changed with the horizontal inner bottom extending to the turn of the bilge, and wide under deck wing tanks arranged almost to the ships centreline. The double bottom and upper wing tanks were used for water ballast. No side water ballast tanks were fitted and the side hull formed the secondary barrier. Single transverse bulkheads were fitted between the cargo tanks.[7, 8, 9, 10]

The cargo tanks were built simultaneously with the hull structure, which reduced the building time and labour costs, compared to the ingenious transfer of the completed cargo tanks onto the double bottom of *Bridgestone Maru*.

Bridgestone Maru II was sold to breakers, as *Isavana*, in 1984.

MHI delivered 38,161 m³ *Yamahide Maru* to domestic owners Yamashita-Shinnihon Kisen K.K. & Nissho Kisen K.K. on 12 October 1966. The ship had the same hull form as *Bridgestone Maru II* but the cargo tanks were slightly changed to give an additional 2,154 m³ of cargo carrying capacity.

One claim to fame for this ship was that after being sold to joint owners Faran S.A. and Common Brothers in 1982, the ship was renamed *Bo Bengtsson*. Bo Bengtsson was the Norwegian engineer, who worked with Det Norske Veritas and who invented the LNG metallic primary barrier membrane which was, after further development, incorporated into the successful Technigaz membrane system for LNG carriers.[11] *Bo Bengtsson* was sold for demolition in 1985.

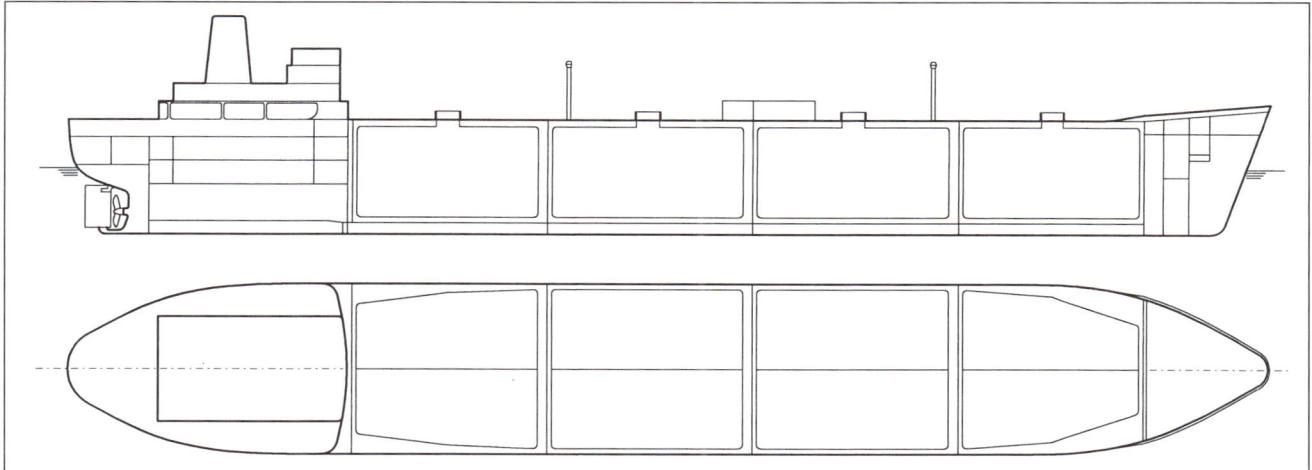

Figure 3-3 Outline Arrangement of *Bridgestone Maru II*

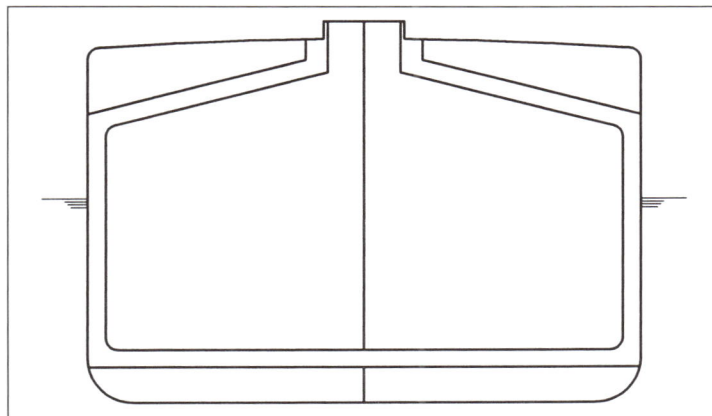

Figure 3-4 Midship Section of *Bridgestone Maru II*

Tatsuno Maru

Principle Particulars	
Length o.a.	202.12 m
Length b.p.	190.00 m
Breadth	30.00 m
Depth	19.90 m
Draught	11.81 m
LPG Capacity	50,542 m³
Engine	Mitsubishi 6UEC85/160C
Power	14,400 hp/10,591 kW
Service speed	15.5 knots

Free from the specific requirements of Bridgestone and Conch, the Yokohama shipyard of Mitsubishi Heavy Industries (MHI) autonomously designed and built the 50,542 m³ *Tatsuno Maru* for domestic owners Nippon Yusen Kaisha (NYK).[12, 13] Delivered on 25 August 1967, the vessel was classed with Nippon Kaiji Kyokai and the ship's distinguishing feature in profile, was the raised main deck above the forward cargo tank.

The four cargo tanks were similar in shape to the tanks on *Bridgestone Maru II*. The under deck water ballast tanks extended well aft into the machinery spaces. The inner hull formed the secondary barrier. The cargo tanks' plating and the flanged plate stiffeners were of quenched tempered carbon steel, and the partially spherical tank corners and pump sumps were of 2¼% nickel steel. The tanks were supported on load bearing insulation and the sides of the tanks were insulated with 80 mm of polyurethane foam. A mid-length dome was fitted at the top of the tank. The dome's polyurethane foam insulation was covered by a polyester treated glass-fibre cloth. Three 336 m³/hr J C Carter submerged electric cargo pumps were fitted in each tank with two used for discharge and the third fitted as a spare. An emergency stern cargo discharge was also fitted.

Tatsuno Maru was broken up in 1985 as *Al-Hada 2*.

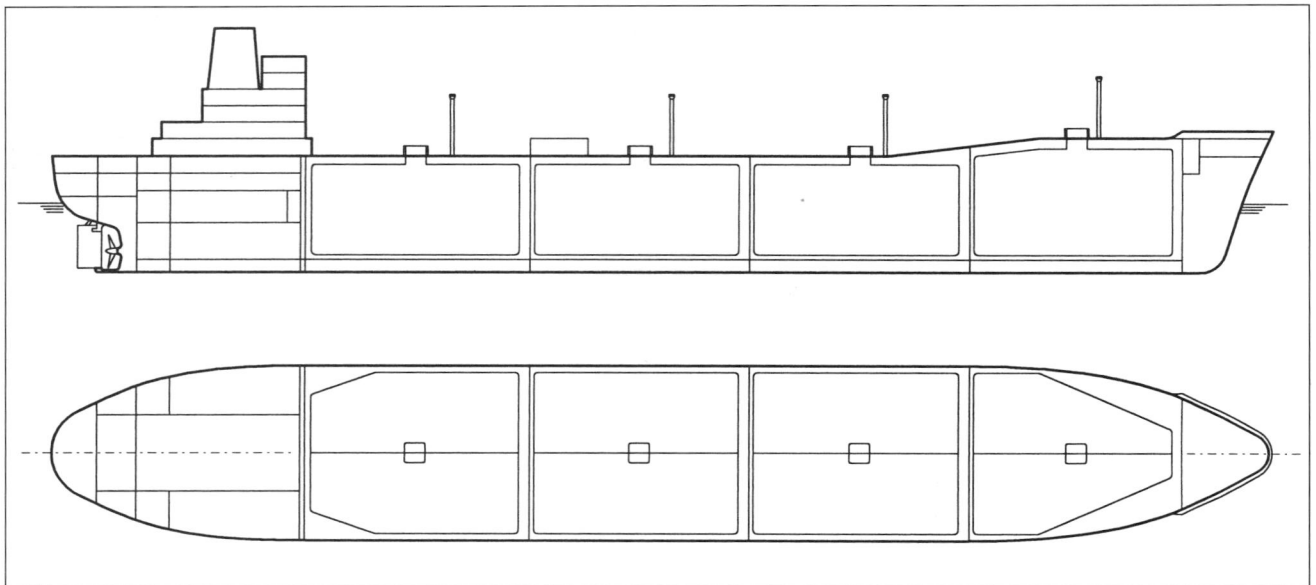

Figure 3-5 Outline Arrangement of *Tatsuno Maru*

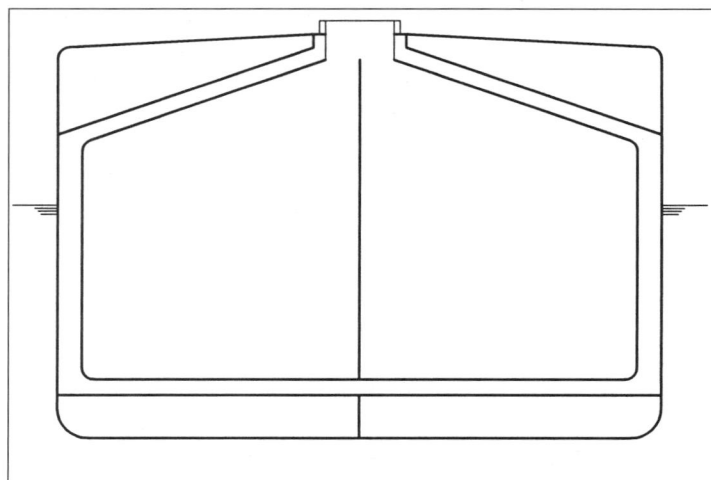

Figure 3-6 Midship Section of *Tatsuno Maru*

Plate 3-3   *Tatsuno Maru*   MHI

Kanayama Maru

Principle Particulars	
Length o.a.	223.96 m
Length b.p.	213.00 m
Breadth	34.60 m
Depth	21.40 m
Draught	11.93 m
LPG Capacity	70,238 m³
Engine	Mitsubishi-Sulzer 6RND90
Power	17,400 hp/12,797 kW
Service speed	15.65 knots

Between 1970 and 1975 the Yokohama yard built a series of six 70,000 m³ LPG carriers for various owners. The lead design ship, 70,238 m³ *Kanayama Maru* was delivered to owners Shinwa Kaiun K.K. and Kyoei Tanker K.K. on 24 August 1970. The four prismatic cargo tanks and water ballast arrangements were similar to the earlier 50,542 m³ *Tatsuno Maru* design, but with a flush main deck from stern to stem. A cargo control room was arranged on the forward part of the bridge deck overlooking the cargo area and a reliquefaction house was located aft of the amidships manifolds. The ship was classed with Nippon Kaiji Kyokai as a Liquefied Flammable Gas Carrier for LPG cargoes at a minimum temperature of -45°C. Two 500 m³/hr and a 250 m³/hr J C Carter submerged electric pumps were fitted in each cargo tank.

Kanayama Maru was sold to breakers in 1985.

Ordered by World-Wide Shipping, *World Rainbow,* which was the second of the series, was delivered to Panamanian affiliated company, Elegance Shipping on 16 December 1971. *World Rainbow* was chartered by Sanko Kisen Kaisha to trade from the Middle East to Japan and was the only ship of the series to have a cargo tank dedicated solely for butane.

World Rainbow was sold to breakers, as *Gaz Coral*, in 2003.

Two Liberian flag vessels followed; *Amvrosios* on 28 February 1974 for Papachristidis Maritime Inc's affiliate Ivory Steamship Corp., and *Pine Queen* on 13 August 1974 for Marubeni America Corp's., affiliate Pine Maritime Corp. The fifth vessel Panamanian flag *Nektar,* was delivered to Texas LPG Transport on 7 February 1975.[14]

Amvrosios was sold to breakers in Taiwan in 1986 and *Nektar* was broken up in 1998.

The sixth and final vessel of the series, *Ogden General,* was delivered to Ogden Tagus Transport on 30 September 1975. The power was increased for a service speed of 17 knots, with an eight cylinder Sulzer diesel engine, rated at 23,200 hp (17,064 kW).

Ogden General was sold to Chinese breakers, as *Gaz Marmara,* in 2003.

Plate 3-4   *Nektar*   MHI

3 March 1988 – Salvage Balancing Act

World Rainbow was fully loaded with 29,000 tonnes of butane and 10,000 tonnes of propane. Bound for Taiwan from the Middle East, the ship ran aground at Pulau Tekong Kechil in Indonesian waters, two miles south of Raffles Light.[15] Dutch specialists Wijsmuller, Salvindo of Singapore and Marine Salvage Offshore of Jakarta were jointly contracted to salvage the vessel. Initial attempts to re-float the gas carrier with three tugs were unsuccessful.

Wijsmuller chartered Singapore flagged 70,792 m³ *Tatsuta,* originally NKK built as *Tatsuta Maru,* to transfer part of the cargo from *World Rainbow* in order to lighten the ship. With the ships side by side, water ballast was pumped into *World Rainbow* to balance the weight of cargo being transferred. This simple but effective technique was used to keep the vessel hard aground in order to restrict any sudden movement or flotation. It also prevented the ships engaged in the salvage work from being damaged by the stranded vessel.

The grounded ship was re-floated at 01:20 hours local time on 12 March. The temporarily stored cargo on *Tatsuta* was then transferred back to *World Rainbow.* A diving inspection found only minor damages to the bottom hull. At 02:35 hours local time on 13 March *World Rainbow* left the grounding site and arrived at the destination discharge port of Kaohsiung on 24 March. This was an unfortunate incident, but the salvage operation was successful, with no loss of life, no pollution and no cargo lost.

Pioneer Louise

Principle Particulars	
Length o.a.	229.00 m
Length b.p.	215.80 m
Breadth	36.60 m
Depth	21.45 m
Draught	11.60 m
LPG Capacity	77,373 m³
Engine (1)	Mitsubishi-MAN V6V52/55
Engine (2)	Mitsubishi-MAN V7V52/55
Power	26,000 hp/19,123 kW
Service speed	16.95 knots

Shell International Marine Ltd., of London in 1965 began research to develop an internal insulation system for fully refrigerated LPG carriers, with the stated aim to reduce the capital cost.[16] Extensive laboratory work on sprayed polyurethane foam was carried out in the United Kingdom and tests were made on a small land based tank and on shipboard tanks. Two 200 m³ tanks were constructed by the Belfast shipyard Harland & Wolff and were fitted inside the forward cargo tank of 18,000 tonnes deadweight oil tanker *Aulica*. In November 1968, LPG was loaded in the test tanks on *Aulica* and over a period of 18 months, at weekly intervals, LPG was moved between the two tanks. A reliquefaction plant was fitted on the main deck. The tanker traded normally during this period in crude oil service.

Following the tests and sea trials, the internal insulation system was offered for licence to shipyards in 1970. Three ships with the Shell system were constructed at MHI, Yokohama with five cargo tanks. *Pioneer Louise* was delivered to Goldcup Shipping Inc. on 31 August 1976, *Gas Gemini* was delivered to Gas Gemini Shipping Inc. on 26 January 1977 and *Gas Diana* was delivered to Gas Diana Transport Inc. on 1 February 1978. The ships were constructed with a double hull arrangement and transverse cofferdams between each cargo tank. Propulsion power was provided by two medium speed diesel engines through a single shaft and a controllable pitch propeller. The double engine arrangement resulted in a shorter engine room and an increased cargo capacity, compared to a single engine arrangement.

Unfortunately the internal insulation system was not successful in service. Using the remarkable technical expertise of Mitsubishi Heavy Industries, the original cargo area and fore end of each of the three ships were rebuilt with five independent steel prismatic cargo tanks. Most of the original items of specialised and expensive gas equipment and fittings, such as cargo pumps, compressors and cargo relief valves etc., were skilfully removed, with great care, from the original cargo sections and refitted on the new tank bodies. The conversions were completed during 1981 and 1982 and the original forward hull sections were used as self-unloading cement handling storage barges.

On 31 March 1980 the Yokohama yard delivered *Gas Libra* to Gas Libra Transport Inc. The ship was based on the same hull dimensions and double engine arrangement as *Pioneer Louise,* but purpose built with five independent steel cargo tanks.

Gas Libra was the last fully refrigerated LPG carrier to be built at MHI's pioneering Yokohama yard. Shipbuilding finished at the yard in 1980. MHI have retained a dock yard and ship repair facility at Yokohama.

Plate 3-5   *Gas Libra*   MHI

Tenryu Maru

Principle Particulars	
Length o.a.	228.00 m
Length b.p.	217.00 m
Breadth	36.60 m
Depth	21.45 m
Draught	10.98 m
LPG Capacity	77,290 m^3
Engine	Mitsubishi-Sulzer 6RLA90
Power	21,600 hp/15,887 kW
Service speed	16.6 knots

The first fully refrigerated LPG carrier to be constructed at the Nagasaki Shipyard & Engine Works of Mitsubishi Heavy Industries was 77,290 m^3 *Tenryu Maru*.[17] The keel was laid in January 1981, the ship was launched on 26 June 1981 and delivered to Nippon Yusen Kaisha on 2 February 1982.

The ship was arranged with a raked transom stern, a flush main deck with aft machinery and accommodation spaces, four cargo tanks and a bulbous bow. The ship was classed with Nippon Kaiji Kyokai as a Tanker for Liquefied Gases at a maximum pressure of 0.21 kg/cm^2 and a minimum temperature of -46°C. The vessel also complied with the United States Coast Guard requirements. Two 550 m^3/hr main and a 250 m^3/hr spare electric submerged pumps were fitted in each cargo tank. Five reliquefaction plants were fitted on the main deck aft of the manifolds and a cargo control room was located in the aft accommodation house.

Plate 3-6   *Tenryu Maru*   MHI

Nichizan Maru

Principle Particulars	
Length o.a.	192.00 m
Length b.p.	182.00 m
Breadth	30.80 m
Depth	18.90 m
Draught	9.80 m
LPG Capacity	43,671 m³
Engine	Mitsubishi-Sulzer 6RLB76
Power	13,600 hp/10,003 kW
Service speed	15.5 knots

Three months after completing *Tenryu Maru,* the Nagasaki yard delivered on 21 May 1982, a smaller, but similar ship with four cargo tanks, the 43,671 m³ *Nichizan Maru.* The joint owners were Nissho Shipping Co. Ltd. and Yamashita-Shinnihon Steamship Co. Ltd.[18] The new ship replaced 38,161 m³ *Yamahide Maru* built for the same owners at MHI Yokohama in 1966.

The vessel was designed for the carriage of butane and propane and was to be engaged on a long term charter, shipping LPG from Vancouver, Canada to Mizushima, Japan. With this trading route in mind, breakwaters were fitted on the main deck, forward of cargo tank domes Nos. 1, 2 & 4. Two 300 m³/hr and a 100 m³/hr electric submerged pumps were fitted in each cargo tank. Four reliquefaction plants were fitted on the main deck forward of the manifolds and a cargo control room was located in the aft accommodation house.

Joyama Maru

Principle Particulars	
Length o.a.	225.50 m
Length b.p.	214.00 m
Breadth	36.00 m
Depth	22.30 m
Draught	11.50 m
LPG Capacity	82,513 m^3
Engine	Mitsubishi-Sulzer 7RTA76
Power	18,600 hp/13,680 kW
Service speed	15.5 knots

The Nagasaki yard completed the third and the largest of a trio of individually tailor-made designs with the delivery of the 82,513 m^3 Joyama Maru to Shinwa Kaiun Kaisha Ltd. on 31 January 1986.[19] All three ships had a similar profile with four cargo tanks. An aft lower deck was introduced on Joyama Maru. This new ship replaced the first 46,469 m^3 Joyama Maru built for the same owners by IHI at Nagoya in 1965.

Nichiyuh Maru

Principle Particulars	
Length o.a.	230.00 m
Length b.p.	219.00 m
Breadth	36.60 m
Depth	20.40 m
Draught	10.60 m
LPG Capacity	78,508 m^3
Engine	Mitsubishi-6UEC60LS
Power	13,100 hp/9,635 kW
Service speed	15.6 knots

Mitsubishi Heavy Industries Ltd. introduced a new design concept for four tank fully refrigerated LPG carriers with their V-Series.[20] The concept of the V-Series, an abbreviation of Variable Common Design, was a range of ships based on the following; a constant beam and depth, a standard aft module, a variable cargo tank and hold module, and a standard bow module. Initially, four cargo capacities were offered; 71,500, 75,000, 78,000 and 82,000 m^3 with a speed of about 17 knots for LPG, NH$_3$ and naphtha cargoes. The concept proved a remarkable, and ongoing success story for the Nagasaki shipbuilders with, up to the time of publishing, a single 71,500 m^3 and twenty eight 78,000 m^3 V-Series LPG carriers having been delivered, with a further two 78,000 m^3 currently on order.

Yuyo Steamship Co. Ltd., signed the first contract for a V-Series ship on 21 December 1987. Débutante 78,507 m^3 Nichiyuh Maru was delivered from Nagasaki on 21 September 1989. This record breaking 78,000 m^3 version, with an overall length of 230 m and an arrival draught of 10.5 m, was designed for world wide trading and able to enter most of the larger LPG terminals. The cargo handling systems were arranged with two segregation of cargo in four prismatic cargo tanks. All bunker tanks were located aft of the cargo area. Refined lines with a Mitsubishi developed bulbous bow and Mitsubishi Reaction Fin, added for the first time on a LPG carrier, made for an energy saving hull arrangement.[21]

The ship was classed with Nippon Kaiji Kyokai as a Tanker for Liquefied Gases at a maximum pressure of 0.28 kg/cm^2 and a minimum temperature of -46°C. The vessel was an IMO type 2G and complied with the United States Coast Guard requirements. The cargo tanks were insulated with polyurethane foam protected with galvanised steel sheeting. Two Ebara 550 m^3/hr electric submerged pumps and a 125 m^3/hr emergency eductor were fitted in each cargo tank. Cargo handling equipment included a 2,000 m³/hr LPG vaporiser, an inert gas generator and four reliquefaction plants. The cargo compressors and motors were housed on the main deck aft of the cargo manifolds. Reflecting the good design, the cargo piping was tidily arranged, leaving a generally open, neat and uncluttered main deck. A cargo control room was located on A-deck in the aft accommodation, facing the cargo area.

A second similar vessel, *Sunny Hope*, was delivered to Sunny Gas Transportation SA on 19 June 1990 under the management of Yuyo Steamship Co. Ltd.

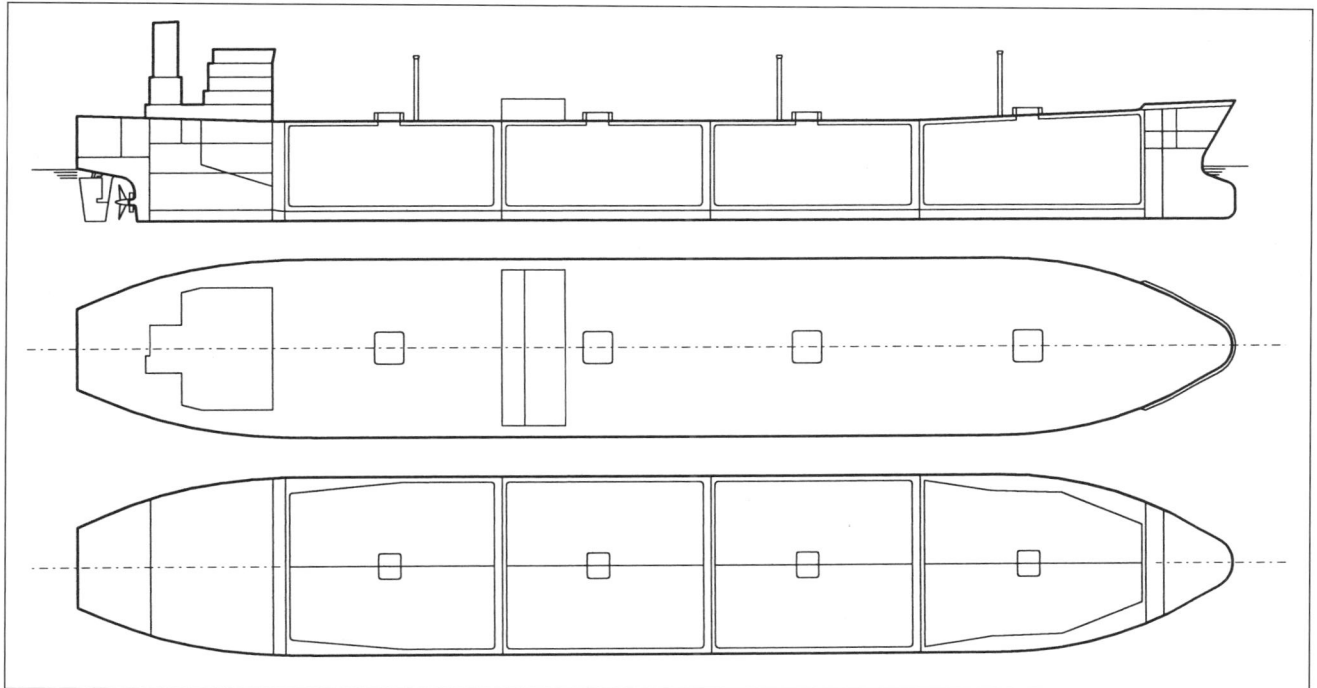

Figure 3-7 Outline Arrangement of *Nichiyuh Maru*

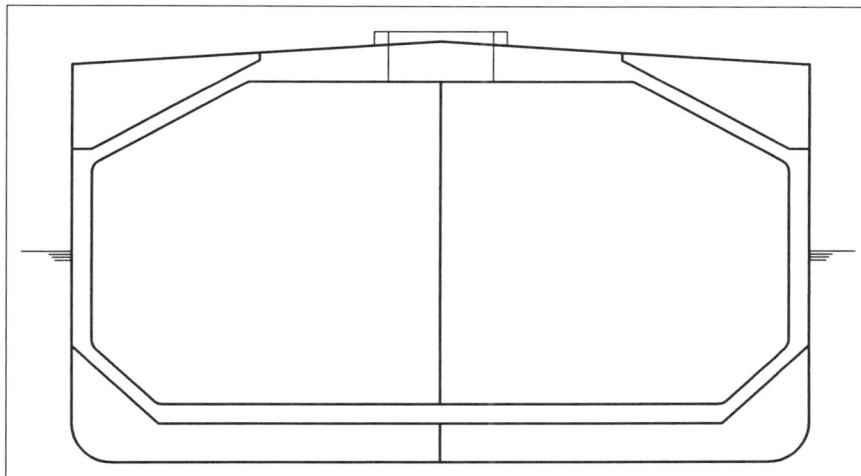

Figure 3-8 Midship Section of *Nichiyuh Maru*

| Plate 3-7 | *Nichiyuh Maru* | MHI |

Gohshu

Principle Particulars	
Length o.a.	217.40 m
Length b.p.	206.40 m
Breadth	36.60 m
Depth	20.40 m
Draught	11.03 m
LPG Capacity	71,913 m³
Engine	Mitsubishi-7UEC60LS
Power	16,800 hp/12,356 kW
Service speed	16.6 knots

The only smaller version of the *V-Series* was the 71,913 m³ *Gohshu*.[22] The seven cylinder Mitsubishi-7UEC60LS main engine was introduced for the first time, and this was to become the standard propulsion unit for the *V-Series* 78,000 m³ ships. *Gohshu* was ordered on 29 August 1988 by Sea Express Transport S.A. and delivered on 20 September 1990, to be operated under Mitsui OSK Lines Ltd. management.

Plate 3-8 *Gohshu* MHI

Plate 3-9 *Gohshu* looking aft MHI

Plate 3-10 *Gohshu* from bridge front MHI

The first two 78,000 m³ carriers with the Mitsubishi-7UEC60LS main engine, and a service speed of 16.7 knots, were ordered by Gas Diana Transport Inc.[23] Under the Panama flag, *Gas Leo* was delivered on 13 December 1990 and *Gas Aries* was delivered on 13 June 1991. Two Ebara 550 m³/hr electric submerged pumps and an Ebara 250 m³/hr stripping pump were fitted in each cargo tank. Five reliquefaction plants were fitted, with three used during normal loaded passage at sea, and two fitted as standby units.

A further two Panama flag vessels followed, with *Gas Roman* being delivered to Holy Light Shipping on 19 December 1990 and *Sunway* to Golden Gas Carrier SA on 28 February 1991. *Pacific Century,* the eighth ship of the *V-Series,* was delivered to Gas Asia Shipping Inc on 27 November 1991 and placed under Sanko Line management. *Inger* was delivered to Orient Gas Transport Inc. on 27 March 1992, and was modified in 1996 into the Floating Storage and Offloading (FSO) vessel *N'Kossa II* and positioned off the Congo coast.

Golden Gas Transport SA added *Sunny Green* to the Yuyo Steamship Co. Ltd. fleet on 17 March 1992 and *Gas Miracle* was added to the Holy Light Shipping fleet on 27 November 1992. The round dozen for the *V-series* was achieved with the delivery of *Energy Orpheus* on 27 January 1993, to an Idemitsu Kosan SA affiliated company Orpheus Tanker Corp.

The first LPG carriers to be built at Mitsubishi for non-Japanese ownership were ordered by the Kuwait Oil Tanker Company.[24] *Gas Al-Mutlaa* was delivered on 25 March 1993 with *Gas Al-Gurain* following on 29 June of the same year.

On 22 July 1993, Oriental Gas Transport took delivery of *Oval Nova* as the fourth 78,000 m³ LPG carrier to be efficiently completed at Nagasaki in a seven month period of that year. The 16th and 17th *V-Series* ships were completed in 1995 with *G Leader* for IMS Navigation SA on 20 November and *Gas Scorpio* added to the Gas Diana Transport Inc fleet on 21 December.

The succession of 78,000 m³ LPG carriers from Nagasaki continued into 1996 with the delivery of *Gas Vision* to Turtle Shipping on 31 January and *Lavender Passage* to Brighton Shipholding SA on 19 July. The next *V-Series* ship, *Toyosu Maru,* was delivered on 28 January 1997 to the joint ownership of Iino Kaiun Kaisha Ltd., and Tokyo LNG Co. Ltd., as a replacement for 39,113 m³ *Toyosu Maru* built at IHI, Aioi, in 1984. The small ship had been designed to trade to the Tokyo Gas terminal at Toyosu. With the planned phase out of the Toyosu plant, the new ship would trade to the larger import terminals of Tokyo Gas Company, at Negishi and Sidegaraura.

Two more ships with this MHI standard design were ordered for the Yuyo Steamship Co. Ltd. fleet. *Yuhsho* was delivered to Bull Transport Inc. on 15 February 1999 and *Sunny Joy* to Lealty Marine Corp. on 31 October 2000. Mitsu OSK Lines through Windmill Shipping SA took delivery of *Great Tribune* on 29 November 1999. Jasper Shipholding SA took delivery of *Linden Pride* in January 2001. Another ship was ordered by Gas Diana Transport Inc. and delivered as *Gas Diana* on 30 June 2000. *Gas Taurus* was delivered to Orient Gas Transport on 29 June 2001.[25] Pacific Gas Transports SA took delivery of *Yuhsan* on 15 January 2002.[26] The twenty-eighth ship of the *V-Series,* *Lycaste Peace* was delivered to Quailwood Enterprise on 28 February 2003. *Gas Capricorn* was delivered to Gas Diana Transport on 30 June 2003.

Currently, MHI have a further two ships on order with their 78,000 m³ design. Hull 2182 is due for delivery to Hawthorne Shipping in December 2003 and Hull 2188 is due for delivery to Ocean Gas Transports SA in September 2004.

Mitsubishi Heavy Industries have delivered or have on order, thirty-one LPG carriers based on a single design concept. This is a remarkable achievement. In total, over fifty fully refrigerated LPG carriers have been delivered from the Yokohama and Nagasaki shipyards, beginning with *Bridgestone Maru,* which was completed in 1962.

Plates 3-11 a-f *Lilac Princess* to *Havdrott* LPG trans shipment

Brugge Venture

Principle Particulars	
Length o.a.	169.90 m
Length b.p.	162.00 m
Breadth	27.40 m
Depth	18.20 m
Draught	11.10 m
LPG Capacity	35,418 m³
Engine	Mitsubishi-7UEC50LSII
Power	13,092 hp/9,630 kW
Service speed	16.7 knots

In 1997 the Nagasaki yard completed three 35,418 m³ multi-purpose LPG carriers for three different owners. The first of the trio, *Brugge Venture*, was delivered on 9 May 1997 to an Exmar NV affiliated company, Blackbeard Shipping Ltd.[27] The ship profile was similar to the 78,000 m³ series, but 104 m³ and 335 m³ deck tanks were added and forward deck sheer introduced. Like the *V-Series* ships the energy saving Mitsubishi bulbous bow and Reaction Fin were fitted.

The ship was classed with Lloyd's Register of Shipping for the carriage of a full range of petroleum and chemical gases including anhydrous ammonia, butane, butadiene, butylene, dimethylamine, ethyl chloride, propane, propylene and VCM. The three prismatic tanks were designed for a minimum temperature of -50°C, a maximum pressure of 0.28 kg/cm² and a maximum specific gravity of 0.97.

Two 400 m³/hr Svanehøj deep-well pumps, mounted on a second tank dome, were fitted at the aft part of each cargo tank. Cargo tanks Nos. 1 & 3 were liquid tight at the centreline with a swash bulkhead fitted at the centreline of cargo tank No. 2. Two 400 m³/hr Svanehøj centrifugal booster pumps and a cargo heater were fitted on the main deck. A combined cargo heater and vaporiser was fitted. A breakwater was fitted on the main deck forward of No. 1 cargo tank dome. Three reliquefaction plants were housed on the main deck aft of the cargo manifolds with a forward facing cargo control room above the reliquefaction house.

The second of the series, *Gas Columbia,* was delivered to Northern Hawk Maritime SA on 30 July 1997 under the classification of Nippon Kaiji Kyokai.

Originally ordered by Exmar NV., the third ship, *Oxfordshire,* was sold before delivery on 25 November 1997 to Bibby affiliated company, Huskisson Shipping Ltd.

Another 35,000 m³ multi-purpose LPG carrier, Hull No. 2186, is on order at Nagasaki, for owners Rolling Hills Maritima S.A. Delivery is due in January 2004.

Carli Bay

Principle Particulars	
Length o.a.	155.00 m
Length b.p.	148.00 m
Breadth	25.80 m
Depth	16.30 m
Draught	10.20 m
LPG Capacity	25,302 m³
Engine	Mitsubishi-7UEC50LSII
Power	13,092 hp/9,630 kW
Service speed	17.2 knots

An Exmar NV affiliated company, Ama Shipping, took delivery on 29 October 1998 of a multi-purpose vessel, the 25,302 m³ *Carli Bay*.[28] The ship was a smaller version of 35,418 m³ *Brugge Venture* and designed to carry a similar range of petroleum and chemical gases in three cargo tanks. Two 300 m³/hr Svanehøj deep-well pumps were fitted in each cargo tank and two similar sized booster pumps were fitted on the main deck. The same main engine propulsion unit was fitted on both ships.

Plate 3-12   *Carli Bay*   MHI

Eupen

Principle Particulars	
Length o.a.	179.92 m
Length b.p.	172.00 m
Breadth	27.40 m
Depth	18.20 m
Draught	11.13 m
LPG Capacity	38,961 m³
Engine	Mitsubishi-7UEC50LSII
Power	13,092 hp/9,630 kW
Service speed	16.85 knots

A third ship for the Exmar fleet was delivered to Aiola Shipping on 31 March 1999. The 38,961 m³ *Eupen* was a slightly larger version of *Brugge Venture*.

In November 2003 BP Shipping placed an order with four 83,000m³ LPG carriers. The first ship is scheduled for delivery in 2006.

[1] Yamamoto, Katsuro, *Bridgestone LPG Carriers and Terminals,* Le Pétrole et la Mer, Section III – No. 318, 1965.

[2] Banister, Montgomery, and Filstead C. G., *Low-Temperature Liquefied-Gas Transportation,* Society of Naval Architects and Marine Engineers Annual Meeting 1961.

[3] Ffooks, Roger, *Gas Carriers,* Fairplay Publications, 1974.

[4] The Shipping World, *Launch of Refrigerated Propane Carrier,* 22 November 1961.

[5] The Shipping World, *Bridgestone Maru,* 14 March 1962.

[6] Japan Line Press Release, *Japan Line Starts Large LPG Carrier Operation,* 13 February 1965.

[7] MHI Review, New Products, *Refrigerated LPG Carrier Bridgestone Maru II,* 1965.

[8] The Motor Ship, *Bridgestone Maru II, A 36,007 m³ LPG Carrier,* August 1965.

[9] Shipbuilding & Marine Engineering in Japan, JSEA, *LPG Carrier Bridgestone Maru II,* 1966.

[10] Bridgestone brochure, *Gas Carriers,* 1971.

[11] Jean, Pierre, and Petit, Henri, *Quand le Méthane prend la mer,* Gaz Transport & Technigaz, 1998.

[12] Mitsubishi Heavy Industries Ltd., Shipbuilding Report No. 18, *World's Largest LPG Carrier, Tatsuno Maru,* November 1967.

[13] Zosen, *Tatsuno Maru, World's Biggest Refrigerated LPG Carrier,* January 1968.

[14] Shipbuilding & Marine Engineering in Japan, JSEA, *LPG Carrier, Nektar,* 1976.

[15] Lloyd's List Casualty Reports, *World Rainbow,* March 1988.

[16] Worboys, R. V., and Young, S. F., *The Development of an Internal Insulation System for LPG Carriers,* Gastech 74, Amsterdam.

[17] Mitsubishi Heavy Industries Ltd., Technical Review, *Tenryu Maru, A 77,000 m³ LPG Carrier of Independent Prismatic Tank Type,* October 1984.

[18] Mitsubishi Heavy Industries Ltd., Shipbuilding Report No. 201, *43,500 m³ Low Temperature LPG Carrier Nichizan Maru,* 6 August 1982.

[19] Mitsubishi Heavy Industries Ltd., Shipbuilding Report No. 248, *Mitsubishi 18th Refrigerated LPG Carrier Joyama Maru,* 31 October 1986.

[20] Mitsubishi Heavy Industries Ltd., brochure, *Mitsubishi V series LPG Carriers,* 1 May 1989.

[21] Mitsubishi Heavy Industries Ltd., Shipbuilding Record No. 42, *A 78,000 m³ Advanced LPG Carrier, Nichiyuh Maru,* 20 December 1989.

[22] Mitsubishi Heavy Industries Ltd., Shipbuilding Record No. 54, *A 71,900 m³ Advanced LPG Carrier, Gohshu,* 20 February 1991.

[23] Mitsubishi Heavy Industries Ltd., Shipbuilding Record No. 57, *A 78,000 m³ Advanced LPG Carrier, Gas Leo,* 20 February 1991.

[24] Mitsubishi Heavy Industries Ltd., Shipbuilding Record No. 80, *A 78,000 m³ Advanced LPG Carrier, Gas Al-Mutlaa,* 1 June 1993.

[25] Mitsubishi Heavy Industries Ltd., Shipbuilding Record No. 148, *A New 78,500 m³ LPG Carrier, Gas Taurus,* 15 February 2002.

[26] Shipbuilding & Marine Engineering in Japan JSEA, *Yuhsan, 78,500 m³ LPG Carrier,* 2003.

[27] Mitsubishi Heavy Industries Ltd., Shipbuilding Record No. 123, *A 35,000 m³ Multi-Purpose LPG Carrier, Brugge Venture,* 25 September 1997.

[28] Mitsubishi Heavy Industries Ltd., Shipbuilding Record No. 138, *A 25,000 m³ Multi-Purpose LPG Carrier, Carli Bay,* 20 August 1999.

Chapter 4

First Refrigerated LPG from Ras Tanura Terminal

The Chiba and Tamano works of Mitsui Shipbuilding and Engineering Co. Ltd., have constructed semi-pressurised and fully refrigerated LPG carriers, and spherical and membrane type LNG carriers. In 1961, *Gohshu Maru,* delivered from the Tamano yard was the first ship to carry refrigerated LPG from the Aramco terminal at Ras Tanura, Saudi Arabia, to Japan. On this first historic voyage, 3,200 m³ of butane and 4,800 m³ of propane were carried concurrently with a full cargo of crude oil.

Gohshu Maru

Principle Particulars	
Length o.a.	221.44 m
Length b.p.	212.00 m
Breadth	30.40 m
Depth	15.15 m
Draught	11.84 m
LPG Capacity	11,300 m³
Engine	Mitsui-B&W 8 84 VT2BF 180
Power	16,800 hp/12,356 kW
Service speed	16 knots

The Tamano yard of Mitsui Shipbuilding and Engineering Co. Ltd., delivered on 31 October 1961, a combined crude oil and LPG carrier, *Gohshu Maru,* to General Kaiun K.K., based on guidance plans from the Standard Oil Co. of New Jersey, (Esso).[1, 2] The vessel had dual classification with the American Bureau of Shipping and Nippon Kaiji Kyokai. About 10% of the tanker's deadweight was dedicated to loading LPG and the ship was arranged with cruiser stern, poop deck, aft superstructure, trunk deck, amidships bridge house and forecastle deck. Five independent LPG cargo tanks were fitted at centre amidships, with crude oil carried in the remaining centre tanks and in the wing tanks.

In 1976, as *Great Crane,* the vessel was converted to carry only crude oil and in 1982, as *Contovello,* was sold to Taiwanese breakers.

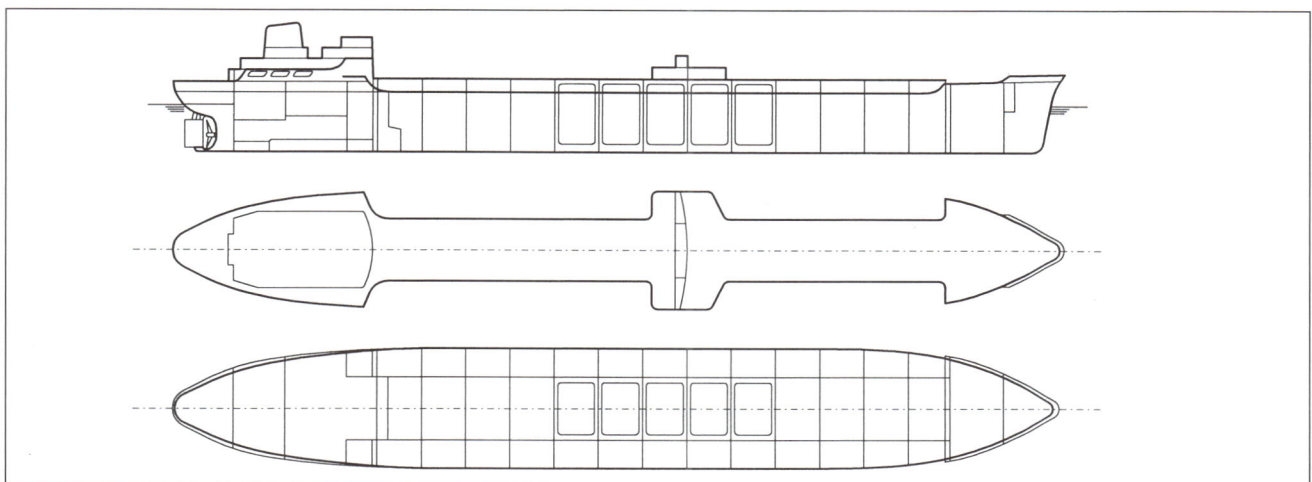

Figure 4-1 Outline Arrangement of *Gohshu Maru*

Plate 4-1   *Gohshu Maru*   Mitsui

Izumisan Maru

Principle Particulars	
Length o.a.	215.07 m
Length b.p.	203.00 m
Breadth	32.00 m
Depth	21.50 m
Draught	11.03 m
LPG Capacity	60,990 m³
Engine	Mitsui-B&W 6K84EF
Power	15,500 hp/11,400 kW
Service speed	16 knots

The first purpose built fully refrigerated LPG carrier to be constructed at the Tamano shipyard was 60,990 m³ *Izumisan Maru*.[3] The keel was laid on 4 November 1969, the ship was launched on 11 April 1970, and delivered to owners Mitsui OSK Lines Ltd. on 31 August 1970. Classed with Nippon Kaiji Kyokai as a tanker for Liquefied Flammable Gas, at a minimum temperature -48°C, the ship was designed to carry butane or propane in all four cargo tanks.

The ship was arranged with a cruiser stern, aft machinery spaces/accommodation house, flush main deck with forward sheer, and a bulbous bow. Each prismatic cargo tank, with large rounded edges and corners, had a small cargo dome just aft of the mid-length swash bulkhead, with an in-line pump sump at the base of the tank. Two 500 m³/hr submerged electric pumps and a similar 200 m³/hr stripping pump were fitted in each tank. Generous room for access was provided in the void spaces around the cargo tanks. The cargo tanks were insulated with 100 mm thick polyurethane foam. A reliquefaction house, with a cargo control room above it, was located on the main deck above Nos. 3 and 4 cargo tanks.

Izumisan Maru was sold to breakers in 1986.

A second ship, 61,203 m³ *Tokuho Maru,* with the same hull dimensions and main propulsion unit as *Izumisan Maru,* was ordered by Iino Kaiun K.K. from Mitsui.[4] The keel was laid on 14 September 1973, the ship was launched on 26 December 1973, and delivered on 31 August 1974. One aspect which made this vessel different from the first ship was that No. 3 cargo tank was dedicated for butane only. *Tokuho Maru* was reported as scrapped as *Rainbow Gas* in 2003.

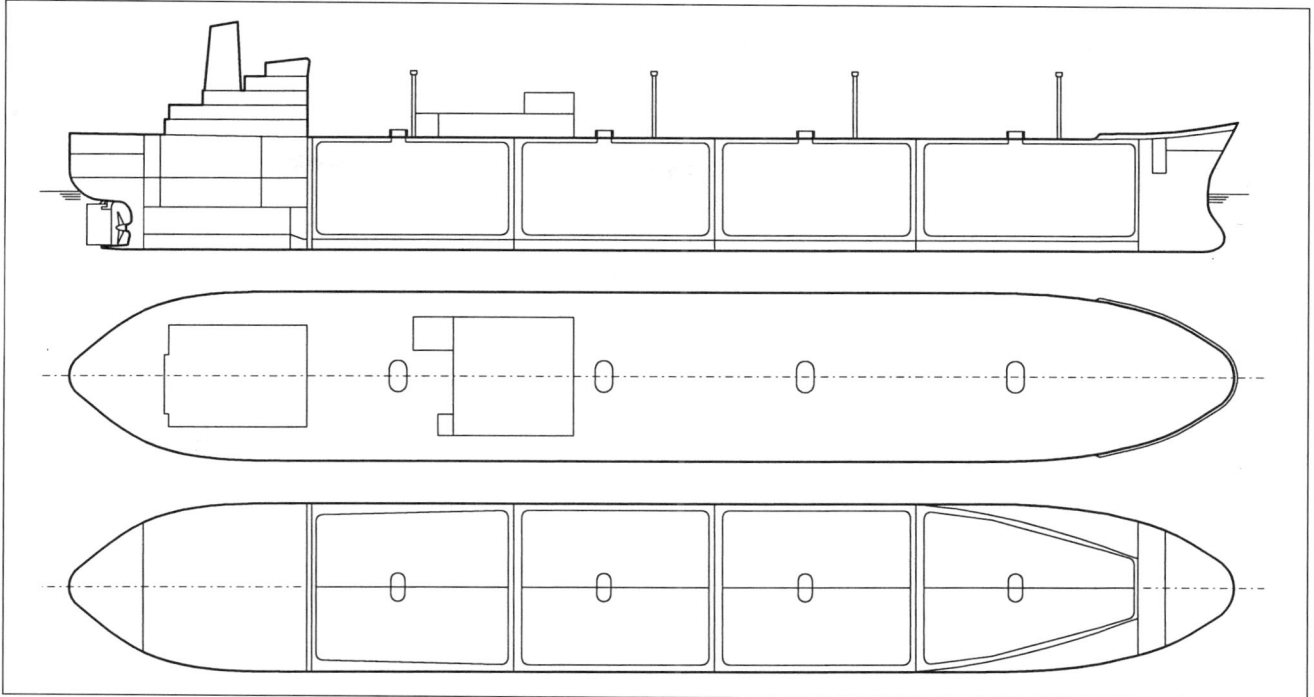

Figure 4-2 Outline Arrangement of *Izumisan Maru*

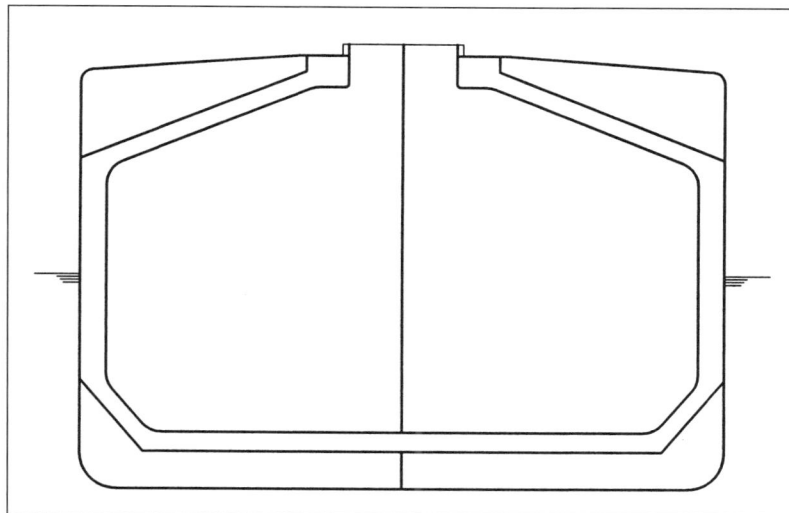

Figure 4-3 Midship Section of *Izumisan Maru*

Plate 4-2   *Izumisan Maru*   Mitsui

Plate 4-3   *Tokuho Maru*   Mitsui

[1] The Motor Ship, *Three LPG Tankers Under Construction in Japan,* October 1961.
[2] The Shipping World, *Gohshu Maru, Japanese Combined Tanker and LPG Carrier,* 14 March 1962.
[3] Shipbuilding & Marine Engineering in Japan, JSEA, *Izumisan Maru, LPG Carrier,* 1972.
[4] Shipbuilding & Marine Engineering in Japan, JSEA, *Tokuho Maru, LPG Carrier,* 1976.

Chapter 5

Secondary Barrier Side Hull from A G Weser

German shipbuilders Akitien-Gesellschaft Weser (A G Weser) of Bremen, started their studies on the sea transportation of liquefied gases in 1955. The shipyard's design engineer Jürgen Rehling perfectly summed up the approach of the time in his honest statement;

> Besides the development of Weser's own gas carrier designs, the yard carefully watched the activities of other yards, shipowners and consultants in the growing field of sea transportation of liquefied gases.[1]

The now closed Bremen shipyard was only involved with two fully refrigerated LPG carriers; *Esso Centro America* and *Antilla Cape.* However, both of these ships were to have a major influence on future gas ship designs. On *Esso Centro America,* the side hull was utilised as the secondary barrier for the first time on a fully refrigerated LPG carrier. The side hull was again the secondary barrier on *Antilla Cape* with the ship arranged, for the first time, with the now almost standard FRLPG's cross section having lower and upper side wing tanks for water ballast.

Esso Centro America

Principle Particulars	
Length o.a.	116.50 m
Length b.p.	111.56 m
Breadth	14.69 m
Depth	9.99 m
Draught	6.07 m
LPG Capacity	5,748 m³
Engine	Nordberg
Power	1,400 hp/1,030 kW
Service speed	9.5 knots

In 1961, the Bremen yard received an order to convert a T1-M-BT 2 type tanker, *Esso Venezuela,* into an LPG/ammonia carrier.[2, 3] *Esso Venezuela* was originally built as *Tarauca* in 1945 by Todd Houston in Texas. In a complex conversion, the existing aft end and machinery spaces, aft accommodation and fore end were retained. The original amidships deckhouse was moved aft and connected to the existing aft superstructure. A new mid-body with four holds was built for the four prismatic shaped self-supporting cargo tanks. *Esso Centro America* was delivered to the Panama Transport Company on 28 September 1962.

The conversion was completed under the classification of American Bureau of Shipping and the requirements of the US Coast Guard. The tanks were designed for a minimum temperature of -45° C and a maximum pressure of 0.28 kg/cm². The dynamic loads for the cargo tanks were designed to withstand an inclination of 30° to port or starboard within 7 seconds, a pitching of 6° from the horizontal within 7 seconds and a heaving of L/80 in an 8 second period. Each cargo tank and the hull structure in way of the cargo holds were constructed with low carbon fine grain steel. The side hull, inner bottom and transverse bulkheads formed the secondary barrier. The main deck in the cargo area was constructed with mild steel.

The cargo tanks were supported and centred on the inner bottom by several longitudinal and transverse sliding timber bearers. Timber supports, to retain the cargo tanks during rolling and pitching, were fitted on the upper sides and ends of the tanks, with five supports fitted on the sides and four supports fitted on the ends.

The insulation work was carried out by the Bremen firm of Kaefer, who were also involved in the same year with applying mineral wool insulation to the cargo tanks of 908 m³ LPG carrier *Kirsten Tholstrup* building at the Jos. L. Meyer shipyard in Papenburg. Two historical events of note; Meyer's first gas carrier and Kaefer's first step into insulating gas ship tanks.

Sprayed polyurethane foam insulation was applied to the outer surfaces of the cargo tanks.[4] The technique presented two basic problems; the adhesion of the approximately 100 mm thick foam to the cargo tank and the uneven crater like surface of the foam. To level this surface with available knives, milling machines and saws proved to be especially difficult and a levelling machine was built, which combined both sawing and milling operations. After the surface was levelled, the insulation was protected from mechanical damage with a sprayed glass fibre polyester resin covering, which also acted as a vapour seal. To provide a good working environment, for the cutting work and to ensure the correct reaction between the polyurethane foam and the polyester resin, a dome shaped inflatable and heated tent was used. The tent, cutting machine, heaters and related equipment were moved four times, for each of the cargo tanks in turn. The insulated cargo tanks were each positioned on board by using the shipyard's 150 tonne floating crane. The underside of the main deck was also insulated.

A single deep-well cargo pump was fitted in each cargo tank with an inline horizontal booster pump, with bypass, fitted in the loading and discharge line, for each deep-well pump. In the event of failure of a deep well pump, a built-in eductor system was available, which was primed by the booster pump of another tank. Cargo loading and discharge from either side of the ship were through a common articulated pipeline arm, positioned on a derrick between Nos. 2 and 3 cargo tank. A two stage R22 reliquefaction plant was fitted.

More major surgery for the hull in 1984, when the cargo section was converted into a barge for Mundogas and renamed *Monomer Venture*. This important ship was broken up as *Gas Venture* in 1993.

Plate 5-1   Sprayed polyurethane foam insulation before levelling on one of the cargo tanks on *Esso Centro America*   Kaefer

Plate 5-2   Surface levelling of the polyurethane foam insulation   Kaefer

Plate 5-3   Dome shaped inflatable and heated tent providing a good working environment in which to apply the insulation   Kaefer

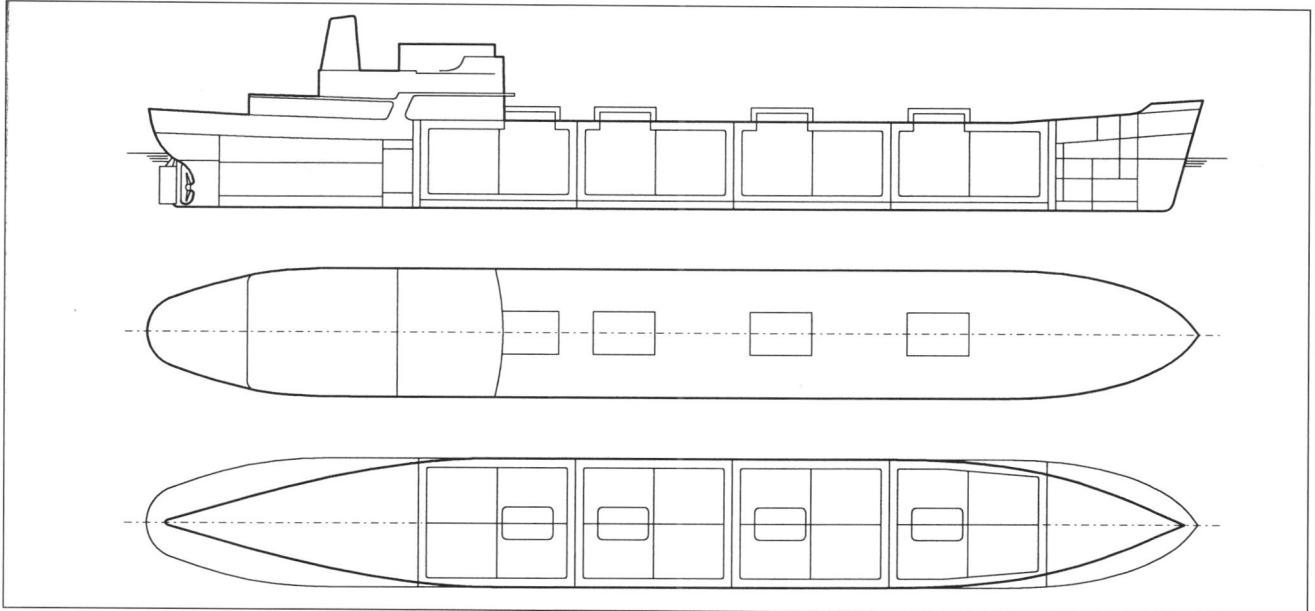

Figure 5-1 Outline Arrangement of *Esso Centro America*

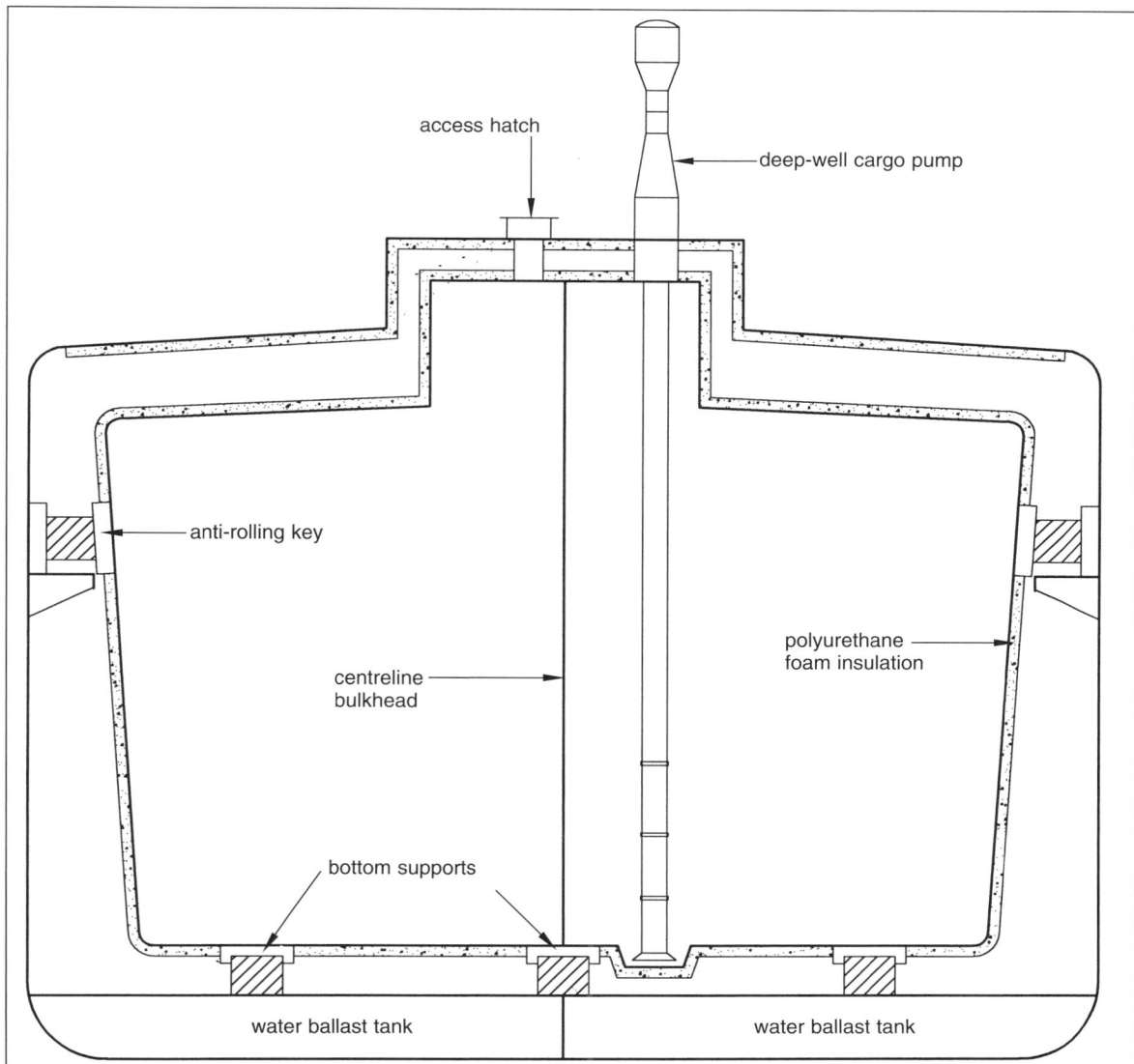

access hatch

deep-well cargo pump

anti-rolling key

polyurethane
foam insulation

centreline
bulkhead

bottom supports

water ballast tank

water ballast tank

Figure 5-2 Midship Section of *Esso Centro America* showing Insulation,
Tank Supports and Deep-well Pump

Antilla Cape

Principle Particulars	
Length o.a.	173.84 m
Length b.p.	164.00 m
Breadth	25.80 m
Depth	17.10 m
Draught	10.22 m
LPG Capacity	29,540 m³
Engine	Winterthur-Sulzer 8RD76
Power	13,200 hp/9,709 kW
Service speed	17 knots

The only fully refrigerated LPG carrier to be built by A G Weser, 29,540 m³ *Antilla Cape,* was delivered in August 1968 to Scheepvaart Maatschappij Volharding of Willemstad, Curaçao, Netherlands Antilles.[5, 6, 7, 8] The owners were a consortium of three Dutch companies; Nederland Line, Royal Interocean Lines and Royal Rotterdam Lloyd, each owning 30% of the capital, with the remaining 10% share taken by Compagnie Worms of Paris. The same consortium members funded the construction of *Hypolite-Worms*, which was delivered from CNIM in December 1968.

Marine Service GmbH of Hamburg, following their involvement with 25,102 m³ *Paul Endacott,* built at Kockums in 1964, again provided design and supervision services for the A G Weser newbuilding (See Chapter 7). This ice strengthened vessel was classed with the American Bureau of Shipping and complied with the US Coast Guard requirements for LPG/ammonia cargoes for a minimum temperature of -51°C and a maximum pressure of 0.28 kg/cm².

The ship was arranged with a cruiser stern, a flush main deck with an aft accommodation house, a reliquefaction house with cargo control room amidships and a raked stem. Twin cargo vents fitted over No. 1 cargo tanks were an eye catching feature. A breakwater was fitted on the main deck forward. Aft of the reliquefaction plant house there were four pressurised cylindrical deck tanks, two at 35 m³ for the inert gas system and two at 33 m³ for LPG.

The four prismatic cargo tanks were constructed with low carbon steel and were arranged with the bottom of the tanks sloping downwards towards the ship's centreline. Water ballast spaces were arranged in the double bottom with lower side wing tanks and upper side under deck wing tanks. Single transverse bulkheads were fitted between each cargo tank. The inner bottom, inner hull and transverse bulkheads formed the secondary barrier and were constructed with the same low carbon steel as the cargo tanks. The cargo tanks were supported at the centreline and at the side by three longitudinal rows of steel and azobé timber supports. The cargo tanks were held in position against rolling and pitching by four sets of vertical keys, two on the centreline at the ends of the tanks and two at the mid-length of the sides of the tanks. The keys, a patented A G Weser system, were constructed around access trunks to the inner bottom at the centre, and access trunks to the lower ballast tanks at the side. Good access was provided around the sides of the cargo tanks with three 980 mm wide horizontal stringers fitted at the side hull.

The tanks were insulated with 110 mm slabs of polyurethane foam bonded to the tanks and externally covered with glass fibre reinforced epoxy sheathing. Two 310 m³/hr J C Carter submerged electric cargo pumps were fitted in each tank. Each pump was fitted inside a vertical cylindrical trunk and could be removed from the tank, for repair or servicing, without cargo discharge or gas-freeing. Two Worthington booster pumps were also fitted. Three reliquefaction plants were installed, each included a Sulzer labyrinth oil free LPG compressor, a Sabroe R22 compressor and associated condensers. An inert gas plant, designed by Gasellschaft fur Inertgas Anlagen (GIA) was located at the main deck level in the accommodation deckhouse.

Antilla Cape started trading with propane cargoes from Houston, Texas, to Felixstowe, United Kingdom, on a six month charter from the Worms Group. This was followed by a three year charter for Phillips Petroleum, transporting propane and butane from Ras Tanura, Saudi Arabia, to Yokohama, Japan.

Antilla Cape, as *Egypt Gas* was sold to Indian breakers in 2003.

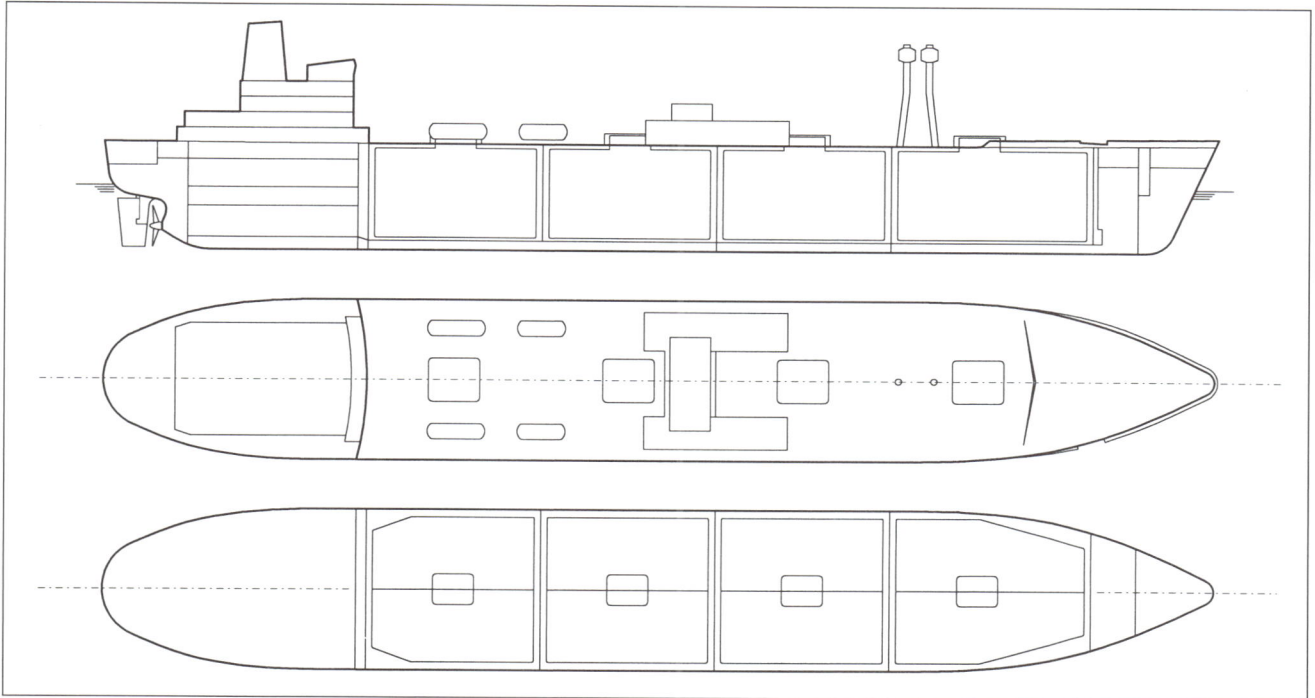

Figure 5-3 Outline Arrangement of *Antilla Cape*

Plate 5-4   *Antilla Cape* waits in the north lock   Marine Service GmbH,
                   at Bremerhaven prior to sailing to   Hamburg
                   Felixstowe, England, for gas trials

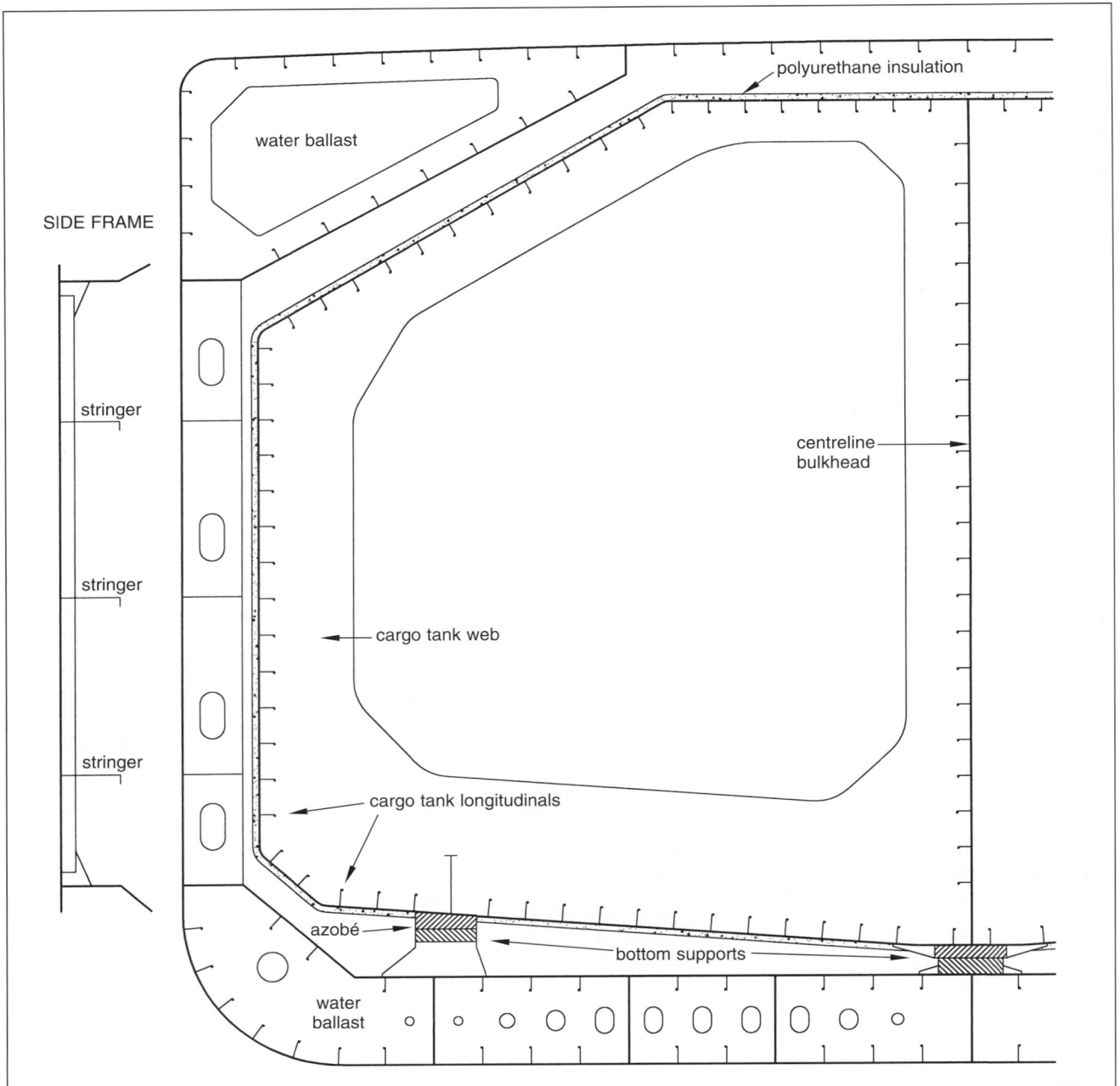

Figure 5-4 Midship Section of *Antilla Cape* at Web Frame

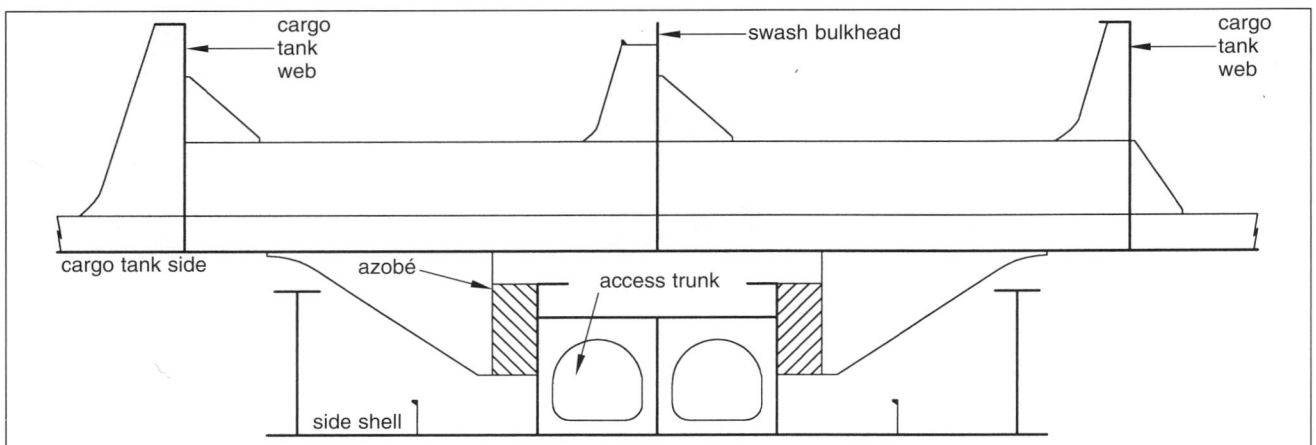

Figure 5-5 *Antilla Cape* – Combined Side Shell Access Trunk and Tank Supports

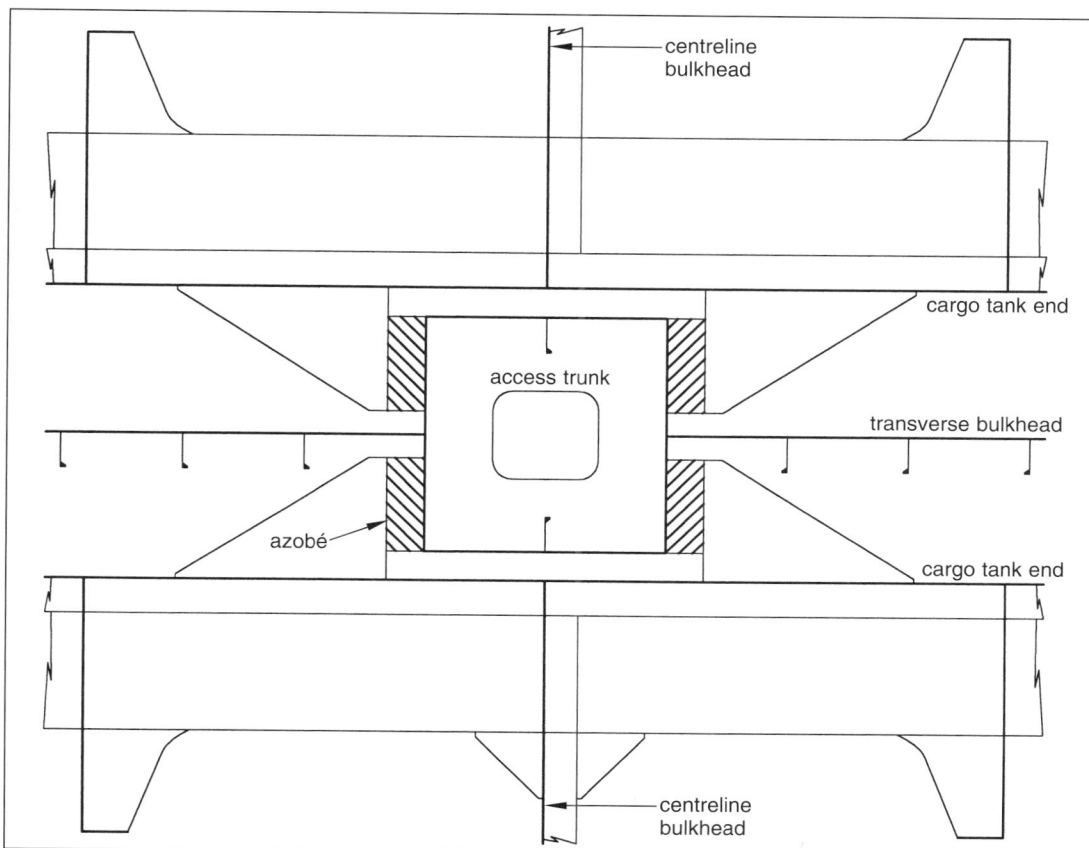

Figure 5-6 *Antilla Cape* – Combined Transverse Bulkhead Access Trunk and Tank Supports

[1] Rehling, Jürgen, *A G Weser's Activities in the Transportation of Liquefied Gas,* Shipbuilding & Shipping Record, 30 May 1969.
[2] Volger, Manfred, *Seetransport von flüssigen Gasen bei tiefen Tempersturen,* A G Weser, 12 February 1963.
[3] International Marine Design and Equipment, *Esso Centro America,* 1963.
[4] Nullmeier, Edgar, *Overseas Transport of Liquefied Natural Gas,* Kaefer Isoliertechnik GmbH & Co. KG.
[5] Rehling, Jürgen, *Gastankerbau bei der A G Weser, Bremen,* Hansa 105 Jahrgang 1968 Nr. 21.
[6] Shipbuilding & Shipping Record, *Antilla Cape, A 30,000 m³ LPG Carrier with Fully Automated Gas Control Room and Provision for Unmanned Engine Room Operation,* 18 October 1968.
[7] The Motor Ship, *Antilla Cape, The Largest European LPG Tanker,* October 1968.
[8] Shipping World & Shipbuilder, *Antilla Cape, German-built LPG Carrier,* October 1968.

Chapter 6

Conversions and Newbuildings from Hitachi Zosen

The design team, naval architects and engineers from the Innoshima yard of Hitachi Zosen can be justifiably proud of their achievements with LPG carriers. Since the late nineteen fifties, the yard has converted T2 tankers to LPG carriers, built combined LPG/crude oil tankers and constructed fully refrigerated LPG carriers with semi-membrane, integral and independent IMO type A and B tanks. The yard also designed and completed the smallest and the largest fully refrigerated LPG carriers with prismatic cargo tanks, which were built in Japan; 8,082 m³ *Iwakuni Maru,* and 100,213 m³ *Esso Fuji.*

Nisseki Maru

Principle Particulars	
Length o.a.	183.54 m
Length b.p.	177.24 m
Breadth	22.86 m
Depth	14.40 m
Draught	9.75 m
LPG Capacity	9,470 m³
Engine	General Electric
Power	7,800 hp/5,737 kW
Service speed	14.5 knots

With technical assistance from Caltex, extensive work was carried out by Hitachi Zosen in Innoshima to convert a T2-SE-A1 type tanker, *Caltex Johannesburg,* into a combined LPG/crude oil tanker. This Second World War built tanker was completed as *Carlsbad* by the Kaiser Company, in Portland, Oregon, in February 1945.

The existing cargo section of the tanker was scrapped and a new wider and longer mid-body was built and fitted to the existing bow, stern and accommodation. Crack arresting riveted hull seams were fitted in the new mid-body at the bottom and side shell, gunwale and deck. The new main deck height was the same as the original poop and forecastle. The increased freeboard for LPG trading was considered sufficient to eliminate the need for a forecastle. The three centre insulated prismatic LPG tanks were constructed with 2½% nickel steel and located 1200 mm above the double bottom. The cargo capacities were 9,470 m³ (32%) for LPG and 20,560 m³ (68%) for crude oil. An indirect reliquefaction system was fitted using R12 as the coolant.

On completion, *Carlsbad* renamed as *Nisseki Maru* was delivered to Nippon Oil Co. Ltd. on 5 March 1962 and classed with the American Bureau of Shipping. Operated by Tokyo Tanker K.K., the converted vessel began trading by importing crude oil and LPG from Aramco's Ras Tanura terminal to Nippon's subsidiary, Nippon Petroleum Gas Co.

After completing 29 years of service, the tanker was scrapped as *Beava* in 1974.

A second similar conversion was completed by Hitachi Zosen from *Caltex Lisbon,* another Kaiser T2 tanker, originally delivered in February 1945 as *Sunset.* The resulting combined LPG/crude oil tanker, *Toyosu Maru,* had the same hull dimensions as *Nisseki Maru.* Four LPG cargo tanks were fitted with an increased total LPG capacity. The cargo capacities were 13,145 m³ (45%) for LPG and 15,807 m³ (55%) for crude oil. The converted tanker was delivered to Tokyo Ekikagasu Yusosen K.K. in October 1963.

Forty years after originally being delivered, the tanker was broken up in 1985 as *Toyosu*.

Yuyo Maru No 10

Principle Particulars	
Length o.a.	227.10 m
Length b.p.	215.00 m
Breadth	35.80 m
Depth	20.75 m
Draught	12.00 m
LPG Capacity	47,424 m³
Engine	Hitachi-B&W 884-VT2BF-180
Power	18,400 hp/13,533 kW
Service speed	15.85 knots

After successfully converting two T2 tankers during the years 1962 and 1963, into combined crude oil and LPG tankers, *Nisseki Maru* and *Toyosu Maru,* Hitachi Zosen moved on to build a 52,839 deadweight combined tanker for Japanese owner Yuyo Kaiun K.K. Delivered on 26 July 1966, *Yuyo Maru No 10* was the largest combined crude oil and LPG tanker ever to be constructed.[1]

The tanker was classed with Nippon Kaiji Kyokai and had four fully refrigerated centre tanks for LPG, and eight wing tanks and a forward deep tank for crude oil. The cargo capacities were 47,424 m³ (58%) for LPG and 33,983 m³ (42%) for crude oil. The prismatic cargo tanks were constructed with a low carbon steel YND-37, compared with the more expensive 2½% nickel steel, which had been used on the conservatively designed converted tankers. Grade F killed steel was used for the inner bottom plating and the longitudinal and transverse bulkheads, in way of the LPG cargo tanks. The LPG cargo tanks were insulated with polyurethane foam.

A refrigeration machinery room was located on the main deck, at the superstructure front, with a pump room below. Two reliquefaction plants, using R12 as a refrigerant, were fitted, and the LPG compressors were steam driven. The main LPG liquid cargo piping was made from 3½% nickel steel and insulated with polyurethane foam.

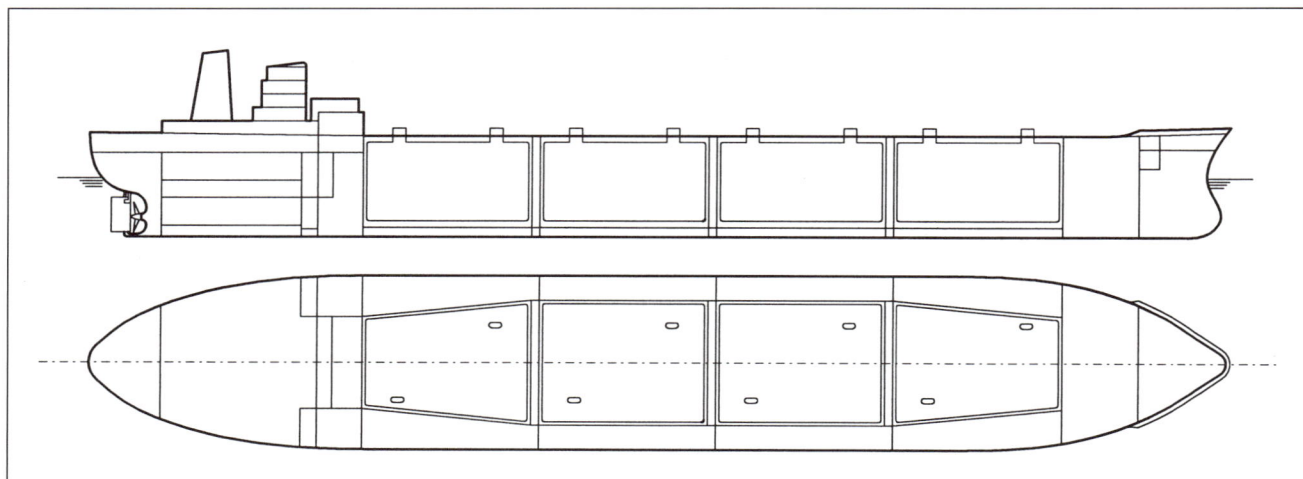

Figure 6-1 Outline Arrangement of *Yuyo Maru No 10*

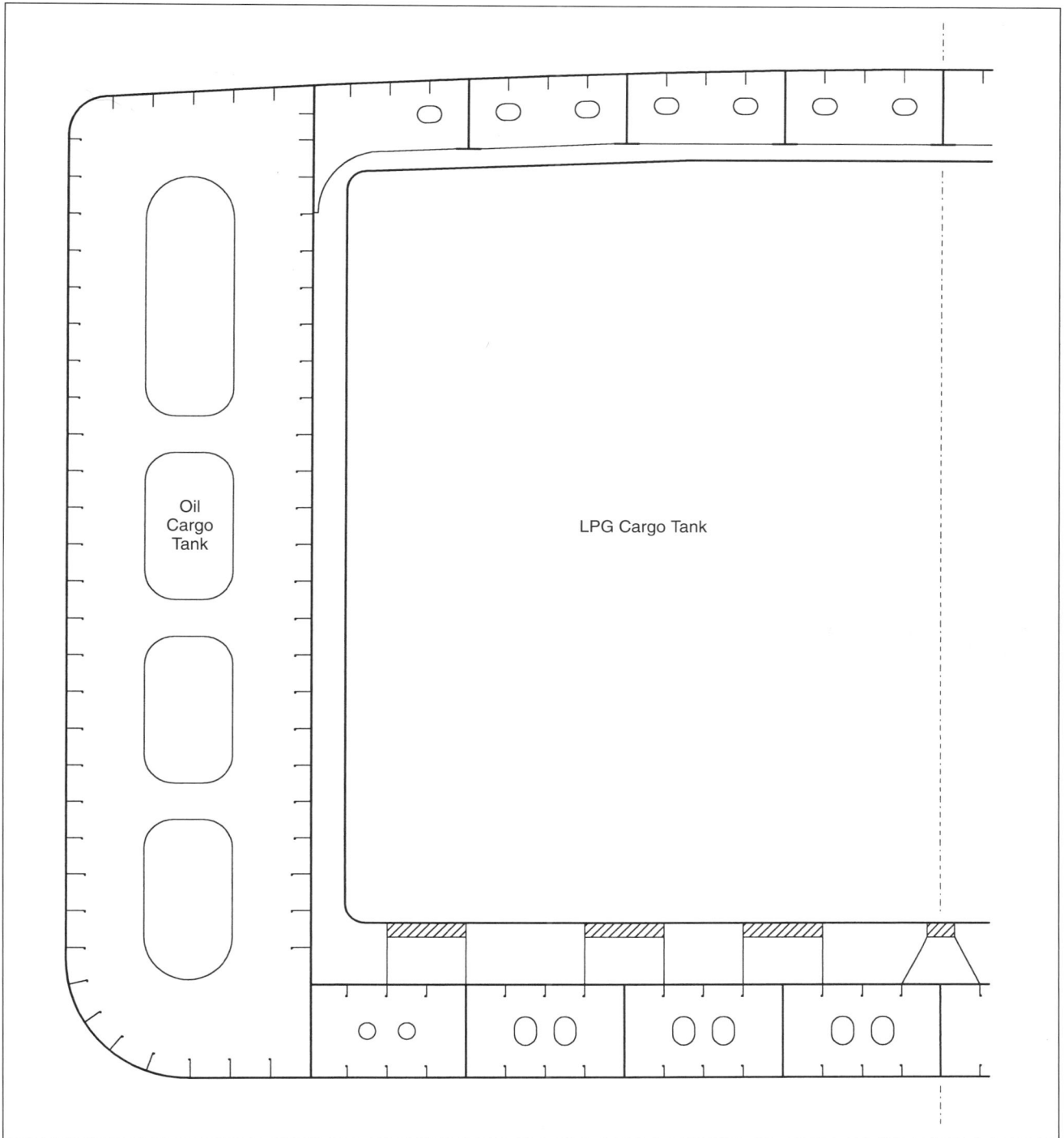

Figure 6-2 Midship Section of *Yuyo Maru No 10*

9 November 1974 – Lessons Learnt from Carrying Naphtha in Wing Tanks

Yuyo Maru No 10 was destroyed after a fatal collision in Tokyo Bay. Inbound for Kawasaki, on 9 November 1974, and fully loaded with a cargo of butane, propane and naphtha, the tanker was struck on the starboard side, almost at a right angle to the hull, by the bow of bulk carrier *Pacific Ares*.[2, 3, 4, 5]

The tanker's load port was Ras Tanura, Saudi Arabia, and on the final part of the passage to Japan, the ship was loaded with 20,200 tonnes of propane and 6,400 tonnes of butane in the centre tanks, and 30,800 tonnes of naphtha in the wing tanks and forward deep tank. The bulk carrier was also fully loaded, with 14,000 tonnes of steel products, and bound for Los Angeles, after loading at Kimitsu on the eastern side of Tokyo Bay.

The bow of the bulk carrier penetrated the hull plating in way of the forward deep tank and No. 1 starboard wing tank containing naphtha. Naphtha from both tanks spilled into the sea, immediately ignited and engulfed the bulk carrier. The fire was so intense on the water surface and on *Pacific Ares* that an approach was impossible. Tragically, all but one of the 29 crew on *Pacific Ares* were killed. The next day the sole survivor, the second engineer, was sighted on deck after remaining in the engine control room during the fire. Five crew from *Yuyo Maru No 10* also died.

The fire on *Yuyo Maru No 10* burned for almost three weeks, spreading to the other starboard wing tanks containing naphtha. The four independent LPG cargo tanks located almost six meters inboard from the side hull plating were not damaged during the initial impact and remained intact despite the intense heat from the burning naphtha. The fire did spread to the propane vapours released through deck mounted relief valves and damaged deck fittings and pipe work.

On 28 November, the combined forces of the Japanese Air Force and Navy, after two days of bombardment from shells, bombs, rockets and torpedoes, finally sunk *Yuyo Maru No 10* in deep water, some 300 miles off the Chiba coast. It is believed that the butane in No 4 tank and the naphtha in the port wing tanks remained unaffected until the military action.

Lessons have been learnt from this devastating and tragic collision. The last combined crude oil and LPG tanker to trade was *Toyosu,* and this vessel was scrapped in 1985. What cannot be emphasised enough is the fact, that there are no gas carriers in service which carry cargoes of LPG, chemical gases, ammonia, ethylene or LNG in tanks adjacent to the side hull.

Kazutama Maru

Principle Particulars	
Length o.a.	199.95 m
Length b.p.	188.00 m
Breadth	31.40 m
Depth	21.00 m
Draught	11.63 m
LPG Capacity	51,824 m³
Engine	Hitachi-B&W 874-VT2BF-160
Power	13,200 hp/9,709 kW
Service speed	15.55 knots

Progressing from the conversion and construction of three combined LPG/crude oil tankers, the Innoshima yard of Hitachi Zosen delivered its first purpose built fully refrigerated LPG carrier, 51,824 m³ *Kazutama Maru,* to domestic owners on 30 September 1967. Built for the joint ownership of Yamashita-Shinnihon Kisen K.K., Nissho Kisen K.K. and Sanwa Shosen K.K., the vessel was classed with Nippon Kaiji Kyokai.

The ship was arranged with cruiser stern, flush main deck, aft accommodation deckhouse and a bulbous bow. The reliquefaction house was on the main deck at the deckhouse front. The four prismatic cargo tanks were constructed to the shipyard's own design, with horizontal stringers and insulated with polyurethane foam sheathed with polyvinyl sheets. Two J C Carter 300 m³/hr submerged electric cargo pumps were fitted in each cargo tank.

Kazutama Maru was broken up in 1983.

Yusho Maru

Principle Particulars	
Length o.a.	227.00 m
Length b.p.	215.00 m
Breadth	34.80 m
Depth	23.20 m
Draught	11.51 m
LPG Capacity	73,211 m³
Engine	Hitachi-B&W 7K84EF
Power	17,500 hp/12,871 kW
Service speed	15.9 knots

The second purpose built fully refrigerated LPG carrier from the Innoshima yard, 73,211 m³ *Yusho Maru,* was delivered on 27 August 1971.[6] The propane and butane carrier owned by Yuyo Kaiun K.K., was a larger version of *Kazutama Maru* with four cargo tanks constructed with KT-500 modified carbon manganese steel. Two J C Carter 500 m³/hr submerged electric cargo pumps were fitted in each cargo tank.

Yusho Maru was sold to Taiwanese breakers in 1985 as *Yusho*.

Esso Fuji

Principle Particulars	
Length o.a.	246.13 m
Length b.p.	234.00 m
Breadth	39.90 m
Depth	25.50 m
Draught	12.70 m
LPG Capacity	100,213 m³
Engine	Hitachi-B&W 8K84EF
Power	20,000 hp/14,710 kW
Service speed	15.4 knots

Esso Fuji, with a capacity of 100,213 m³, has the distinction of being the largest LPG carrier built in Japan.[7, 8, 9] Unlike most fully refrigerated LPG carriers, *Esso Fuji* was assigned to operate to a designated trade i.e. from the loading ports of Ras Tanura, Saudi Arabia and Westernport, Australia, to Japanese import terminals at Sodegaura near Chiba in Tokyo Bay, and Sakai near Osaka.

Delivered to Esso Transport Co. Inc. on 2 February 1973, *Esso Fuji* was classed with Nippon Kaiji Kyokai as a Tanker for Flammable Gas at a minimum temperature of -46°C. The ship had a transom stern, aft accommodation house, a flush main deck, four independent prismatic cargo tanks, a bow thruster and a bulbous bow. The reliquefaction plant was located on the main deck at the accommodation house front, with a cargo control room above it. Double bottom and lower, and upper wing ballast tanks were arranged in the cargo area, with dry transverse cofferdams located between each cargo tank. The cargo tank plating was N-TUF33 steel and the tank rolled sections were N-TUF30N steel. The cargo tanks were insulated externally with 75 mm of polyurethane foam with a minimum core density of 32 kg/m³. Two J C Carter 500 m³/hr submerged electric cargo pumps were fitted in each cargo tank.

The two reliquefaction plants each included a R12 refrigerating compressor, a R12 condenser and a LPG condenser, with three LPG blowers, two LPG receivers and three condensate pumps. Separate systems were provided for butane and propane, but both could be used in parallel when a single gas cargo was carried. Cargo manifolds were arranged on the port side above No. 3 cargo tank and above No. 2 cargo tank on the starboard side.

Esso Fuji was sold to Taiwanese breakers in 1986.

Based on the same overall dimensions as *Esso Fuji,* but with a slightly smaller cargo capacity, a second ship, 100,181 m³ *Palace Tokyo,* was delivered from Hitachi Zosen on 18 October 1974 to Palace Shipping. In December 1972, Hitachi Zosen and Yuyo Kaiun Kaisha established a joint stock company, Palace Shipping, and *Palace Tokyo* was the company's first vessel. The ship's keel was laid on 10 December 1973 with a launching on 5 June 1974. The second ship's propulsion unit was a B&W 9K84EF diesel engine with a power output of 23,200 hp/17,064 kW, for a service speed of 16.5 knots. Cargo manifolds were fitted on both sides of the ship above No. 3 cargo tank, unlike the staggered arrangement on *Esso Fuji.*

Palace Tokyo was sold to Taiwanese breakers in 1986.

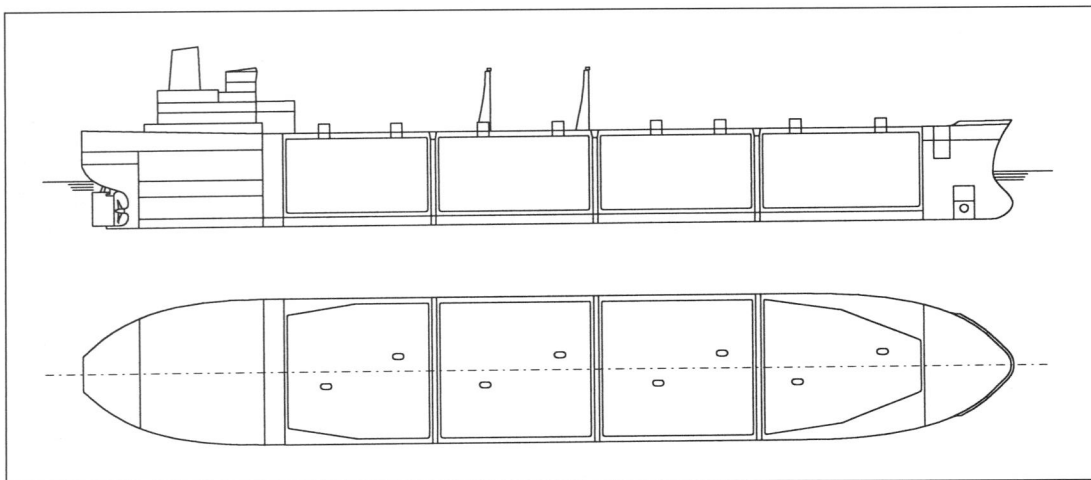

Figure 6-3 Outline Arrangement of *Esso Fuji*

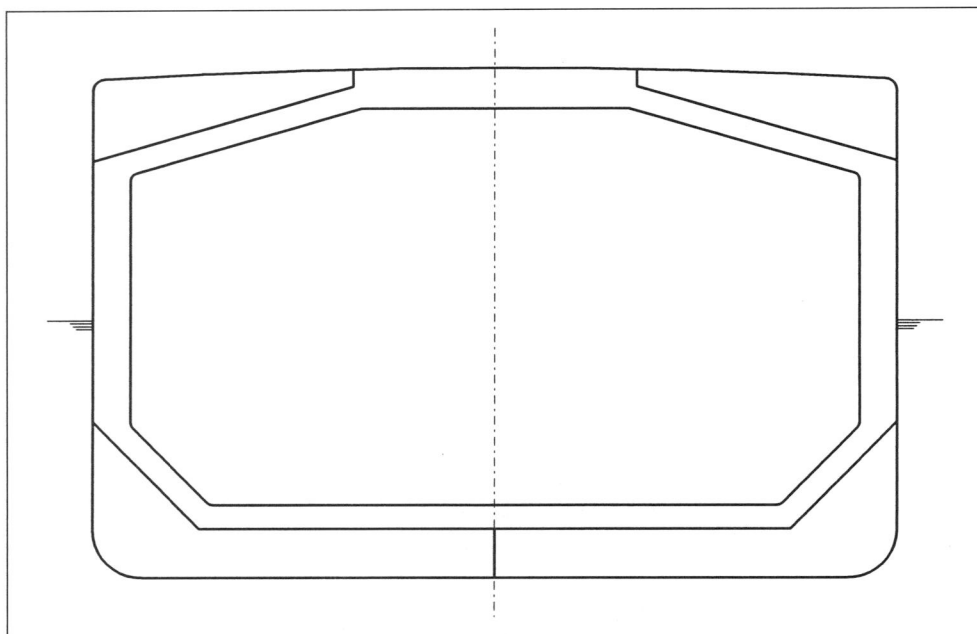

Figure 6-4 Midship Section of *Esso Fuji*

Plate 6-1   *Esso Fuji*   Hitachi Zosen

Yuyo Maru

Principle Particulars	
Length o.a.	228.00 m
Length b.p.	216.00 m
Breadth	35.40 m
Depth	22.60 m
Draught	11.75 m
LPG Capacity	83,070 m³
Engine	Hitachi-B&W 6K90GF
Power	20,500 hp/15,078 kW
Service speed	16.3 knots

In 1977, a licence agreement was made between Hitachi Zosen and Bridgestone Liquefied Gas Co. Ltd., for the semi-membrane LPG tank system. The first and only semi-membrane LPG carrier built by Hitachi Zosen 83,070 m³ *Yuyo Maru* was delivered from the Innoshima yard on 28 May 1979 to Yuyo Kaiun K.K.[10, 11]

Like the *Kasmet* series from the Kobe works of Kawasaki, as described in Chapter 17, *Yuyo Maru* was arranged with integral tanks for butane at -5°C and semi-membrane tanks for propane at -46°C. Nos. 2 – 4 cargo tanks, with a total capacity of 59,672 m³, were for propane. No. 1 cargo tanks and the uniquely narrow centre tank between Nos. 2 – 4 semi-membrane tanks, were for butane, with a total capacity of 23,398 m³.

KT 50N low temperature steel was used for the 8 mm flat parts of the membrane and for the 10 mm cylindrical parts. 2¼% nickel steel was used for the 10 mm spherical corners. A total of fifteen J C Carter electric submerged cargo pumps were fitted; eight at 500 m³/hr, six at 250 m³/hr and one at 150 m³/hr. The first direct reliquefaction system from Hitachi Zosen was fitted with five LPG compressors and electric motors housed on the main deck above Nos. 3 and 4 cargo tanks. A cargo control room was fitted above the reliquefaction house.

Plate 6-2   *Yuyo Maru* showing centreline panel and corner saddles for semi-membrane tank system   Hitachi Zosen

Iwakuni Maru

Principle Particulars	
Length o.a.	109.88 m
Length b.p.	104.00 m
Breadth	20.00 m
Depth	11.90 m
Draught	5.90 m
LPG Capacity	8,082 m³
Engine	Kobe Diesel-Mitsubishi 6UET45/80D
Power	4,500 hp/3,310 kW
Service speed	13.5 knots

For coastal service, the smallest fully refrigerated LPG carrier with prismatic tanks to be built in Japan, 8,082 m³ *Iwakuni Maru,* was delivered from the Innoshima yard to Shimaza Kaiun Co. Ltd. on 25 November 1981. Classed with Nippon Kaiji Kyokai, the ship was designed with three IMO type B independent cargo tanks for butane and propane.

Plate 6-3   *Iwakuni Maru*   Hitachi Zosen

Co-op Sunshine

Principle Particulars	
Length o.a.	220.00 m
Length b.p.	210.00 m
Breadth	38.40 m
Depth	22.80 m
Draught	11.30 m
LPG Capacity	83,127 m³
Engine	Hitachi-B&W 6L80GFCA
Power	18,400 hp/13,533 kW
Service speed	16.1 knots

With a similar capacity to earlier built *Yuyo Maru,* the 83,127 m³ *Co-op Sunshine* was designed with four independent IMO type B prismatic cargo tanks and a pair of integral cargo tanks, as compared to the four semi-membrane tanks and similar integral tanks of *Yuyo Maru.* A comparison can be made between the two systems, as with almost the same length and depth, the breadth of the ship with independent tanks is three metres wider for the same cargo carried. *Co-op Sunshine* was delivered to Kumiai Kosan on 25 February 1983. Four reliquefaction plants were fitted.

Hourai Maru

Principle Particulars

Length o.a.	219.74 m
Length b.p.	210.00 m
Breadth	38.40 m
Depth	21.00 m
Draught	11.02 m
LPG Capacity	77,755 m³
Engine	Hitachi-B&W 7L80GBE
Power	19,400 hp/14,275 kW
Service speed	16.1 knots

The next fully refrigerated LPG carrier from Innoshima was 77,755 m³ *Hourai Maru,* which was delivered on 2 July 1985 to Kumiai Senpaku K.K. This ship returned to the standard four tank design with conventional IMO type A cargo tanks for butane and propane. Four reliquefaction plants were fitted.

A second vessel, *Co-op Sunrise,* with the same cargo capacity and same hull dimensions as *Hourai Maru* was delivered to Kumiai Senpaku K.K. on 25 March 1987. The main propulsion unit was changed to a Hitachi-B&W 8S60MC diesel with a service speed of 16.1 knots. *Co-op Sunrise* was the last ship to be build at Hitachi Zosen, Innoshima.

Plate 6-4   *Hourai Maru* showing cargo tank dome and aft accommodation front   Hitachi Zosen

Antwerpen Venture

Principle Particulars

Length o.a.	195.93 m
Length b.p.	186.00 m
Breadth	29.40 m
Depth	17.00 m
Draught	10.07 m
LPG Capacity	39,270 m³
Engine	Hitachi-MAN B&W 6S60MC
Power	14,300 hp/10,518 kW
Service speed	16.0 knots

The first fully refrigerated LPG carrier to be constructed at the Ariake works of Hitachi Zosen was 39,270 m³ *Antwerpen Venture.* The vessel was originally ordered by Norwegian owner Christian Haaland and built to Det Norske Veritas classification. Delivered to Cedonia Shipping Ltd., on 28 November 1996, the ship with three prismatic cargo tanks, was designed for the carriage of propane, butane, anhydrous ammonia, propylene, butadiene and vinyl chloride monomer (VCM). Three reliquefaction plants were fitted. A 110 m³ pressurised tank for change of grades was fitted on the main deck forward. A combined cargo heater and vaporiser was fitted.

Agri Viking

Principle Particulars

Length o.a.	153.92 m
Length b.p.	147.00 m
Breadth	24.60 m
Depth	13.10 m
Draught	9.37 m
LPG Capacity	18,152 m³
Engine	Hitachi-MAN B&W 6S50MC
Power	9,300 hp/6,840 kW
Service speed	15.5 knots

In 1997, the Ariake works delivered two multi-purpose LPG carriers 18,152 m³ to Norsk Hydro A.S.[12] *Agri Viking* was delivered on 31 March and *Euro Viking* was delivered on 1 October. A half-size version of *Antwerpen Venture,* the vessels were each classed with Det Norske Veritas as Tankers for Liquefied Gas, at a minimum temperature of -48° C, a maximum pressure of 0.275 kg/cm² and a maximum specific gravity of 0.972. Butylene, ethylchloride and hydrocarbon mixtures were additional cargo carried compared to *Antwerpen Venture.* Three reliquefaction plant were fitted. For change of cargo, 50 m³ and 120 m³ pressurised tanks were fitted on the forward main deck. A combined cargo heater and vaporiser was fitted. A free fall lifeboat was fitted at the stern.

| Plate 6-5 | *Agri Viking* | Hitachi Zosen |

On 1 October 2002, Hitachi Zosen Corporation and Nippon Kokan K. K. (NKK Corporation) combined their shipbuilding operations to form Universal Shipbuilding Corporation.

[1] Shipping World & Shipbuilder, *Yuyo Maru No 10, Combined Crude Oil & Liquefied Gas Carrier,* January 1967.
[2] Lloyd's List Casualty Reports, *Yuyo Maru No 10,* November 1974.
[3] Zosen, *How Terrible LPG Tanker Collision Is,* December 1974.
[4] Shipping World & Shipbuilder, *Yuyo Maru No 10 Disaster,* January 1975.
[5] Thomas, William duBarry, *Spectacle Blurs Issues,* Hazardous Cargo Bulletin, October 1984.
[6] Shipbuilding and Marine Engineering in Japan, JSEA, *Yusho Maru LPG Carrier,* 1972.
[7] Exxon Marine, *Giant of the LPG Trade,* Volume 18, Number 2.
[8] Marine Engineers Review, *Esso Fuji, World's Largest LPG Carrier Delivered by Hitachi Zosen,* April 1973.
[9] SEA-Japan, *Esso Fuji, World's Largest LPG Carrier,* No. 50, 1973.
[10] Zosen, *Yuyo Maru, Semi-membrane LPG tanker,* September 1979.
[11] Hitachi Zosen brochure, *LPG Carriers of Hitachi Zosen, Outline of Independent Prismatic Tank and Semi-membrane Tank,* February 1980.
[12] Shipbuilding and Marine Engineering in Japan, JSEA, *Agri Viking 18,000 m³ Gas Carrier,* 1999.

Chapter 7

European First from Kockums

By chance, a meeting took place in 1959 in New York between Frans Malmros, Managing Director of Trelleborgs Ångfartygs AB, Trelleborg, Sweden and Peter Burbank, President of A L Burbank & Co. Ltd., New York.[1] During this meeting the basic idea of refrigeration for the transportation of LPG by sea was discussed with the potential seen, if the transport costs could be reduced, to open up large new markets for the use of LPG.

For this new business venture, Trelleborgs Ångfartygs AB enlisted the services of consultants Marine Service GmbH of Hamburg for the design work on a purpose built 25,000 m³ LPG carrier. The contract for the newbuilding was placed with Swedish shipbuilders Kockums Mekaniska Verkstads of Malmö. Through A L Burbank & Co. Ltd., a long-term charter was obtained from Phillips Petroleum Company of Bartlesville, Oklahoma, USA., to export LPG from the Gulf of Mexico on transatlantic trading routes.

Paul Endacott

Principle Particulars	
Length o.a.	180.53 m
Length b.p.	166.70 m
Breadth	25.00 m
Depth	14.70 m
Draught	10.62 m
LPG Capacity	25,102 m³
Engine	Kockums-MAN K8Z 78/140D
Power	10,350 hp/7,763 kW
Service speed	16 knots

The original design from Marine Service GmbH was further developed by the shipyard, owners, regulatory authorities and subcontractors.[2, 3, 4] The ship was classed with the American Bureau of Shipping and also built to the requirements of the United States Coast Guard and the Svenska Sjöfartsstyrelsen. Cargoes carried were anhydrous ammonia, propane, butane, butadiene and ethylene oxide, at a minimum temperature of -51°C and a maximum pressure of 0.3 kg/cm².

Many new techniques were required, relating to the special steels, welding and insulation materials, which had not previously been encountered in conventional shipbuilding. A laboratory was set up in the shipyard for testing, problem solving and the evolution of instruments and cargo handling equipment.

The profile of the ship was distinctive with a forecastle deck, trunk deck, large amidships deckhouses for the cargo control room and gas plant with the cargo vents grouped above it, four large cylindrical deck tanks and an aft superstructure. The hull was of all welded construction, except for double riveted crack arresting seams located at the bottom shell, at the lower turn of the bilge, at the deck sheer strake and at the trunk deck.

The prismatic cargo tanks were each located in the five hold spaces below the main deck. A double bottom and a double side hull were used for water ballast. Transverse cofferdams were fitted between each hold space. In addition, two 106 m³ vertical cylindrical/conical shaped pressure vessel tanks were fitted in the forward part of No. 1 hold space. Four 300 m³ horizontal cylindrical pressure vessel tanks were fitted at the sides of the main deck.

Domnarvet Steel Works, in co-operation with Kockums, produced the special steel for the main cargo tanks and inner hull, which formed the secondary barrier. This was a fully-killed fine-grained manganese low carbon steel with minimum impact properties of 2.8 kpm/cm^2 at -57°C.

The tanks' were supported by steel foundations and brackets on the bottom of the tanks, cushioned with tropical azobé hardwood and Swedish pine. Azobé was also used for the rolling and pitching keys as well as the anti-lift chocks.

The hold spaces were insulated with two 50 mm thick layers of polyurethane foam which were glued to the inner hull, the cofferdams and the underside of the main and trunk decks. The arrangement with the insulation on the inner hull rather than on the cargo tank made for some interesting design features. It was possible to have direct access to inspect the outside plating of the cargo tanks where walkways were installed. In normal service the hold spaces would be filled with inert gas produced from an on board system with two nitrogen generating plants. For the carriage of chemicals which could not be handled by the reliquefaction plant, cooled nitrogen gas could be circulated in the spaces around the cargo tanks. This alternative cooling system was designed to maintain the cargo at -7°C. Fans were used to circulate the nitrogen gas after passing through a cooling battery connected to one of the reliquefaction plants.

The vessel was fitted with three reliquefaction plants, each consisting of an oil free two-stage Sulzer compressor, a Stal refrigeration unit using Freon 22 as a coolant, a gas condenser, a receiver and related valves, gauges and controls.

Named after the vice-chairman of Phillips Petroleum Company, the vessel was christened by Mrs. Endacott, his wife, on 27 November 1963. *Paul Endacott* was delivered to the owners on 28 May 1964 and was the first purpose built fully refrigerated LPG carrier constructed in Europe.

On 29 May 1964 *Paul Endacott* left Malmö bound for Mena al Ahmadi, Kuwait, to load the first of four consecutive LPG cargoes for Japan, under a sub-charter to the Bridgestone Liquefied Petroleum Company Ltd., of Tokyo.[5] Delays in the preparations of the terminals for the planned regular transatlantic LPG service, opened up the opportunity for this temporary trade to the Far East.

On 1 April 1965, onboard *Paul Endacott,* the first shipment of propane, under the Phillips Petroleum contract, reached the Phillips United Kingdom's terminal at Felixstowe, for delivery to the Eastern Gas Board.[6] The building of this new import terminal was made feasible late in 1962, when the Felixstowe Dock and Railway Company agreed to construct a deep-water jetty. The contract was finally agreed when an offer was made, by Phillips, to deliver gas from the Gulf of Mexico, at a competitive price. That decision must have given great satisfaction to the forward thinking entrepreneurs Frans Malmros and Peter Burbank.

The new 33 m high and 52 m diameter refrigerated storage tank at Felixstowe provided facilities for road and ship loading as well as a non insulated pipeline connection to Norwich. The Eastern Gas Board Cremore Gas Works in Norwich was equipped with five high pressure reforming plants and the piped liquefied propane was used to enrich the local town gas. By an odd coincidence, the Norwich end of the pipeline was located about ten kilometres from where these words have been typed.

Paul Endacott as *Petrogas I* was reported broken up in 1986.

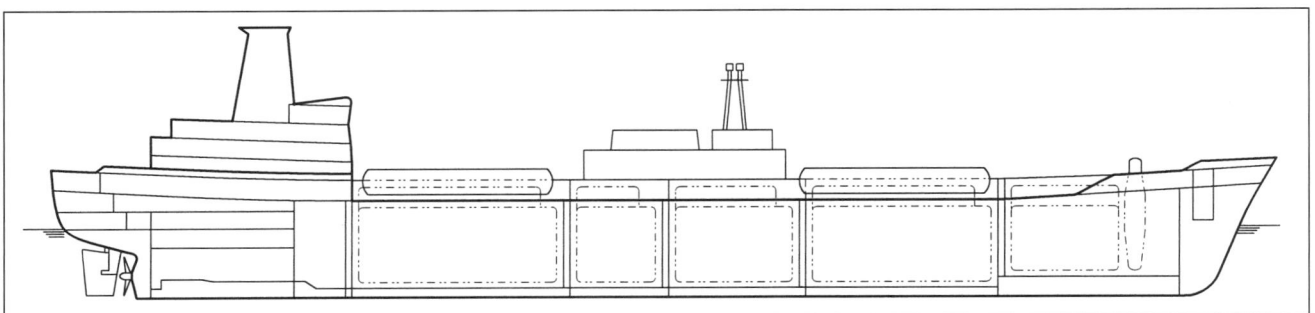

Figure 7-1 Profile of *Paul Endacott*

300m³
deck cargo tank

anti-roll key

inner hull
insulation

LPG Cargo Tank

anti-lift
chock

centreline
bulkhead

anti-roll key

bottom
supports

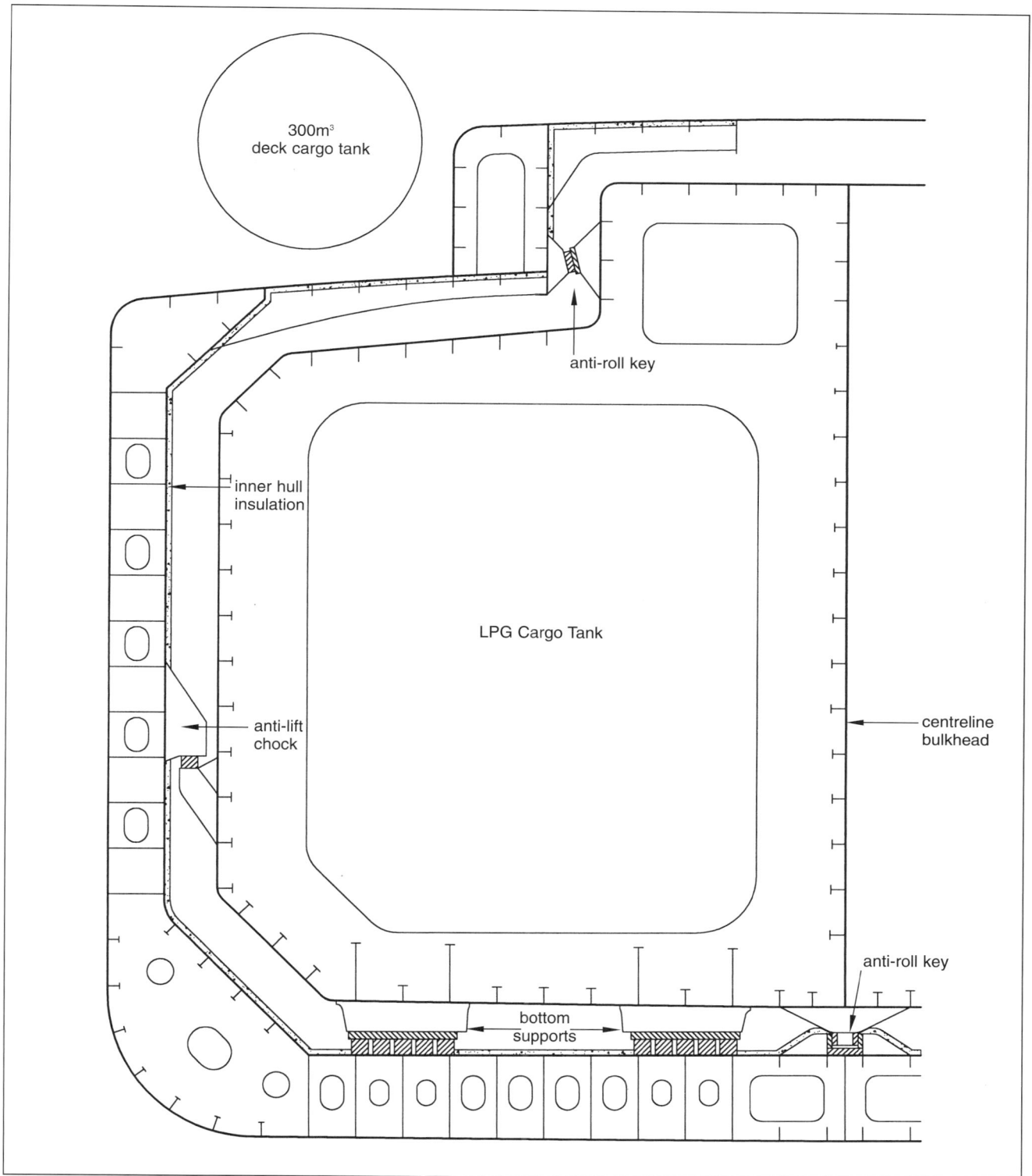

Figure 7-2 Midship Section of *Paul Endacott* showing Inner Hull Insulation and Tank Supports

Plate 7-1   *Paul Endacott*   Marine Services GmbH,
              under construction   Hamburg
              with two pressure vessel
              change of grade tanks forward
              of the main prismatic cargo tanks

Plate 7-2   Painting of *Paul Endacott* by marine artist Georg Holm   York Refrigeration

Phillips Arkansas

Principle Particulars	
Length o.a.	184.79 m
Length b.p.	172.52 m
Breadth	25.50 m
Depth	16.10 m
Draught	9.70 m
LPG Capacity	26,505 m³
Engine	Kockums-MAN K9Z 78/155E
Power	15,750 hp/11,584 kW
Service speed	17 knots

Phillips Arkansas was the first vessel to be constructed in Kockums new building dock, where the impressive 140 m tall Krupp gantry crane, with a lifting capacity of 1,500 tonne, was to become a familiar feature of the Malmö skyline for many years.[7, 8, 9] At the same time, for Phillips/Marathon, the 71,500 m³ Gaz Transport membrane LNG carriers *Polar Alaska* and *Arctic Tokyo* were also being built in the dock. Quite a trio and all with a Phillips connection.

Delivered on 21 January 1969 to Philtankers Inc. of Monrovia, an operating subsidiary of Phillips Petroleum Company, the 26,505 m³ *Phillips Arkansas* was classed with the American Bureau of Shipping and built to the requirements of US Coast Guard and Svenska Sjöfartsstyrelsen. The cargo capacity was similar to 25,102 m³ *Paul Endacott,* built five years earlier, but the design was generally simplified and improved, reflecting the progress made in gas ship technology at the time. The cargo handling systems were designed for the carriage of propane, butane, butadiene and anhydrous ammonia, at a minimum temperature of (-51.6°F) -46.45°C, a maximum pressure of 0.3 kg/cm² and a maximum specific gravity of 0.72. No. 2 cargo tank was arranged for the carriage of butadiene in addition to LPG and ammonia.

Constructed with three prismatic cargo tanks, *Phillips Arkansas* was arranged with a cruiser stern, poop deck, flush main deck, bow thruster and a bulbous bow. Water ballast was arranged in the inner bottom with side lower wing tanks and under deck upper wing tanks. The inner bottom, inner sloping sides of the water ballast tanks, single transverse bulkheads and the side hull formed the secondary barrier. The reliquefaction house, with a cargo control room and a 30 m³ pressurised liquid nitrogen tank above it, were fitted on the main deck in the aft part of the cargo area. 85 m³ and 170 m³ pressurised LPG tanks were fitted on the main deck forward. An enclosed passageway at poop deck level, with an airlock, connected the cargo control room to the aft accommodation.

The tanks and secondary barrier were constructed with a fully-killed silicon-aluminium fine grain treated low carbon-manganese steel with minimum impact properties of 4.15 kpm/cm² at -52°C. In collaboration with Kockums, the steel was developed and produced by Domnarvet Steel Works. For welding the steel, a special electrode OK 73.52, containing 1.6% nickel was developed by ESAB and the Kockums laboratories. The tanks were supported and positioned with steel and azobé chocks and keys. The tanks were insulated with two 100 mm thick overlapping layers of prefabricated Gullfiber glass wool slabs, secured by plastic pins to the tank surface. Cargo deck pipework was insulated with polyurethane foam jackets faced with fibre-reinforced polyester resin.

The Krupp gantry crane was put to good use during the construction of the cargo tanks. Before being insulated, each tank was temporarily lifted out of the assembly shop for hydrostatic testing. The cargo tanks were then returned to the assembly shop to be finished off and for the insulation to be applied. When finished, the cargo tanks were lifted to the building dock with No. 1 tank, at 7,807 m³ capacity weighing 712 tonnes and No. 2 tank at 9,632 m³ capacity weighing 735 tonnes.

Tank domes were located towards the aft end of each cargo tank. Six 300 m³/hr J C Carter electric submerged pumps were fitted, with two in each tank. The pump and motor assemblies were mounted within steel casings extending from the tank dome to the tank sump. Each pump could be removed from the tank, for overhaul or repair, even when the tank was loaded. The system was designed to discharged a full cargo in 16 hours.

Three reliquefaction plants were fitted with each containing a Sulzer oil free cargo compressor, a Sabroe R22 compressor, condensers, receivers, separators and controls. Each unit had a capacity of 138,000 Kcal/hr in propane service.

Phillips Arkansas was broken up as *Gaz Kandla* in 2001.

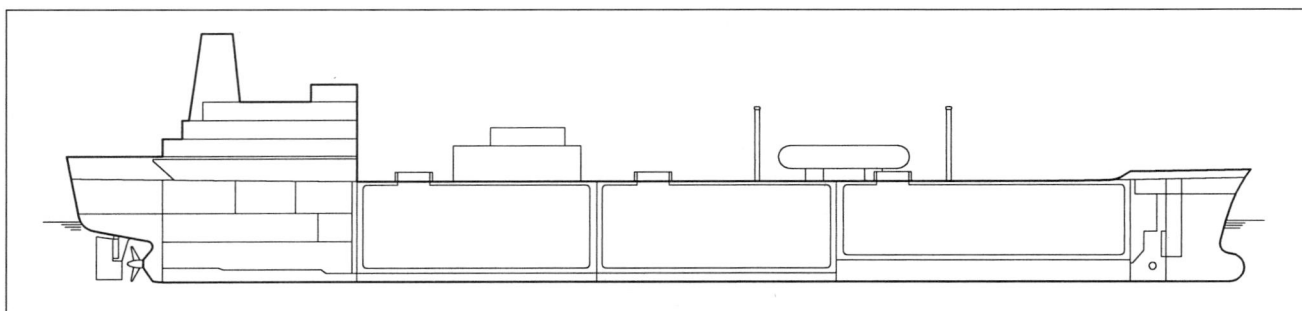

Figure 7-3 Profile of *Phillips Arkansas*

Plate 7-3   Cargo tank for *Phillips Arkansas*   Kockums/Archives of Pat Craig
being lifted through the roof
of the assembly shop

Plate 7-4   *Phillips Arkansas* under   Kockums/Archives of Pat Craig
construction in the building dock
(left) with LNG carrier *Polar Alaska* alongside

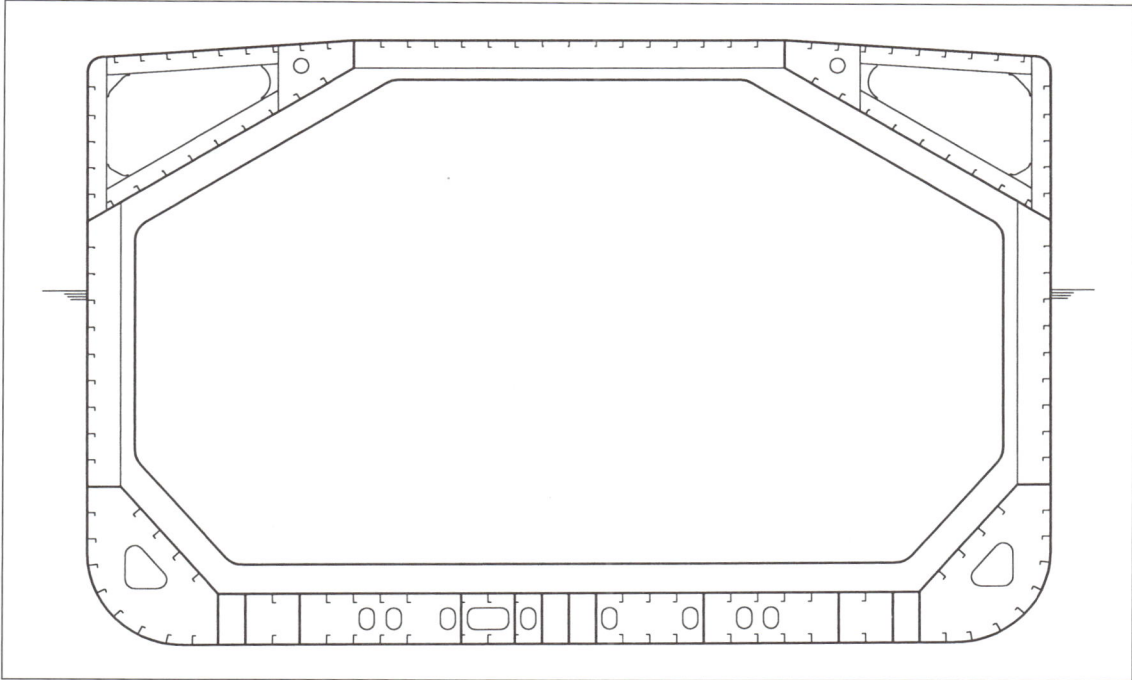

Figure 7-4 Midship Section of *Phillips Arkansas*

Plate 7-5   *Phillips Arkansas*   Common Brothers
                   as *Danian Gas*   Limited

Kockums shipyard closed to commercial shipbuilding in February 1986. In 2002, the Kockums Krupp gantry crane was sold to the offshore division of Hyundai Heavy Industries, Ulsan. When reassembled in South Korea, as at Malmö, the giant crane will dominate the shoreline and become a new prominent landmark. With Hyundai's expertise with gas carrier construction this globe trotting crane may well lift LPG cargo tanks again.

1   Trelleborgs Ångfartygs AB brochure, *Newbuilding LPG Carrier of about 25,000 m³ Cargo Capacity,* 1961.
2   Shipping World, *Launch of Large Swedish LPG Carrier,* 11 December 1963.
3   Shipbuilding & Shipping Record, *The LPG Carrier Paul Endacott,* 12 December 1963.
4   Shipping World & Shipbuilder, *First Europe-Built Refrigerated LPG Carrier,* 2 July 1964.
5   The Engineer, *Liquefied Petroleum Gas Carrier Paul Endacott,* 14 August 1964.
6   Gas Times, *Eastern Gas Ship Comes Home,* April 1965.
7   Shipbuilding & Shipping Record, *Phillips Arkansas, First Ship from Kockums' Building Dock* – 28 February 1969.
8   Shipping World & Shipbuilder, *Phillips Arkansas, Liquid Petroleum Gas Carrier from Sweden's Giant Building Dock,* March 1969.
9   Hannah, F. J., *ESAB and Kockums Collaborate on LNG/LPG Tanker Production,* ESAB, Göteborg, Sweden.

Chapter 8

Verolme Pair for the Ammonia Trade

Anhydrous ammonia was first transported by ship between Norsk Hydro plants across a deep Norwegian fjord on board *Heroya* and *Hydro*, built in 1949 and 1950 at Horten, Norway, by Marinens Hovedverft. The ammonia was carried on these ships in vertically mounted pressurised cylindrical cargo tanks. However, the large scale movement in bulk of anhydrous ammonia by sea began in 1964, with the delivery of two 12,975 m³ fully refrigerated NH_3/LPG carriers from the Dutch shipbuilders Verolme United Shipyards of Rozenburg near Rotterdam.

William R Grace

Principle Particulars	
Length o.a.	156.45 m
Length b.p.	142.65 m
Breadth	21.18 m
Depth	12.50 m
Draught	7.53 m
LPG Capacity	12,975 m³
Engine	MAN K8Z 70/120D
Power	9,600 hp/7,061 kW
Service speed	16 knots

The American industrial company W R Grace & Company, and its subsidiaries, were instrumental in setting up a complete production, marketing, storage and transportation chain for anhydrous ammonia.[1] Ammonia was manufactured by Federation Chemicals Ltd., at their plant at Point Lisas, Trinidad. In the United States, distribution facilities were established at Tampa, Florida and Wilmington, North Carolina, while in Europe, Fredericia in Denmark, Avonmouth in the UK and Uusikaupunki in Finland, were to become regular destination ports for the Grace ships.

The two sister ships, *William R Grace* and *Joseph P Grace*, were completed on 19 June and 28 December 1964 and named respectively after the founder of the company and his grandson, who headed the firm from 1945 to 1989. Delivered to the owners Oswego Chemical Carriers, the ships were operated by Marine Transport Lines, under a long-term charter to the Nitrogen Products Division of the W R Grace Company.[2, 3, 4, 5, 6]

The ships were designed jointly by Verolme and Maryland Shipbuilding & Drydock Co., of Baltimore, in close co-operation with Marine Transport Lines and the Grace Company, to carry anhydrous ammonia at -33°C or propane at -42°C. Built to American Bureau of Shipping classification, the vessels also complied with the US Coast Guard regulations.

Underway at sea the vessels were of pleasing and neat appearance with flared bow, forecastle deck, an uncluttered main deck, curved aft superstructure front, poop deck and cruiser stern. Riveted crack arresting seams were fitted at the bottom shell and deck gunwale. Built with four independent insulated prismatic cargo tanks, the ships also had dry spaces forward for 300 tonnes of solid nitrogen fertiliser in the form of urea or ammonium sulphate. The inner bottom and inner side hull formed the secondary barrier. Each cargo tank was fitted with three hatches; a single deep-well pump on the centre hatch and pipe connections and instruments fitted on the side hatches.

A cargo control room was fitted on the main deck at the superstructure front. The York Refrigeration plants, supplied by Bailey Distributors, and an inert gas room, were fitted in an amidships deckhouse. Seven vertically mounted cylindrical nitrogen storage tanks were located on the main deck aft of the amidships deckhouse.

Joseph P Grace as *Savonetta* was sold to Indian breakers in 1998 with *William R Grace* as *Amelina* suffering the same fate in the following year.

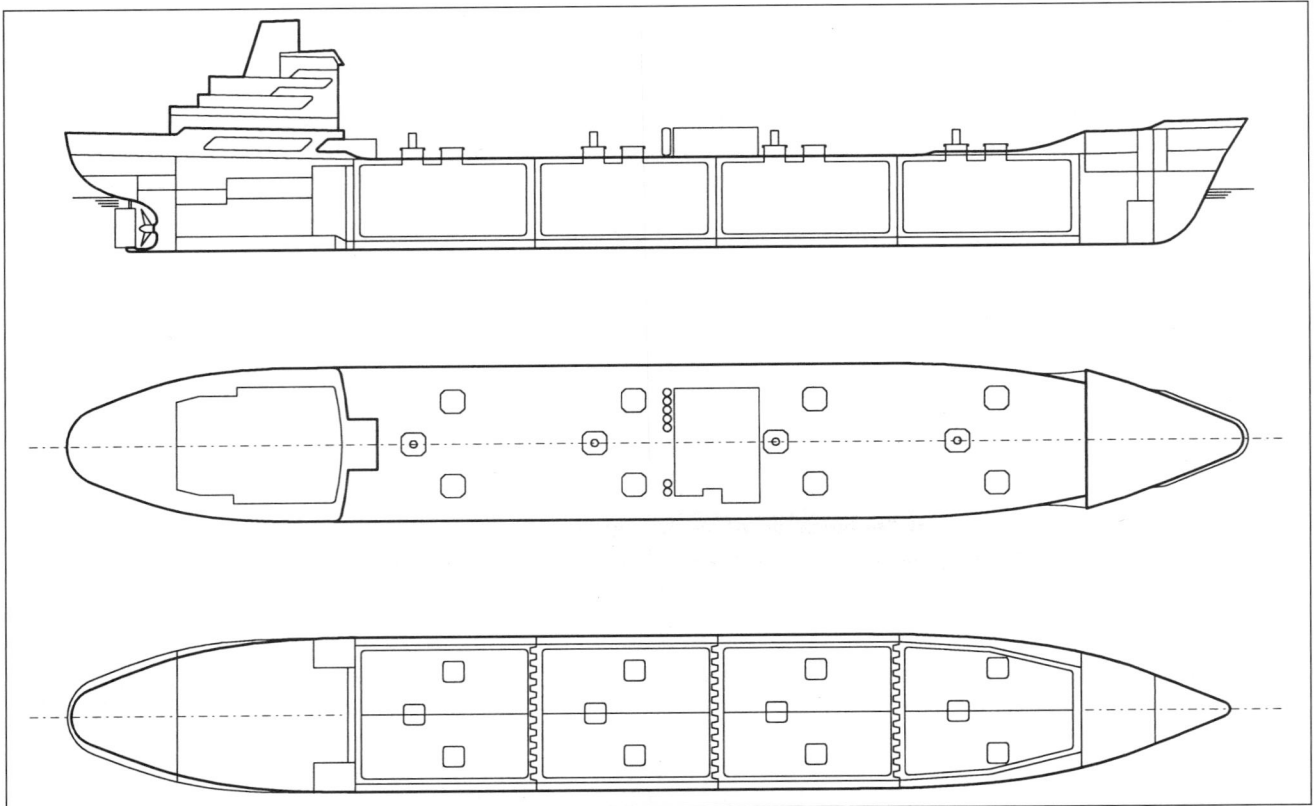

Figure 8-1 Outline Arrangement of *William R Grace*

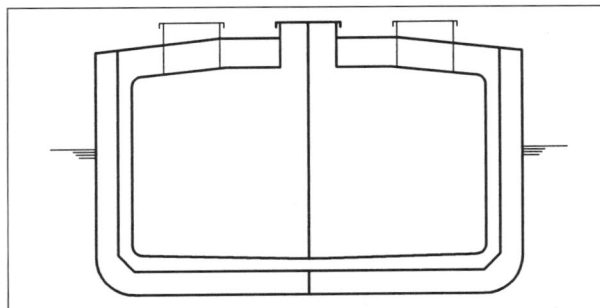

Figure 8-2 Midship Section of *William R Grace*

[1] Hautefeuille, Roland with Clayton, Richard, *Gas Pioneers,* Paris, 1998.
[2] Verolme United Shipyards Press Release, *mv William R Grace,* 1964.
[3] Holland Shipbuilding, *Atmospheric Pressure-refrigerated Ammonia Tanker William R Grace,* August 1964.
[4] Shipbuilding & Shipping Record, *William R Grace the First Ocean-going Refrigerated Ammonia Carrier,* 3 September 1964.
[5] Shipping World & Shipbuilder, *William R Grace World's First Atmospheric Pressure-refrigerated Ammonia Tanker,* 1 October 1964.
[6] Marine Engineering/Log, *World's First Refrigerated Ammonia Tanker delivered by Verolme's Rotterdam Shipyard,* October 1964.

Chapter 9

Home Town Shipyard Hawthorn Leslie

J B Priestley, in his book *English Journey,* which is an account of his rambling through England in the autumn of the year 1933, visited the author's home town Hebburn, at one of the lowest points of the depression years on Tyneside. He sadly wrote; "You felt that there was nothing in the whole place worth a five-pound note."[1] 1933 was the year that only one vessel, a 250 ton coaster, *Rock,* was to leave the Hawthorn Leslie slip way.[2] What a pity he had not walked down Ellison Street two years earlier when he could have witnessed the delivery of the first purpose built LPG carrier, *Agnita,* to the Anglo-Saxon Petroleum Company. The ship was fitted with 12 riveted cylindrical pressure vessel tanks for butane, mounted vertically in her oil cargo tanks.

Plate 9-1   *Agnita*   Hawthorn Leslie

Clerk-Maxwell

Principle Particulars	
Length o.a.	140.70 m
Length b.p.	131.07 m
Breadth	19.21 m
Depth	11.89 m
Draught	8.25 m
LPG Capacity	11,750 m³
Engine	Hawthorn-Sulzer 7RD68
Power	8,000 hp/5,884 kW
Service speed	16 knots

Thirty five years later, on 20 October 1966, the first purpose built fully refrigerated LPG carrier to be constructed in the United Kingdom, 11,750 m³ *Clerk-Maxwell,* was delivered from Hawthorn Leslie to the Nile Steamship Company.

The shipbuilders made a decision in 1961 to commence design studies into ships for the carriage of LPG and chemicals in bulk. On 26 January 1961, Lloyds Register of Shipping first published their Rule Section 70 titled *Provisional Requirements for the Carriage of Liquefied Petroleum and Natural Gases at or near Atmospheric Pressure.*[3] In 1962, Hawthorn Leslie obtained approval from Lloyd's Register of Shipping, the American Bureau of Shipping and the US Coast Guard for a 12,000 ton deadweight fully refrigerated propane carrier.[4, 5, 6] This first project did not materialise into a newbuilding, but it did influence the development of the design of *Clerk-Maxwell.*

Cargo tank drawings for Hawthorn Leslie projects, specifying Lloyd's Register of Shipping classification, referred to the then key British reference work relating to cargo tank design:

> Scantlings derived from method outlined in J B Davies paper, March 1962, *The Carriage of Liquefied Petroleum and Natural Gases.*[7]

Prior to the work on *Clerk-Maxwell,* the Tyneside shipyard converted the 'tween deck dry cargo vessel *Broughty* into 757 m³ *Abbas* for Stephenson Clarke Limited, London.[8] This important semi-refrigerated vessel was the first gas ship from an United Kingdom shipyard to have a reliquefaction plant installed. Designed for the carriage of LPG, butadiene or anhydrous ammonia, *Abbas* loaded her first cargo at Grangemouth in January 1964.

Clerk-Maxwell, launched on 6 May 1966, was chartered to Ocean Gas Transport, a company jointly owned by Houlder Brothers and Gazocéan. Gas specialists Technigaz, the technical arm of Gazocéan, completed the French connection, with design help and supervision of the reliquefaction plant and cargo handling system. For efficient gas-freeing when changing cargo, the owners required, that the inert gas supply should be totally independent of shore facilities. In addition, the vessel was to be able to discharge fully refrigerated or semi-refrigerated cargo at a minimum temperature of +23°F (-5°C).

The ship was classed with Lloyd's Register of Shipping, for the carriage of propane, butane, butadiene and anhydrous ammonia, at a maximum vapour pressure of 4 lb/in² (0.28 kg/cm²) and a minimum temperature of -50°F (-45.6°C). *Clerk-Maxwell* had a distinctive profile with a raked stem, cruiser stern, forecastle, trunk and poop, reliquefaction house and a cylindrical liquid nitrogen storage tank at the superstructure front.

The double bottom was arranged as water ballast tanks with the inner bottom and side shell forming the secondary barrier. The three cargo tanks and the secondary barrier were constructed with *Arctic D* steel, a perfectly named steel for low temperature applications. After years of trials, welding X-rays and impact testing, it was claimed at the time by the shipyard to be "...the finest steel of its type which was available." Developed by the South Durham Steel & Iron Company, West Hartlepool, who had worked closely with the shipyard since 1961, *Arctic D* was a niobium treated, control rolled, carbon manganese steel.[9]

The cargo tanks were insulated with mineral wool and polyurethane, with a glass reinforced polyester vapour seal, supplied and installed by the Mersey Insulation Company. Each cargo tank was fitted with two Sigmund Pulsometer single stage centrifugal deep-well pumps, discharging through three Sigmund centrifugal booster pumps, with a combined total discharge capacity of 1,225 m³/hr. Two Roots vapour boosters, supplied by George Waller & Son Ltd. were fitted for use when a shore vapour return line was available.

The influence of Technigaz was evident regarding equipment suppliers. The three reliquefaction plants, each rated at 186,000 BTU/hr in propane service, were supplied by Chantiers de l'Atlantique. 2% nickel steel, supplied by Lorraine Escaut of Paris and fabricated locally by Blackett Charlton, was used extensively throughout the cargo handling system including the loading and discharge liquid lines, vapour lines, condensate lines, vent risers and nitrogen tank loading line.[10] A liquid nitrogen steam vaporiser was supplied by Ateliers et Chantiers de la Seine Maritime (ACSM), of Le Trait, and the Icare automatic gas detection system was from Marseille.

The Anglo-French *Clerk-Maxwell* was sold to Spanish breakers in 1986, twenty years after leaving the Hebburn shipyard. The cancellation of a Gazocéan charter at the time was a primary cause of this premature scrapping.

A further two 11,750 m³ LPG carriers, *Mariano Escobedo* and *Gas Lion,* were built with the same hull dimensions, cargo tanks geometry and Sulzer 7RD68 main propulsion as *Clerk-Maxwell.* However, the combination of new innovations, three different owners and three types of cargo plant, meant that the vessels were far from being sister ships.

Mariano Escobedo was delivered from Hawthorn Leslie in December 1967, to the state oil and gas company Petroleos Mexicanos (PEMEX). Changes compared to *Clerk-Maxwell* included; polyurethane foam insulation for the cargo tanks from Newalls Insulation & Chemical Company, a J & E Hall Ltd. reliquefaction plant including V-block compressors and a W C Holmes inert-gas generator. An inert-gas generator room was added on the main deck, at the superstructure front, in place of the liquid nitrogen storage tank.

Mariano Escobedo traded exclusively for PEMEX and was reported laid up in 2003.

Gas Lion was built, based on the Hawthorn Leslie design, at Scotts' Shipbuilding & Engineering Company Limited, Greenock, Scotland, for Norwegian owners Kristian Gerhard Jebsen Skipsrederi of Bergen. Classed with Det Norske Veritas and built with a Scott-Sulzer 7RD68 main engine, *Gas Lion* was delivered on 16 August 1968. The three reliquefaction plants each included a Sulzer Labyrinth two-stage cargo compressor, rated at 397,000 BTU/hr in propane service, and a Sabroe R22 compressor. Two submerged electric J C Carter cargo pumps were fitted in each cargo tank with a total discharge capacity of 1,260 m³/hr. A sea-water cargo heater and a David Brown booster pump were also fitted.

Gas Lion was broken up in 1986 as *Gas Pilot*.

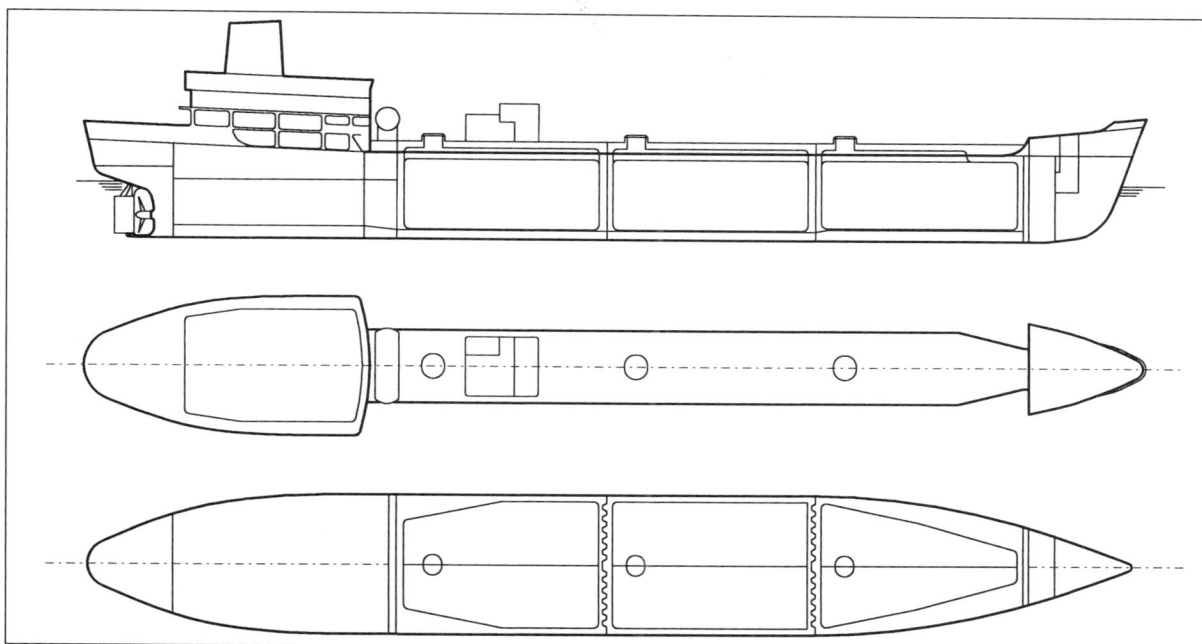

Figure 9-1 Outline Arrangement of *Clerk-Maxwell*

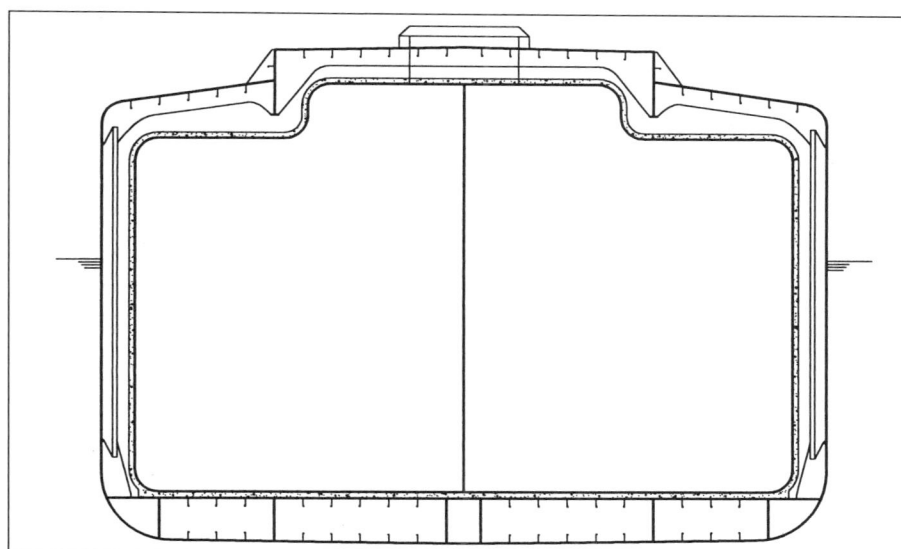

Figure 9-2 Midship Section of *Clerk-Maxwell*

Plate 9-2   Nitrogen storage tank   Hawthorn
at the superstructure front   Leslie

Plate 9-3   Reliquefaction house   Hawthorn
Leslie

Plate 9-4   *Clerk-Maxwell* on sea trials   Hawthorn Leslie

Plate 9-5   Cargo crossover   Hawthorn
Leslie

Plate 9-6   Trunk deck   Hawthorn
Leslie

Petroquimico I

In addition to the contract for *Mariano Escobedo,* Petroleos Mexicanos also placed an order with Hawthorn Leslie for a non-propelled ocean-going fully refrigerated LPG barge, for service on both the east and west coasts of Mexico.[11, 12] The barge, 3,499 m³ *Petroquimico I,* was delivered to PEMEX in the summer of 1967 and classed with Lloyd's Register of Shipping. Both the ship and the barge were built to transport the same gas and chemical gas cargoes, and many of the design features were similar.

The towed barge was arranged with stern twin skegs, main deck and trunk, and a double bottom and double side hull. The inner bottom and inner side formed the secondary barrier. The barge was built with three insulated independent prismatic cargo tanks. Each tank was fitted with two Sigmund deep-well pumps. A small accommodation deck house was fitted aft and a reliquefaction house, control room and electric motor room were fitted on the main deck, forward of the cargo tanks. A four cylinder Davey Paxman diesel engine provided the electrical power at sea and in port when discharging cargo.

In 1989, *Petroquimico I* was sold to Naviera Armamex, renamed *Macuiltepetl* and was used as a water supply barge for offshore drilling work in the Campeche Bay oil field. The barge was scrapped in 1996.

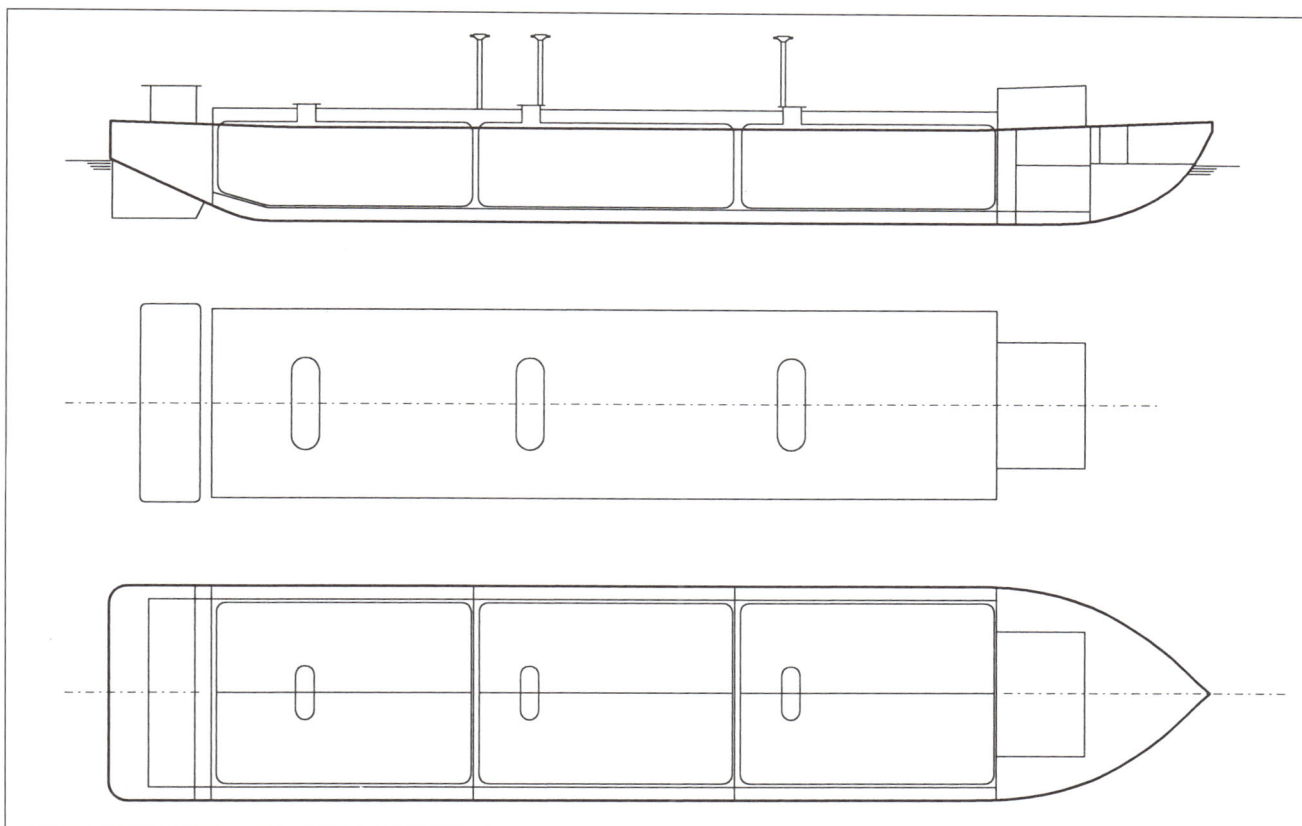

Figure 9-3 Outline Arrangement of Barge *Petroquimico I*

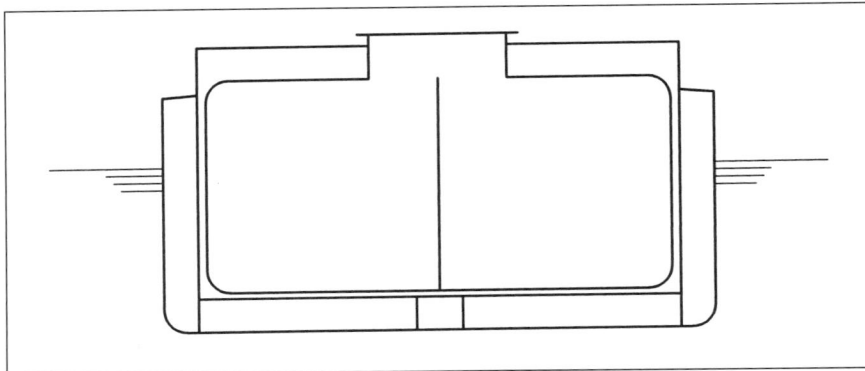

Figure 9-4 Midship Section of Barge *Petroquimico I*

Wiltshire

Principle Particulars	
Length o.a.	151.73 m
Length b.p.	141.74 m
Breadth	21.34 m
Depth	12.50 m
Draught	8.23 m
LPG Capacity	15,495 m³
Engine	Hawthorn-Doxford 76 J4
Power	8,380 hp/6,163 kW
Service speed	16 knots

As with so many major decisions in the gas shipping business the beginning of Bibby Line's involvement in owning gas ships was remarkably unplanned and happened by sheer chance. "Would you like to buy an LPG ship being built?" was the telephone question to the late Derek Bibby from his London broker.

The ship under discussion had been ordered by George Gibson & Company of Leith, on the strength of an anticipated charter, which had not been confirmed.[13, 14] An agreement was reached between Bibby Line and Hawthorn Leslie in which the shipyard would cover the cost of construction until delivery, and the vessel, 15,495 m³ *Wiltshire*, would then be time-chartered to George Gibson.

Delivered to the owners on 6 September 1968, *Wiltshire*, with three cargo tanks, was an improved and larger version of the earlier built *Clerk-Maxwell*.[15, 16] The ship was also built to Lloyd's Register of Shipping classification and to US Coast Guard requirements. The cargo tank design temperature of -58°F (-50°C) was slightly lower than on *Clerk-Maxwell*. *Arctic D* steel was again used for the cargo tanks and secondary barrier.

The cruiser stern became a raked transom stern and the cargo tanks were constructed without trunks, which resulted in a flush main deck. The poop and forecastle remained, and additional protection from heavy seas was provided by a main deck breakwater in way of No. 1 cargo tank. The double bottom and upper wing tanks were used for water ballast. The cargo tanks were insulated with polyurethane foam with a fire-resistant vapour seal. Two David Brown centrifugal deep-well pumps were fitted in each cargo tank, with a total discharge capacity of 1,392 m³/hr. Three reliquefaction plants were fitted. Each plant included a Sulzer labyrinth oil-free cargo compressor, a Sabore R22 compressor and a heat exchanger.

Wiltshire was broken up as *Zallaq* in 1998.

Wiltshire was the last vessel to be delivered with the Hawthorn Leslie builder's plate, thereby completing an intriguing 112 year gas connection, which flowed steadfastly through the shipyard's history. During the early years of the shipyard, with a scarcity of local labour, the founder

Andrew Leslie brought skilled men from his home town Aberdeen and labourers from Ireland.[17] Not an ideal combination which often resulted in violence in "Little Aberdeen" as the town became known. In 1856, houses were built for the workers. Most of the homes had only one room, but gas lighting was supplied from a gas-producing plant in the shipyard.

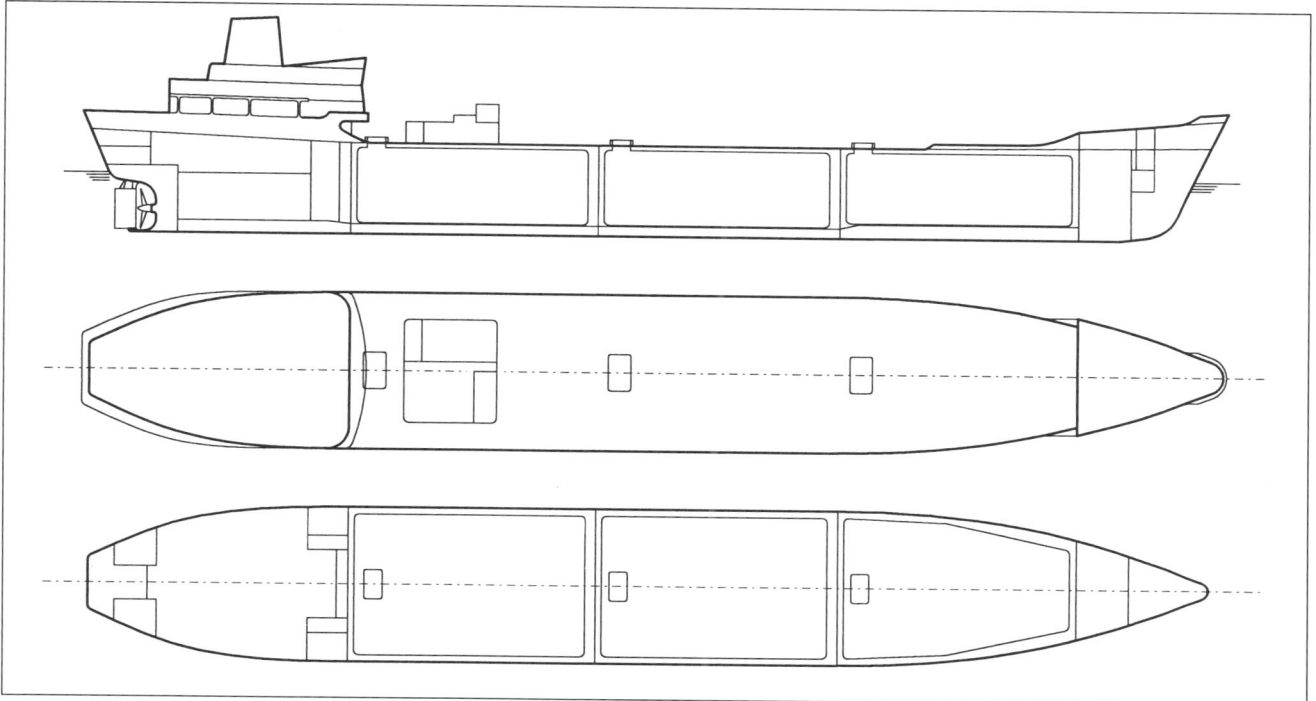

Figure 9-5 Outline Arrangement of *Wiltshire*

Plate 9-7   *Wiltshire* on sea trials   Hawthorn Leslie

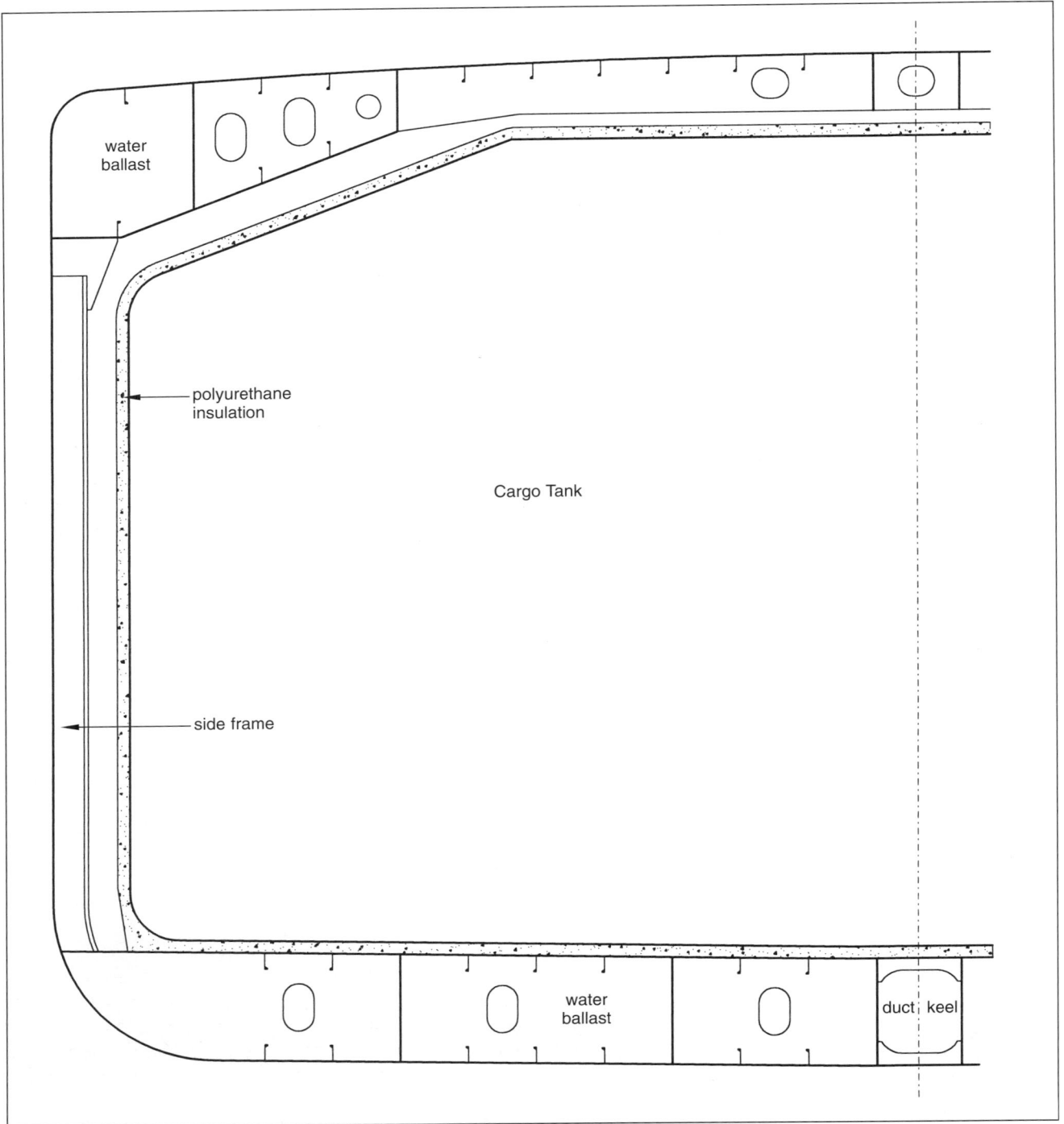

water
ballast

polyurethane
insulation

Cargo Tank

side frame

water
ballast

duct keel

Figure 9-6 Midship Section of *Wiltshire*

Faraday

Principle Particulars	
Length o.a.	186.84 m
Length b.p.	178.31 m
Breadth	26.83 m
Depth	15.40 m
Draught	9.75 m
LPG Capacity	31,215 m^3
Engine	Hawthorn-Doxford 76 J6
Power	15,000 hp/11,032 kW
Service speed	17 knots

On the same building berths on the south bank of the Tyne, but under the Swan Hunter name, two fully refrigerated LPG carriers, *Faraday* and *Lincolnshire,* were launched and delivered, each with some differences but with the same hull and cargo tank dimensions.

For Anglo-French owners Nile Steamship Company Ltd., *Faraday* followed *Clerk-Maxwell,* when delivered from the Hebburn yard on 4 January 1971. Famous names and famous people were connected with the naming of this ship. Mrs. Paulette Boudet, wife of gas pioneer René Boudet, performed the naming ceremony on 19 June 1970, and with the name *Faraday* continued the splendid Gazocéan custom of giving gas ships the names of prominent scientists and engineers.

Built to the requirements of Lloyd's Register of Shipping and the US Coast Guard, the 31,215 m^3 *Faraday* was designed for the carriage of LPG, butadiene and NH_3, with a maximum cargo pressure of 4¼ lb/in^2 (0.293 kg/cm^2) and a minimum temperature of -49°F (-45°C). The vessel was delivered on 4 January 1971 and arranged with a curved transom stern, aft accommodation house, flush main deck with forward sheer and a small bulbous bow.[18]

The arrangement of the windows in the accommodation house front gave an unusual visual effect. Bridge windows were fitted with centreline "V" shaped windows and below the bridge, at the third deck level, a single line of six 355 mm diameter portlights, with fire resisting glass, were fitted. This gave the ship a sinister appearance, almost like a warship rather than a gas carrier. Perhaps the idea came from the Ministry of Defence Fleet Replenishment Tanker series built by the shipyard. The portlights were not repeated on *Lincolnshire.* Three pressurised tanks for cargo changes, one 140 m^3 for ammonia and two 120 m^3 for propane, were located on the main deck above No. 1 cargo tank and protected by a breakwater.

The three cargo tanks and the secondary barrier were constructed with *Arctic D* steel, with the cargo tanks insulated with fine filament glass wool. Two J C Carter submerged electric pumps were fitted in each cargo tank, with a total discharge capacity of 2,400 m^3/hr. The double bottom and lower and upper wing tanks formed the water ballast tanks. High tensile steel was used for the sheerstrake, double bottom floors and girders, and lower and upper wing tanks internal structures.

The gas handling equipment was designed and supplied by Liquid Gas Equipment Ltd. of Edinburgh. Three reliquefaction plants were fitted and each included a Sulzer cargo compressor, a J & E Hall Ltd. R22 compressor and related equipment.

Not a lot of people know that *Faraday* made a cameo appearance alongside Michael Caine in the 1971 crime thriller *Get Carter. Faraday* was being fitted out at the Hebburn shipyard whilst Michael Caine and Ian Hendry were involved in a shootout on the Mid-Tyne Ferries landing at Wallsend.

Faraday was sold to Chinese breakers in 1993.

For Bibby Line Ltd., *Lincolnshire*, at double the capacity, followed *Wiltshire* from the Hebburn yard, and was delivered on 9 March 1972. The range of cargoes carried on *Lincolnshire* was increased, compared with *Faraday*, and the Bibby ship was also able to load isobutane, butylene, isobutylene and propylene. The minimum cargo design temperature was reduced to -50°C.

Lincolnshire was sold for scrap in 2002.

Plate 9-8   *Lincolnshire* with three change of   Bibby Line Limited
                                grade tanks above No 1 cargo tank

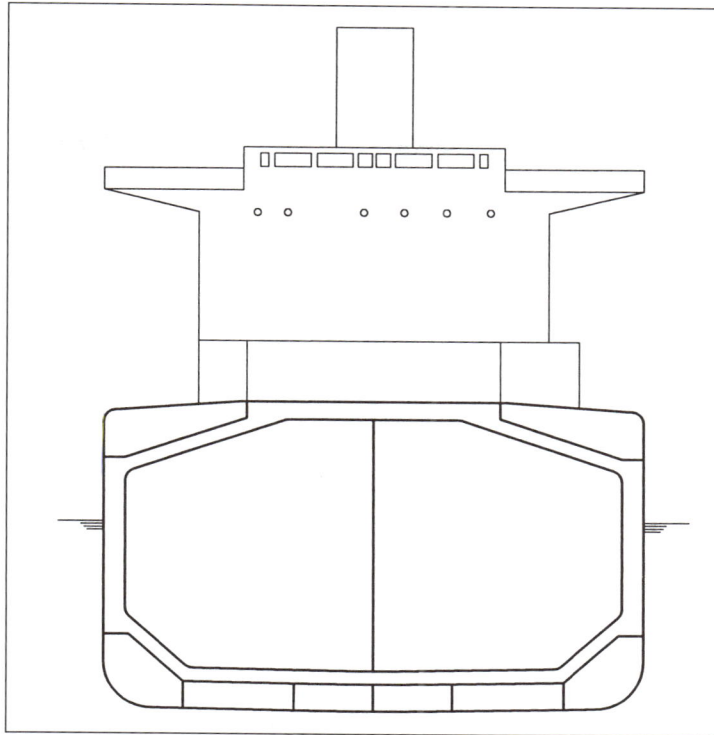

Figure 9-7 *Faraday* – Midship Section and Accommodation House Front

Gandara

Principle Particulars

Length o.a.	160.51 m
Length b.p.	152.00 m
Breadth	24.00 m
Depth	16.20 m
Draught	9.82 m
LPG Capacity	22,711 m^3
Engine	Kincaid-B&W 7K74EF
Power	14,600 hp/10,738 kW
Service speed	16.5 knots

The final gas carrier to be built at the Hebburn yard was one of a pair of 22,700 m^3 LPG/ammonia carriers ordered at the time by the P&O Group. Moss Værft delivered 22,764 m^3 *Garbeta* to P&O Lines Ltd. on 21 October 1975 and Swan Hunter delivered 22,711 m^3 *Gandara* to P&O Bulk Shipping on 30 March 1976.

Gandara was classed with Lloyd's Register of Shipping and the gas handling plant was supplied by Liquid Gas Equipment Ltd. of Edinburgh. The four cargo tanks and the secondary barrier were constructed with *Arctic D* steel.

[1] Priestley, J. B., *English Journey*, Mandarin, 1994.

[2] Clarke, J. F., *Power on Land & Sea, A History of R & W Hawthorn Leslie*, 1977.

[3] Lloyd's Register of Shipping, *Rules and Regulations for the Construction and Classification of Steel Ships*, London, 1962.

[4] Shipbuilding & Shipping Record, *Clerk-Maxwell, First UK built ✠ 100 A1 Liquefied Gas Carrier*, 6 July 1967.

[5] Shipbuilding & Shipping Record, *Engineering for Gas Tankers*, 30 May 1969.

[6] Gray, R. C., and Johnson, L., *The Design & Construction of Liquefied Gas Carriers*, North-East Coast Institution of Engineers & Shipbuilders, 7 December 1970.

[7] Davies, J. B., *The Carriage of Liquefied Petroleum and Natural Gases*, Lloyd's Register Staff Association, No. 20, March 1962.

[8] Shipbuilding & Shipping Record, *Abbas, First UK Conversion to LPG Carrier*, 6 February 1964.

[9] Green, G., and Turner M. J., *The Construction of Ships Tanks for the Transport of Liquid Gas*, International Institute of Welding, Annual Assembly 1971.

[10] Charlton, Robert B., *Specialised Piping for Gas Tankers*, Shipbuilding & Shipping Record, 30 May 1969.

[11] Shipbuilding & Shipping Record, *Tyne-built LPG Barge for Mexico*, 24 November 1966.

[12] Shipbuilding & Shipping Record, *LPG Barge for Mexico*, 31 August 1967.

[13] Somner, Graeme, *George Gibson & Company*, World Ship Society, May 1988.

[14] Watson, Nigel, *The Bibby Line 1807-1990, Story of Wars, Booms and Slumps*, James & James, 1990.

[15] Shipbuilding & Shipping Record, *Wiltshire, A Basically Simple LPG Carrier from Hawthorn Leslie*, 18 October 1968.

[16] Shipping World & Shipbuilder, *Wiltshire, Liquefied Gas Carrier for the Bibby Line*, November 1968.

[17] Dougan, David, *The History of North East Shipbuilding*, George Allen & Unwin, 1968.

[18] Shipping World & Shipbuilder, *Faraday, Liquefied Gas Carrier from Swan Hunter*, February 1971.

Chapter 10

LPG and LNG Technologies Intertwined at IHI

Japanese shipbuilders Ishikawajima-Harima Heavy Industries (IHI) are a perfect example of how LPG and LNG shipbuilding technologies have developed, intertwined and complemented each other.[1] One of the final ships to bear the Harima Zosensho K.K., Aioi, builders plate was the pressurised 990 m³ *L P Maru No. 1,* with 13 vertical cylindrical tanks, which was delivered to Nippon Ekika Gas Yuso K.K. in 1960. Since then IHI have steadily progressed to the present day with an impressive variety of gas ship types, built to carry LPG, NH_3, VCM, ethylene and LNG.

The design of the successful IHI SPB (Self-supporting Prismatic shape IMO type B) LNG carrier has its roots in the design of the fully refrigerated LPG carrier. Over many years, materials, techniques and new ideas have been tried, tested and proven in service, before moving on to the -163°C cargoes. The first IHI-SPB LNG carriers, 88,000 m³ *Polar Eagle* and *Arctic Sun* were commissioned in 1993.

Joyama Maru

Principle Particulars	
Length o.a.	198.04 m
Length b.p.	190.00 m
Breadth	29.00 m
Depth	19.40 m
Draught	11.03 m
LPG Capacity	46,548 m³
Engine	IHI-Sulzer 8RD76
Power	12,000 hp/8,826 kW
Service speed	15.8 knots

IHI's first fully refrigerated LPG carrier was 46,548 m³ *Joyama Maru,* which was delivered on 25 October 1965, to Japanese owners and operators Shinwa Kaiun K.K., to carry propane and butane from Kuwait to Japan. The vessel's keel was laid on 26 November 1964 and *Joyama Maru* was launched on 29 June 1965.[2] Classed with Nippon Kaiji Kyokai, the ship had four independent self-supporting prismatic tanks.

The cargo tanks, constructed with N-TUF 33 notch tough steel and 2¼% nickel steel, were supported on plywood blocks and insulated with polyurethane foam. The side hull formed the secondary barrier. Water ballast tanks were arranged in the double bottom and in upper wing tanks. Nippon Steel Corporation developed a cost saving steel, under the trade name N-TUF 33. N for Nippon, with TUF standing for low-temperature toughness and 33 kg/mm² being the minimum yield point.[3, 4] N-TUF 33 was a quenched and tempered low-carbon aluminium-killed steel, which was to be used extensively in later years for the construction of LPG cargo tanks in Japan.

Two 330 m³/hr J C Carter submerged cargo pumps were fitted in each tank, being the first time this type of pump had been exported to Japan for installation on an LPG carrier.

Joyama Maru traded successfully for twenty years for Shinwa Kaiun K.K. and was scrapped in 1985. On 31 January 1986, Shinwa Kaiun K.K. took delivery from Mitsubishi, Nagasaki, of a larger 80,863 m³ LPG carrier, bearing the same name, to replace the smaller vessel.

Plate 10-1   *Joyama Maru*   IHI

Bridgestone Maru No. 3

Principle Particulars

Length o.a.	187.50 m
Length b.p.	180.00 m
Breadth	29.00 m
Depth	18.00 m
Draught	10.52 m
LPG Capacity	47,124 m³
Engine	IHI-Sulzer 7RD76
Power	11,200 hp/8,238 kW
Service speed	15 knots

Bridgestone Maru and *Bridgestone Maru II* were completed at the Yokohama works of Mitsubishi Heavy Industries Ltd., with prismatic cargo tanks in 1962 and 1964. The third ship in the Bridgestone trilogy was quite different and had a unique design with integral tanks for butane, and an independent self-supporting tank forward for propane.[5] *Bridgestone Maru No. 3* was delivered to Japan Line Ltd., on 14 May 1966 from the Nagoya yard of Ishikawajima-Harima Heavy Industries Co. Ltd. (IHI).

Bridgestone LPG Co. Ltd. were involved with the design, and compared with the previous two Bridgestone ships they were successful in achieving a major cost reduction. A building cost of U.S. $5.30 million for *Bridgestone Maru No. 3* was quoted by Katsuro Yamamoto. The ship was constructed with four cargo hold spaces with a prismatic tank in the forward hold for propane at -45°C and seven integral tanks for butane at -5°C, arranged in the other spaces. The ship was classed with Nippon Kaiji Kyokai.

The internal structure in way of the integral tanks was similar to a conventional oil tanker, but with inner hull void spaces arranged around the butane tanks. Mild steel Grade B was used for the integral tanks, as the cargo temperature was considered no more severe than for an oil tanker trading in the Arctic Ocean during winter. A below deck pump room was fitted between the machinery spaces and the cargo spaces. The aft two butane spaces were arranged with a centre tank and wing tanks, with the centre tank also used for water ballast. The integral tanks were externally insulated with polyurethane.

This ship had many technical innovations and another one was added in 1981. As *Ribagorça,* when owned by Trans-Offshore Inc., a deck mounted booster pump module was installed, with a second hand J C Carter submerged electric cargo pump, which had to be primed with cargo before use.

This unique ship traded for 27 years and was scrapped in 1993. The Arctic Ocean winter theory must have been accurate.

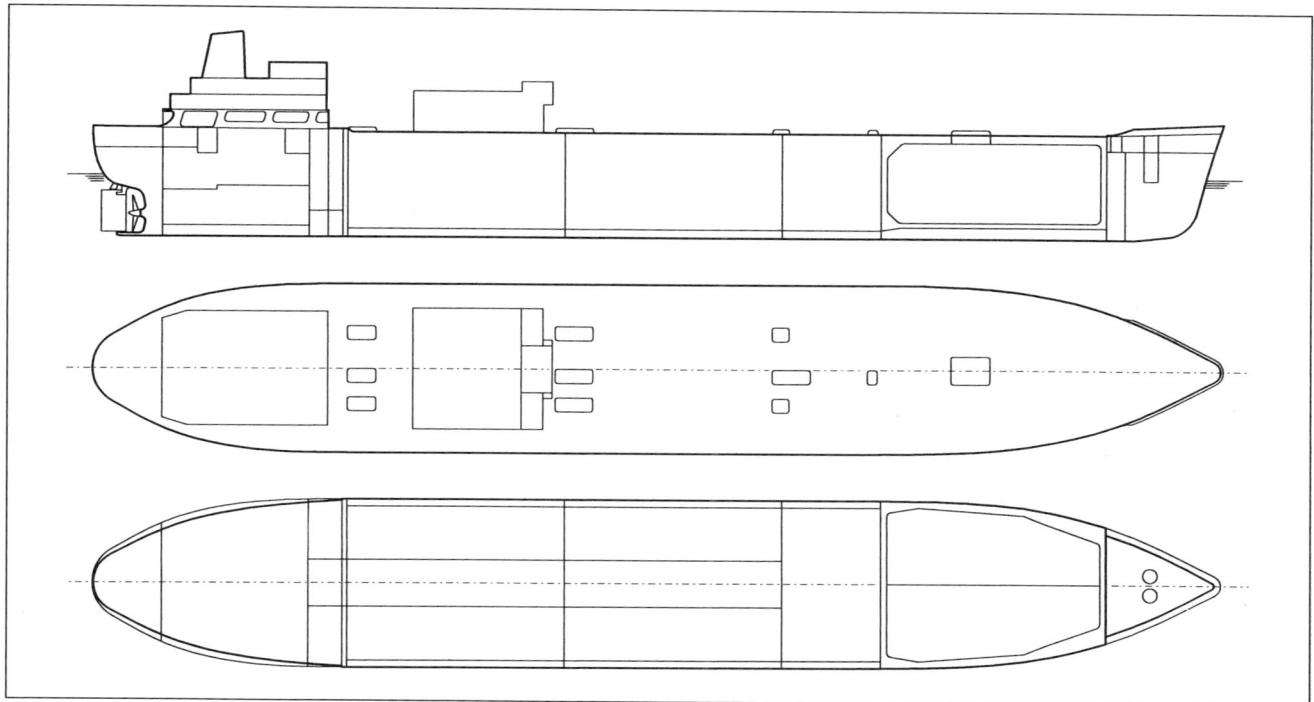

Figure 10-1 Outline Arrangement of *Bridgestone Maru No. 3*

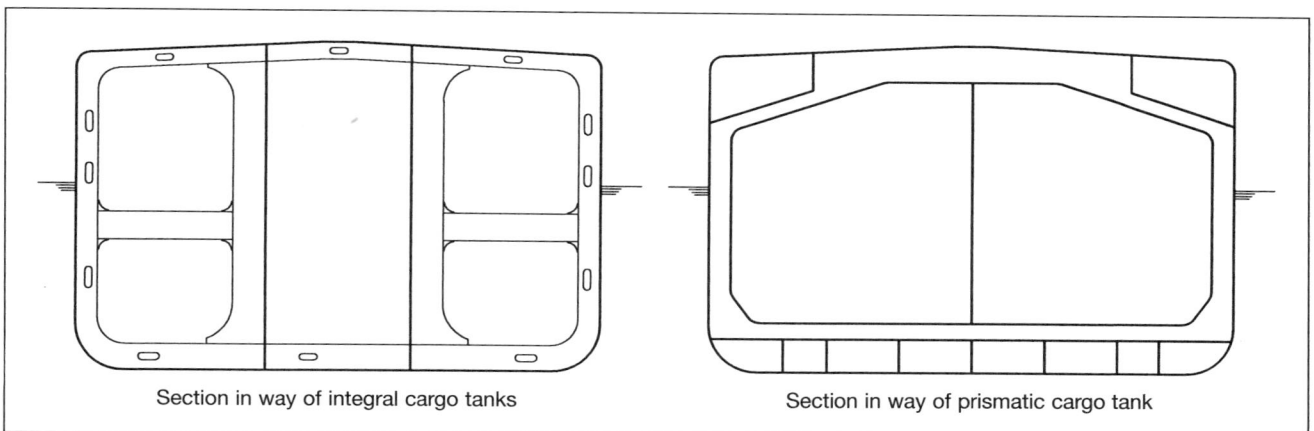

Section in way of integral cargo tanks

Section in way of prismatic cargo tank

Figure 10-2 Cross Sections of *Bridgestone Maru No. 3*

Plate 10-2   *Bridgestone Maru No. 3*   IHI

M P Grace

Principle Particulars	
Length o.a.	162.84 m
Length b.p.	154.00 m
Breadth	23.31 m
Depth	14.35 m
Draught	8.39 m
LPG Capacity	19,450 m³
Engine	IHI-Sulzer 7RND76
Power	11,200 hp/8,238 kW
Service speed	16 knots

On 29 September 1967, IHI delivered 19,450 m³ *M P Grace* to Oswego Chemical Carriers Corp. This was the third FRLPGC from the Nagoya yard, and was also Oswego's third gas ship, having taken delivery of 12,975 m³ *William R Grace* and *Joseph P Grace* from Verolme in 1964. *M P Grace,* like the smaller Grace ships, was built to American Bureau of Shipping classification and complied with the US Coast Guard regulations.

There are many similarities between the Verolme and IHI designs, but on the later ship there were some noteworthy improvements. Propylene was added as a cargo. Crack arresting riveted seams were fitted at the hull and deck of the first ships. The IHI ship was all welded. All three ships had four cargo tanks, with the inner bottom and inner side forming the secondary barrier and the outer hull spaces used as water ballast tanks.

On the Dutch ships, the inner hull was chamfered at the inner bottom at side, whereas on the Japanese ship the inner bottom was curved and parallel to the lower corner radius of the cargo tank. In addition, on the IHI ship, the water ballast tanks extended to an under deck upper wing tank.[7] The cargo tanks were constructed with 2¼% nickel steel and N-TUF 33 tough notched steel and stiffened internally with large horizontal stringers. The tank insulation was glass fibre.

Unusually, the Verolme ships were fitted with a single deep-well pump in each cargo tank. How quickly lessons are learnt in the gas shipping business. *M P Grace* had two deep-well pumps fitted in each cargo tank. The flush deck vessel did not have the protection provided by a forecastle and poop.

M P Grace was sold for scrap as *Calina* in 1999.

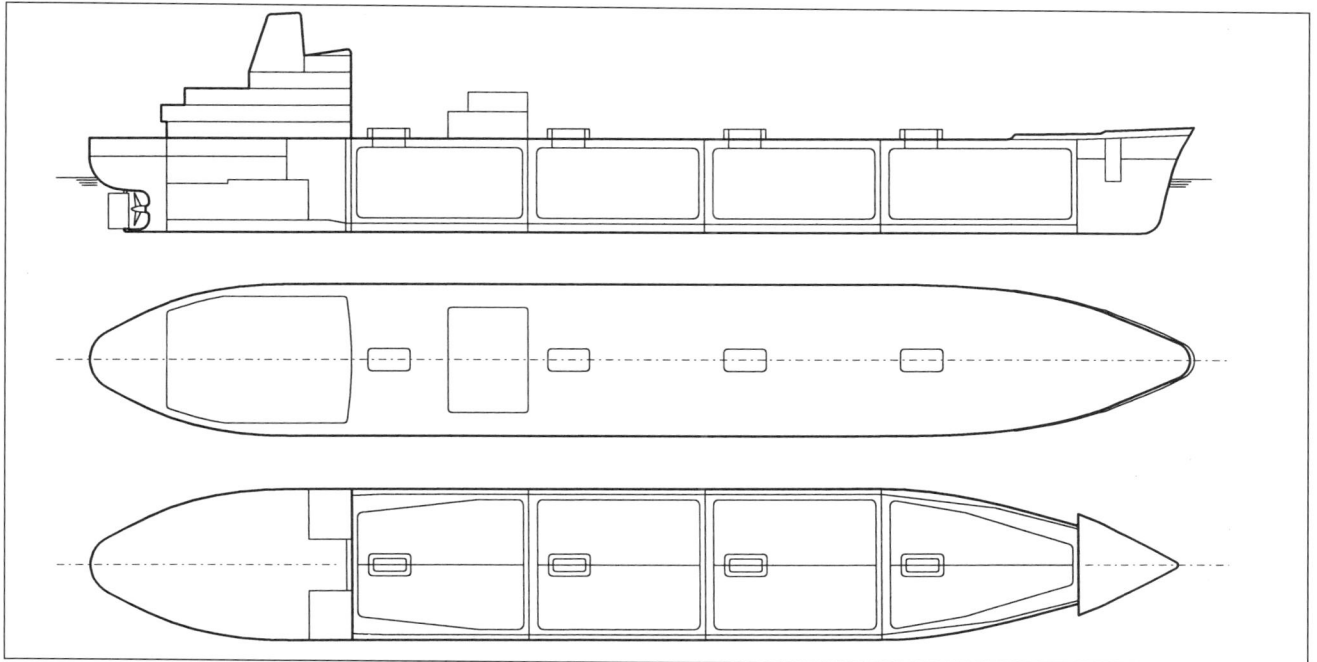

Figure 10-3 Outline Arrangement of *M P Grace*

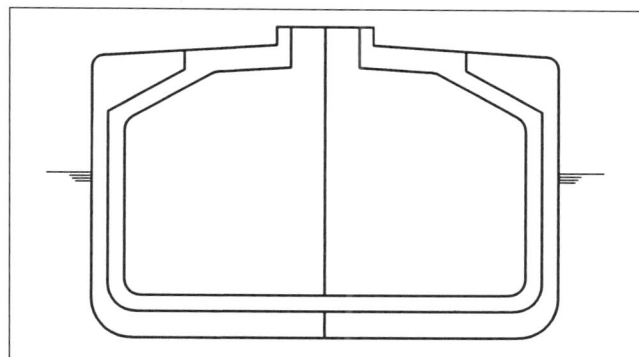

Figure 10-4 Midship Section of *M P Grace*

Genkai Maru

Principle Particulars	
Length o.a.	224.00 m
Length b.p.	212.00 m
Breadth	36.00 m
Depth	22.30 m
Draught	11.40 m
LPG Capacity	80,311 m³
Engine	IHI-Sulzer 6RND90M
Power	19,080 hp/14,033 kW
Service speed	16.25 knots

The first fully refrigerated LPG carrier to be built with IMO type B cargo tanks was completed by IHI, Aioi, on 15 November 1980, as 80,311 m³ *Genkai Maru*.[8, 9, 10, 11] The philosophy behind the IMO type B concept is that the cargo tanks are designed and constructed to such high standards that the secondary barrier is not required, and provided a partial secondary barrier is fitted, the ship's adjacent structures can be constructed with normal shipbuilding steels. Cargo tanks must be designed using model tests and sophisticated computer analysis to determine stress levels, fatigue life and crack propagation characteristics. The partial secondary barrier, in the form of splash barriers and drip trays, must be fitted to contain any envisaged small gas leak from cracks in the tanks. An effective gas leak detection system is required.

Genkai Maru was ordered by Idemitsu Tanker Co. Ltd. to transport LPG from the Middle East to Japan and was classed with Nippon Kaiji Kyokai as a Tanker for Liquefied Gases at a maximum pressure of 0.28 kg/cm² and a minimum temperature of -45°C. The four independent tanks were constructed with aluminium killed steel NK-KL24B with 3½% nickel steel used for the corner sections.

The ship was arranged with an upright transom stern with lower aft deck, aft machinery and living quarters, main deck, four cargo tanks and a bulbous bow. Water ballast tanks were arranged in the inner bottom and upper wing tanks, with the inner bottom extending to the turn of bilge. No lower wing ballast tanks were fitted.

Internally, the cargo tanks were constructed with top and bottom transverse webs and two large horizontal stringers. To satisfy the IMO type B criteria regarding the generation and propagation of fatigue cracks, great attention was paid to design details of webs, stringers, stiffeners and brackets within the cargo tanks. The care taken with the design and construction was evident in the following feature; brackets and flat bars were curved into an arc at their extremities, lap joints were eliminated, internal stiffening edges were shaped smooth and free of notches, stiffeners with curved ends were not fixed to brackets and the shape of stringers and webs were smoothly curved.

A cargo dome was arranged at the mid-length of each tank. Electric submerged pumps were used for cargo discharge, with two 550 m³/hr main pumps and a 100 m³/hr stripping pump fitted in each tank. The ship was fitted with four 2-stage reliquefaction plants housed on the main deck, offset to starboard, above No. 4 cargo tank, with a central cargo control room above. Deck cargo pipework was arranged below the fore and aft walkway on the port side, which resulted in a neat and uncluttered main deck arrangement.

The cargo tanks were insulated with 100 mm of polyurethane foam, which was applied on-site and covered with thin steel sheets. To satisfy the requirements for an effective gas leak detection system, strips of soft polyurethane were attached to the cargo tanks to provide an encased passageway in the polyurethane foam for any escape of gas from a crack, which could be detected by sensors in the void spaces. The thin steel covering sheets provided the splash barrier to guide any possible small leak downwards towards drip trays, arranged around the tank bottom supports.

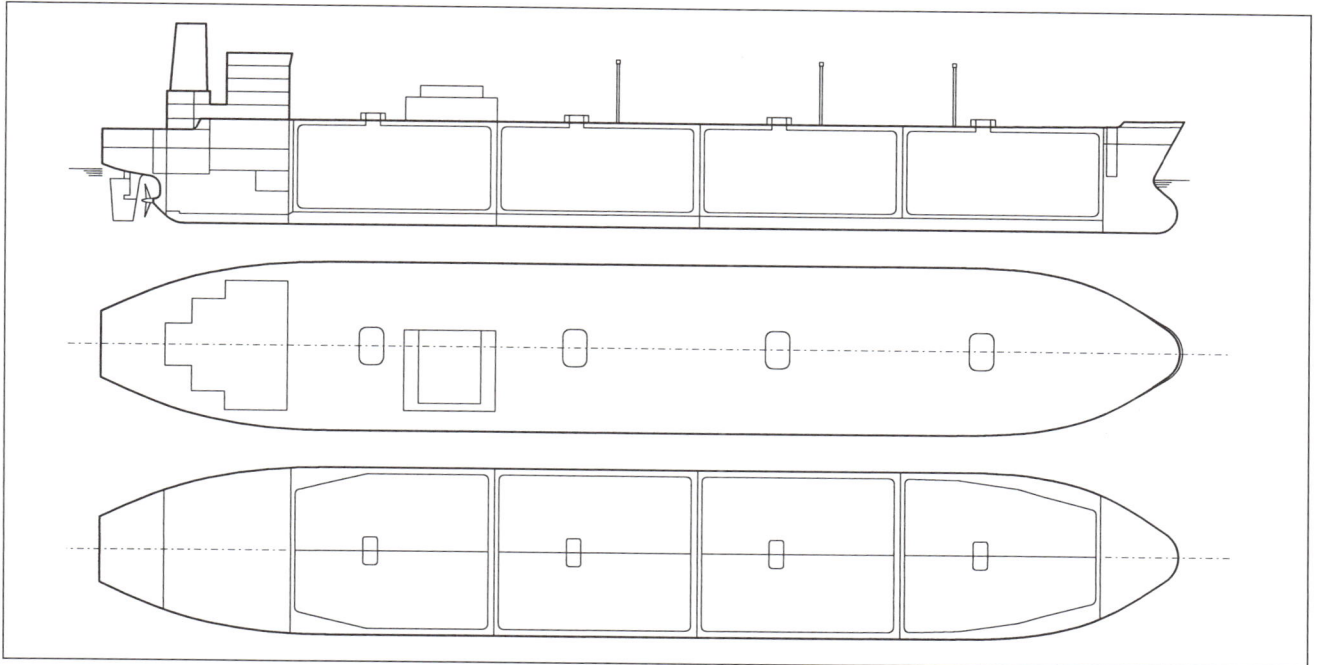

Figure 10-5 Outline Arrangement of *Genkai Maru*

Plate 10-3   *Genkai Maru*   IHI

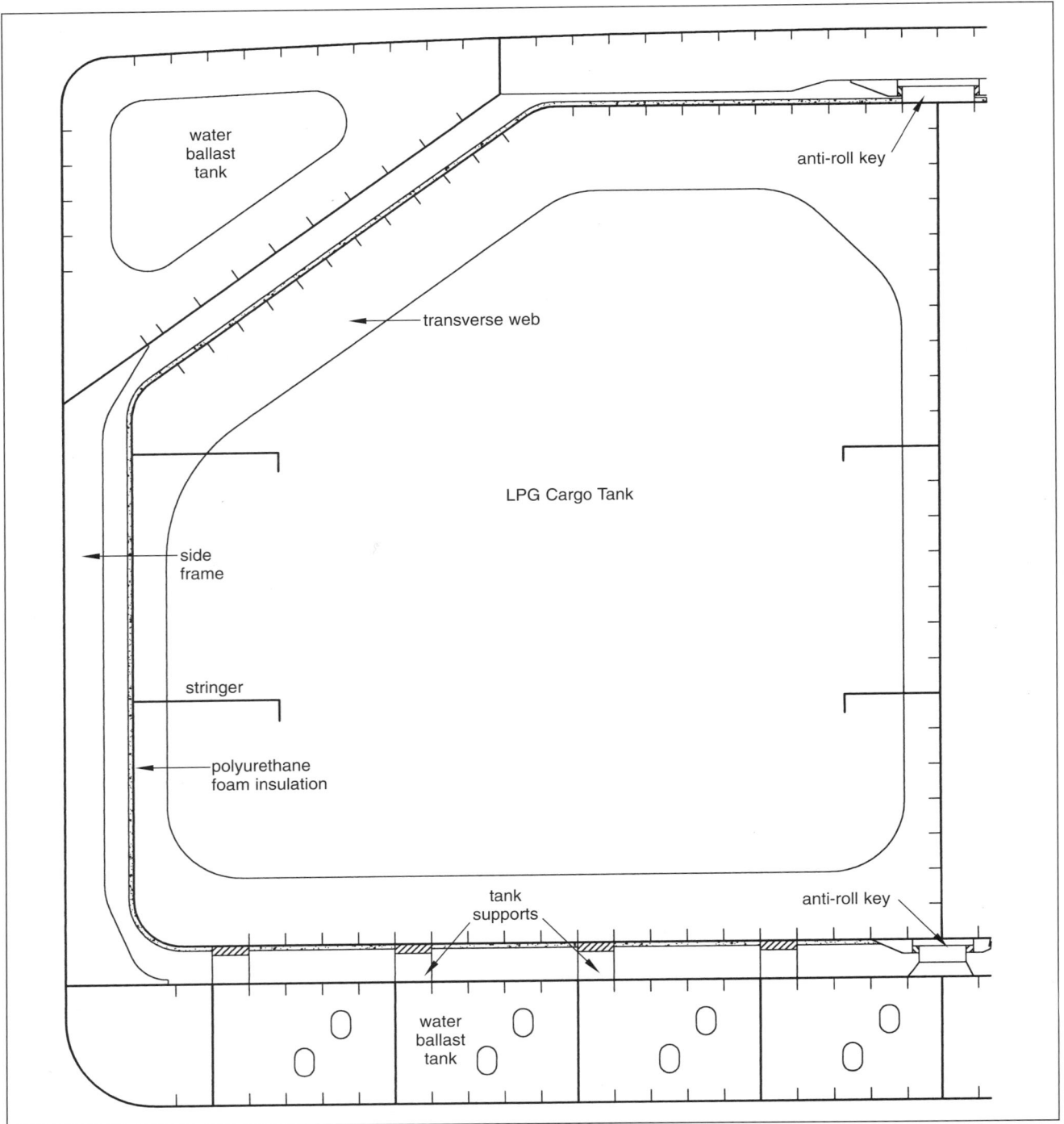

Figure 10-6 Midship Section of *Genkai Maru*

Plate 10-4   *Toyosu Maru*   IHI

Toyosu Maru

Principle Particulars	
Length o.a.	176.70 m
Length b.p.	169.00 m
Breadth	30.00 m
Depth	17.60 m
Draught	9.20 m
LPG Capacity	39,113 m³
Engine	IHI-Sulzer 6RTA58
Power	8,200 hp/6,031 kW
Service speed	14.5 knots

The next fully refrigerated LPG carrier from the Aioi yard was a smaller version of *Genkai Maru,* designed as the optimum size to trade to the Tokyo Gas terminal at Toyosu in Tokyo Bay. Launched on 18 June 1984, 39,113 m³ *Toyosu Maru* was delivered to the owners Iino Kaiun Kaisha on 25 October 1984. The cargo tanks were designed as IMO type A tanks, unlike the IMO type B tanks on *Genkai Maru,* and many features of the larger ship were incorporated in the latest newbuilding from IHI.[12]

The ship was arranged with upright transom stern, lower aft deck, aft machinery and accommodation spaces, main deck, four cargo tanks, raised forward deck above No. 1 cargo tank and a bulbous bow. The offset reliquefaction house and the neat port side piping layout were retained, as were electric submerged pumps, with two 330 m³/hr main pumps and a 50 m³/hr stripping pump fitted in each tank.

Koho Maru

Principle Particulars	
Length o.a.	221.50 m
Length b.p.	209.00 m
Breadth	36.00 m
Depth	22.60 m
Draught	11.60 m
LPG Capacity	80,681 m³
Engine	IHI-Sulzer 6RTA76
Power	13,550 hp/9,966 kW
Service speed	16 knots

In 1985 IHI, Aioi delivered 80,681 m³ *Koho Maru* to domestic owner Iino Kaiun Kaisha.[13] The ship had a similar capacity to *Genkai Maru,* but with slightly different hull dimensions and like *Toyosu Maru* had IMO type A cargo tanks. Launched on 10 February 1985 and completed on 21 June 1985, the ship combined some features from the two previously built fully refrigerated LPG carriers. The main deck extended aft to the stern and was raised forward, and the distinctive offset reliquefaction house was retained. The electric submerged cargo pumps increased in capacity to 650 m³/hr and a 100 m³/hr stripping pump was fitted in each tank.

Plate 10-5   *Koho Maru*   IHI

Kelvin

Principle Particulars	
Length o.a.	146.09 m
Length b.p.	137.00 m
Breadth	23.00 m
Depth	14.70 m
Draught	8.55 m
LPG Capacity	17,900 m³
Engine	IHI-Sulzer 4RTA52
Power	6,000 hp/4,413 kW
Service speed	14.65 knots

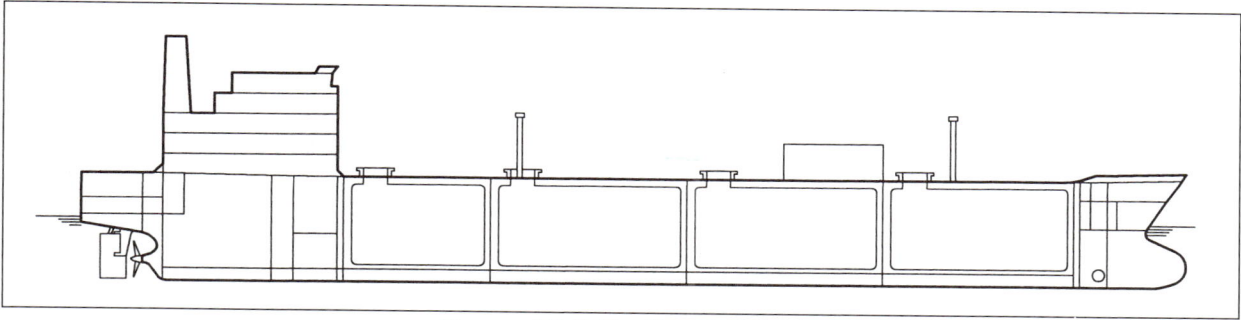

Figure 10-7 Profile of *Kelvin*

Plate 10-6　　　　　　　　　　　　　　　　*Kelvin*　　　　　　　　　　　　　　　　IHI

ICI Australia ordered a LPG/NH₃ carrier from the Kure works of IHI, as a replacement for the 1968 Hawthorn Leslie built, 15,495 m³ *Wiltshire*, owned by Bibby, which was under charter to ICI Australia. The ship was launched on 29 September 1989 and handed over to Teuton Pty. Ltd., an ICI Australia affiliated company, on 19 January 1990, as 17,900 m³ *Kelvin*.[14]

The Australian flagged vessel was classed with Lloyd's Register of Shipping as a Liquefied Gas Carrier for cargoes at a minimum temperature of -48°C, a maximum pressure of 0.28 kg/cm² and a maximum specific gravity of 0.69. The ship was arranged with upright transom stern with free-fall lifeboat, aft machinery and living quarters, flush main deck, four cargo tanks, bow thruster and a bulbous bow. The IHI offset reliquefaction house was located on the main deck above No. 2 cargo tank. Each of the three reliquefaction plant were rated at 150,000 kcal/hr in propane service. Domes were arranged at the aft ends of each tank to accommodate two 190 m³/hr deep-well pumps. A 380 m³/hr booster pump was fitted on the deck together with a cargo heater. Also fitted was a shell and tube vaporiser.

In a similar way to all of the fully refrigerated LPG carriers built by IHI since *M P Grace,* the water ballast spaces were arranged in the full beam double bottoms and upper wing tanks.

In October 1996, the Aichi shipyard of IHI completed 54,000 m³ *Escravos LPG FSO,* for Chevron Nigeria Limited, as the world's first purpose built steel LPG Floating Storage & Offloading (FSO) vessel.[15] The vessel was towed to Nigeria after completing gas trials in Japan. Final installation and commissioning took place on the offshore Escravos oil field approximately 33 km east of Lagos, Nigeria. Operations in the Chevron Nigeria Limited/Nigerian National Petroleum Corporation oil field started in July 1997, with the vessel utilising an external bow turret mooring system at the site.

The LPG FSO has an overall length of 172.1 m, a breadth of 36 m and a depth of 23.4 m and was constructed with three equally sized prismatic cargo tanks based on the IHI SPB system. The vessel is designed to operate continuously for twenty years without dry-docking. In a tandem operation, a floating LPG hose is used to transfer cargo to the export LPG carrier at the stern of the FSO.

On the 1st October 2002, IHI Marine United Inc. was formed as a result of combining the shipbuilding and offshore businesses of Ishikawajima-Harima Heavy Industries Co. The new company also included the Marine United Inc., which was the result of an earlier merger between IHI and Sumitimo Heavy Industries Ltd.(SHI).

Currently, IHI Marine United Inc. have on order the world's first LPG Floating Production, Storage & Offloading (FPSO) vessel.[16] The unit, 135,000 m³ *Sanha LPG FPSO,* is due for delivery from the Kure shipyard in mid-2004, for a joint venture company formed by Single Buoy Mooring Inc., Monaco, and Sonagol, the national oil company of Angola. Part of the Sanha Condensate Project, the vessel will be located in the Cabinda oil field off Angola.

The first delivery of LPG from the field is scheduled for the beginning of 2005. The LPG FPSO has an overall length of 260 m, a breadth of 49 m and a depth of 29.3 m. The six prismatic cargo tanks will be based on the IHI SPB system, like the 54,000 m³ LPG FSO.

1   Fujitani, Takashi, *Gas Carrier Technology, Development of SPB LNG Carrier at IHI,* IHI Engineering Review, January 1995.
2   Shipbuilding & Shipping Record, *Largest Japanese LPG Carrier Launched,* 29 July 1965.
3   Nippon Steel Corporation Specification, *Properties of N-TUF 33 & N-TUF 37 Low Temperature Steels,* January 1975.
4   Nippon Steel Corporation Specification, *Low Temperature Steels N-TUF,* April 1978.
5   Yamamoto, Katsuro, *Experience in the Development of Gas Tankers,* Shipbuilding & Shipping Record LNG/LPG Conference, London, 21-22 March 1972.
6   Lloyd's Weekly Casualty Reports, *Bridgestone Maru No. 3,* 22 February 1966.
7   Kinkead A. N., *Further Study of Cargo Protection Afforded by Ships Structures in Collision,* 6th International Symposium on Transport of Dangerous Goods by Sea and Inland Waterways, Tokyo, October 1980.
8   Miyanari, Takayoshi, Ushirokawa, Osamu, Yashima, Hisayoshi and Ando, Akitoshi, *Structural Design of LPG Carrier – In Accordance with the Design Standards for Independent Tank Type B with a Prismatic Configuration,* IHI Engineering Review, July 1981.
9   Sekiguchi, Kenji, Nakayama, Shoji and Shida, Akito, *80,000 m³ Low Temperature Liquefied Petroleum Gas Carrier, Genkai Maru, for Idemitsu Co. Ltd.,* IHI Engineering Review, July 1981.
10 Fujitani, T., Miura, M., Motozuna, K., Minoda, K., and Miyanari, T., *Gas Carriers with Self-Supporting Prismatic-Type Cargo Tanks,* Gastech 82, Paris.
11 IHI brochure, *80,000 m³ Low Temperature Liquefied Petroleum Gas Carrier, Genkai Maru,* April 1983.
12 IHI brochure, *39,000 m³ LPG carrier, Toyosu Maru,* July 1989.
13 IHI brochure, *80,000 m³ LPG carrier, Koho Maru,* August 1989.
14 IHI brochure, *17,900 m³ LPG/NH₃ carrier, Kelvin,* February 1998.
15 Yamagishi, Naoto, Nakajima, Hironobu, Taru, Masahiro and Manabe, Hideo, *Design of LPG FSO,* IHI Engineering Review, Vol. 30 No. 4, October 1997.
16 Shipbuilding & Marine Engineering in Japan, JSEA, *Sanha 135,000 m³ LPG FPSO,* 2003.

Chapter 11

Moss Værft and Dokk

Moss Værft and Dokk of Moss, Norway, were acquired by the Kværner Burg Group in 1961 with the stated aim "To build technologically advanced and specialised ships." This decision was made to combat the then generally reduced profit margins in the shipbuilding industry. It was a historically significant move because it was the first step for the Kværner Group to progress, in the intervening years, to become internationally famed for their designs of LPG/ammonia carriers, ethylene carriers, a chlorine carrier, and the LNG carriers with the familiar spherical cargo tanks.

Havgas

Principle Particulars	
Length o.a.	141.30 m
Length b.p.	130.00 m
Breadth	19.20 m
Depth	12.00 m
Draught	9.52 m
LPG Capacity	11,071 m³
Engine	Kockums-MAN K7Z 70/120D
Power	8,400 hp/6,178 kW
Service speed	16 knots

The first gas ship to be completed was initially built to Moss Værft's own account as Hull No. 150. On 2 July 1963, an agreement was signed in Oslo between Kværner Brug, P Meyer and Hjalmar Bjørge, regarding Hull No. 150, which later was to result in the founding of A/S International Gas Carriers. The keel of Hull No. 150 was laid on 25 April 1964, the ship was launched on 31 May 1965 and delivered to A/S International Gas Carriers on 25 November 1965, as *Havgas*. The 11,071 m³ LPG/NH_3 carrier *Havgas* was operated by P Meyer of Oslo and was the first fully refrigerated LPG carrier built in Norway.[1] Produced by the Moss design team, with contributions from consultants Marine Service GmbH of Hamburg, the vessel had many design features similar to the larger 25,102 m³ *Paul Endacott,* delivered from the Swedish yard of Kockums in the previous year.

The ice strengthened ship was built to Det Norske Veritas classification as a Tanker for Liquefied Gas and met the requirements of The Norwegian Ships Control and the US Coast Guard, for a minimum cargo temperature of -51°C and a maximum pressure of 0.3 kg/cm². Det Norske Veritas had published, for the first time, in their 1962 Rules for the Construction and Classification of Steel Ships, a comprehensive Chapter 14 headed *Recommendations for the Design and Construction of Ships for Transportation of Liquefied Gas.*[2, 3]

Havgas was constructed with three prismatic cargo tanks with upper trunks, and the insulation was fitted on the inner hull. The low carbon steel for the cargo tanks and secondary barrier were manufactured by the German firm Hüttenwerk Oberhausen. The inner bottom was insulated with a layer of Onazote, and a 760 mm thick layer of glass wool covered the upper parts of the holds. The double bottom tanks for fuel oil were arranged either side of a centreline duct keel with the double side hull and transverse cofferdams used as water ballast tanks. Two David Brown Bingham type deep-well pumps were fitted in each cargo tanks with capacities of 110m³/hr in No. 1 tank and 220 m³/hr in Nos. 2 & 3 tanks, giving a total discharge capacity of 1,100 m³/hr.

Three cascade reliquefaction plants were fitted, with each plant containing a Sulzer K140-2B oil free compressor and Kværner R22 condenser and receiver.

Havgas was sold to Houlder Brothers in 1974 and was scrapped by Chinese breakers as *Joule* in 1984.

A second similar vessel, 11,396 m³ *Havfrost,* was delivered from Moss Værft on 1 November 1966 to A/S International Gas Carriers. How quickly the learning curve rises; the cargo tanks' capacity was increased by 325 m³ on *Havfrost,* with the hull dimensions remaining the same as on *Havgas.*

Havfrost as *Gaz Channel* was sold to Indian breakers in 1996.

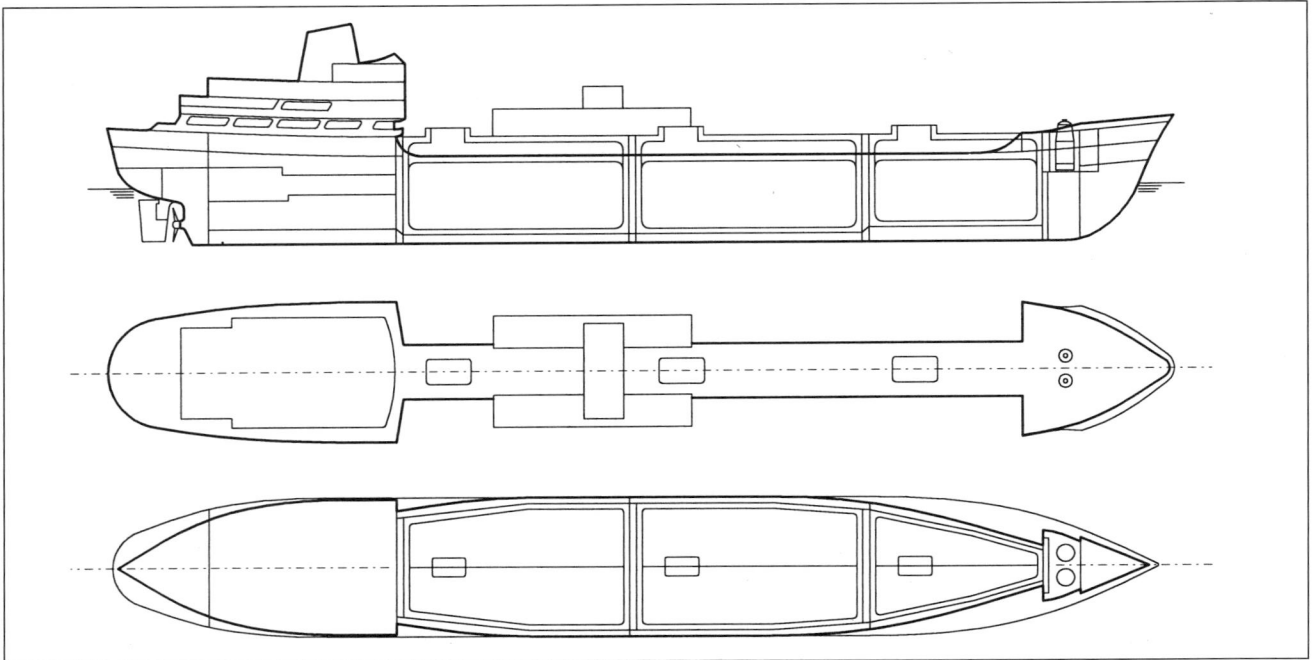

Figure 11-1 Outline Arrangement of *Havgas*

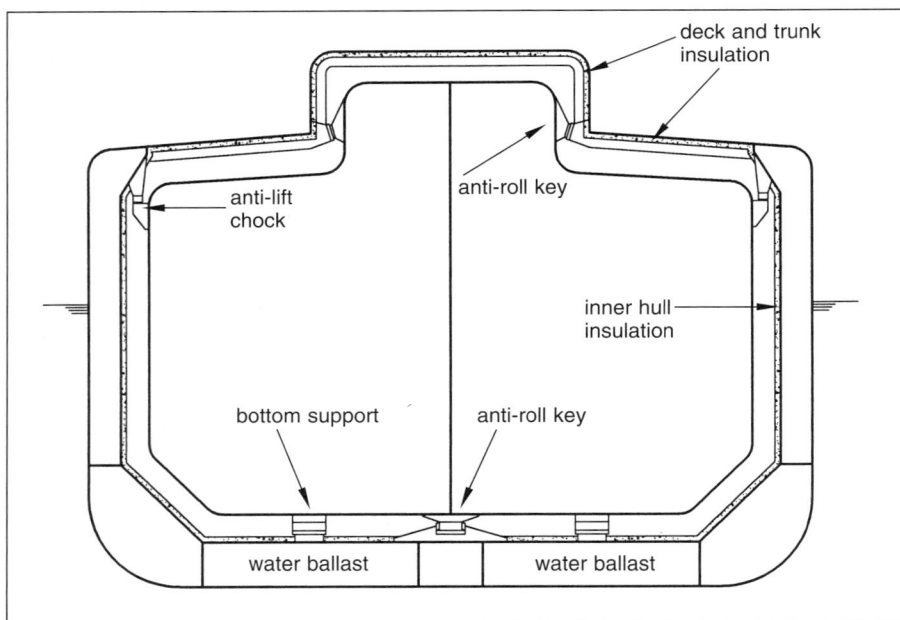

Figure 11-2 Midship Section of *Havgas* showing Inner Hull Insulation and Tank Supports

Plate 11-1 *Havgas* under construction   Moss

Plate 11-2   *Havgas* at sea   Moss

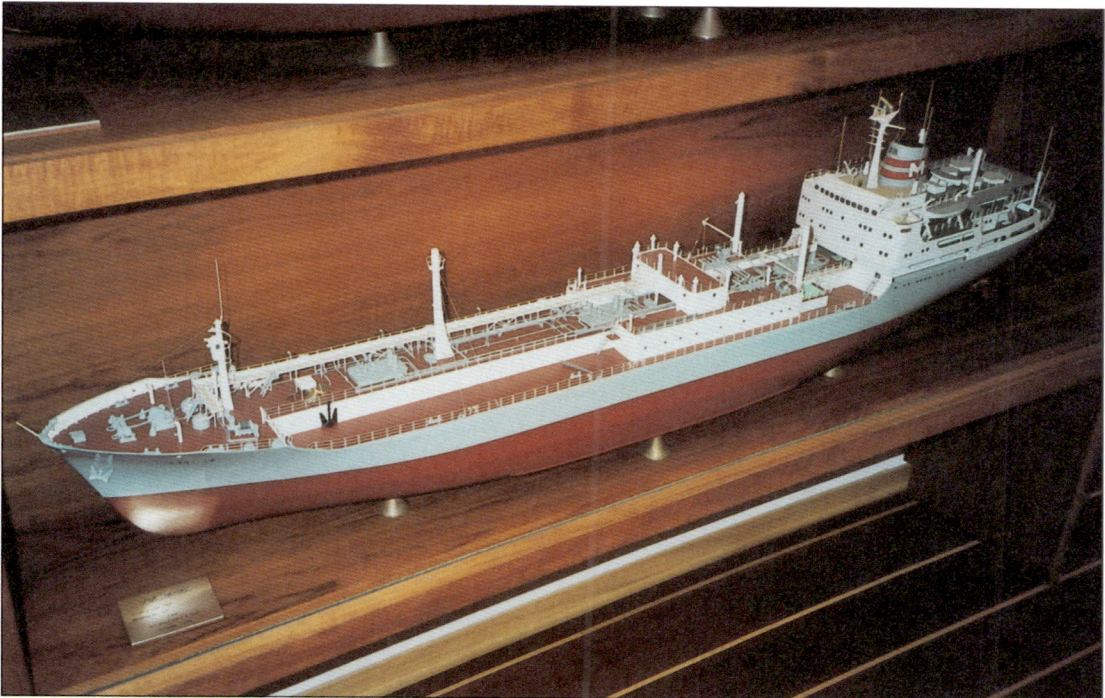

Plate 11-3   Model of *Havgas* in the office of The Havinvest Group, Oslo

Plate 11-4   *Mundogas Rio*   Moss

Mundogas Rio

Principle Particulars	
Length o.a.	162.55 m
Length b.p.	150.00 m
Breadth	22.50 m
Depth	14.50 m
Draught	9.52 m
LPG Capacity	19,462 m³
Engine	Horten-Sulzer 6RD90
Power	13,800 hp/10,150 kW
Service speed	17 knots

The third fully refrigerated LPG carrier delivered from Moss Værft, 19,462 m³ *Mundogas Rio,* had a different design to the previous two ships built for A/S International Gas Carriers.[4] The keel for *Mundogas Rio* was laid on 13 June 1966, she was launched on 2 June 1967 and delivered on 14 November 1967 to A/S Gasskib, a company controlled by shipowners Øivind Lorentzen of Oslo, one of the founding members of Mundogas SA. Classed with Det Norske Veritas and built to the requirements of Norway's Skipskontrollen and the US Coast Guard, the LPG/NH_3 carrier was designed for a minimum cargo temperature of -51°C and a maximum pressure of 0.25 kg/cm².

The two main design differences, compared with the earlier Moss ships, were that no cargo tank trunks were fitted and the insulation was on the cargo tanks, rather than on the ship's inner hull. In place of the trunks, the relatively large cargo tank domes appeared for the first time, designed to be at least 2% of the cargo tank capacity, with the result that when fully loaded at 98% capacity, the liquid surface and cargo vapours would be inside the dome. These 2% capacity Kværner domes were to become a distinctive feature of the later series of designs for fully refrigerated LPG carriers. Less gas boil-off with less work for the reliquefaction plants being the philosophy behind the 2% capacity dome arrangement.

A double bottom and double side were fitted throughout the cargo area with the inner bottom and inner side longitudinal bulkheads forming the secondary barrier. The forecastle remained but the poop had gone from the stern. The four cargo tanks, arranged in three hold spaces, and the secondary barrier were constructed with fine grain carbon manganese steel. Cargo tank Nos. 2 and 3 were fitted in a single hold amidships. Each cargo tank was fitted with two David Brown deep-well pumps with a total discharge rate of 2,000 m³/hr. The cascade reliquefaction plant included; three Rheinhaelte Dravn cargo compressors, and three Kværner R22 refrigeration units.

Mundogas Rio was sold for demolition in India in 2002 as *Gaz Hudson*.

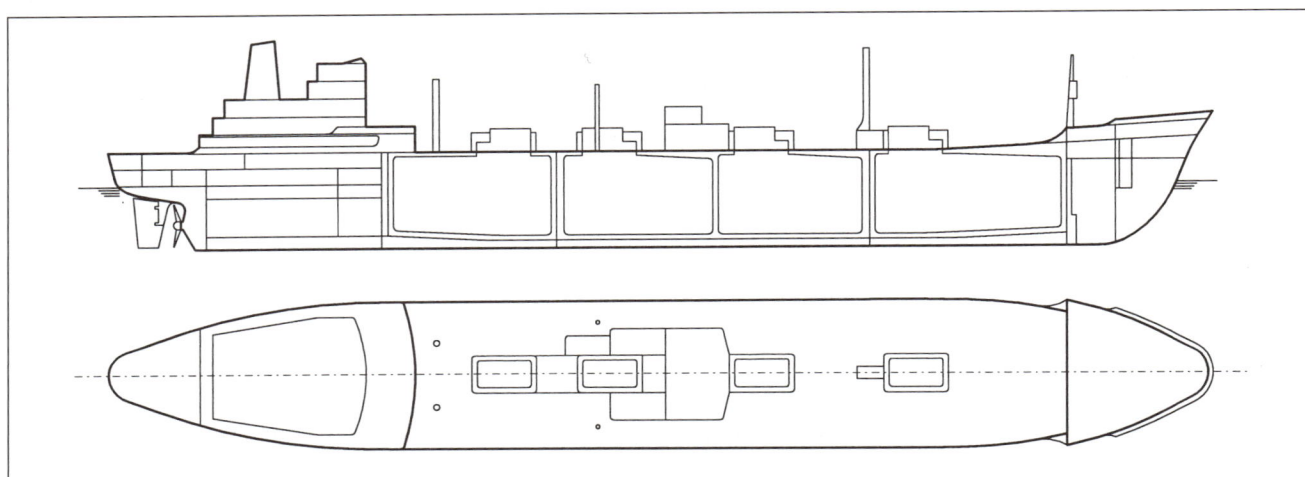

Figure 11-3 Outline Arrangement of *Mundogas Rio*

15 June 1985 – Alert Crew

Mundogas Rio was superficially damaged on 15 June 1985, when berthed at Pajaritos, Mexico, after a fire which had started on nearby 57,000 m³ LPG carrier *Ahkatun*, spread to the ship. Quick action by the crew on *Mundogas Rio*, in closing all accommodation openings and operating the water spray and water curtain protection systems kept the damage to a minimum. See a more detailed account of the incident under *Ahkatun* in Chapter 20.

26 May 1988 – Eerie Salvage

During the Iran/Iraq war, *Mundogas Rio* was attacked east of the Straits of Hormuz, early in the evening of 26 May 1988, with rocket propelled grenades fired from two Iranian gunboats. The vessel was en route from Saudi Arabia to India, fully loaded with almost 13,000 tonnes of anhydrous ammonia, for Rashtriya Chemicals and Fertilisers. The upper parts of the machinery spaces and the accommodation, including the wheelhouse, were set on fire. The aft cargo tank was punctured, with a resulting cloud of ammonia vapour drifting over the vessel.[5]

As the bridge and engine controls were lost in the blaze, the vessel continued underway out of control under its own power. Columbian Captain Orlando Garcia and his Spanish officers, engineers and crew were unable to contain the fire and all were safely evacuated from the ship, but not before ingeniously stopping the ship by adding water ballast to the fuel bunkers, which in turn knocked out the main engine.

The next day, fire-fighters from the Dutch company Wijsmuller Salvage BV boarded the vessel using breathing apparatus. The fire was extinguished on 28 May with the use of three fire-fighting vessels. Two days later there was a spontaneous explosion in the void space around No. 4 cargo tank. There were no casualties amongst the salvage team on board and no fire, but a vaporised ammonia cloud enveloped the vessel and it listed to about 11 degrees. On 4 June, salvage tugs towed the vessel 30 miles out into the Gulf of Oman from the anchorage 4 miles off Fujairah. After being cleared free of explosive devices by bomb disposal experts, the vessel returned to the Fujairah anchorage in preparation for a transfer of the ammonia still on board, to 21,794 m³ *Mundogas Pacific*. The transfer commenced on 29 July and was completed the next day, and the saved 6,950 tonnes of anhydrous ammonia on board *Mundogas Pacific*, continued its passage to India. The salvage operation ended on 2 August 1988.

When viewed at the end of August 1988 off Fujairah, the damage to *Mundogas Rio* was both extensive and dramatic. The ship was dead in the water and silent. The tangled pipework, domed deck and white dusting left from the ammonia created an eerie scene.[6] It is truly remarkable that no lives had been lost in the fire and explosion.

Four rocket propelled grenades were fired at the starboard side of the ship. Two penetrated the side hull in way of No. 4 cargo tank, at about the summer load line. A third grenade penetrated the accommodation house side and the fourth missile penetrated one side of a deck derrick post. Holes from small arms fire were found on the accommodation house side. The internal accommodation spaces and forward upper part of the machinery spaces were gutted by fire. The machinery space was flooded to approximately the height of the top of the main engine.

The main deck in way of No. 4 cargo tank was domed to a height of approximately 1.5 metres at the centre with the dome extending to the side longitudinal bulkheads and the transverse bulkheads. Deck storerooms, lockers, swimming pool, access hatches and the poop deck were buckled. A pair of derrick posts were inclined approximately 10 degrees out of upright. The cargo tank hatch, liquid, condensate and vapour pipe work, inert gas piping, deep-well pumps, gauges and relief valves were damaged, fractured or twisted. Electric cables, deck lights, fire main and fire-fighting systems and walkway were extensively damaged.

Cargo information data sheets on anhydrous ammonia advise that it is toxic, but for practical purposes ammonia is non-flammable, even though ammonia can be burnt, but the flames have a low heat, and with mercury, ammonia can form a high explosive which is very sensitive to *impact*. A great comfort to Captain Garcia, his crew and the salvage teams.

The damaged ship was declared a constructive total loss and sold at scrap value to Arbross Shipping Ltd. of Hong Kong, who had a penchant for operating former Mundogas ships. Singapore's Sembawang shipyard won the contract for the major refitting and damage repairs. A new superstructure block was built, 700 tonnes of steel were replaced, including 550 tonnes of low temperature steel, damaged cargo pipework and safety systems were replaced, and the machinery spaces and equipment were completely overhauled.

On 11 October 1989, as *Hudson River,* this Moss ship left Singapore, refreshed and refurbished, bound for Vladivostok.

Looking at the 1985 Pajaritos incident described previously and this second devastating fire, we should applaud the actions of the ship's captain, officers and crew, when in both cases, through no fault of their own, their lives were put in danger. Experience, training, good seamanship, intelligence, speed of thought and a working knowledge of the ship's layout and equipment, all combined in each case, to save the ship and more importantly, to prevent loss of life.

Plate 11-5   *Mundogas Rio* off Fujairah – August 1988

Plate 11-6   Rocket entry into accommodation

Plate 11-7   Domed main deck

Plate 11-8   No 4 cargo tank dome

Plate 11-9   Top of No 4 cargo tank dome

Plate 11-10   Wheelhouse

A second vessel *Nyhavn* was built by Moss Værft to the same design as *Mundogas Rio,* for domestic owners Christian Haaland, and delivered on 15 October 1968 to an affiliate firm A/S Nygass & Company. The keel for *Nyhavn* was laid on 19 June 1967 with a launching ceremony taking place on 22 May 1968.

Havis

Principle Particulars	
Length o.a.	146.75 m
Length b.p.	136.30 m
Breadth	21.75 m
Depth	13.50 m
Draught	10.61 m
LPG Capacity	15,285 m³
Engine	Augsburg-MAN K7Z 70/120E
Power	9,800 hp/7,208 kW
Service speed	17 knots

Moss Værft delivered a third fully refrigerated LPG/NH_3 carrier to A/S International Gas Carriers on 29 December 1970. 15,285 m³ *Havis*, like the earlier delivered *Havgas* and *Havfrost*, was constructed with three cargo tanks, but with no cargo tank trunks. The ship was arranged with a poop, a forecastle and a flush main deck with Kværner 2% domes. Two pressurised horizontal cylindrical tanks for cargo changes were fitted on the main deck.

Havis was broken up in 1994 as *Nelina*.

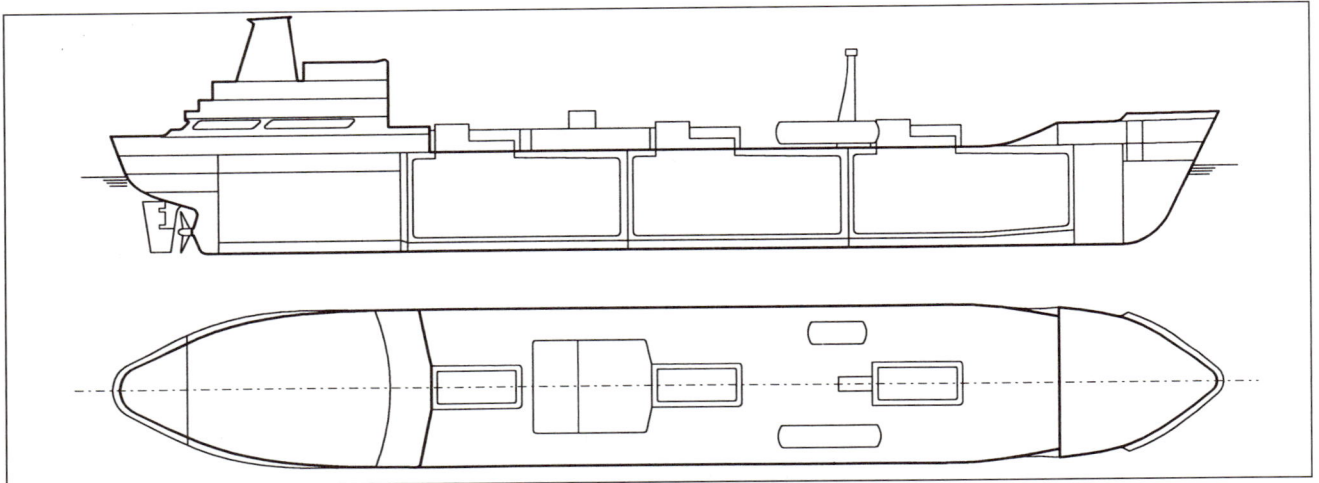
Figure 11-4 Outline Arrangement of *Havis*

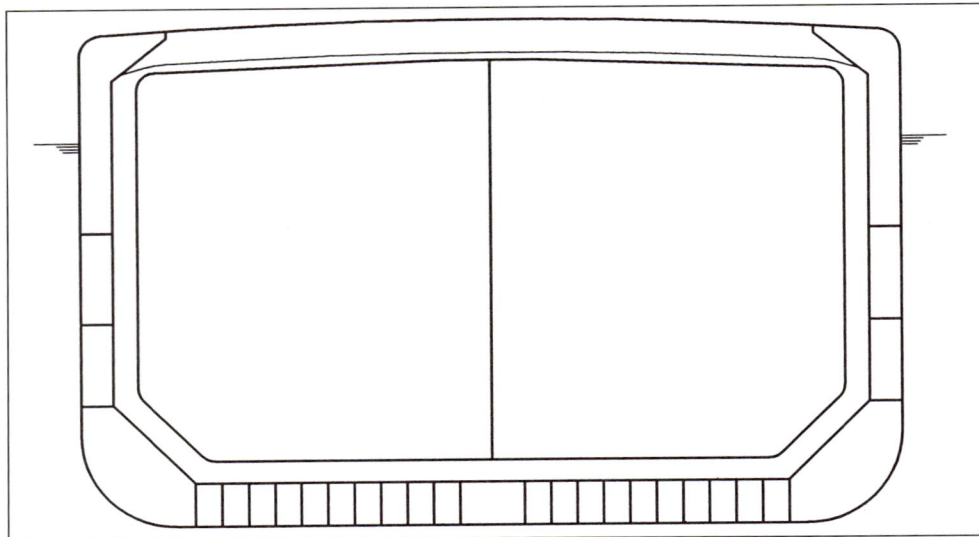
Figure 11-5 Midship Section of *Havis*

Plate 11-11   *Havis*   Moss

Höegh Multina

Principle Particulars	
Length o.a.	207.08 m
Length b.p.	196.00 m
Breadth	31.40 m
Depth	18.60 m
Draught	11.32 m
LPG Capacity	52,647 m³
Engine	Horten-Sulzer 7RND90
Power	20,300 hp/14,931 kW
Service speed	17.5 knots

At the beginning of 1970, the Kværner Group took over the Stavanger shipyard of Rosenberg Mekaniske Verkstad.[7] The first gas carrier designed in close co-operation with Moss Værft, from the renamed Rosenberg Verft, was 52,647 m³ *Höegh Multina*.[8] The LPG/NH$_3$ carrier was delivered to Leif Höegh & Co. A/S of Oslo on 12 October 1971. The ship was classed with Det Norske Veritas as a Tanker for Liquefied Gas, at a minimum temperature of -48°C, a maximum pressure of 0.25 kg/cm² and a maximum specific gravity of 0.69.

This ground breaking design was to be the foundation on which the Kværner Group developed a series of ships, which would be built at Norwegian yards at Moss, Fredrikstad and Stavanger, and also by overseas yards in Finland, France and Poland. The 24,000 m³, 52,000 m³ and 75,000 m³ sizes of LPG standard ship designs proved to be extremely successful. Designs for FRLPG carriers in these three different capacity groups were produced by many competing shipyards.

The ship was arranged with raked transom stern, aft machinery and accommodation, flush main deck with forward sheer, large cargo tank domes and a flared bow. The four prismatic cargo tanks had become the standard arrangement for fully refrigerated LPG carriers, with water ballast tanks arranged in lower and upper wing tanks and the side hull forming the secondary barrier. However, a number of features were incorporated into the design, which were to become unique to all of this generation of LPG carriers.

The most visible of these special features were the large 2% Kværner domes fitted over each cargo tank. Two 360 m³/hr David Brown deep-well cargo pumps were fitted on each tank dome. Under the main deck, with cargo vapours in mind, the forward tops of each cargo tank sloped slightly downwards. To provide a better flow to the pump sumps, the aft end of the bottom of the aft tank and the forward end of the bottom of the forward tank sloped slightly upward. This arrangement also gave a good forward and aft entry for the hull form. The tanks and secondary barrier were constructed with carbon manganese steel NV 2-4 with a minimum yield point of 30 kg/mm².

Three cascade reliquefaction plants were housed on the main deck above the forward end of No. 3 cargo tank with a cargo control room above it. Each plant included a cargo compressor, a R22 compressor and associated equipment. The arrangement of the electric motor and compressor rooms, and cargo control room, just forward of the cargo manifolds was another distinctive feature of the standard series of Kværner LPG carriers.

Höegh Multina was broken up as *Havgast* in 2001.

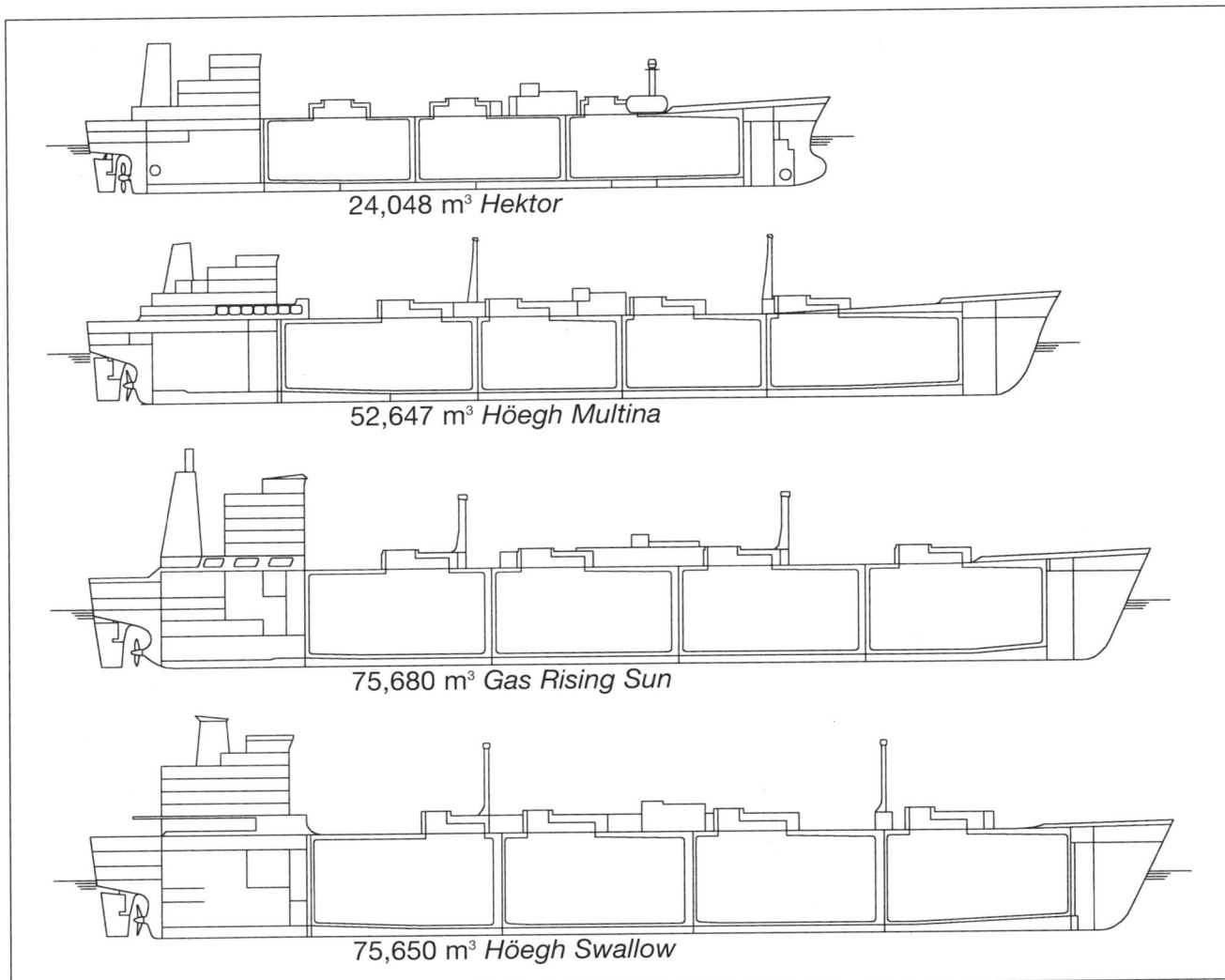

24,048 m³ *Hektor*

52,647 m³ *Höegh Multina*

75,680 m³ *Gas Rising Sun*

75,650 m³ *Höegh Swallow*

Figure 11-6 Kværner Moss Standard Series Profiles

The second vessel from Stavanger in the 52,000 m³ series was *Garmula*.[9] Delivered to P&O Steam Navigation Company on 17 July 1972, *Garmula* had similar hull dimensions and cargo tanks arrangements as *Höegh Multina* but with some changes in propulsion, navigation, accommodation and cargo handling specifications for the British owners. Two 370 m³/hr J C Carter submerged electrical pumps were fitted in each cargo tank. For change of grades, 180 m³ and 300 m³ pressurised storage tanks were fitted on the main deck forward.

Garmula was named after a village in the Skeikhpura district of Pakistan, west of Lahore. In 2002, as *OGC America*, the gas carrier was sold to Bangladesh breakers on the eastern side of the Indian subcontinent.

Six years after *Garmula*, the third and final of Kværner's Norwegian built 52,000 m³ LPG/NH₃ carrier *Centum*, was delivered on 21 October 1978 to P Meyer of Oslo, under A/S Havtor management. The stern profile changed on *Centum* with a lower aft deck arrangement. Two 420 m³/hr Thune Eureka deep-well cargo pumps were fitted in each cargo tank.

22 March 1988 – Plugs for Cargo Tanks

Centum, as *Havglimt*, when fully loaded with anhydrous ammonia, was twice attacked during the Iran/Iraq war, by Iranian gunboats at 0522 and 0600 hours local time on 22 March 1988, in the southern Gulf, 12 miles off Dubai.[10] The gas ship, operated by A/S Havtor Management of Norway, was raked with gunfire from all sides and the attackers also fired on tugs approaching to aid the stricken vessel. The bridge and hull of *Havglimt* were riddled with holes from the attack rockets. The ship was ablaze in the machinery spaces and accommodation and leaking ammonia vapours spread over the ship and the sea.

Two of the Singapore crew members were killed and nine other men, including the Norwegian master and chief officer, were injured. The injured were taken off the vessel by Wijsmuller's fire-fighting rescue vessel and landed at Port Rashid. Salvage tugs secured the vessel before the remaining crew all safely abandoned ship.

The fire in the engine room was extinguished at 1125 hours on 22 March and at 1300 hours the same day the accommodation fire was also extinguished. The vessel was without power and the accommodation was completely destroyed. Early on in the morning of 23 March, work began to plug the holes in the cargo tanks. With the temporary repairs completed, the vessel was taken in tow on 29 March with a supply vessel escort, and arrived at Fujairah roads on 31 March.

Under the control of Wijsmuller, on 4 April, the transfer of the remaining ammonia cargo began to the Norwegian operators fleet vessel 54,226 m³ *Havkong*, originally built as *Galconda* by Thyssen Nordseewerke. The ship to ship transfer was successfully completed on 6 April. A tricky operation, considering that the temperature and consequently the pressure of the ammonia cargo would both be continually rising.

Following this tragic incident, fire and subsequent salvage, the Keppel shipyard of Singapore completed the major repairs and rebuilding, over a period of four months, for the Scandinavian Underwriters Agency. The work involved extensive refurbishment to the machinery spaces, engine control room, switchboards and accommodation, as well as hull and cargo tank repairs. On 21 October 1988 *Havglimt* left Singapore bound for Port Kelang, Malaysia, for further trading.

Gazana

Principle Particulars	
Length o.a.	178.00 m
Length b.p.	165.00 m
Breadth	26.00 m
Depth	17.00 m
Draught	10.02 m
LPG Capacity	29,791 m³
Engine	Kincaid-B&W 8K74EF
Power	15,000 hp/11,032 kW
Service speed	16.25 knots

The P&O Group's first LPG carrier, 29,791 m³ Gazana, was delivered from the Birkenhead Merseyside shipyard of Cammell Laird on 28 February 1972.[11] This was the first gas ship to be built by the Birkenhead yard and design assistance was provided by Kværner and Marine Service GmbH. Additional help was also acquired in the United Kingdom and the author clearly remembers a fact finding trip by Cammell Laird representative to Tyneside shipbuilders Hawthorn Leslie, with many photographs being taken of a gas ship under construction. The LPG/NH₃ carrier was arranged with transom stern, aft superstructure, flush main deck without sheer and a bulbous bow. The ship was classed with Lloyd's Register of Shipping as a Liquefied Gas Carrier for a minimum cargo temperature of -51°C and a maximum pressure of 0.30 kg/cm².

The four prismatic cargo tanks and the secondary barrier were constructed with *Arctic D* steel. The tanks were insulated with 100 mm of polyurethane foam manufactured by Honeywell-Atlas. Permawood and Permali were used for the tanks' supports and keys. Two 316 m³/hr J C Carter submerged electric pumps were fitted in each cargo tank. Three cascade reliquefaction plants were fitted, each with Sulzer cargo and J & E Hall R22 compressors with liquid receivers and separators.

Gazana was sold for scrap in 2002 as *Havjarl*.

A sister vessel *Gambada* was delivered to the P&O Group from Birkenhead on 2 March 1973.

Gambada was sold for demolition to Chinese breakers in 2003 as *Hesiod*.

Plate 11-12   Launch of *Gazana*   P&O

Plate 11-13   Builder's plate for Hull 1342 – Gambada

Plate 11-14   *Gazana* at sea   P&O

Hampshire

Principle Particulars	
Length o.a.	207.02 m
Length b.p.	196.00 m
Breadth	31.40 m
Depth	18.60 m
Draught	11.28 m
LPG Capacity	52,647 m³
Engine	Atlantique-Sulzer 7RND90
Power	20,300 hp/14,931 kW
Service speed	17.5 knots

The first gas carrier to be built by Chantiers de France-Dunkerque, 52,647 m³ *Hampshire*, was built under a license from Moss Rosenberg Værft.[12] The ship, the first of two ordered by Bibby Line of Liverpool, was delivered from the French yard to Bibby subsidiary company Britain Steamship Co. Ltd. on 24 January 1974. The ship was the first of the Kværner 52,000 m³ series to be built outside Norway and was based on the design of *Höegh Multina*. The second ship of the pair *Devonshire*, was delivered to Bibby Bulk Carriers Ltd. on 25 November 1974. For the British owner, both ships were classed with Lloyd's Register of Shipping.

Devonshire was the fifth and final ship of the Kværner 52,000 m³ series.

Garbeta

Principle Particulars	
Length o.a.	165.00 m
Length b.p.	155.00 m
Breadth	23.00 m
Depth	15.50 m
Draught	10.32 m
LPG Capacity	22,764 m³
Engine	Nylands-B&W 7K74EF
Power	14,600 hp/10,738 kW
Service speed	16.5 knots

The P&O Group ordered two similar sized, B&W powered, LPG/ammonia carriers from Moss Værft and British shipbuilders Swan Hunter. Both yards produced designs with four cargo tanks. Moss Værft delivered 22,764 m³ *Garbeta* to P&O Lines Ltd. on 21 October 1975 as a smaller version of the 52,000 m³ series. Three cascade reliquefaction plants were fitted. *Gandara* was delivered from Swan Hunter on 30 March 1976.

Plate 11-15   *Garbeta* in port   P&O

Höegh Swallow

Principle Particulars	
Length o.a.	229.30 m
Length b.p.	217.00 m
Breadth	32.20 m
Depth	22.50 m
Draught	12.92 m
LPG Capacity	75,650 m³
Engine	Cegielski-Sulzer 8RND90
Power	23,200 hp/17,064 kW
Service speed	16.7 knots

Double firsts for the Gdynia Shipyard with 75,650 m³ *Höegh Swallow*, which was delivered on 31 Dec 1976, as the first gas ship to be built in Poland and the first of a five ship Kværner 75,000 m³ series of LPG carriers.[13] The design was essentially an enlarged version of the Kværner 52,000 m³ series and in the case of the Polish built hulls, was based on the maximum beam suitable for passage through the Panama Canal. Three cascade reliquefaction plants were fitted. Two David Brown-Bingham 525 m³/hr deep-well pumps were fitted in each cargo tank.

Three ships were built for Leif Höegh & Co. A/S and like *Höegh Multina* built at Stavanger, had four prismatic cargo tanks and were classed with Det Norske Veritas. The second ship, *Höegh Swift* was delivered on 30 June 1977. The third ship for the Norwegian owners, *Höegh Sword* was delivered on 30 November 1978.

During 1977 and 1978, two similar vessels, *Northern Arrow* and *Northern Eagle I,* were delivered to Northern Natural Gas Company of Omaha, Nebraska, and were the first ships built at Gdynia Shipyard for American owners. *Northern Arrow* was delivered on 29 December 1977 and *Northern Eagle* was delivered on 30 June 1978.

Plate 11-16   *Höegh Swallow* at fitting out quay   Stocznia Gdynia

Plate 11-17   *Northern Arrow* & *Northern Eagle 1*   Stocznia Gdynia
laid up in the Oslofjord at
Holmstrand after delivery

23/24 November 2002 – Role Reversal for Secondary Barrier

The structural integrity of a loaded fully refrigerated LPG carrier was put to the test in a dramatic incident in Chinese waters off Hong Kong.[14] A fire started at the No. 3 diesel generator in the engine room of *Gaz Poem*, built in 1977 as *Höegh Swallow* at the Gdynia Shipyard, when on a partially loaded passage. The machinery spaces were evacuated and within approximately twenty minutes after the fire was first reported, the carbon dioxide system was activated to smother the fire.

Unfortunately, after an explosion in the engine room, the fire rekindled and spread upward into the large accommodation block. In the early hours of 24 November the 34 crew abandoned ship and were all safely rescued some sixty minutes later by a passing Chinese vessel *Dong Wei*. Before the evacuation, the crew had been able to anchor the vessel. At the time of the outbreak of the fire *Gaz Poem* was loaded with 9,740 tonnes of propane and 10,210 tonnes of butane.

In strong winds with the vessel at the anchor, the flames and smoke from the engine room and aft accommodation fire were directed away from the cargo tanks. The Shenzhen port authority enforced a 10 nautical miles exclusion zone around the vessel. Fire and salvage teams were at the scene and on 26 November the fire was reported as being under control. The ship was made safe and by 20 December all liquid cargo had been removed from *Gaz Poem*.

The expertise of the technical and salvage teams in bringing this incident to a safe close should be applauded, especially after the initial extensive media coverage given of the potential danger the ship posed, in contrast to the limited reporting of the safe outcome.

The basic good design of *Gas Poem* also contributed greatly to the successful conclusion. The cargo in the aft tank, which was most at risk, was protected from the fire by three separate steel divisions; the aft end of the cargo tank, the transverse secondary barrier and the engine room transverse bulkhead. A transverse cofferdam and the aft part of the void space separated the engine room from the aft cargo tank. The secondary barrier and insulation, in a reversal of the intended design, protected the cargo tanks from the fire. The insulation on the cargo tanks remained effective, provided a heat shield, and was not in direct contact with the fire. The top of the nearest cargo vent mast was some eighteen metres above the main deck and approximately forty one metres forward of the accommodation house front. The liquid cargo and vapours in the cargo tanks and pipework were totally enclosed. When on passage, the partially loaded ship had water ballast in some of the double bottom and lower and upper wing tanks, adding more protection for the cargo tanks.

Gaz Poem was sold for scraping in 2003.

Gas Rising Sun

Principle Particulars	
Length o.a.	224.75 m
Length b.p.	213.00 m
Breadth	34.20 m
Depth	21.60 m
Draught	13.02 m
LPG Capacity	75,680 m³
Engine	Wärtsilä-Sulzer 7RND90M
Power	23,450 hp/17,247 kW
Service speed	16.7 knots

As well as the five ship series being built in Poland, a seven ship Kværner 75,000 m³ series of LPG carriers were order in Finland in 1974.[15] The deal at the time for Oy Wärtsilä Ab, was the largest single contract placed with an individual Finnish enterprise. Originally Fearnley & Eger were to take five of the ships, with Sig. Bergesen dy & Co. and Gotaas-Larsen each taking a single vessel. On the basis of these orders, Wärtsilä financed and constructed its new shipyard at Perno as a hull and cargo tank assembly site, with the Turku shipyard used for all fitting out.

The oil crisis of 1973 was a contributing factor in the financial difficulties incurred by Fearnley & Eger, which resulted in the company withdrawing from the Finnish contract. The contract for the first ship was taken over by Japanese traders Nissho Iwai, and 75,680 m³ *Gas Rising Sun* was delivered to a subsidiary company Rising Sun Gas Carriers Corp. on 18 September 1978. This gas carrier was the first ship to be built in Finland for Japanese owners.

All seven ships of the series were classed with Det Norske Veritas. The ship's dimensions differed from the Gdynia series, being shorter in length, shallower in depth, but with the beam increased to 34.20 m. Three cascade reliquefaction plants were fitted. Two Thune Eureka 525 m³/hr deep-well pumps were fitted in each cargo tank. The four cargo tanks were insulated by Kaefer with 125 mm thick panels of Styropor, covered by seawater resistant aluminium foil.

Sig. Bergesen added two of the Fearnley & Eger ships to its single order, and took the next three of the series as *Berge Sisu* in December 1978, *Berge Sisar* in April 1979 and *Berge Saga* in September 1979. The delivery of *Berge Sisu* was number one in the Bergesen gas fleet, which has, by steady growth in the intervening years, become the world's largest fleet of fully refrigerated LPG carriers.

The fourth ship of the series, *Golar Frost* was delivered to Gotaas Larsen in March 1980. In 1989, *Golar Frost* was added to the Bergesen fleet as *Berge Spirit*.

In 1979, Bergesen agreed to take over the contract of the final Fearnley & Eger pair and took delivery of *Berge Sund* in October 1981 and *Berge Strand* in May 1982.

After delivering the Kværner 52,000 m³ series *Hampshire* and *Devonshire* to Liverpool's Bibby, Chantiers de France-Dunkerque built a Kværner 75,000 m³ design under license for United Gas Carrier Corp., a subsidiary company of Bibby Line. *Staffordshire* was completed at Dunkerque in September 1977 and was commissioned in July 1979. *Staffordshire* had the same hull dimensions as the Wärtsilä 75,000 m³ series.

In total, thirteen Kværner 75,000 m³ series were completed, without any being built in Norway.

Hampshire was sold to breakers in 2002 as *Hermes*.

Gas Rising Sun was sold to Chinese scrap buyers in 2003.

Staffordshire was broken up in 2003 as *Yuan Da*.

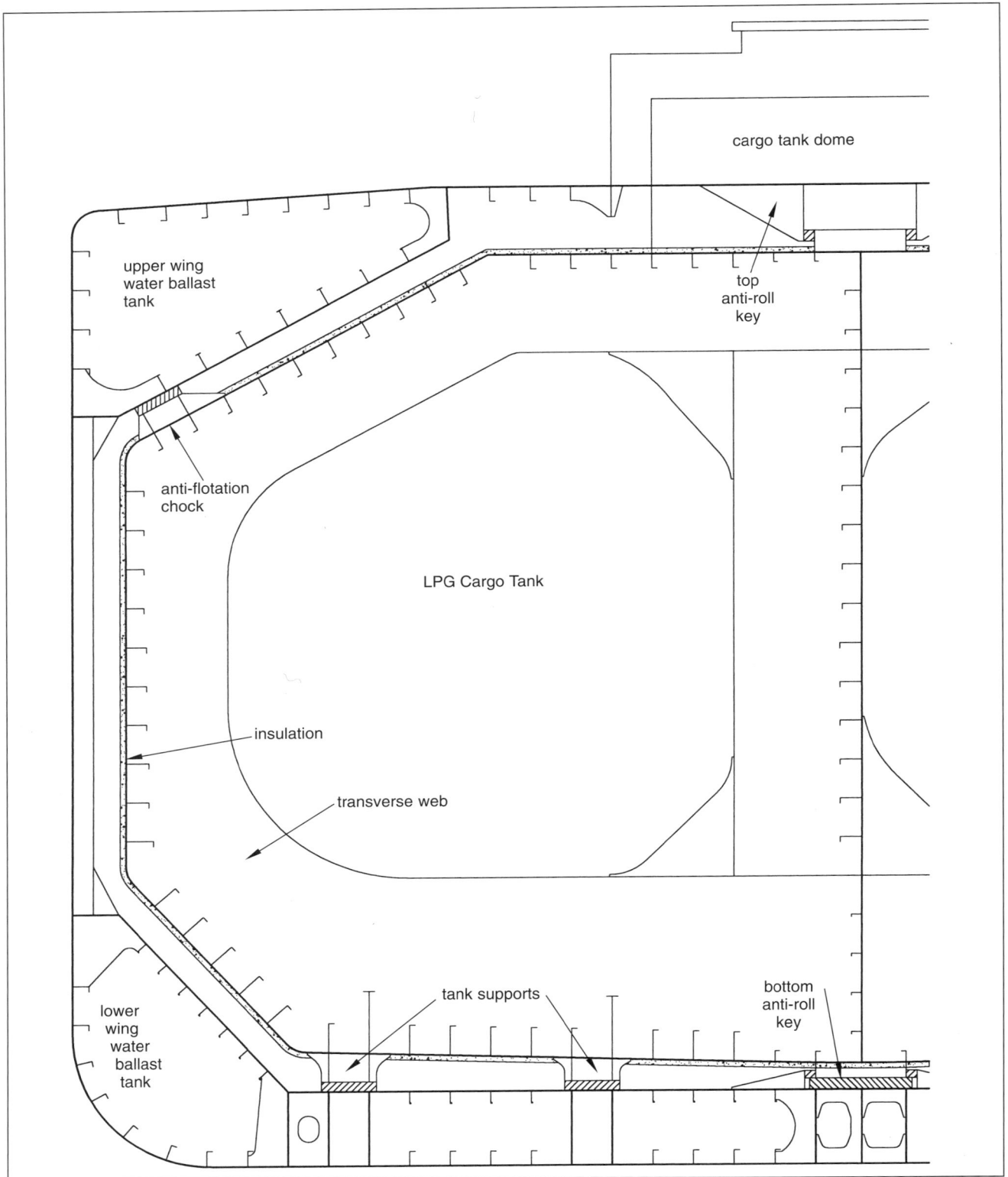

cargo tank dome

upper wing
water ballast
tank

top
anti-roll
key

anti-flotation
chock

LPG Cargo Tank

insulation

transverse web

tank supports

bottom
anti-roll
key

lower
wing
water
ballast
tank

Figure 11-7 Midship Section of *Gas Rising Sun*

Plate 11-18   75,000m³ series under construction at Wärtsilä Perno yard   Wärtsilä

19 May 1988 – Gunboats in the Strait of Hormuz

Berge Strand was attacked twice on the morning of 19 May 1998 by Iranian gunboats in the Strait of Hormuz, on a ballast passage from the Far East to Ras Tanura, Saudi Arabia. The ship was slightly damaged in the first attack and was heading, under power, for Dubai for repairs when attacked again. Rocket propelled grenades were fired at the vessel hitting the crew's quarters. One person was injured in the second raid and damages caused the loss of engine power. Salvage tugs quickly extinguished the on board fire. *Berge Strand* was initially taken in tow, but later propulsion power was restored and the gas carrier was escorted to Dubai. After repairs were carried out, *Berge Strand* continued on passage and arrive for loading at Ras Tanura on 25 May.[16]

3 July 1988 – Helpers Attacked

More Iran/Iraq war problems for *Berge Strand*. Following a radio appeal from Dubai, *Berge Strand* was helping in the search for survivors of an Iranian Airbus A300 passenger aircraft carrying 290 people, accidentally shot down by USA cruiser *Vincennes* on 3 July 1988. The gas carrier was in ballast and bound for Ras Tanura from Yokohama. Ironically, after changing course to assist in the area of the shot down jet, *Berge Strand* was attacked, about ten miles off the coast of Sharjah, by two Iranian gunboats. The ship was hit by rocket propelled grenades. The initial fire was quickly extinguished and there were no injuries to the crew. The rockets punctured two holes in the ship's deep tank and three holes in a cargo tank. *Berge Strand* left the search area without assistance, and later the same day anchored off Dubai for an assessment of the damage. Following repairs at Dubai *Berge Strand* arrived at Ruwais for cargo loading on 13 July.[17]

16 November 1991 – Double Atlantic Tow

Gas Rising Sun was reported on 16 November 1991 to be drifting in Cape Verde territorial waters between the islands of Boa Vista and Maio with a steering problem. The gas carrier, owned by Navix Line of Tokyo, had loaded a full cargo of LPG at Yanbu, Saudi Arabia for Salvador, Brazil.

Initial assistance was given by local tugs from St. Vincent, followed by an underwater examination at Praia roads, undertaken by a specially flown-in Northern Divers team from the United Kingdom. The semi-balanced rudder supported on a rudder horn was found jammed with a part missing. The damaged rudder was positioned to give the best steerage for towing.

The Polish Ship Salvage company, Polskie Ratownictwo Okrętowe (PRO) was contacted through United Towing Ltd. of Hull to assist. PRO's anchor handling tug, *Baltic Amber* departed from Praia roads on 20 November with *Gas Rising Sun* under tow, to deliver the ship and LPG cargo to Brazil.

Throughout the tow, the gas tanker's main engine was not used and the ship's auxiliary engines provided the necessary power to keep the ship's reliquefaction plants operating. The discharge of a full cargo of LPG was completed at the Arutu Gas Bulk Terminal at Salvador on 12 December.

With the task now only half completed, *Baltic Amber* departed from Salvador on 15 December with *Gas Rising Sun* in tow and heading for Europe. The couple were finally parted when the troubled gas carrier was successfully handed over at Elbe Pilot Station on 25 January. German tugs from Kiel towed the gas carrier up the River Elbe to the Hamburg shipyard of Bloom & Voss for repair.

Careful plans for bunkering the tug were required throughout this mammoth Atlantic round trip. Bunkers were taken at Las Palmas prior to departure, at Fortaleza on the Brazilian coast in both directions, again at Las Palmas and finally at Ijmuiden. At each of the bunkering stops the tow was disconnected with *Gas Rising Sun* waiting on anchor.

An average speed of six knots was achieved in both directions due to good weather and sea conditions and the considerable navigational skills of the tug's master.

There are times in the gas shipping industry when a significant chain of events occurs, which somehow slip through the daily shipping news without great notice. This double Atlantic tow in mid-winter deserves a special mention. Here we have a testimony to the confidence, knowledge and experience of all concerned on board the gas carrier, as well as highlighting the quality of the basic design and cargo containment to monitor and control the systems which prevented the loss of cargo. Master and crew of *Baltic Amber* should also be praised for a difficult job well done. Overall just another salvage statistic, but hidden behind the successful outcome, lies a wealth of expertise, hard work and good seamanship.[18, 19]

Hektor

Principle Particulars	
Length o.a.	157.79 m
Length b.p.	149.00 m
Breadth	24.40 m
Depth	16.00 m
Draught	10.78 m
LPG Capacity	24,048 m³
Engine	Horten-Sulzer 5RLB76
Power	14,400 hp/10,591 kW
Service speed	16 knots

The smallest of the 2% capacity Kværner dome series was a medium sized 24,000 m³ three cargo tank design, of which five newbuildings were shared between Moss Værft and A/S Nye Fredrikstad Mek. Verksted. *Hektor* was delivered from the Moss yard on 17 September 1980 to a Rederiet Helge R Myhre A/S company, K/S A/S Nordsjøgas. As on the larger Kværner 52,000 m³ and 75,000 m³ series, the slightly sloped tops and bottoms of the cargo tanks were also incorporated into the smaller series.

The ship was classed with Det Norske Veritas for the carriage of propane, butane, anhydrous ammonia and vinyl chloride. A neat looking ship with raked transom stern, flush main deck with forward sheer, aft machinery and accommodation, a reliquefaction house/control room forward of the manifolds, 75 m³ and 150 m³ deck tanks, aft and bow thrusters and a bulbous bow. The cargo tanks were insulated with polyurethane. Cargo handling equipment included three cascade reliquefaction plants with Howden LPG and R22 compressors, six 400 m³/hr Thune-Eureka deep-well pumps, two 500 m³/hr Thune Eureka booster pumps, a cargo heater and an inert gas plant. In 1981 *Hektor* was sold to Petroleos Mexicanos and renamed *José Colomo*.

The next two ships of the series, another *Hektor*, just to confuse archivists and traders alike, and *Hebris*, were also for Helge R Myhre companies and were built at Fredrikstad. *Hektor* was delivered to K/S A/S Hektorgas on 21 June 1982 and *Hebris* was delivered to K/S A/S Nordsjøgas II on 22 June 1983. K/S A/S Gas Traders, a company controlled by Rederiet Christian Haaland of Haugesund took delivery of the fourth of the series, *Concordia Fjord*, from Moss on 31 August 1983.

The fifth and final vessel of the 24,000 m³ series, *Hermion*, was delivered from Moss on 29 June 1984 to K/S A/S Hermion for Helge R Myhre and was powered by a MAN B&W 6L67GB diesel engine rated at 15,050 hp (11,069 kW).

Plate 11-19   *Hektor*   Kværner Group

Berge Fister

Principle Particulars	
Length o.a.	158.25 m
Length b.p.	149.75 m
Breadth	27.60 m
Depth	18.20 m
Draught	13.61 m
LPG Capacity	30,455 m³
Engine	Horten-Sulzer 6RLB76
Power	13,230 hp/9,731 kW
Service speed	15.75 knots

In the month previous to taking delivery of *Berge Strand*, the last of the Wärtsilä 75,000 m³ series, Sig. Bergesen d/y A/S took delivery of *Berge Fister*, a one-off 30,455 m³ design from Rosenberg Værft, Stavanger. Completed on 1 April 1982, the ship was classed with Det Norske Veritas as a Tanker for Liquefied Gas with a minimum temperature of -50°C, a maximum pressure of 0.25 kg/cm² and a maximum specific gravity of 0.97.

The three prismatic cargo tank ship followed the Kværner 2% capacity cargo tank dome style. However, the position of the reliquefaction house/control room was change to be aft of the manifolds rather than forward of the manifolds. Three cascade reliquefaction plant were fitted.

Helice

Principle Particulars	
Length o.a.	205.00 m
Length b.p.	193.60 m
Breadth	32.20 m
Depth	20.00 m
Draught	13.02 m
LPG Capacity	57,214 m³
Engine	Kincaid-Sulzer 6RTA62
Power	15,500 hp/11,400 kW
Service speed	16 knots

In 1988, the Kværner Group bought Goven Shipbuilders Ltd. from the UK Government for a nominal sum. The first vessel to be contracted and completed on the Clyde under the Kværner Goven Ltd. banner was 57,214 m³ Helice. This gas carrier, the first of a series of four, was also the first to be built at Goven, and the largest from a Scottish shipyard. Classed with Det Norske Veritas, Helice was delivered to Spey Marine Ltd. for Helge R Myhre A/S, part of Kværner Shipping, Norway, on 5 April 1991.[20, 21, 22]

Like in the Kværner 52,000 m³ series, the 32.20 m Panamax beam was a design consideration, and the Kværner 2% capacity cargo tank domes appeared again. The ship was arranged with transom stern, lower aft deck, aft machinery and accommodation, flush main deck with forward sheer, a reliquefaction house/control room aft of the manifolds, 150 m³ and 300 m³ deck tanks, a bow thruster and a bulbous bow.

The four independent cargo tanks and the secondary barrier were constructed with fine grain carbon manganese steel. Although in outward appearance this latest design seemed little different to previous Kværner designs, subtle changes could be found throughout the cargo handling systems, compared to Kværner's first generation of fully refrigerated LPG carriers. These changes reflect equipment development, trading lessons learned, environmental considerations and the mandatory requirements of the time.

The comprehensive list of products which could be carried was as follows; anhydrous ammonia, butane, butadiene, butylene, naphtha derivatives, propane, propylene and vinyl chloride monomer. The cargo systems were designed for a minimum temperature of -50°C, a maximum pressure of 0.25 kg/cm² and a maximum specific gravity of 0.68 or 0.97. Vinyl chloride monomer with a specific gravity of 0.97 could be carried at 98% filling in Nos. 2 & 3 tanks and at 70% filling in Nos. 1 & 4 tanks. The naphtha derivatives required additional foam monitors to be fitted in the cargo area. The Autronica GL 90 cargo tank radar level gauging system was the first to be fitted on an LPG carrier newbuilding.

The cargo tanks were insulated by Ticon Isolering, using 100 mm thick panels of low CFC polyurethane foam, clad with galvanised steel sheeting. Cargo was discharged with two 500 m³/hr Eureka deep-well pumps in each tank. If required, two 500 m³/hr Eureka booster pumps were available and were protected from the sea and the elements in a deck shelter near the cargo manifolds. There was no cooling R22, as the four modular reliquefaction plants were designed for direct condensation of the cargo, each with an oil-free Sulzer labyrinth cargo compressor, a cargo condenser with receiver and an intermediate cooler. An intrinsically safe MTL 901 emergency shutdown (ESD) link was fitted, which inter-connected the ship and shore shutdown systems during cargo transfer and ensured that pumps and valves shut down safely in an emergency.

Havfrost was delivered to Spey Marine Ltd for Havtor A/S Mangement in June 1991, Helios was delivered on 29 July 1992 to Helge Shipping for Kværner Shipping A/S and the final ship of the series, Havis, was delivered to Havgas Partners Ltd., for A/S Havtor Management on 27 April 1993.

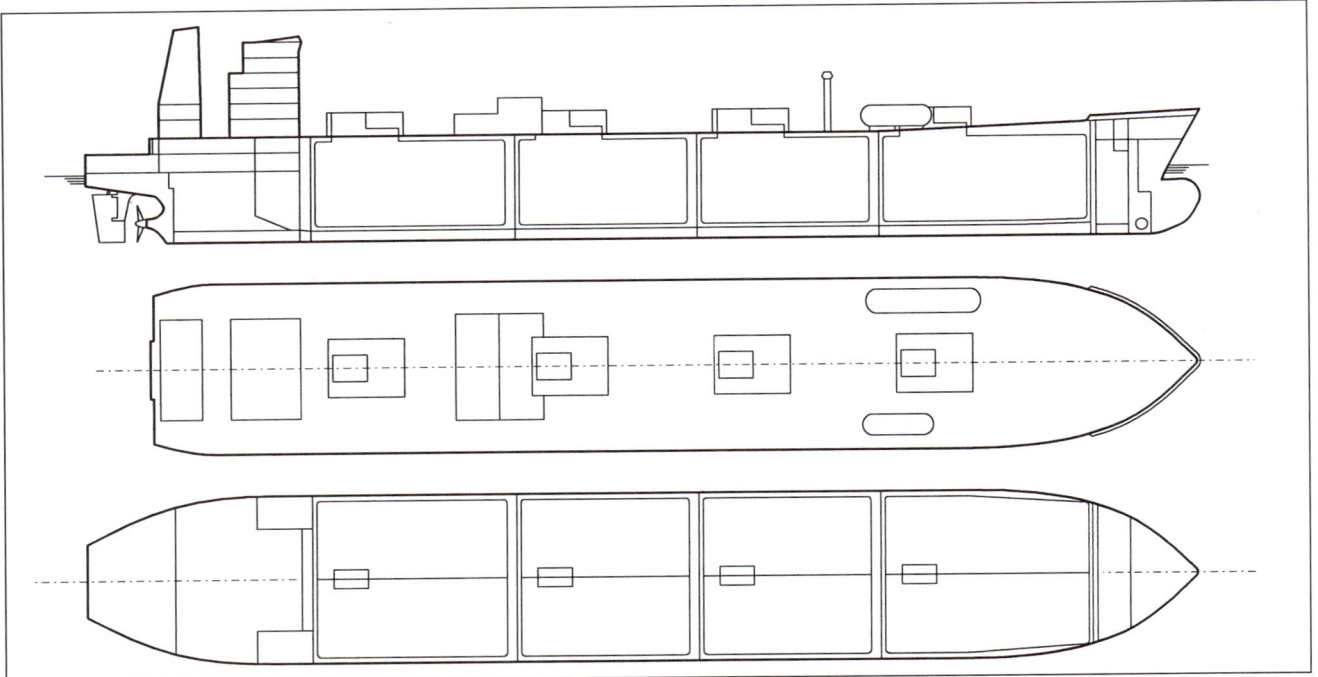

Figure 11-8 Outline Arrangement of *Helice*

Plate 11-20 Positioning of *Helice* cargo tank

Plate 11-21   Midship construction of *Helice*   Kværner Goven

Berge Danuta

Principle Particulars	
Length o.a.	225.57 m
Length b.p.	218.58 m
Breadth	36.40 m
Depth	22.00 m
Draught	11.25 m
LPG Capacity	78,550 m³
Engine	H Cegielski-Sulzer 6RTA68TB
Power	23,982 hp/17,640 kW
Service speed	18 knots

After a gap of over twenty years, Norwegian owners turned again to Poland for gas ship newbuildings, when on 20 May 1988, Bergesen dy ASA awarded Stocznia Gdynia a contract for two 78,550 m³ LPG carriers. The first of the pair, *Berge Danuta*, was named on 5 September 2000 and delivered to the owners on 28 September 2000. Classed with Det Norske Veritas the ship's cargo systems were designed for a minimum temperature of -50°C, a maximum pressure of 0.275 kg/cm² and a maximum specific gravity of 0.69 for the carriage of anhydrous ammonia, butadiene and LPG.[23, 24, 25]

The ship was arranged with a transom stern, aft machinery and accommodation, flush main deck and a bulbous bow. A duct keel was fitted in the double bottom. A reliquefaction house was located above the forward end of No. 4 cargo tank and a cargo control room was arranged in the aft accommodation. A free-fall lifeboat was fitted at the stern. The four independent cargo tanks and the secondary barrier were constructed with NV 2-4 grade steel supplied by the Huta Czestochwa steel mill. The tanks were insulated with 200 mm thick polyurethane foam supplied by Unitor, using a new purpose built workshop. Much of the stainless steel cargo piping was supplied in prefabricated and pre-insulated form by I R Industries of Denmark.

The cargo handling system was designed and supplied by Hamworthy KSE. The four direct reliquefaction plants, each rated at 222 kW, included a new type of compact Alfa Laval AlfaRex gasket-free all welded plate heat exchanger, used instead of the more conventional shell and tube type. The plate heat exchangers were fitted with titanium plates which are impervious to corrosion from sea water. Two 600 m³/hr Hamworthy KSE centrifugal deep-well pumps were fitted in each cargo tank and two similar sized booster pumps were fitted on the main deck.

On time charter to Navion, *Berge Danuta* left Kaarstø, Norway, on 26 November 2000, bound for Turkey, loaded with a first cargo of butane and propane. The vessel was joined on the trade route between Kaarstø or Mongstad and Izmit, by the second ship of the pair, *Berge Denise*, which was delivered to Bergesen dy ASA on 29 December 2000.

Plate 11-22   Skid mounted reliquefaction   Hamworthy KSE
plant for *Berge Danuta*

Plate 11-23   Vaporiser on *Berge Danuta*   Hamworthy KSE

Plate 11-24   Pre-insulated pipework on *Berge Danuta*   IR Industries Denmark

Plate 11-25   Cargo heater on *Berge Danuta*   Hamworthy KSE

[1] The Motor Ship, *A Norwegian-built and Owned LPG/Ammonia Carrier,* February 1966.
[2] Det Norske Veritas, *Rules for the Construction and Classification of Steel Ships,* Oslo, 1962.
[3] Tobiesen, Tryggve, and Riksheim, Jens B., *Classification of Gas Carriers,* Det Norske Veritas, February 1996.
[4] The Motor Ship, *Norway's Largest LPG Tanker,* August 1967.
[5] Lloyd's List Casualty Reports, *Mundogas Rio,* May/Oct 1988.
[6] Author's on site observations, *Mundogas Rio,* Fujairah, 29/30 August 1988.
[7] Iversen, Hafdan H., *Specialisation at Moss Værft,* Shipbuilding and Shipping Record, 30 July 1969.
[8] Shipping World & Shipbuilder, *Höegh Multina, LPG/Ammonia Carrier with Computer Controlled Engine Room,* April 1972.
[9] Shipping World & Shipbuilder, *Garmula, P&O's Largest LPG Carrier,* October 1972.
[10] Lloyd's List Casualty Reports, *Havglimt,* March 1988/January 1989.
[11] The Motor Ship, *P &O's First Step in a £15 million Liquefied Gas Transportation Project,* April 1972.
[12] Shipbuilding & Marine Engineering International, *Bibby Line LPG Tanker, Hampshire,* April 1974.
[13] Shipping World & Shipbuilder, *Höegh Swallow, First of a Series of LPG Carriers for Poland,* February 1978.
[14] Lloyd's List Casualty Reports, *Gas Poem,* November 2002/Mar 2003.
[15] Fairplay International, *First Finnish Newbuilding to Japan, Instead of Norway,* 5 October 1978.
[16] Lloyd's List Casualty Reports, *Berge Strand,* May/June 1988.
[17] Lloyd's List Casualty Reports, *Berge Strand,* July 1988.
[18] Lloyd's List Casualty Reports, *Gas Rising Sun,* November 1991/March 1992.
[19] Personal correspondence from M. Leszczynski of PRO to the author, *Baltic Amber,* 4 February 1992.
[20] The Motor Ship, *Helice, Accuracy Controls Increases Cargo Carrying Capacity,* July 1991.
[21] Significant Ships of 1991, *Helice: Kværner's First Ship from Goven,* Royal Institution of Naval Architects, London, February 1992.
[22] Richardson, Doug, *A Shipyard Reborn on the Clyde – Kværner Goven,* Shipbuilding Technology International, 1993.
[23] Lloyd's List, *Bergesen Break for Sulzer RTA68T Diesel Engine,* 12 January 1999.
[24] Significant Ships of 2000, *Berge Danuta: Gdynia Shipyard re-enters the LPG Market,* Royal Institution of Naval Architects, London, February 2001.
[25] Horizon, *Berge Danuta Loads at Kaarstø: Impressive Design, Happy Crew,* Issue 4, 2000.

Chapter 12

Scottish Ammonia Carrier Conversion

Scottish ship owners George Gibson & Company of Leith, entered the gas shipping business in 1965 after successfully obtaining a contract in April 1964 to carry liquefied anhydrous ammonia across the Irish Sea.[1, 2, 3, 4] Until then, the George Gibson fleet had consisted of small dry cargo vessels engaged in short sea trading. Under a seven year charter, to Imperial Chemicals Industries (ICI), a ship was required to transport 450 tonnes of ammonia from Heysham, Lancashire, England, to Belfast, Northern Ireland, and later, as the trade developed, to Arklow in the Republic of Ireland. This contract was to result in the conversion of George Gibson's single deck coaster *Quentin* into a refrigerated ammonia carrier. Up to the present time, 679 m³ *Quentin*, holds the distinction of being the smallest capacity refrigerated gas carrier, built or converted, with cargo transported at just above atmospheric pressure.

Quentin

Principle Particulars	
Length o.a.	52.95 m
Length b.p.	49.70 m
Breadth	8.54 m
Depth	4.22 m
Draught	3.44 m
NH₃ Capacity	679 m³
Engine	British Auxiliaries M 471
Power	650 hp/478 kW
Service speed	10.25 knots

The motor vessel *Quentin* was originally delivered from the Grangemouth Dockyard Company in June 1940. Conversion work was carried out at Leith, at the Henry Robb shipyard, and was completed in September 1966. A single prismatic cargo tank was constructed with Lloyd's Register of Shipping special grade E steel and was fabricated in six sections. The upper sides of the tank sloped inwards, above the level of the original main deck, and a steel weather cover was fitted over the tank. The tank was launched, floated alongside the shipyard and then lifted by crane into the single hold of *Quentin*. Insulation was secured by lugs welded onto the tank.

Due to the location of the storage tanks at Heysham, some four kilometres from the jetty, with the pipeline installed above the ground across an undulating route, stringent requirements were specified by the charterers for loading the ammonia. The vessel was required to be able to load the first 50 tonnes of *warmed-up* ammonia at 23°F (-5°C) at about 20 tonnes/hour. The remaining cargo was then to be loaded at the fully refrigerated temperature of -27.4°F (-33°C) at about 80 tonnes/hour. No vapour return line was available for loading.

The charterers also required that the vessel was to be able to discharge a full cargo in about six hours. A discharge rate of about 40 tonnes/hour was required and a cargo heater was to be installed to raise the temperature at the ship's manifold from -27.4°F (-33°C) to 32°F (0°C). As with loading, no vapour return line was available for discharging.

With the charterers' criteria to be satisfied, the tank was designed for a maximum pressure of 10 lb/in² (0.703 kg/cm²), a minimum temperature of -27.4°F (-33°C) and a comparatively large gas plant for the size of ship was fitted. The plant, rated at 1,360,000 BTUs/hr., included two J & E Hall six cylinder V-block compressors, a four cylinder compressor, condensers and associated equipment. The ammonia plant was housed forward of the machinery space and above the aft end of the cargo tank. The aft end of the prismatic cargo tank was shaped to fit underneath the gas plant.

A deep-well pump and two booster pumps, supplied by Sulzer, England, were used for discharge. The booster pumps were arranged to operate in series, or parallel, depending on the shore conditions. As a backup arrangement for the deep-well pump, cargo could be discharged by using the booster pumps only. A steam ammonia heater, also supplied by J & E Hall, was fitted with the steam produced by a Stone Vapour Generator. In the first year of operation, about 60 cargoes were carried.

At the time of the conversion of *Quentin*, the senior superintendent with George Gibson was Jim Whyte, who two years later, in 1967 was instrumental in setting up Liquid Gas Equipment Limited (LGE) at Loanhead, at the foot of the Pentland Hills. In the intervening years, LGE has developed from a few skilled and knowledgeable engineers to an internationally known and highly respected company serving the gas, chemical and petrochemical industries. The company is currently trading as LGE Process within the Weir Group.

Jim Whyte, in describing the first year of operation of *Quentin* and the company's experience with their first ethylene carrier, 833 m³ *Teviot*, recalled training requirements, problems with the heavy ammonia smell and high frequency generator engines' noise. He remarked;

> Having now operated small fully refrigerated gas tankers for over a year, it would seem that the technical and human problems which are encountered on larger vessels tend to become accentuated. ... These and other such human problems must be given equal priority with technical problems if these complex and expensive ships are to attract the type and calibre of men who are necessary for their continued successful operation.

With such attention to detail it is not surprising that LGE prospered.

Thirty-six years after originally being built, *Quentin* was scrapped in 1976.

Plate 12-1   *Quentin* before conversion   Archives of Jim Whyte

Plate 12-2   *Quentin* after conversion   Archives of Jim Whyte

[1]   Somner, Graeme, *George Gibson & Company*, World Ship Society, May 1988.
[2]   Shipbuilding & Shipping Record, *Coaster to Ammonia Carrier*, 16 December 1965.
[3]   Whyte, J., *Operation of Small Gas Tankers*, Shipbuilding & Shipping Record, 24 November 1966.
[4]   Baroutakis, M. A., *LPG/LNG Handling*, Piraeus, 1971.

Chapter 13

Single Invar LPG Membrane from CNIM

In 1982, three major French shipbuilders, all with extensive experience in building a full range of LPG and LNG gas carriers were merged to form Chantiers du Nord et de la Méditerranée. The three yards were; Chantiers de France-Dunkerque in the north, and in the south Chantiers Navals de la Ciotat (CNC) and Constructions Navales et Industrielles de la Méditerranée (CNIM), La Seyne-sur-Mer.

Up to the time of the merger the two southern yards, situated some 30 km apart on the Mediterranean coast, had for many years been great rivals in competing for both LPG and LNG newbuilding work. Gazocéan was one of CNC's major clients and as such, Technigaz, the technical arm of Gazocéan had a great influence over the ships delivered from the yard. (See Chapter 2). CNIM., with connections to the Worms Group, and with a 25% share in Gaz Transport, in 1968 built a prototype LPG carrier, *Hypolite-Worms,* based on the Gaz Transport membrane system, which was to be a important step in the development of LNG invar membrane technology.

La Seyne shipyard closed in June 1986.

Aeolos

Principle Particulars	
Length o.a.	154.50 m
Length b.p.	144.00 m
Breadth	23.00 m
Depth	12.80 m
Draught	7.70 m
LPG Capacity	14,805 m^3
Engine	CCM-Sulzer 6RD76
Power	9,600 hp/7,061 kW
Service speed	16 knots

The first purpose built gas carrier to be finished at Constructions Navales et Industrielles de la Méditerranée (CNIM), La Seyne-sur-Mer, was 14,805 m^3 *Aeolos*. Originally ordered by Northern Ship Agency Inc., *Aeolos*, and a second vessel *Aeolos II*, were completed in 1967. In 1968, *Aeolos* was delivered to Gazocéan as *Mariotte* and *Aeolos II* was delivered to Nouvelle Compagnie Havraise Penisulaire de Navigation as *Cerons*.

Dual classed with American Bureau of Shipping and Bureau Veritas the ships also complied with the requirements of the United States Coast Guard. Design assistance was provided by Marine Service GmbH of Hamburg. The ships were designed for the carriage of LPG and anhydrous ammonia for a minimum temperature of -45°C and a maximum pressure of 0.28 kg/cm^2.

The ships were arranged with a cruiser stern, machinery spaces, aft superstructure, flush main deck, forecastle and a flared stem. A double bottom and double side hull were fitted in way of the three prismatic cargo tanks. The cargo tanks were constructed with a high tensile strength, fine grain, fully killed, aluminium treated, carbon manganese steel, manufactured by Le Creusot. Insulation was provided by loose perlite in the void spaces around the cargo tanks.

Transverse azobé hardwood planks in line with each double bottom floor supported the cargo tanks. Oak anti-flotation chocks were located at the upper outboard corners of each tank. Top and bottom azobé anti-rolling keys were fitted at each tank at the centreline and transverse bottom azobé anti-collision keys were fitted at the mid-length of the tank.

The reliquefaction house was located on the main deck between Nos. 1 and 2 cargo tanks with a cargo control room above. Each of the three cascade reliquefaction plants included a Sulzer cargo compressor, a Sabroe R22 compressor, a condenser and heat exchangers. Two 165 m³/hr J C Carter electric submerged pumps were fitted in each cargo tank.

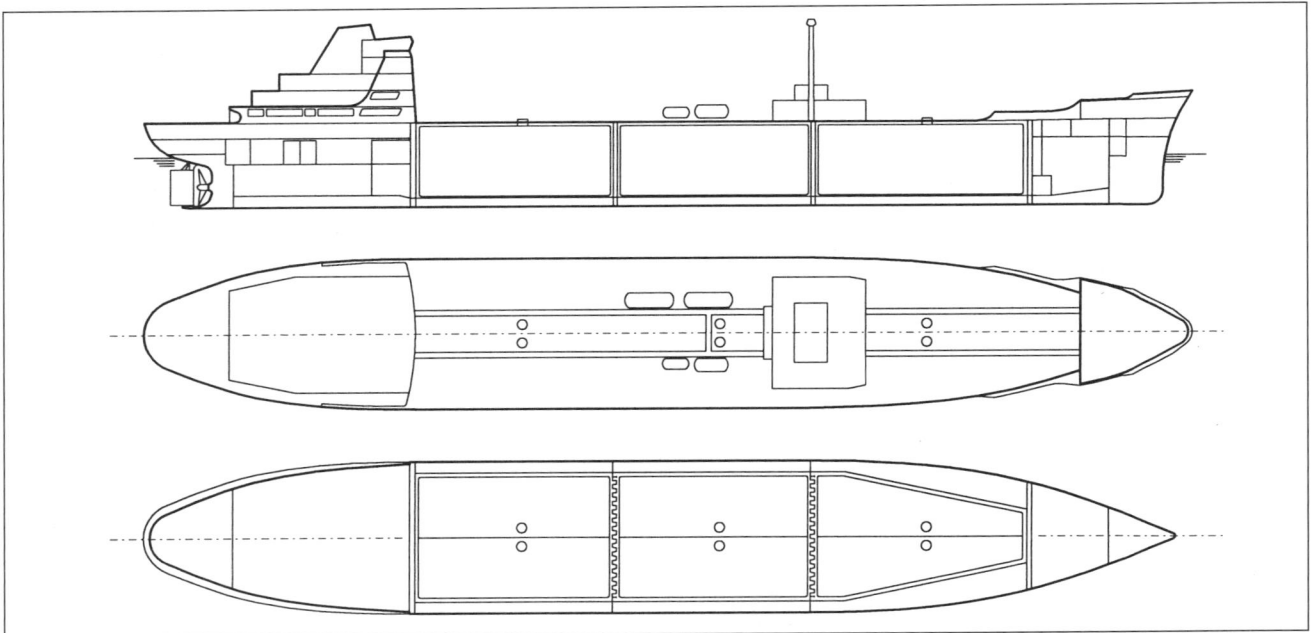

Figure 13-1 Outline Arrangement of *Aeolos*

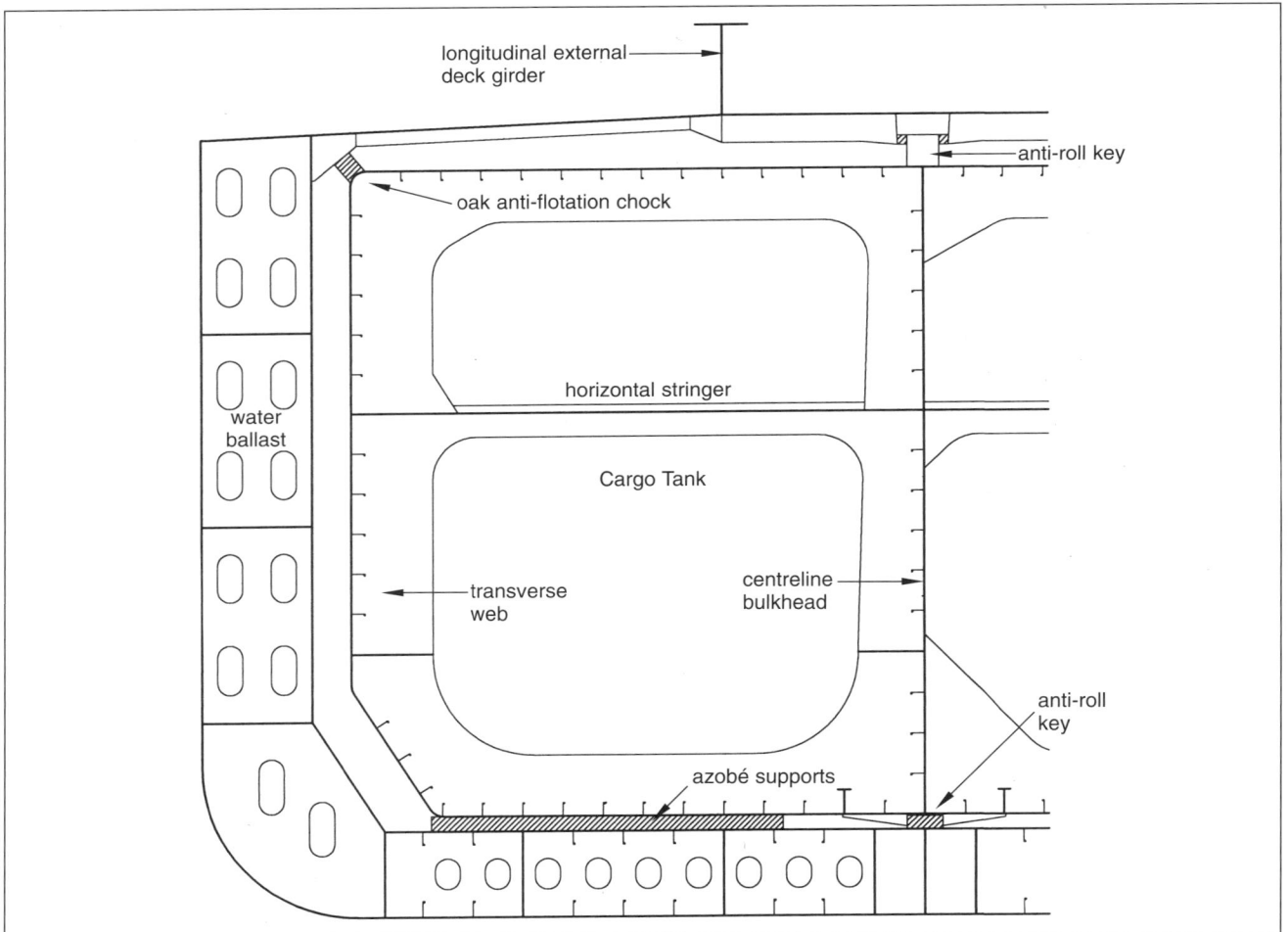

Figure 13-2 Midship Section of *Aeolos* showing Tank Supports

26 December 1982 – In the Wake of Nelson and Magallanes

Cerons, as *Galileo,* grounded when transiting the Pasa Grey in Chilean waters, in the early afternoon of 26 December 1982, due to damaged steering gear jamming the rudder at 10° to port. The vessel was fully loaded with LPG and on the southern section of a north bound Chilean coastal passage from Cabo Negro, near Punta Arenas to Quintero, north of Valparaiso. Against the backdrop of the rugged, ever changing coastal scenery of the southern tip of the Andes, this was a dramatic Christmas incident, as the ship navigated past islands, under cliffs and through tight canals. Fortunately, there were no injures reported on board.

The machinery space was partially flooded to just above the floor plates, with Nos. 1 & 2 starboard double bottom tanks open to the sea and No. 3 starboard double bottom flooded. On board pumps controlled the water ingress in the machinery spaces, estimated at 200 tonnes/per hour. By discharging water ballast and because the tide was rising the vessel was re-floated within 90 minutes, and drifted free of rocks. The starboard anchor was lost during the re-floating and the vessel was held in position by the port anchor.

Navy divers reported bottom damage extending from the break of the forecastle to the machinery space. The divers and the crew were able to plug and patch the ruptured bottom shell. The cargo reliquefaction plants were operating and normal cargo temperatures were maintained.

As *Galileo* was blocking the shipping channel, the maritime authorities required a move to approximately 22 miles north of the stranded position. The vessel proceeded to a safe anchorage off Bahia Año Nuevo, on 31 December, at reduced speed under her own power, with a Navy tug assisting. The internal structure supporting No. 3 cargo tank was found to be severely damaged, but the perlite insulation in the void space around the cargo tank prevented any inspection of the timber tank supports and tank alignment. There was no loss of LPG or leakage from the cargo tanks.

Galileo sailed north to Talcahuano, where the LPG cargo was discharged before the ship entered dry dock for an examination of the full extent of the damage in a gas free condition. The extensive structural damages were not repaired, and in February the vessel was sold to Taiwan interests. For the cross Pacific passage to Taiwan, some minor repairs were carried out to made the vessel seaworthy. *Galileo* arrived at Kaohsiung on 2 May 1983 for breaking up.[1]

December 1993 – Alaska winter waters

Mariotte as *Asia Rainbow* encountered heavy weather damage when on a ballast passage from Kenai, Alaska to South Korea. Water ingress in way of No. 1 cargo tank caused the empty tank to float which resulted in damage to the main deck. The vessel was not repaired and was broken up in 1994.

Hypolite-Worms

Principle Particulars	
Length o.a.	177.90 m
Length b.p.	165.00 m
Breadth	24.50 m
Depth	15.50 m
Draught	10.42 m
LPG Capacity	29,866 m³
Engine	CCM-Sulzer 6RD90
Power	13,800 hp/10,150 kW
Service speed	17 knots

Of major importance in the development of the Gaz Transport membrane system for LNG carriers was the 29,866 m³ LPG carrier *Hypolite-Worms*. After much pioneering work, the Worm Group wanted to build a prototype ship before proposing its membrane technology to shipowners. The ship was ordered from Forges et Chantiers de la Méditerranée (FCM) in mid 1966, and was delivered in December 1968. In the same year, FCM became Constructions Navales & Industrielles de la Méditerranée (CNIM).

Aiming to convince an international LNG market of viability of their membrane technology, the owners built the LPG ship under the dual classification of American Bureau of Shipping and Bureau Veritas. The owning company was Compagnie Havraise Peninsulaire de Navigation, which was an international consortium with Compagnie Worms, holding 90% of the capital. The remaining 10% share was taken by Dutch companies; Nederland Line, Royal Interocean Lines and Royal Rotterdam Lloyd. The same consortium members funded the construction of *Antilla Cape,* which was delivered from A G Weser in August 1968.

Hypolite-Worms was constructed with four cargo spaces with a double bottom and double side hull, and a trunk deck. The cargo spaces were separated by transverse cofferdam bulkheads. The cargo containment consisted of a layer of plywood boxes filled with perlite with a single 0.5 mm invar membrane as the primary barrier. Invar is a 36% nickel steel with a very low thermal coefficient of expansion. The ship's inner hull and cofferdams were constructed with low temperature steel, forming the secondary barrier.

In the book, *Quand le Méthane prend la mer*, co-authored by Henri Petit, Pierre Jean gives a delicious account of his personal involvement with the design, construction and first commercial voyage of *Hypolite-Worms*.[2] Some of his recollections are worth repeating.

> *Hypolite-Worms* was sarcastically nicknamed the *Hypocrite* by the engineers who were involved in its construction and later in the operations, probably because of all the problems that it posed for them.

A bonus for the crew when 300 m³ of propane needed to be jettisoned at sea to gas free the ship.

> Our chief cook took the fortunate initiative to place an improvised trawl behind the ship. Made of a large wicker basket and a mooring line, it turned out to be most effective: each time the basket was raised, we took five or six lobsters.

Old techniques helped new techniques at the Cape Town docks.

> I needed to find a way to set up the scaffolding in tank No. 1 as soon as possible. The tank was about 20 meters deep, 20 meters wide at the rear, 10 meters wide at the front and 18 meters long. This represented a huge surface to be covered, especially when all of the scaffolding components had to pass through a single manhole on the deck measuring about 1 meter in diameter. After quickly examining the facilities available from companies at the port, I had to face the fact that only bamboo could be used for the scaffolding.

Secret message ending codes when reporting back to chairman Audy Gilles.

> The more polite sounding the ending, the greater the difficulties. On the other hand, when the message ended on an informal tone, this meant that things were going better and better and that most of the problems were solved.

Pierre Jean's hands on tale of the many problems encountered, perfectly combines an engineer's individual joy in solving seemingly impossible technical challenges, with the satisfaction such tasks gives to all involved.

This first successful voyage, with propane, from Ras Tanura to Tokyo Bay, proved that the unique primary barrier of invar was able to contain the liquefied cargo, and with some ingenuity, could be repaired if necessary.

In July 1967, a contract was signed to build two 71,500 m³ LNG carriers for Phillips/Marathon, at the Kockums shipyard in Malmö, Sweden. These two sisters, the first to be built using the Gaz Transport membrane system, with a double layer of insulating boxes and two invar membranes, traded from Kenai, Alaska, to Negishi, Japan as *Polar Alaska* and *Arctic Tokyo*. Today, thanks to the pioneering work on *Hypolite-Worms*, the Gaz Transport membrane design is well established and internationally successful. Currently, ultra large LNG carrier invar membrane designs of 250,000 m³, and above, are on the drawing boards and computer screens.

Hypolite-Worms was converted in 1974 for the owners Compagnie Navales Worms by Compagnie Marseillaise de Réparations (CMR) into a Ro-Ro/containership, and renamed *Ile de la Réunion*. Appropriately, No. 1 LPG cargo space was used for refrigerated cargo. Nos. 2 – 4 LPG cargo tanks space became, between the original transverse cofferdams, holds for containers with side access hatches to Ro-Ro ramps. *Ile de la Réunion* was broken up in 1984.

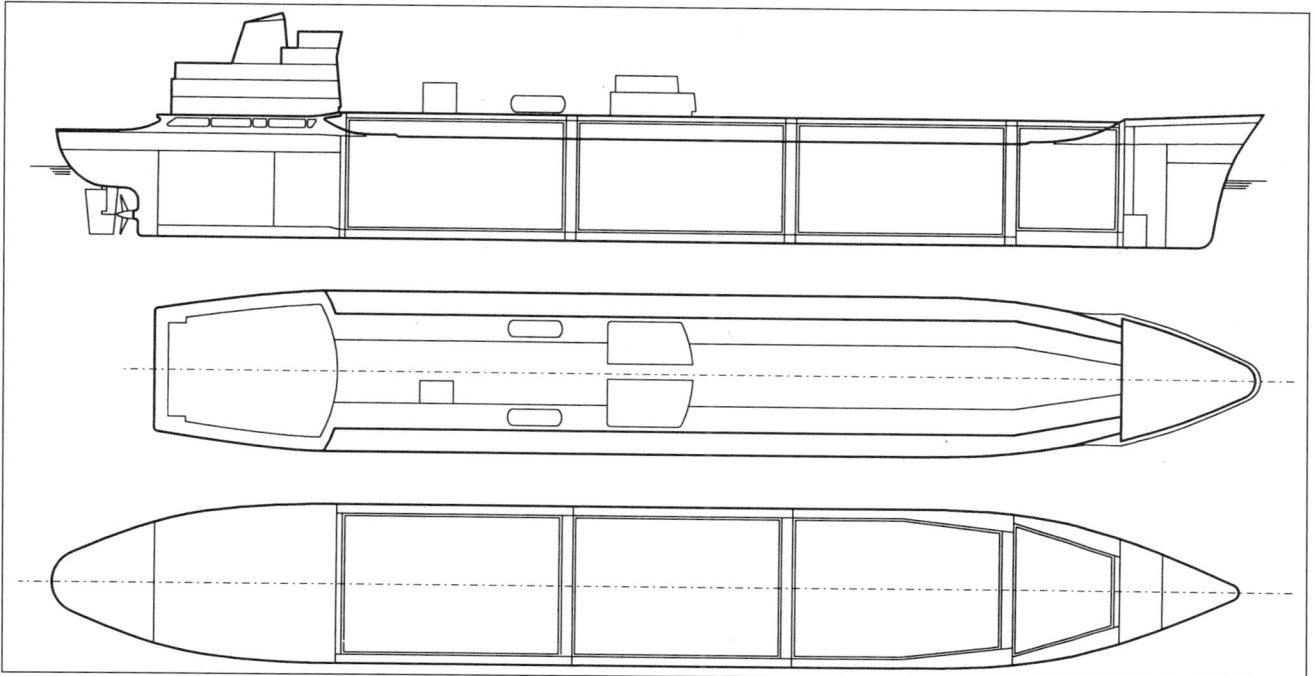

Figure 13-3 Outline Arrangement of *Hypolite-Worms*

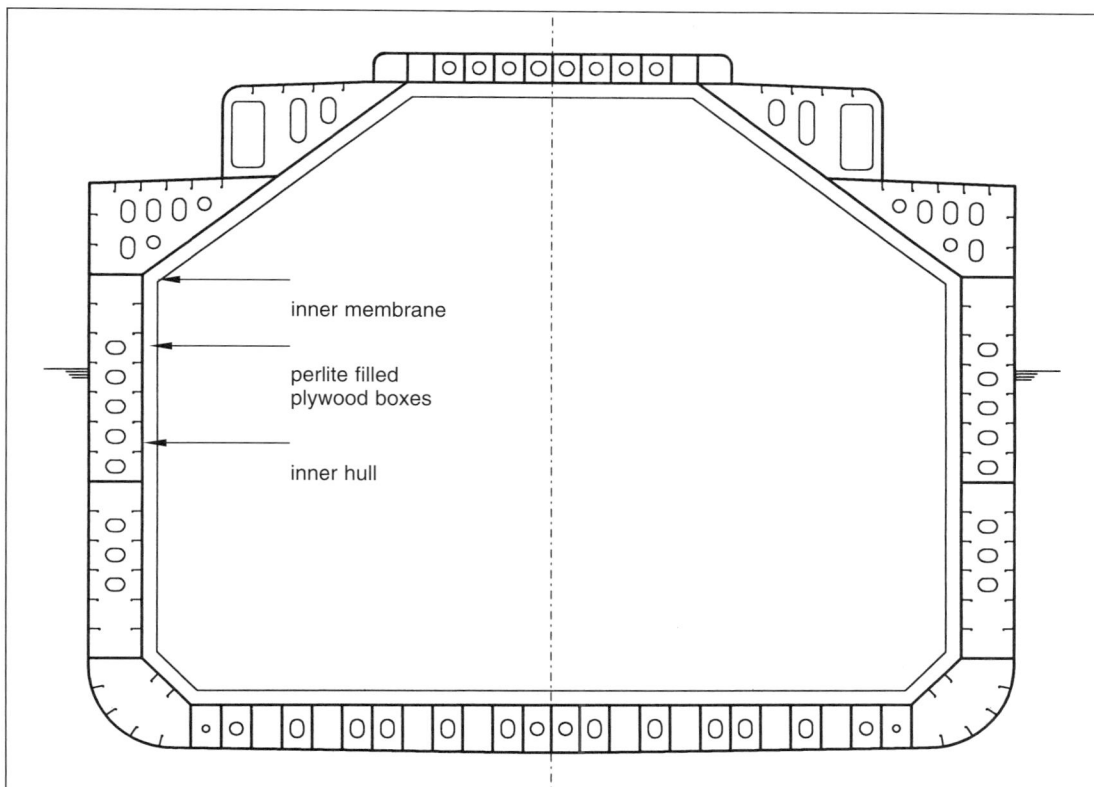

Figure 13-4 Midship Section of *Hypolite-Worms* showing Invar Membrane

Plate 13-1 *Ile de la Réunion*

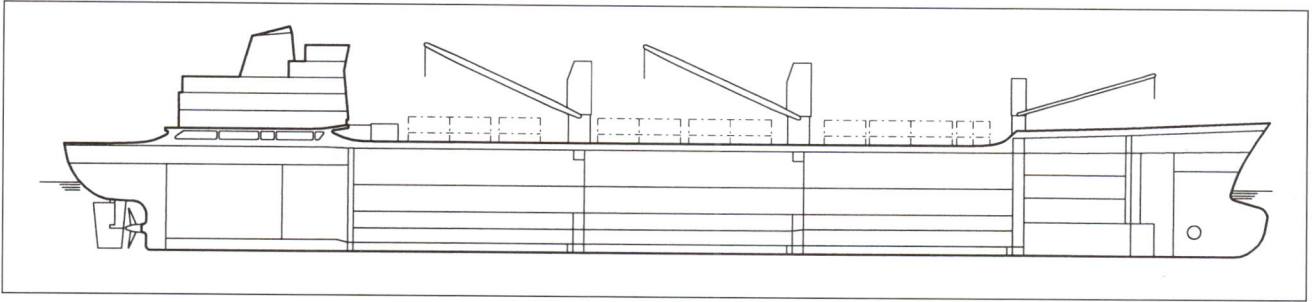

Figure 13-5 Profile of *Hypolite-Worms* after conversion to Ro-Ro/containership *Ile de la Réunion*

Antilla Bay

Principle Particulars	
Length o.a.	216.52 m
Length b.p.	203.00 m
Breadth	32.25 m
Depth	18.40 m
Draught	11.02 m
LPG Capacity	53,400 m³
Engine	CCM-Sulzer 7RND90
Power	20,300 hp/14,931 kW
Service speed	17 knots

53,400 m³ *Antilla Bay,* was the first of five similar sized LPG/NH₃ carriers to be delivered from La Seyne in a period from 1973 to 1978.[3, 4, 5] This was a difficult period for ship owners with the oil crisis of 1973 causing many shipping company casualties, and for the gas shipbuilders, the forthcoming introduction of the IMCO Gas Ship Code in 1976 was beginning to require a little tweaking of ships' equipment and layout.

With design assistance from Marine Services GmbH of Hamburg, the series hull dimensions were based on the Panamax beam of 32.25 m. All five ships were classed with Lloyd's Register of Shipping and *Antilla Bay* was handed over to Scheepsvaart Maatschappij Volharding of Willemstad, Curaçao, Netherlands Antilles on 18 June 1973.

The ship was designed for the carriage of anhydrous ammonia, butane, butadiene, propane and propylene, at a minimum temperature of -48°C and a maximum pressure of 0.29 kg/cm².

Antilla Bay was constructed with four prismatic cargo tanks, and using the now most common arrangement for fully refrigerated LPG carriers, of lower and upper wing ballast tanks and the side hull forming the secondary barrier. The lower wing tanks' cross section was much smaller than the upper wing tanks' cross section. The cargo tanks, cargo tank foundations and secondary barrier were constructed with a high tensile strength carbon manganese steel.

The tanks were externally insulated with 2 m x 1 m x 100 mm panels of Klegecell 33 which were secured to the tank with adhesive and welded pins. The joints between the panels were filled with polyurethane foam and the complete insulation system was protected and sealed with a mastic reinforced with glass fibre cloth. Azobé hardwood provided the sliding cushion between the cargo tanks and the support foundations and keys.

Pipework on the deck for cargo, fire protection and other systems were neatly arranged longitudinally each side of the ship's centreline and running between two side reliquefaction houses above Nos. 3 and 4 cargo tanks. A large cargo control room was built between and above the electric motor rooms of the reliquefaction houses, with clear views forward over the main deck and amidships cargo manifolds. Four cascade type reliquefaction plants were fitted, two on each side of the ship. One good safety design feature was a small circular escape hatch, at main deck level, at the aft end of each compressor house.

Two 380 m³/hr J C Carter submerged electric pumps were fitted in each cargo tank. Other equipment fitted included a 1,800 m³/hr inert gas generator and a 80 m³/hr gaseous nitrogen generator.

Antilla Bay was sold to Chinese breakers in 2004 as *Havmann*.

The next pair in the 53,400 m³ series were originally ordered by Universal Gas and Oil Company and launched as *Dorsetown* and *Dovertown*. *Dorsetown* was delivered from the yard to Sofrangaz as *Providence Multina* in October 1973 and *Dovertown* was delivered to Malmros Rederi A/B as *Malmros Multina* in May 1974.

Dorsetown was sold to Indian breakers in 2003 as *Hesperus*.

The final two ships in the 53,400 m³ series were also ordered by and delivered to different owners. The original order was placed by Multinational Gas and Petrochemical Company with the contract being taken over by Petroleos Mexicanos (PEMEX). Multinational Gas was declared bankrupt in 1977. The first ship was completed in 1978. Both ships were commissioned in August 1979 for PEMEX as *Reynosa* and *Monterrey*.

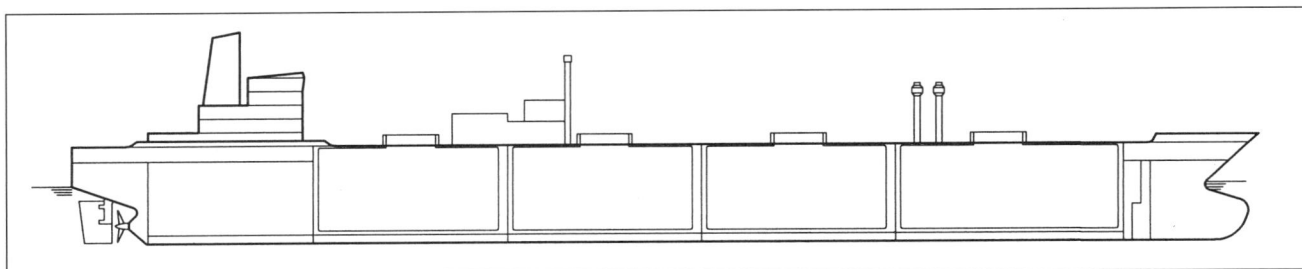

Figure 13-6 Profile of *Antilla Bay*

Plate 13-2   *Providence Multina* under construction   Marine Services GmbH, Hamburg

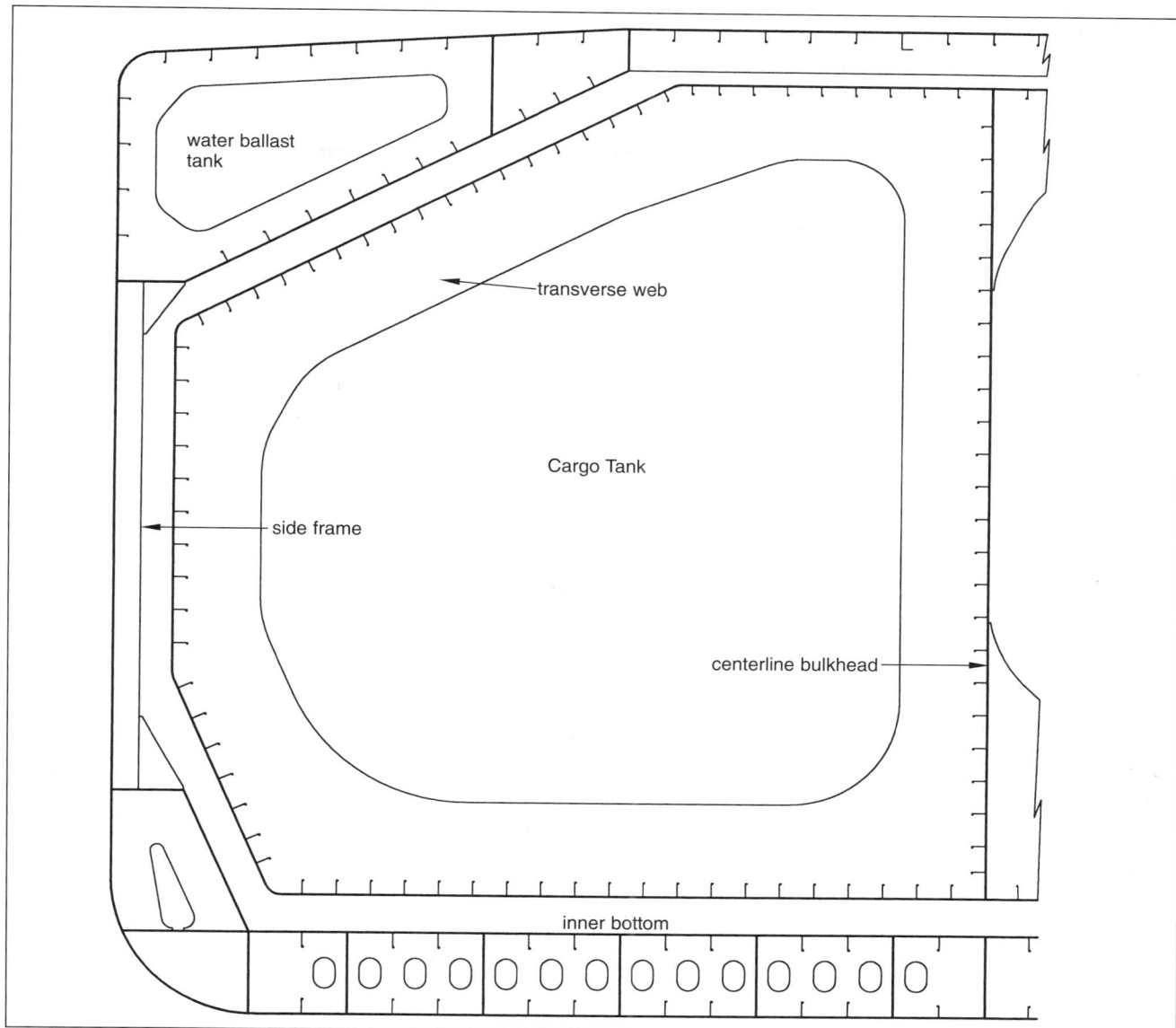

Figure 13-7 Midship Section of *Antilla Bay* showing Cargo Tank Transverse Web

Plate 13-3   *Malmros Multina*   Marine Services GmbH, Hamburg

Plate 13-4   *Antilla Bay* as *Havmann*

Plate 13-5   Cargo vents on *Havmann*

Plate 13-6   Compressor room escape hatch on *Havmann*

[1]   Lloyd's List Casualty Reports, *Galileo,* December 1982/June 1984.
[2]   Jean, Pierre, and Petit, Henri, *Quand le Méthane prend la mer*, Gaz Transport & Technigaz, 1998.
[3]   CNIM brochure, *Transports de Gaz de Pétrole Liquéfiés, LPG Carrier,* January 1977.
[4]   Tanker & Bulker International, *Building LPG Ships at La Seyne,* September 1977.
[5]   Lloyd's Register of Shipping 100A1, *Petroleos Mexicanos,* October 1981.

Chapter 14

Spanish First from Euskalduña

The Spanish state-owned company Butano SA, with a monopoly on LPG distribution throughout the country, first began selling LPG in 1958.[1] Initially, small converted ships with pressurised cargo tanks were used to trade between the refineries on the Canary Islands and those on the mainland, as well as between coastal refineries on the mainland itself. The Bilbao shipyard of Tomas Ruiz de Velasco SA built the first LPG carrier in Spain in 1963, with the delivery of semi-refrigerated 1,245 m³ *Vinci* to Navigas SA of Madrid. In 1965 Butano took delivery of its first newbuildings, with orders placed in two Spanish shipyards for four 2,042 m³ semi-refrigerated vessels. The ships, *Butauno* and *Butados* were delivered from Sociedad Española de Construcción Naval at Matagorda, near Cadiz, and *Butatres* and *Butacuatro* were delivered from Compania Euskalduña de Construcción y Reparación de Bugues SA, of Bilbao.

Spanish shipyards have also been involved in the design and construction of LNG carriers. In 1970, Astilleros y Talleres del Nordeste SA (ASTANO) delivered 39,782 m³ LNG carrier *Laieta*, which was constructed with prismatic aluminium cargo tanks. The Sener spherical tank prototype LNG/ethylene carrier 5,000 m³ *Sant Jordi* was delivered from Tomas Ruiz in 1976. Izar have recently re-entered the LNG market, with the construction and delivery of *Inigo Tapias* from the Sestao yard in 2003. This ship is the first of a series of five 138,000 m³ Gaz Transport membrane type ships on order from the Sestao and Puerto Real yards of Izar.

Two fully refrigerated LPG carriers have been built by Spanish shipbuilders, 11,188 m³ *Alexander Hamilton* in 1968, and 14,103 m³ *Butanueve* in 1969.

Alexander Hamilton

Principle Particulars	
Length o.a.	143.92 m
Length b.p.	132.44 m
Breadth	19.60 m
Depth	11.30 m
Draught	7.67 m
LPG Capacity	11,188 m³
Engine	Euskalduña-MAN K6Z 70/120D
Power	8,400 hp/6,178 kW
Service speed	15.75 knots

The first fully refrigerated LPG carrier to be built in Spain was the 11,188 m³ *Alexander Hamilton*. The ship was delivered on 14 February 1968 to A L Burbank & Co. Ltd. of New York, from Compania Euskalduña de Construcción y Reparación de Bugues SA, Bilbao. The vessel was built to Lloyd's Register of Shipping classification and to the regulations of the US Coast Guard. Consultants from Germany's Marine Services GmbH, Spain's Sener and France's Technigaz helped the shipyard with technical advice.

The ship was constructed with three prismatic cargo tanks, each with full length trunks, and the insulation was on the cargo tanks. The vessel had a double bottom and a double side hull with transverse cofferdams between each cargo tank. The double bottom spaces at the centre below the cargo tanks were used as fuel tanks. The LPG/NH_3 carrier was designed for a minimum cargo temperature of -45°C and a maximum pressure of 0.2 kg/cm².

The now closed Euskalduña shipyard was nearby and on the same side of the inner curve of the Nervión River as the architecturally acclaimed Guggenheim Museum Bilbao.[2] This building was designed by Frank O. Gehry and opened in 1997. With its multiplicity of curves, when viewed from the site of the old shipyard, it does conjure up to a naval architect's eye many nautical shapes. How fitting for such a location. The pronounced flared bow of *Alexander Hamilton* would not have been out of place amongst the museum's curves.

Alexander Hamilton was sold to Aegis Shipping, Greece, in 1973 and renamed *Aegis Diligence*.

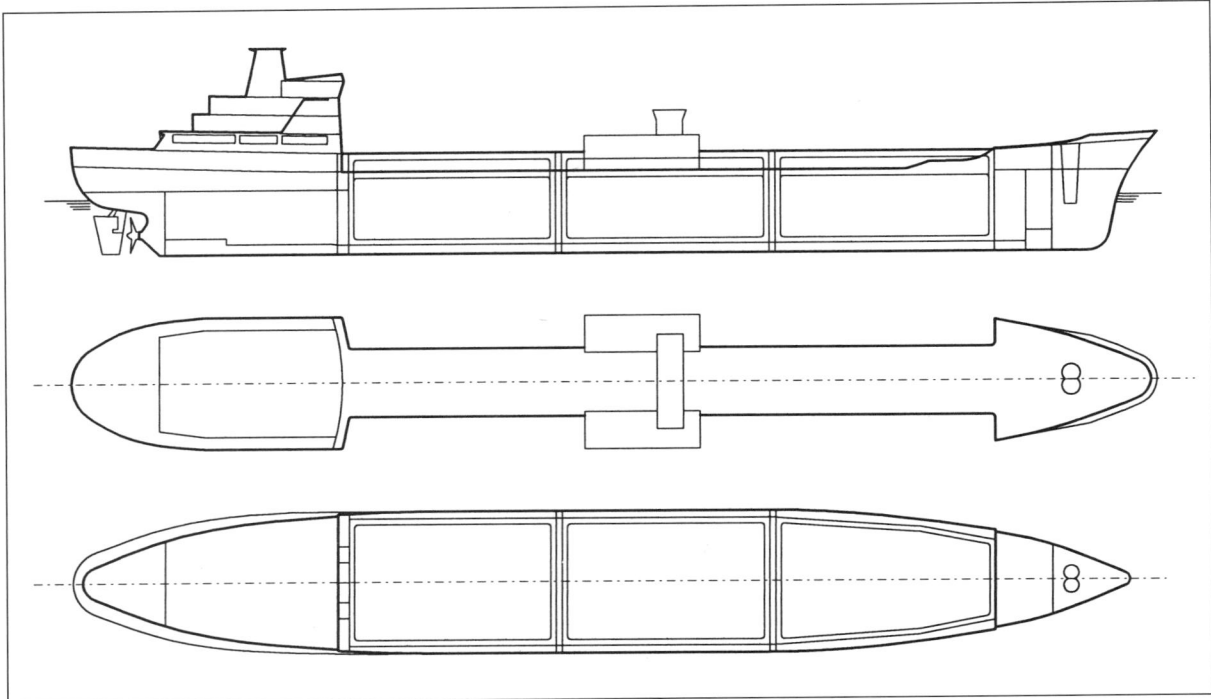

Figure 14-1 Outline Arrangement of *Alexander Hamilton*

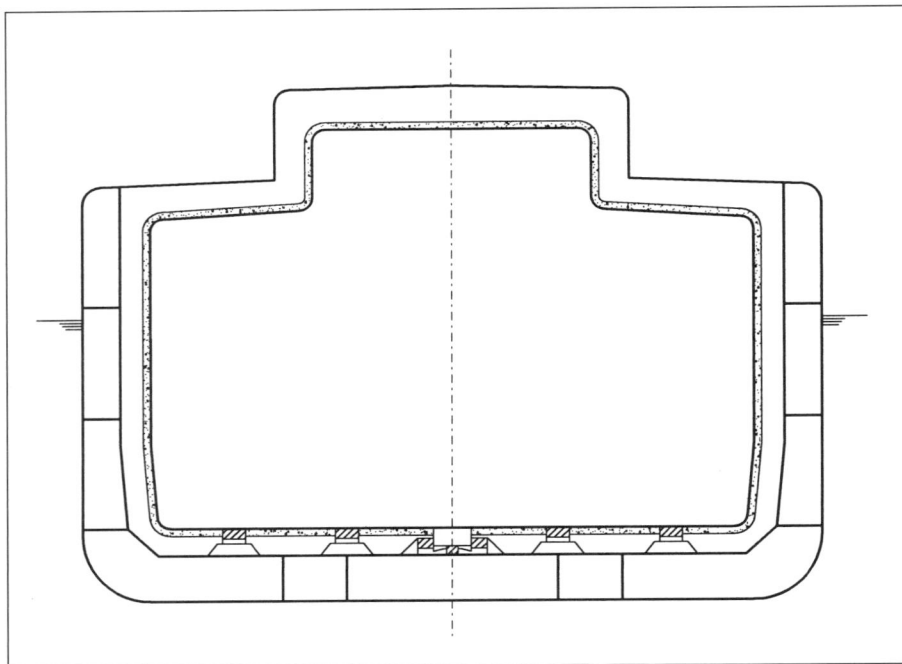

Figure 14-2 Midship Section of *Alexander Hamilton*

28 October 1975 – Cargo Tanks' Uplift

A fire started about midday, after an explosion at the forward part of the engine-room of *Aegis Diligence,* when the vessel was at anchor off Laurium, Greece.[3] The vessel was in ballast with approximately 30 tonnes of LPG on board, and was quickly abandoned by the crew. One crew member was killed. Fire fighters were initially unable to extinguish the fire, which spread to the double bottom tanks. A further small explosion occurred in the engine-room on 30 October and on the same day vibrations and noise were observed in way of No. 3 cargo tank. The next day the anchor cables were released and the vessel was towed, still ablaze, and beached in an isolated cove north of Laurium. The fire was extinguished on 13 November. All void spaces around the cargo tanks had flooded, which may have been from the water used in the fire fighting or from damaged water ballast tanks and piping connections. The cargo tanks floated, which in turn caused the deck to bulge and distort in way of each cargo tank. The aft tank lifted about 300 mm and the vertical movement of the forward two tanks was slightly less than 300 mm. The deck distortion also put stresses and strains on the deck pipe work. *Aegis Diligence* was declared a constructive total loss in 1976.

Butanueve

Principle Particulars	
Length o.a.	153.20 m
Length b.p.	139.80 m
Breadth	21.26 m
Depth	12.35 m
Draught	8.52 m
LPG Capacity	14,103 m³
Engine	Manises-Sulzer 6RD76
Power	9,600 hp/7,061 kW
Service speed	16.5 knots

On 14 April 1969, Astilleros de Cadiz, Seville, delivered 14,103 m³ *Butanueve* to Butano SA.[4] With design help from Kværner, the vessel was of similar appearance and arrangement to 11,396 m³ *Havfrost*, built at Moss Værft, Norway, in 1966, with a cruiser stern, poop, trunk and forecastle decks with a bulbous bow and an additional forth aft cargo tank added, approximately half the size of the other tanks. Classed with Lloyd's Register of Shipping the ship was designed for LPG and ammonia at a minimum temperature of -48°C and a maximum pressure of 0.3 kg/cm².

Water ballast tanks were arranged in the inner bottom and double side hulls. The inner bottom and longitudinal inner side bulkheads formed the secondary barrier.

The four cascade reliquefaction plants and CO_2 room were housed on the port side of the trunk, above No. 3 cargo tank with an inert gas plant and hydraulic pump room on the starboard side. A cargo control room was arranged at centre at the trunk deck level.

Like *Havfrost*, the insulation was on the ship's inner hull rather than on the cargo tanks, with polyurethane foam on the inner bottom and rock wool on the longitudinal side bulkheads and transverse bulkheads.

In 1971 *Butanueve* was sold to Arcadia Reederei GmbH and renamed *Butanaval*. Between 1973 and 1986, as *Gambhira*, the vessel was operated within the P&O Group. In 1987 the vessel was sold to Bostock Co. Ltd. and under A/S Havtor Management was renamed *Havpil*. In 1991 the vessel was sold to Italian owners Simba Chartering Srl. and renamed *Lulligas*.

Butanueve was broken up as *Kapitan Luca* in 1997.

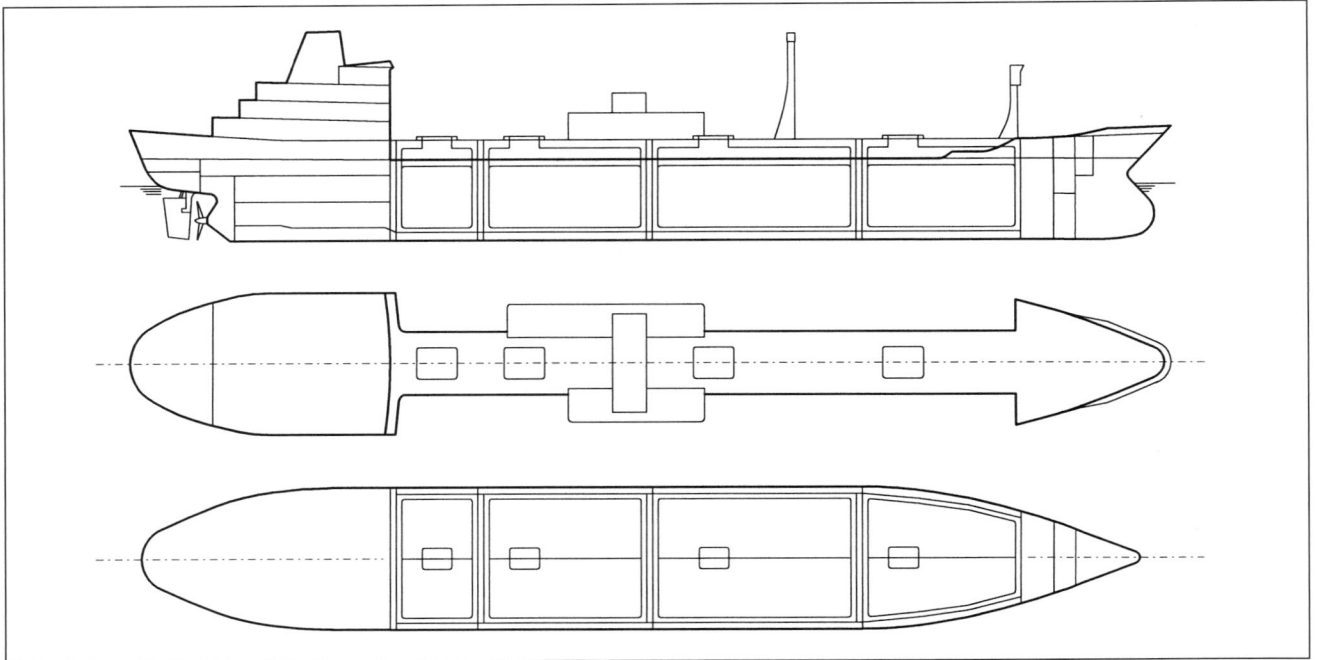

Figure 14-3 Outline Arrangement of *Butanueve*

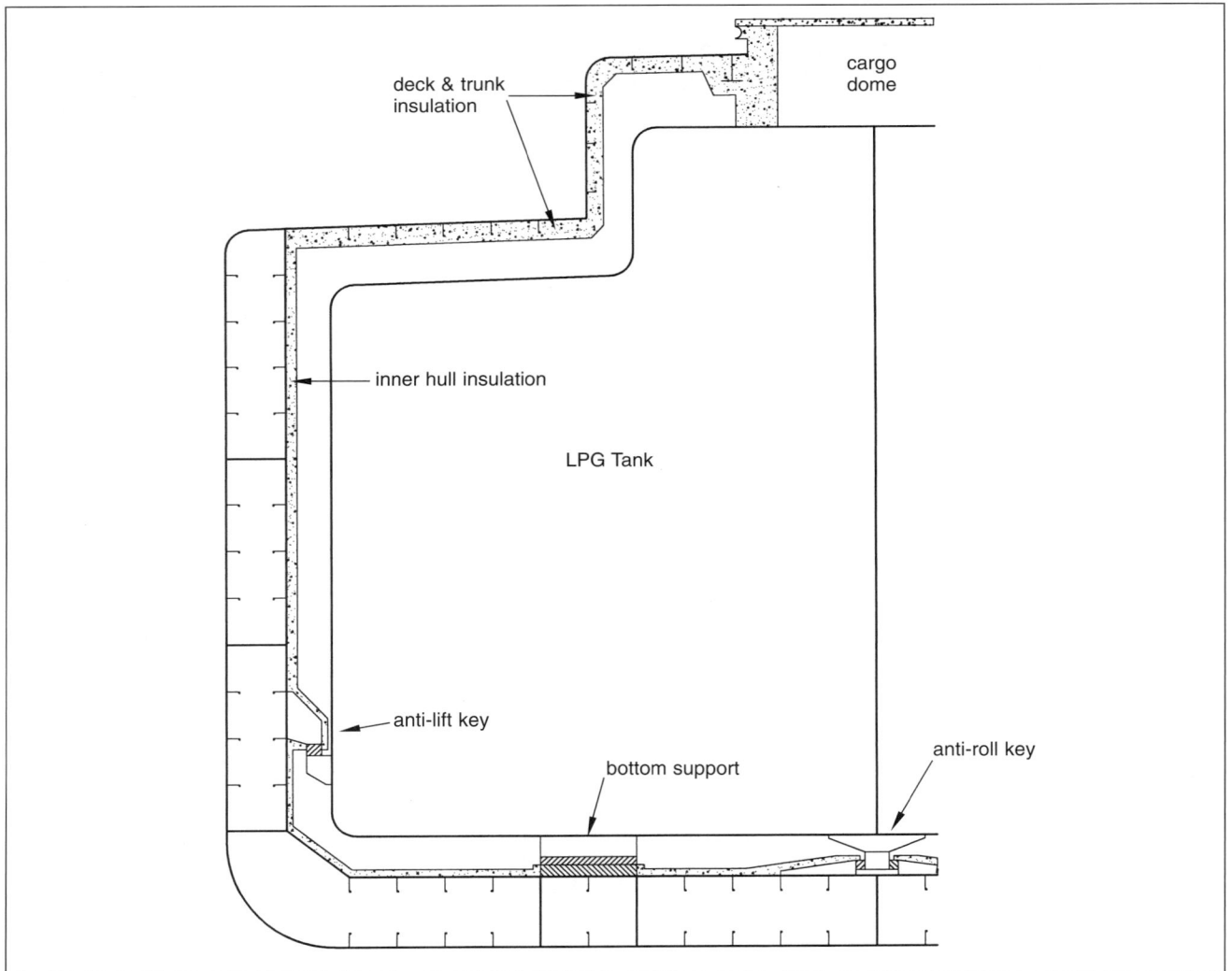

deck & trunk
insulation

cargo
dome

inner hull insulation

LPG Tank

anti-lift key

anti-roll key

bottom support

Figure 14-4 Midship Section of *Butanueve* showing Inner Hull Insulation and Tank Supports

Plate 14-1   *Gambhira*   P&O

22 January 1988 – Mistaken Identity

Havpil was attacked by Iranian gunboats at 0155 hours local time on 22 January 1988 off the port of Mina Saqr during the Iran/Iraq war.[5] An unfortunate case of the wrong target being chosen as the vessel had loaded propane at Jebel Ali, United Arab Emirates, and was bound for the Iranian port of Bandar Abbas. *Havpil* was hit by rocket propelled grenades in way of No. 3 starboard tank. The cargo tank was punctured and propane leaked from the open hole. There was no explosion or fire and no crew were injured.

The vessel under her own power headed for Dubai for a repair assessment and was at Dubai roads by daybreak. Port entry was refused due to the leaking propane and the ship moored 13 miles off Dubai, with tug/supply vessel *Nice Tango* assisting and a Wijsmuller Salvage BV team on board. The work began to transfer the propane remaining in No. 3 cargo tank to other cargo tanks. On 29 February, with propane transferred, the damaged spaces gas freed and the debris from the grenades removed from the cargo tank, the vessel was repaired and redelivered to the owners in a fully operable condition.

The press and media gave relatively brief reports of this event. However, the incident which lasted one week, did give a good demonstration of the professional skills and knowledge of the ship's officers, crew and salvage team. In addition, the propane leaking from the cargo tank into the void space around the cargo tank, highlighted the structural integrity built into LPG carriers, where the secondary barrier proved its worth.

5 July 1993 – Libyan Lightering.

Lulligas grounded one mile off Marsa el Brega, Libya, on 5 July 1993 after loading 9,300 tonnes of anhydrous ammonia for Spain.[6] The pilot had disembarked prior to the grounding. The vessel owned by Simba Chartering Srl. grounded on soft limestone, and tugs were initially able to move the vessel five metres but without the vessel floating free. Smit Tak BV were contracted to render services to the vessel on the evening of 6 July. *Lulligas* was re-floated at 1600 hours on 19 July, after fully pressurised 1,424 m³ *Bubugas*, also from the Simba fleet, had taken on board 755 tonnes of ammonia, in a lightering operation. A diving survey on 20 July found no significant damage and the next day *Lulligas* left the Libyan coast to arrive at Sagunto on 26 July.

[1] Hautefeuille, Roland, with Clayton, Richard, *Gas Pioneers,* Paris, 1998.
[2] Bruggen, van Coosje, *Frank O. Gehry: Guggenheim Museum Bilbao,* Guggenheim Museum Publications.
[3] Lloyd's Weekly Casualty Reports, *Aegis Diligence,* November/December 1975.
[4] Shipbuilding & Shipping Record, *Butanueve, Astilleros de Cadiz Launch an LPG Carrier,* 26 April 1968.
[5] Lloyd's List Casualty Reports, *Havpil,* January/February 1988.
[6] Lloyd's List Casualty Reports, *Lulligas,* July/August 1993.

Chapter 15

Single FRLPG Carrier from Kiel

The Kiel shipyard of Howaldswerke-Deutsche Werft AG (HDW) in northern Germany has a reputation for the design and completion of innovative ships. Impressive firsts have included the submarine *Brandtaucher* and the nuclear powered cargo ship *Otto Hahn*. Research and development studies have covered both membrane and spherical tank type LNG carrier designs as well as hydrogen carriers. In 1977 the yard delivered two 125,000 m³ LNG carriers, *Golar Freeze* for Gotaas-Larsen Limited and *Höegh Gandria* for Leif Höegh & Company A/S.

Roland

Principle Particulars	
Length o.a.	166.18 m
Length b.p.	152.30 m
Breadth	22.60 m
Depth	14.00 m
Draught	9.22 m
LPG Capacity	18,282 m³
Engine	MAN K6Z78/155
Power	9,700 hp/7,134 kW
Service speed	16.5 knots

The only fully refrigerated LPG /NH$_3$ carrier built at Kiel was 18,282 m³ *Roland*. Owned by Ångfartygs A/B of Tirfing, Sweden, the vessel was delivered on 27 August 1968. Classed with American Bureau of Shipping and the requirements of the US Coast Guard, the ship was arranged with a cruiser stern, poop, trunk and forecastle decks, a bow thruster and a flared stem. The three aft cargo tanks each had a capacity of about 5,500 m³. A smaller fourth cargo tank of 1,500 m³ was fitted forward. Transverse cofferdam were fitted between each cargo tank. The ice strengthened vessel was designed for a minimum temperature of -51°C and a maximum pressure of 0.3 kg/cm².

Water ballast tanks were arranged in the inner bottom and double side hull. The inner bottom and longitudinal inner side bulkheads formed the secondary barrier. The insulation for the cargo tanks was on the inner bottom, on the inner side hull, under the main deck and trunk deck and on the transverse cofferdam bulkheads. Later in service the void spaces were filled with loose perlite insulation.

Two deep-well cargo pumps were fitted in each tank with the six aft pumps, each having a capacity of 270 m³/hr and the forward pair having a capacity of 70 m³/hr. In addition a booster pump was fitted. LGA Gastechnik GmbH engineered the gas installations and three reliquefaction plants were fitted. Stal Refrigeration AB designed and supplied the refrigeration plants. The reliquefaction and refrigeration plants were housed on the port side of the trunk above No. 3 cargo tank, with inert gas storage, CO$_2$ and fan rooms on the starboard side. The cargo manifolds and a cargo control room were arranged at centre at the trunk deck level. Two cylindrical pressurised changeover tanks were fitted on the main deck between Nos. 3 and 4 cargo tanks. An inert gas plant was located in the forecastle.

Roland was broken up as *Andesgas* in 1998.

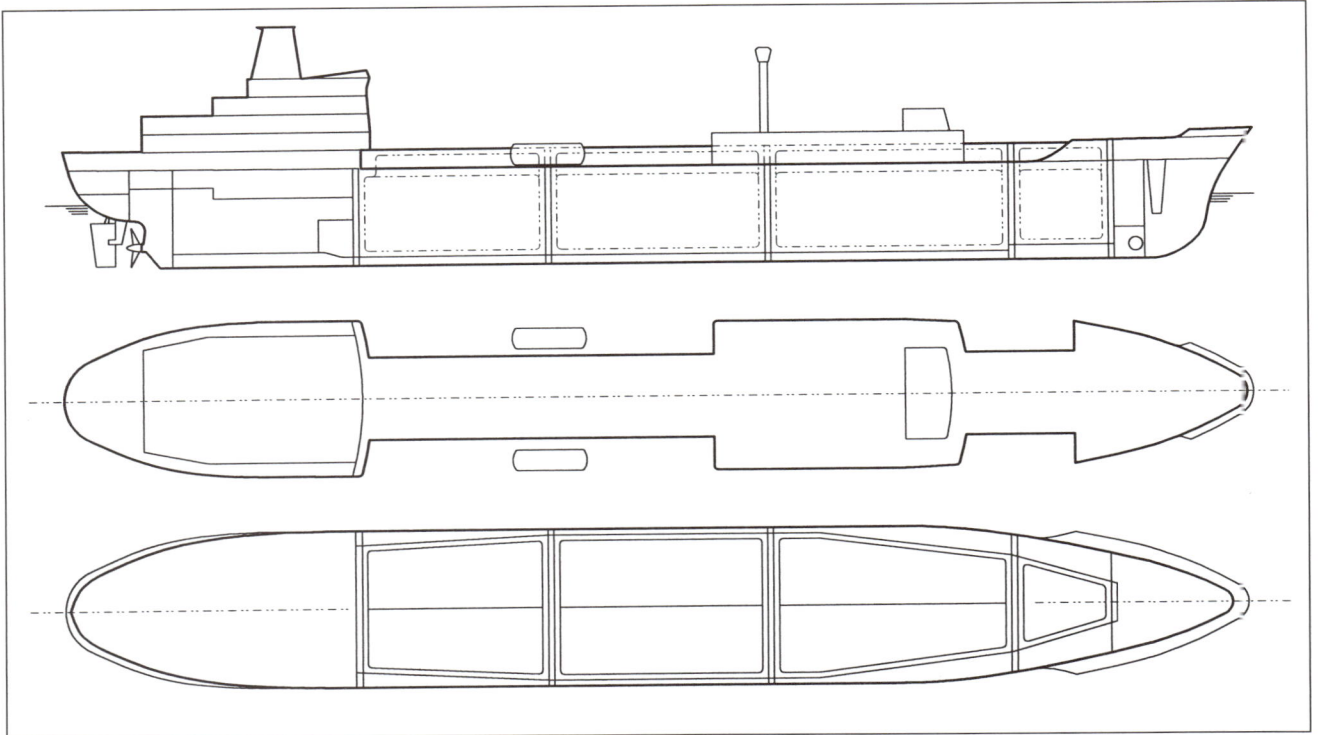

Figure 15-1 Outline Arrangement of *Roland*

Plate 15-1   Stal Reliquefaction plant   York Refrigeration

Plate 15-2　　　　Painting of *Roland* by marine artist Georg Holm　　　York Refrigeration

Chapter 16

Conversions and Combined Carriers from the USA

Ship conversions for the carriage of LNG and pressurised LPG, the construction of combined LPG/NH_3/oil/chemical carriers and LNG carriers have been completed by USA shipyards. The LPG carrier of historical significance was 6,050 m^3 *Natalie O Warren,* converted from C1 type dry cargo ship *Cape Diamond* in 1947, by Bethlehem Steel Shipyards in Beaumont, Texas. Similar conversions with fully pressurised tanks were to follow *Natalie O Warren*. In 1958, Alabama Drydock & Shipbuilding Co., of Mobile, Alabama, converted the general cargo ship *Normarti* into the 5,125 m^3 LNG carrier *Methane Pioneer*. No purpose built fully refrigerated LPG carriers have been constructed in the USA. However, Todd Shipyards Corporation of San Pedro, California, in 1978 did construct a new forebody with prismatic cargo tanks for the conversion of an oil tanker *Sister Katingo* into the FRLPG carrier 31,704 m^3 *Cornucopia*.

Marine Eagle

Principle Particulars	
Length o.a.	187.42 m
Length b.p.	178.52 m
Breadth	24.39 m
Depth	14.41 m
Draught	10.33 m
NH_3 Capacity	12,854 m^3
Engine	Westinghouse Electric
Power	7,240 hp/5,325 kW
Service speed	14.8 knots

In 1969, Virginia shipbuilders and repairers Newport News converted T2-SE-A1 type tanker, *Parkersburg*, into a combined anhydrous ammonia/methanol carrier, *Marine Eagle*. The T2 tanker, as *Fort Conwallis*, was originally delivered from Sun Shipbuilding and Dry Dock Company, Chester, Pennsylvania, in April 1944. Newport News built a new cargo section and forward end with a bow thruster, which was joined to the T2 tanker's stern machinery section.

The converted vessel, *Marine Eagle*, classed with the American Bureau of Shipping was delivered on 1 April 1969 to E I du Pont de Nemours and Company, to be managed by Marine Transport Lines Inc. The ship was arranged with six wing tanks, centre tanks Nos. 2 & 5, and a forward deep tank for methanol, with self-supporting tanks for ammonia fitted in Nos. 1, 3, 4 and 6 centre spaces. The total cargo capacities were 18,254 m^3 for methanol and 12,854 m^3 for ammonia.

The NH_3 cargo tanks were designed for a minimum temperature of -33°C, with a single deep-well pump fitted in each tank. An inner bottom for water ballast was fitted throughout the cargo area.

Marine Eagle was broken up in 1985.

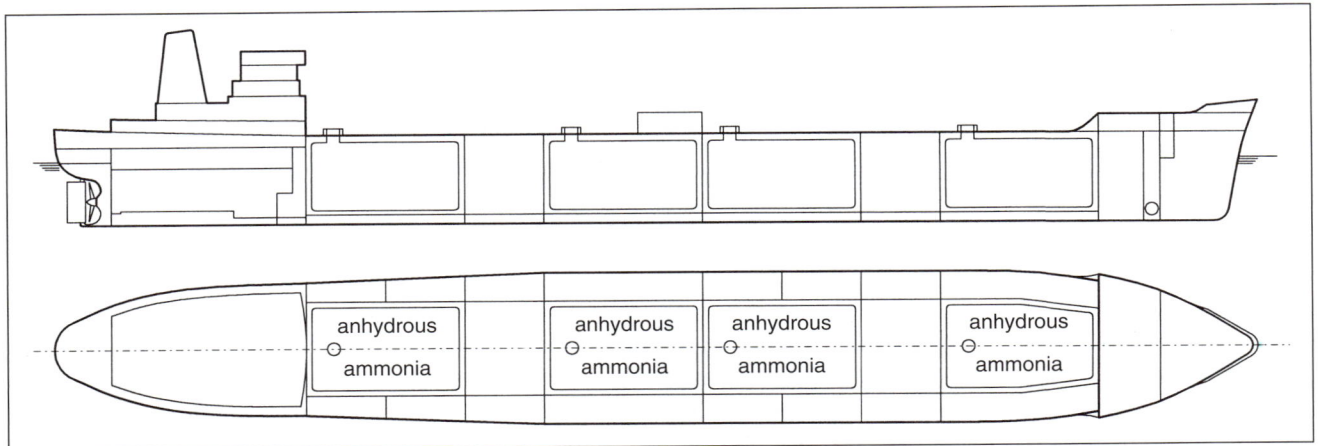

Figure 16-1 Outline Arrangement of *Marine Eagle*

Puerto Rican

Principle Particulars	
Length o.a.	201.27 m
Length b.p.	192.72 m
Breadth	27.46 m
Depth	13.92 m
Draught	11.17 m
LPG Capacity	12,320 m³
Engine	General Electric
Power	15,000 hp/11,032 kW
Service speed	16.5 knots

A unique chemical tanker, *Puerto Rican*, with two insulated independent prismatic cargo tanks, was built at the Sparrows Point, shipyard of Bethlehem Steel Corp., Maryland.[1] The ship was an adaptation of a standard 37,000 deadweight ton oil tanker design, and was handed over to PPG Industries on 15 December 1971. PPG Industries, a leading USA chemical company, was founded in 1883 as the Pittsburgh Plate Glass Company. The new ship was operated by Hendy International Company to carry a variety of chemical products from PPG facilities at Guayanilla, Pañuelas and other Puerto Rican ports, to destinations on the Gulf coast and the east coast of the USA.

Puerto Rican was classed with American Bureau of Shipping with the type description as Chemical and Independent Tank Carrier. The ship had two steel independent centre tanks, numbered 3 and 6 (P&S), each designed for the carriage of butadiene and vinyl chloride monomer (VCM) at a minimum temperature of -14°C, a maximum pressure of 0.28 kg/cm² and a maximum specific gravity of 0.97. The tanks had a centreline bulkhead and were insulated externally with sprayed polyurethane. Two 193 m³/hr J C Carter electric submerged pumps were fitted in each cargo tank. A further 23 centre and wing tanks, some of stainless steel construction, were arranged for other chemical cargoes.

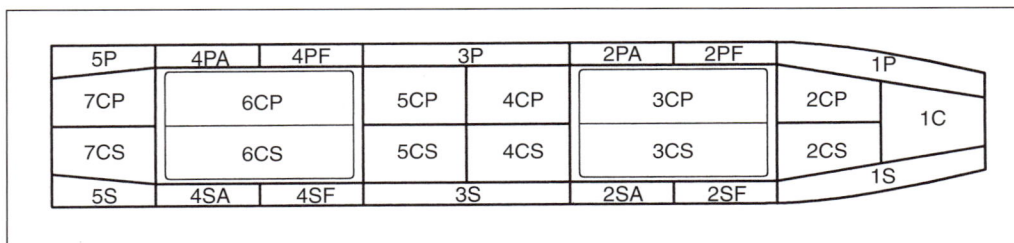

Figure 16-2 Schematic Arrangement of Cargo Tanks of *Puerto Rican*

31 October 1984 – Fatal Chemical Explosions

Puerto Rican left San Francisco, California, loaded with refined petroleum products and chemicals and some caustic soda heel from a previous voyage, bound for Louisiana via the Panama Canal. [2, 3] At approximately 0324 hours local time on 31 October 1984, with the ship 8.5 miles west of the Golden Gate Bridge, a fire and explosions occurred in way of the void space around No. 6 independent tank and the adjacent wing tanks.

At the time of the explosions, a pilot, the third officer and an able seaman were standing on the port side waiting for a pilot boat to come alongside. All three men were thrown overboard. The able seaman was killed and the pilot and third officer were recovered from the water with serious injuries. The deck area over No. 6 tank and the adjacent wing tanks was lifted and landed inverted on the deck immediately forward of its original position. The remaining 26 people onboard abandoned ship safely within about 2 hours.

The fire was extinguished early in the evening of 1 November by salvage teams. When the explosion occurred, the independent cargo tanks were not in use, with the cargo pumps removed. No cargo had been carried in the two independent tanks for approximately five years.

On 3 November, when being towed seaward, the stern section separated from the forebody at about mid-length of No. 6 tank and sank. The forebody was taken in tow to San Francisco, where the remaining cargo was offloaded. During this tow, the empty independent cargo tank floated free, but was recovered and later examined at a ship repair yard at Oakland, California. With permission granted to sell the vessel outside the United States, the forebody under tow arrived on 17 June 1985 at Kaohsiung, Taiwan, for scrapping.

The USCG concluded, that the exact cause of the explosion could not be established, but that the most probable cause was due to caustic soda cargo leaking to the void space around No. 6 cargo tank, which reacted with the zinc coatings in the void space and produced hydrogen gas which ignited.

Media reports of this incident used LPG carrier headlines, when in actual fact there was no LPG on board *Puerto Rican*.

Cornucopia

Principle Particulars

Length o.a.	191.40 m
Length b.p.	179.84 m
Breadth	27.44 m
Depth	16.39 m
Draught	9.47 m
LPG Capacity	31,704 m³
Engine	Bethlehem Steel
Power	15,000 hp/11,032 kW
Service speed	16 knots

For some years Collier Carbon & Chemical Corporation had been using a 1969 built sea-going barge to transport anhydrous ammonia from their production plant at Kenai, Alaska, to Sacramento, California. Unfortunately, the barge sank and the company placed an order in August 1975 for a replacement vessel, with Todd Shipyards Corporation of San Pedro, California. The order resulted in loose perlite being used by a shipyard to insulate shipboard LPG tanks for the first time outside France. [4]

The complex project made use of an existing oil tanker's aft end, which was joined to a new forebody constructed by Todd Shipyards. Technigaz, Paris, developed the design for the four prismatic cargo tanks and the gas handling systems. Keygaz, a company formed by American Technigaz and Keystone Shipping, acted as owners' representatives during the design and construction. The refurbished aft end of *Sister Katingo*, a 34,956 tons deadweight tanker built by Bethlehem Pacific Coast Steel Company of San Francisco in 1958, was used with a new superstructure added. When delivered in 1978 to Union Oil Company of California, *Cornucopia* was classed with American Bureau of Shipping for the carriage of LPG and NH_3.

Cornucopia was broken up in 2002.

Plate 16-1   *Cornucopia*   Todd Shipyards

---

[1] Bethlehem Steel Corporation, *Launching Programme S.S. Puerto Rican,* 19 March 1971.
[2] Lloyd's List Casualty Reports, *Puerto Rican,* November 1984/June 1985.
[3] United States Coast Guard, *Marine Casualty Report No. USCG 16732/0003 HQS 84 Tankship Puerto Rican,* 5 June 1985.
[4] Marine Engineering Log, *L.A. Metropolitan Section Hears Paper on Construction of LPG Vessel,* August 1976.

Chapter 17

Semi-Membrane *Kasmet* from Kawasaki

Kawasaki Heavy Industries first began their research and development of gas carriers in 1956 in a joint study with Gulf Oil Corporation, USA. The first gas carrier built by Kawasaki, *Bridgestone Maru No. 5*, was delivered in 1969. Since then Kawasaki have delivered an impressive quantity of gas ship types, including LPG carriers with semi-membrane and prismatic tanks, ethylene carriers and both small and large Kværner LNG carriers with spherical tanks.

Bridgestone Maru No. 5

Principle Particulars	
Length o.a.	210.50 m
Length b.p.	200.00 m
Breadth	32.50 m
Depth	21.80 m
Draught	12.20 m
LPG Capacity	72,344 m³
Engine	Kawasaki-MAN K8Z 78/155E
Power	14,000 hp/10,297 kW
Service speed	14.75 knots

Gas pioneer and technical innovator Katsuro Yamamoto of Bridgestone Liquefied Gas Co. Ltd., was the driving force behind the first fully refrigerated LPG carrier to be built by Kawasaki Heavy Industries in 1969.[1, 2, 3] In a quest for a less expensive newbuilding than the previous three Bridgestone fully refrigerated LPG carriers, the company developed their own semi-membrane cargo tank design which they described perfectly as "…like a cube with all the edges rounded."

KASMET is an acronym for Kawasaki Semi-Membrane Tank type and was the name chosen for the unique design developed by Bridgestone Liquefied Gas Co. Ltd. and Kawasaki Heavy Industries.[4] The first *Kasmet* ship, 72,344 m³ *Bridgestone Maru No. 5*, was delivered on 13 September 1969 to Showa Kaiun K.K., from the Kobe yard of Kawasaki.

The semi-membrane design was the result of earlier work by Bridgestone, who in 1966 ordered an experimental 895 m³ coastal LPG carrier, *Bridgestone Maru No. 101* with double corrugated membrane tanks. In 1968/1969 they also ordered 785 m³ *Ethylene Daystar* and 1,188 m³ *Ethylene Dayspring*, each with semi-membrane aluminium tanks. Each of these three vessels were constructed at shipyards of Sumitomo Heavy Industries Ltd.

Classed with Nippon Kaiji Kyokai, *Bridgestone Maru No. 5* was arranged with both integral tanks for butane at -10°C and semi-membrane tanks for propane at -46°C. Nos. 1 and 5 cargo tanks were dedicated butane tanks with a total capacity of 31,583 m³. Nos. 2 – 4 cargo tanks, with a total capacity of 40,761 m³, were for propane. The advantage of this combined arrangement is clearly shown by the ratio of cargo tanks capacity compared with the cubic dimensions of the ship's hull. This capacity co-efficient, a good benchmark when comparing gas ship designs, is obtained by dividing the total cargo capacity by the ship's moulded dimensions, as follows:

C_C = Total cargo capacity/Length between perpendiculars x Breadth x Depth

Where $_C$ = cargo.

For *Bridgestone Maru No. 5*, the capacity co-efficient C_C was 0.511. By comparison, C_C for *Bridgestone Maru* was 0.395 and for *Bridgestone Maru II* it was 0.402.

The semi-membrane tanks were arranged in pairs and protected from grounding or collision with a double bottom and double side hull. Transverse cofferdam bulkheads were fitted between each cargo tank and a centreline cofferdam separated the tanks on each side of the ship. The prismatic cargo tanks had six flat surfaces, ¼ cylindrical edges and ⅛ spherical corners. The 8 mm thick membrane was constructed with fine grain aluminium killed steel and was welded from both sides with each weld 100% tested by radiography. The membrane was only fixed to the hull at the dome with the top part of the membrane held in place by supports, which allow horizontal movement but no vertical movement. The cargo load was not taken by the membrane, but was transferred to the inner hull. Wooden joists, secured with stud bolts and glue were fitted in the inner hull, with polyurethane foam fitted between the joists to provide the insulation. Saddle supports were arranged at the curved bottom corners.

At the time of construction, *Bridgestone Maru No. 5* was considered as a prototype for a proposed LNG carrier design, but the idea of a semi-membrane LNG design did not materialise into any firm orders.

Bridgestone Maru No. 5 was broken up in 1985.

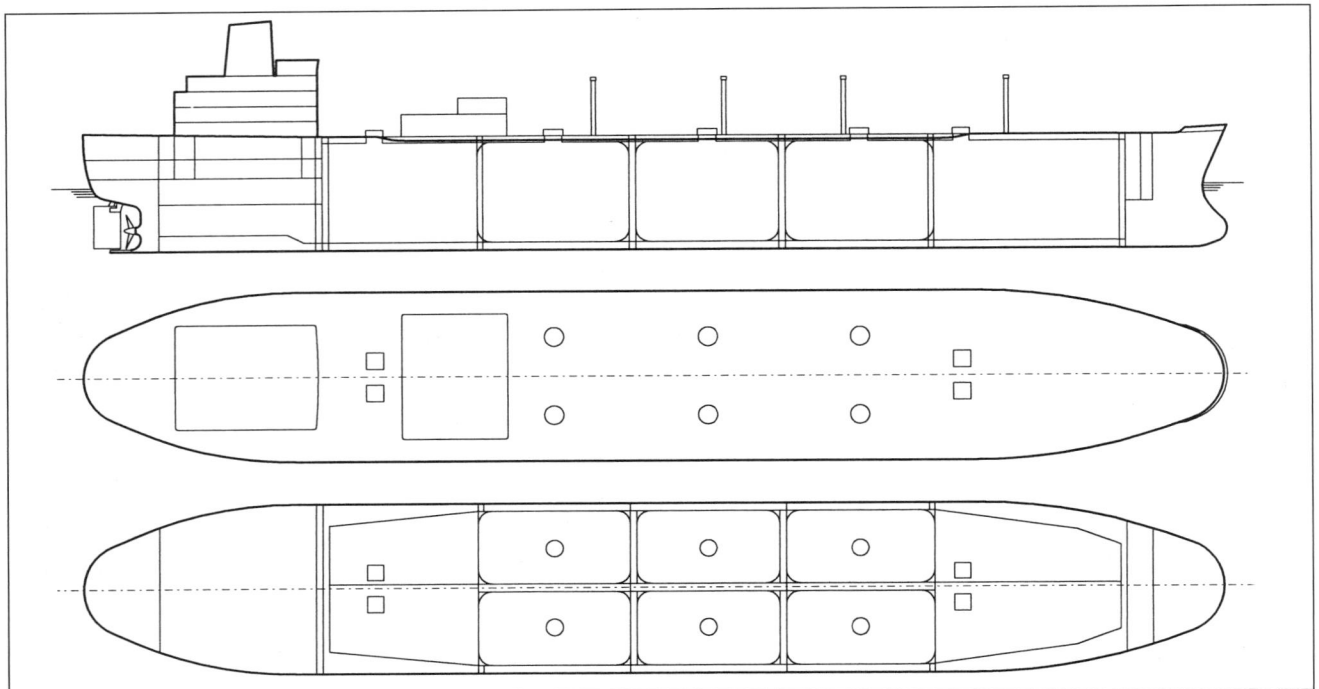

Figure 17-1 Outline Arrangement of *Bridgestone Maru No. 5*

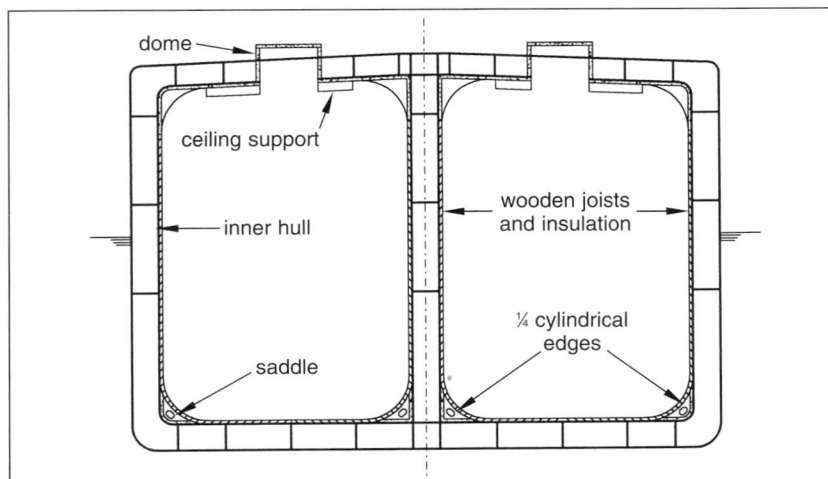

Figure 17-2 Midship Section of *Bridgestone Maru No. 5* showing Semi-membrane Tanks

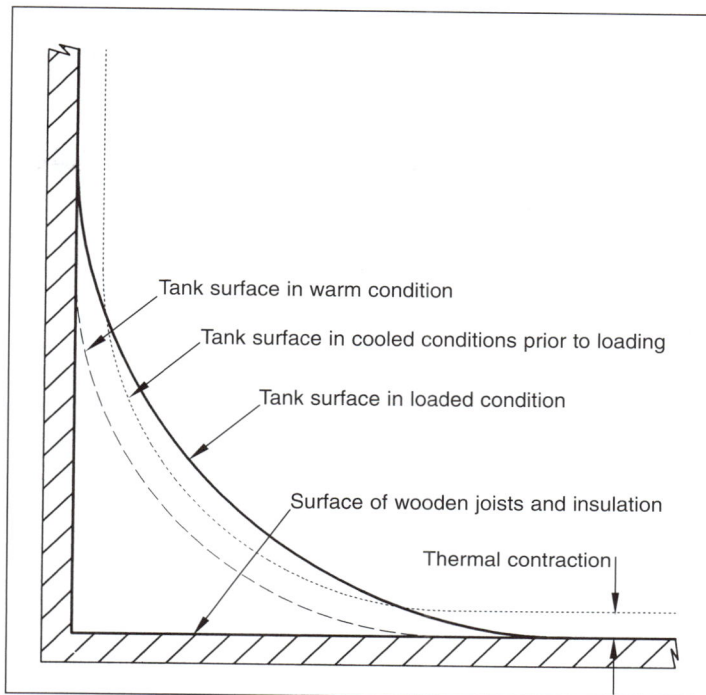

Figure 17-3 *Bridgestone Maru No. 5* – Corner Detail

Labels in figure:
- Tank surface in warm condition
- Tank surface in cooled conditions prior to loading
- Tank surface in loaded condition
- Surface of wooden joists and insulation
- Thermal contraction

Autumn 1968 – Grounding Test

The concept of the semi-membrane system was quickly put to the test when shortly after completion in 1968, *Bridgestone Maru No. 5* ran aground at full speed in the Persian Gulf. 70% of the vessel's hull was grounded with extensive bottom damage in way of the cargo tanks. The semi-membrane cargo tanks remained intact.

The second and third ships of the *Kasmet* series, with the same overall hull dimensions as *Bridgestone Maru No. 5*, were 74,477 m³ *World Bridgestone*, delivered to Credo Shipping on 30 April 1971 and 74,579 m³ *Ogden Bridgestone*, delivered to Ogden Orinoco Transport on 15 February 1973. Compared with *Bridgestone Maru No. 5*, the butane capacity was increased to 33,723 m³ and two external fuel oil tanks were added on the main deck above No. 1 cargo tanks.[5]

World Bridgestone was sold for demolition in 2003 as *Sea Stone*.

Ogden Bridgestone was sold to Chinese breakers in 2002 as *Yuan Xing*.

Plate 17-1   *World Bridgestone*   Kawasaki

Plate 17-2   *Ogden Bridgestone*   Kawasaki

Sun River

Principle Particulars	
Length o.a.	224.00 m
Length b.p.	213.00 m
Breadth	32.50 m
Depth	21.80 m
Draught	11.93 m
LPG Capacity	75,958 m³
Engine	Kawasaki-MAN K7SZ 90/160
Power	20,300 hp/14,931 kW
Service speed	16.2 knots

The fourth *Kasmet* ship was 75,958 m³ *Sun River*. The ship was delivered to Kawasaki Kisen Kaisha Ltd., (K-Line) and Nippon Kisen Kaisha Ltd., (NKK), on 10 September 1974, with No. 1 integral tanks for 15,188 m³ of butane and Nos. 2 – 5 semi-membrane tanks for 60,770 m³ of propane.[6,7] The additional capacity compared to *Bridgestone Maru No. 5* was obtained by increasing the ship's length b.p. by 13.00 m to 213.00 m. A Kawasaki-Strommen nozzle propeller was a new feature fitted on this ship.

World Concord

Principle Particulars	
Length o.a.	224.00 m
Length b.p.	213.00 m
Breadth	32.50 m
Depth	21.80 m
Draught	12.53 m
LPG Capacity	80,026 m³
Engine	Kawasaki-MAN K7SZ 90/160
Power	20,300 hp/14,931 kW
Service speed	16.2 knots

The largest *Kasmet* ship to be built was 80,026 m³ *World Concord* and was the first of three similar vessels for affiliated companies of World-Wide (Shipping) Ltd. *World Concord* was delivered to Liberian Concord Transports Inc., on 3 June 1976, *World Creation* was delivered to Liberian Asteroid Transports Inc., on 28 Dec 1977 and *World Vigour* was delivered to Liberian Viscount Transports Inc., on 28 June 1977. Like *Bridgestone Maru No. 5* the three World-Wide (Shipping) Ltd. ships were arranged with Nos. 1 and 5 integral tanks for butane and Nos. 2 – 4 semi-membrane tanks for propane. Three cascade reliquefaction plants were fitted.

In 1978, Kawasaki Heavy Industries and Bridgestone Liquefied Gas Co. Ltd. received the prestigious Okochi Memorial Prize, which is awarded for new inventions and technology achievement, as described in the paper *Development and Production of an LPG Carrier using Semi-Membrane System*.[8]

Plate 17-3   *World Concord*   Kawasaki

Clean River

Principle Particulars	
Length o.a.	215.00 m
Length b.p.	204.00 m
Breadth	34.00 m
Depth	23.00 m
Draught	12.03 m
LPG Capacity	76,313 m³
Engine	Kawasaki-MAN 14V 52/55A
Power	14,770 hp/10,863 kW
Service speed	16.7 knots

The eighth and final ship of the Kasmet series, all of which were built at the Kobe works, was 76,313 m³ *Clean River*, which was delivered on 30 March 1983 to Kawasaki Kisen Kaisha Ltd., (K-Line). The ship was described by the shipbuilders as a "Super Energy-Saving LPG Carrier".[9, 10, 11] Between building *World Vigour* in 1977 and *Clean River* in 1983, the Sakaide works of Kawasaki built three Kværner Moss LNG carriers, 126,000 m³ *Golar Spirit*, which was the first LNG carrier to be built in Japan, 125,000 m³ *Bishu Maru* and *Kotowaka Maru*.

Compared with the previous *Kasmet* ships, the design of *Clean River* incorporated some noteworthy structural and energy saving features. The ship was the first to be approved with type B semi-membrane tanks as per the IMO Gas Carrier Code. The beam was increased to 34.00 m from 32.50 m and the draught reduced to 12.03 m, with Nos. 1 & 5 integral tanks for 18,508 m³ of butane and Nos. 2 – 4 semi-membrane tanks for 57,805 m³ of propane.

Structural energy saving features included a concave deck edge and side hull in way of No. 1 integral tanks to improve water and air flow to the forward lines, and a near hexagonal shaped deckhouse, in plan view, to reduce the wind resistance.

Propulsion energy savings were provided by the first production version of the Kawasaki Super-Economical (KSE) propulsion plant Mark III. The plant utilised a medium speed diesel engine driving a slow turning controllable pitch propeller through a reduction gearbox and a rudder bulb with radial fins fitted at the leading edge of the rudder.

An innovative electrical power plant arrangement was provided, to supply the large amount of electricity required by the LPG reliquefaction plants when the ship was at sea. Power was supplied by a large capacity shaft generator, which eliminated the need for the conventional parallel operation of the diesel generators. In addition, the system also recovered as much gas energy as possible by the exhaust gas boiler to be used as auxiliary propulsive power via the steam turbine. The system was based on the use of low-grade fuel oil which contributed to reduced running costs.

The shipbuilders claimed that with all of the energy saving features on *Clean River*, the resulting reduction in fuel consumption and running costs was in the order of 34% energy saving, when compared to other similar sized LPG carriers.

Plate 17-4   *Clean River*   Kawasaki

Pacific Harmony

Principle Particulars	
Length o.a.	224.05 m
Length b.p.	212.00 m
Breadth	36.00 m
Depth	20.70 m
Draught	11.02 m
LPG Capacity	75,208 m³
Engine	Kawasaki-MAN B&W 5S70MCE
Power	12,400 hp/9,120 kW
Service speed	16 knots

Seven years on from building the last *Kasmet* semi-membrane ship, *Clean River,* Kawasaki delivered 75,208 m³ *Pacific Harmony* as the lead ship of a series of eight similar LPG carriers with four independent IMO type A cargo tanks of Kawasaki's own design.[12, 13] The 75,000 m³ series was equally shared between Kawasaki's Kobe and Sakaide works, with four ships from each yard. *Pacific Harmony* was handed over to her owners Kumiai Senpaku Company Ltd., on 4 July 1990, from the Sakaide works.

Pacific Harmony was arranged with a raked transom stern, a lower aft deck, a flush main deck from the aft deckhouse to the stem and a bulbous bow. A combined engine and cargo control room was arranged on the second deck in the accommodation, and a reliquefaction house was located on the main deck above No. 3 cargo tank. Four reliquefaction plant were fitted. Two 600 m³/hr Shinko submerged pumps were fitted at the aft part of each cargo tank. One aspect which made this vessel different from the *Kasmet* series was that all four independent cargo tanks were designed for the carriage of propane or butane with no dedicated butane tanks.

The series were all classed with Nippon Kaiji Kyokai as Tankers for Liquefied Gases as a type 2G ships, with a minimum cargo temperature of -45°C and a maximum cargo pressure of 0.25 kg./cm². The prismatic cargo tanks were insulated externally with polyurethane and water ballast was carried in the double bottom with lower wing tanks and under deck upper wing tank. As on *Clean River* a rudder bulb with radial fins was fitted.

The Sakaide works also delivered to Kumiai Senpaku Company Ltd., the second and sixth ship of the 75,000m³ series as *Crystal Mermaid* on 21 December 1990 and *Co-op Akebono* on 23 February 1993 as well as the third ship *Tsaugaru Gloria* on 23 July 1991 for Clio Marine Inc.

The four Kobe built ships were; *Aries Duo* delivered to Holy Rosette Marine SA on 25 September 1992, *Noto Gloria* delivered to Gas Glora Shipping Inc. on 26 February 1992, *Musashi Gloria* delivered to Navix Line Ltd. on 25 March 1993 and *J A Sunshine* delivered to Y K Kumiai Kosan in March 1994.

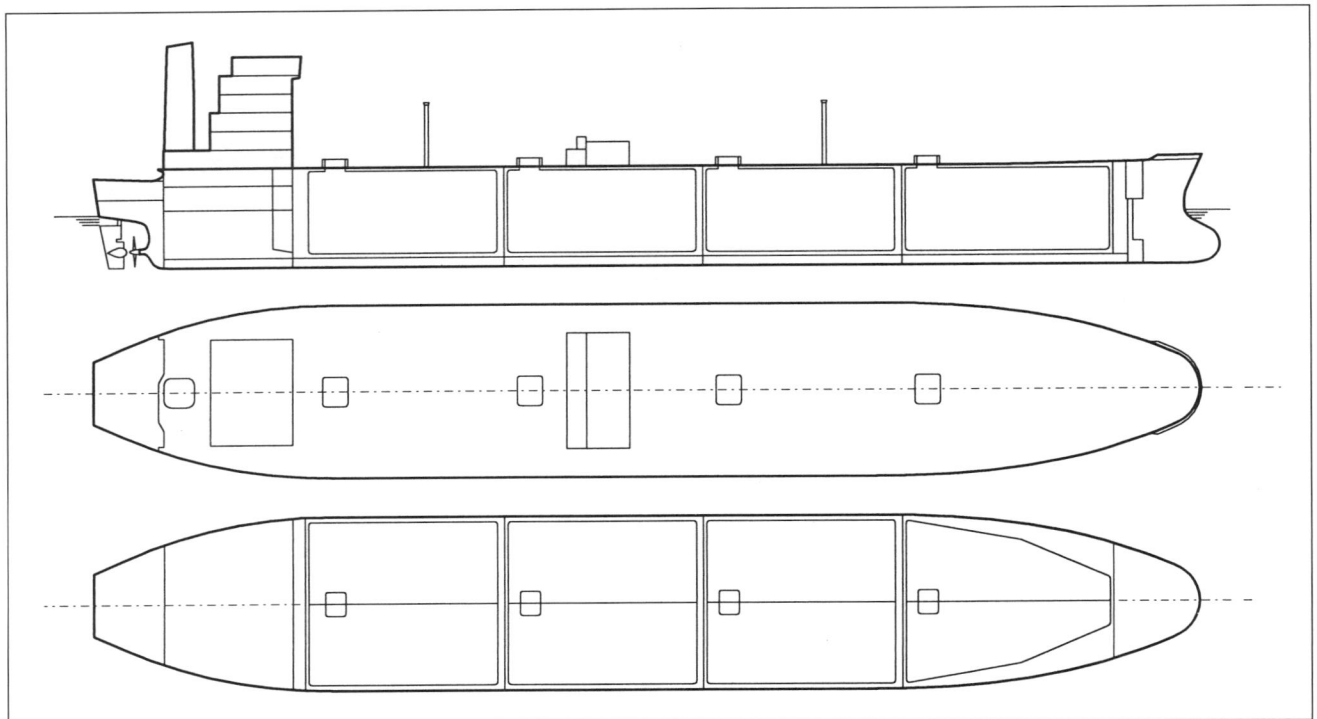

Figure 17-4 Outline Arrangement of *Pacific Harmony*

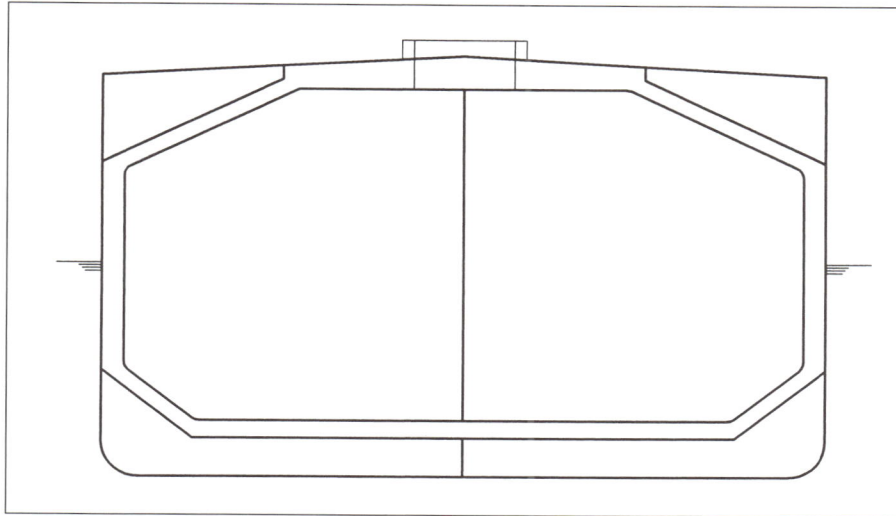

Figure 17-5 Midship Section of *Pacific Harmony*

Plate 17-5   *Pacific Harmony*   Kawasaki

Hedda

Principle Particulars	
Length o.a.	170.00 m
Length b.p.	160.00 m
Breadth	27.36 m
Depth	18.20 m
Draught	12.57 m
LPG Capacity	34,765 m^3
Engine	Kawasaki-MAN B&W 5S60MC
Power	10,800 hp/7,943 kW
Service speed	16.0 knots

Delivered on 8 July 1993, *Hedda* was the first of two 34,765 m³ multi-purpose LPG carriers constructed at the Kobe works for Norwegian owners Kværner A/S.[14] The ships were classed with Det Norse Veritas for the carriage of anhydrous ammonia, butane, butylene, propane, propylene and VCM (80% filling), with a minimum temperature of -48°C, a maximum pressure of 0.25 kg/cm² and a maximum specific gravity of 0.68. The ships were arranged with a transom stern with poop ceck, a flush main deck from the aft deckhouse to the stem, three prismatic cargo tanks below the main deck, a bow thruster and a bulbous bow. The cargo tank section was a similar but smaller version of the Kawasaki 75,000 m³ series, with a double bottom and lower and upper wing tanks for water ballast and the side hull forming the secondary barrier.

Three direct reliquefaction plants were fitted. Two 440 m³/hr deep-well pumps were fitted in each cargo tank and 200 m³ and 100 m³ pressurised deck tanks for change of cargo were fitted on the main deck forward. Similar to the 75,000 m³ series, a combined engine and cargo control room was arranged in the accommodation spaces and a reliquefaction house was located on the main deck above No. 3 cargo tank.

The second ship *Helga* was delivered from the Kobe works on 29 March 1994.

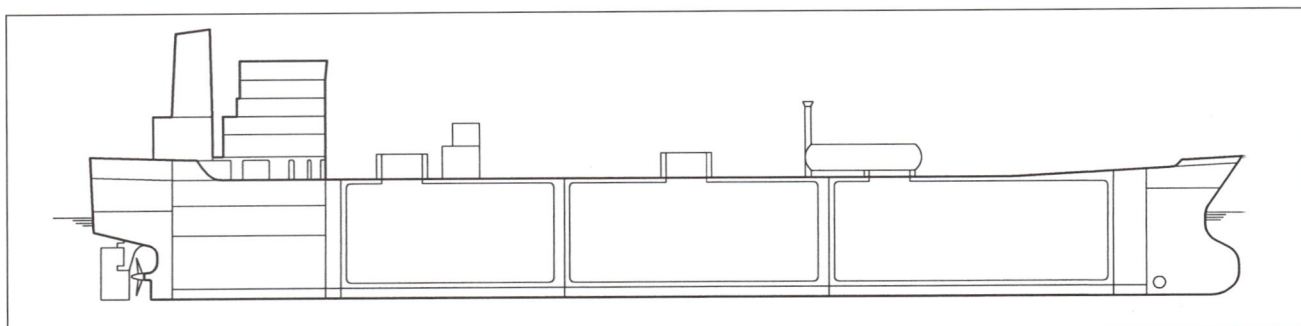

Figure 17-6 Profile of *Hedda*

Plate 17-6   Launch of *Hedda*   Kawasaki

Plate 17-7   *Helga*   Kawasaki

Plate 17-8   Inert gas plant for *Helga*   Hamworthy KSE

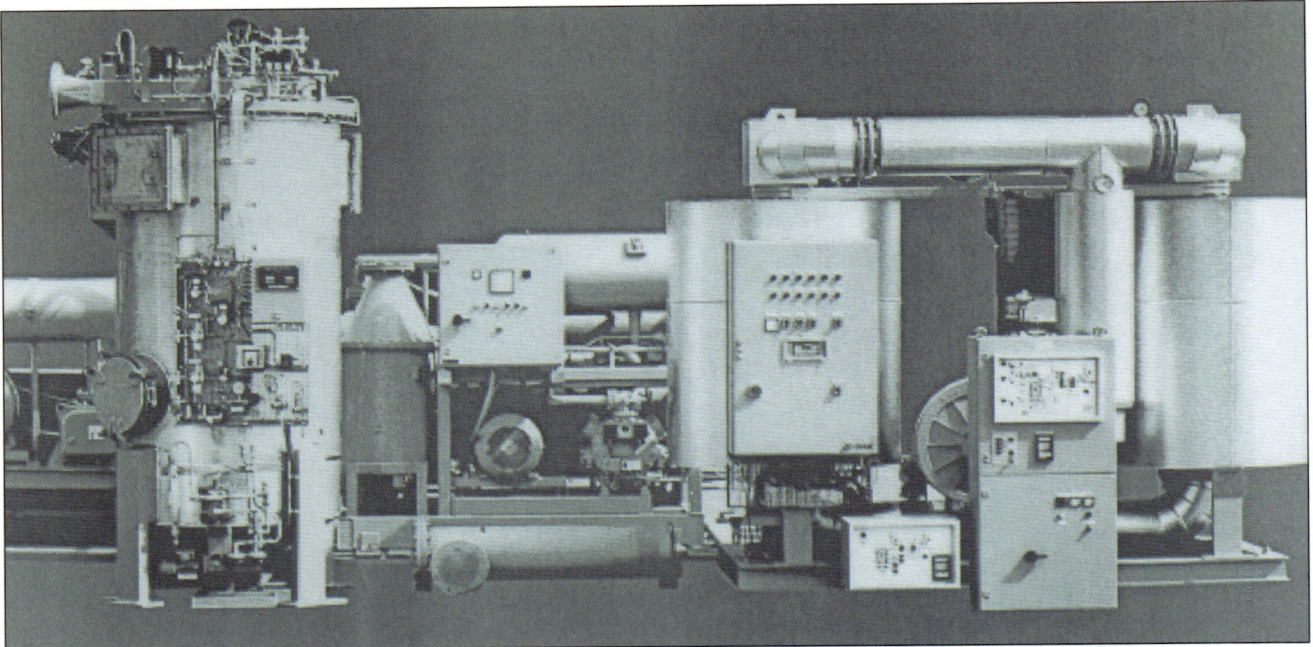

Plate 17-9   Inert gas plant for *Helga*   Hamworthy KSE

Eeklo

Principle Particulars	
Length o.a.	179.00 m
Length b.p.	169.00 m
Breadth	27.36 m
Depth	18.20 m
Draught	11.60 m
LPG Capacity	37,520 m³
Engine	Kawasaki-MAN B&W 5S60MC
Power	12,510 hp/9,202 kW
Service speed	16.1 knots

A devastating earthquake hit the city of Kobe on 17 January 1995 and caused extensive damage at the Kawasaki shipyard.[15] The first of two 37,520 m³ LPG/ammonia/VCM carriers *Eeklo*, ordered by the Belgian company Exmar, was being prepared for the launch when the earthquake struck. Shipyard cranes and other facilities were damaged and a rupture in the building dock gate caused water to flood inwards. The newbuilding was displaced by the earthquake but no significant damage was reported. The colossal damage to the city's infrastructure, resulted in both of the Exmar ships being transferred to Kawasaki's Sakaide works for completion. *Eeklo* was delivered from the Sakaide works on 12 September 1995 and the second vessel *Elversele* was delivered on 10 January 1996.

The ships were classed with Det Norse Veritas for the carriage of anhydrous ammonia, butane, propane and VCM, with a minimum temperature of -48°C, a maximum pressure of 0.25 kg/cm² and a maximum specific gravity of 0.97. The ships were a slightly longer version of 34,765 m³ *Hedda* and *Helga* earlier delivered to Kværner. No bow thruster was fitted.

Three direct reliquefaction plants were fitted. Two 440 m³/hr deep-well pumps were fitted in each cargo tank and 350 m³ and 100 m³ pressurised deck tanks for change of cargo were fitted on the main deck forward. A combined cargo heater and vaporiser was fitted.

Plate 17-10   *Eeklo*   Kawasaki

Flanders Tenacity

Principle Particulars	
Length o.a.	230.00 m
Length b.p.	219.70 m
Breadth	36.00 m
Depth	21.90 m
Draught	11.62 m
LPG Capacity	84,269 m³
Engine	Kawasaki-MAN B&W 5S70MC
Power	18,300 hp/13,460 kW
Service speed	16.8 knots

The next series of LPGC newbuildings from the Sakaide works of Kawasaki had the same 36 metre beam, as the *Pacific Harmony* 75,000 m³ series, but were longer and deeper. The first ship of the series was the 84,269 m³ LPG/NH_3 carrier *Flanders Tenacity,* which was delivered to Exmar NV of Belgium on 29 May 1996.[16] The ship was classed with Det Norske Veritas for the carriage of butane, propane and anhydrous ammonia. The four direct reliquefaction plants were housed on the main deck above No. 4 cargo tank. Each cargo tank was fitted with two 600 m³/hr deep-well pumps. Two 300 m³/hr centrifugal booster pumps were fitted on the main deck. A combined cargo heater and vaporiser was fitted.

The Sakaide works also delivered a further four LPG carriers of this size to Sonatrach Petroleum and Formosa Plastics. The first Algerian LPG ship, *Reggane,* was delivered on 30 November 1999 and the second, *Djanet*, was delivered on 4 October 2000. The first Taiwanese ship *Formosagas Apollo,* was delivered on 29 August 2001 and the second, *Formosagas Bright*, was delivered on 28 December 2001.[17]

Plate 17-11   *Flanders Tenacity*   Kawasaki

Plate 17-12   *Djanet*   Kawasaki

Fountain River

Principle Particulars	
Length o.a.	230.00 m
Length b.p.	219.70 m
Breadth	36.00 m
Depth	20.70 m
Draught	10.77 m
LPG Capacity	79,527 m³
Engine	Kawasaki-MAN B&W 6S70MC
Power	20,630 hp/15,173 kW
Service speed	17 knots

Another design with the 36 metre beam from the Sakaide works was the 79,527 m³ LPG carrier *Fountain River*, delivered on 28 November 1997 to owners River Gas Transport S.A., for Kawasaki Kisen Kaisha Ltd. (K-Line) with a charter to Japan Energy Corp. *Fountain River* was different from the Exmar ship in that the ship had a 20.70 m flush main deck, arranged from stern to stem.

A second similar vessel, *Ocean Orchid*, was delivered to Kumiai Navigation (Pte) Ltd., on 19 March 2001 with a Kawasaki-MAN B&W 5S70MC Mk VI main engine. A third vessel in this series, *Grace River*, was delivered to K-Line on 31 October 2002. All three 79,527 m³ vessels were classed with Nippon Kaiji Kyokai.

Plate 17-13	*Fountain River*	Kawasaki

Dynamic Vision

Principle Particulars	
Length o.a.	227.00 m
Length b.p.	216.62 m
Breadth	36.00 m
Depth	21.90 m
Draught	11.60 m
LPG Capacity	82,200 m³
Engine	Kawasaki-MAN B&W 5S70MC Mk VI
Power	18,899 hp/13,900 kW
Service speed	17 knots

Two 82,200 m³ LPG carriers were ordered from Kawasaki by LPG Transport Service Ltd., and their designs were based on another slight variation of the 36 metre beam. The first vessel of the pair, *Dynamic Vision*, was delivered on 28 September 2001 and the second, *Dynamic Energy*, followed from the Sakaide yard on 27 September 2002.[18, 19, 20]

A third vessel of similar capacity and dimensions was ordered from Kawasaki by domestic owner I S Carriers Inc., and was delivery as *Althea Gas* on 27 January 2003. All three 82,200 m³ vessels were classed with the American Bureau of Shipping.

Clipper Star

Principle Particulars	
Length o.a.	205.00 m
Length b.p.	195.00 m
Breadth	32.20 m
Depth	20.20 m
Draught	10.50 m
LPG Capacity	59,200 m³
Engine	Kawasaki-MAN B&W 5S60MC-C
Power	15,330 hp/11,275 kW
Service speed	16 knots

During 2001 and 2002, Kawasaki Heavy Industries received orders for five 59,200 m³ LPG/NH$_3$ carriers from Norwegian owners Bergesen dy ASA and Solvang ASA. The dimensions were based on a Panamax beam of 32.20 m and each ship was fitted with four prismatic cargo tanks. The shipbuilder introduced a new bow design called Sea-Arrow, to enhance the propulsive performance of the five ships. Sea-Arrow is derived from "Sharp Entrance Angle bow as an Arrow." The designers claim that the new hull entrance will halve the bow resistance.[21] Four direct reliquefaction plant were fitted.

The first vessel of the series, *Clipper Star*, was delivered to Solvang on 26 March 2003. *Berge Nice* and Hull 1530 will follow in 2003 for Bergesen, and Hulls 1531 and 1543 are scheduled to be delivered to Solvang in 2004.

Further orders for two 59,000 m³ LPG carriers were received by Kawasaki from Sonatrach Petroleum Corp., with Hull 1547 due for delivery in 2004 and Hull 1548 due for delivery in 2005.

Crystal Marine

Principle Particulars	
Length o.a.	227.50 m
Length b.p.	222.00 m
Breadth	37.20 m
Depth	21.00 m
Draught	11.20 m
LPG Capacity	80,138 m^3
Engine	Kawasaki-MAN B&W 7S60MC-C
Power	19,035 hp/14,000 kW
Service speed	17 knots

On 30 June 2003, Kawasaki delivered 80,138 m^3 *Crystal Marine* to Kumiai Navigation. The ship was a new design with four cargo tanks based on a 37.20 m beam and like the *Clipper Star* series incorporated the Sea-Arrow bow design. The vessel was classed with Nippon Kaiji Kyokai and registered in Singapore.

On 1 October 2002, the Kawasaki Shipbuilding Corporation started operating.

[1] Bridgestone Liquefied Gas Co. Ltd., brochure, *Gas Carriers, Engineering*, 1970.
[2] Yamamoto, Katsuro, *Experience in the Development of Gas Tankers,* Shipbuilding & Shipping Record LNG/LPG Conference, London, 21-22 March 1972.
[3] Yamamoto, K., *A Semi-Membrane Tank System for Gas Ships,* Shipping World & Shipbuilder, July 1972.
[4] Kawasaki brochure, *Kasmet – Kawasaki Semi-Membrane Tank Type LPG Carriers*, April 1977.
[5] Kawasaki Ship Review No. 15, *World Bridgestone, World's Largest LPG Carrier,* June 1971.
[6] Kawasaki Ship Review No. 31, *Sun River, 75,750 m^3 LPG Carrier*, October 1974.
[7] Zosen, *Kawasaki-Built Large LPG Carrier, Sun River*, November 1974.
[8] The Okochi Memorial Prize Award, Research and Development in Japan, *Development and Production of an LPG Carrier Using Semi-Membrane System,* 1978.
[9] SEA-Japan No. 155, *New Type LPG Carrier, Clean River,* April 1983.
[10] Schiff & Hafen, *LPG Tanker Clean River for K-Line,* 6/1983.
[11] Kawasaki Ship Review No. 45, *Clean River, Super Energy-Saving LPG Carrier,* January 1984.
[12] Kawasaki Ship Review No. 57, *A New Generation LPG Carrier, Pacific Harmony,* October 1990.
[13] Significant Ships of 1990, *Pacific Harmony, A New-design Kawasaki LPG Tanker,* Royal Institution of Naval Architects, London, February 1991.
[14] Kawasaki Ship Review No. 62, *A Multi-purpose LPG Carrier, Hedda,* April 1995.
[15] Lloyd's List Casualty Reports, *Eeklo,* January/March 1995.
[16] Kawasaki Ship Review No. 66, *The 84,000 m^3 LPG/NH$_3$ Carrier, Flanders Tenacity,* March 1997.
[17] Shipbuilding & Marine Engineering in Japan JSEA, *Formosagas Apollo, 84,000 m^3 LPG Carrier*, 2003.
[18] SEA-Japan No. 289, *KHI Delivers LPG Carrier, Dynamic Vision, to LPG Transport,* October – November 2001.
[19] Kawasaki Ship Review No. 71, *Kawasaki's 82,000 m^3 type LPG Carrier, m s Dynamic Vision*, July 2002.
[20] Shipbuilding & Marine Engineering in Japan JSEA, *Dynamic Vision, 82,200 m^3 LPG Carrier*, 2003.
[21] Tinsley, David, *Kawasaki Targets Sea-Arrow Bow Design for LPG Orders,* Lloyd's List, 15 October 2002.

Chapter 18

Thyssen Nordseewerke Four for P&O

The German shipbuilders Nordseewerke GmbH, now part of the Thyssen Krupp Technologies Group, built six ethylene carriers and four fully refrigerated LPG carriers. Located in the inland port of Emden, the yard was involved in the construction of three pairs of ethylene carriers for European owners between 1987 and 1999. Launched as *Gaschem Star* and *Gaschem Moon*, the first pair were delivered in 1987 to Cryotrans Schiffahrts as 10,281 m³ *Igloo Star* and *Igloo Moon*. 11,646 m³ ethylene carriers *Gudrun Maersk* and *Gjertrud Maersk* followed from Emden for A P Møller in 1989. In co-operation with Meyer Werft, also located on the river Ems but upriver at Papenburg, the final pair of ethylene carriers, 12,500 m³ *Clipper Viking* and *Clipper Harald*, were jointly built by the two yards for Solvang.

Garinda

Principle Particulars	
Length o.a.	219.69 m
Length b.p.	208.00 m
Breadth	28.50 m
Depth	20.00 m
Draught	11.80 m
LPG Capacity	54,226 m³
Engine	MAN K6 SZ 290/160A
Power	19,924 hp/14,654 kW
Service speed	16.75 knots

A contract for four 54,226 m³ LPG carriers was signed on 2 July 1974 between P&O Bulk Shipping Division, London, and Thyssen Nordseewerke GmbH.[1, 2] The first ship, *Garinda*, was delivered to Orient Steam Navigation Company on 31 March 1977. The ice strengthened vessel was classed with Lloyd's Register of Shipping as a Liquefied Gas Carrier for a minimum temperature of -50°C, a maximum pressure of 0.28 kg/cm² and a maximum specific gravity of 0.682.

The ship was arranged with transom stern, aft machinery and accommodation spaces, four cargo tanks, a flush main deck with forward breakwater and a bulbous bow. The hull form was based on a successful series of bulk carriers built at the yard. The first ship of the series was Hull No. 390, *Leiv Eiriksson*, delivered to Laboremus A/S, Oslo in 1967. The 28.50 m breadth of *Garinda* was relatively narrow when compared to similar capacity LPG carriers buildings at the time in Europe, such as 52,647 m³ *Höegh Multina* with a breadth of 31.40 m and 53,400 m³ *Antilla Bay* with a breadth of 32.25 m.

The cargo tanks had an unusual internal arrangement with liquid tight bulkheads fitted longitudinally on the centreline and transversely at mid-length. Each of the liquid tight bulkheads had valves at the bottom of the tank, which were open during loading and discharging and closed when the ship was underway. The cargo dome was centred over the intersection of liquid tight bulkheads with colour coded valve controls for the bulkhead valves.

The reliquefaction plants were engineered and supplied by LGA Gastechnik of Remagen-Rolandseck, for the carriage of anhydrous ammonia, butadine, butane, propane and propylene. The four plants, in two parts, reminiscent of a trunk decked ship, were housed symmetrically at the side of the main deck above Nos. 2 & 3 cargo tanks. Each house contained a compressor room and two electric motor rooms, one aft and one forward. A central cargo control room straddled the forward electric motor rooms just aft of the cargo manifolds, with cargo, fire protection and service pipework neatly arranged fore and aft between the compressor houses.

The cargo tanks were insulated by Bremen based Kaefer Isoliertechnik GmbH, using 110 mm thick polyurethane foam panels, covered with aluminium foil. Two 400 m³/hr J C Carter submerged electric pumps were fitted in each cargo tank. A 300 m³ deck tank was fitted on the starboard main deck for change of grades.

The second ship of the series, *Galpara*, was delivered to Orient Steam Ship Navigation Company on 31 March 1978. *Galconda* followed on 29 September 1978, and the final ship, *Garala*, was completed on 2 May 1979. All four ships were managed and operated by P&O Bulk Shipping Division.

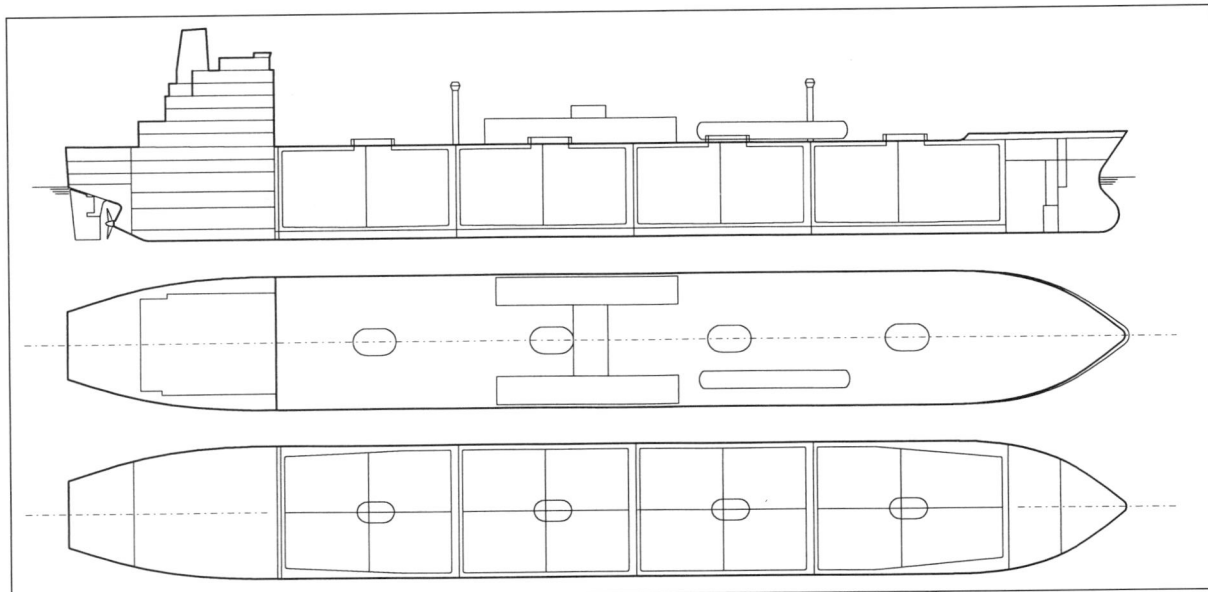

Figure 18-1 Outline Arrangement of *Garinda*

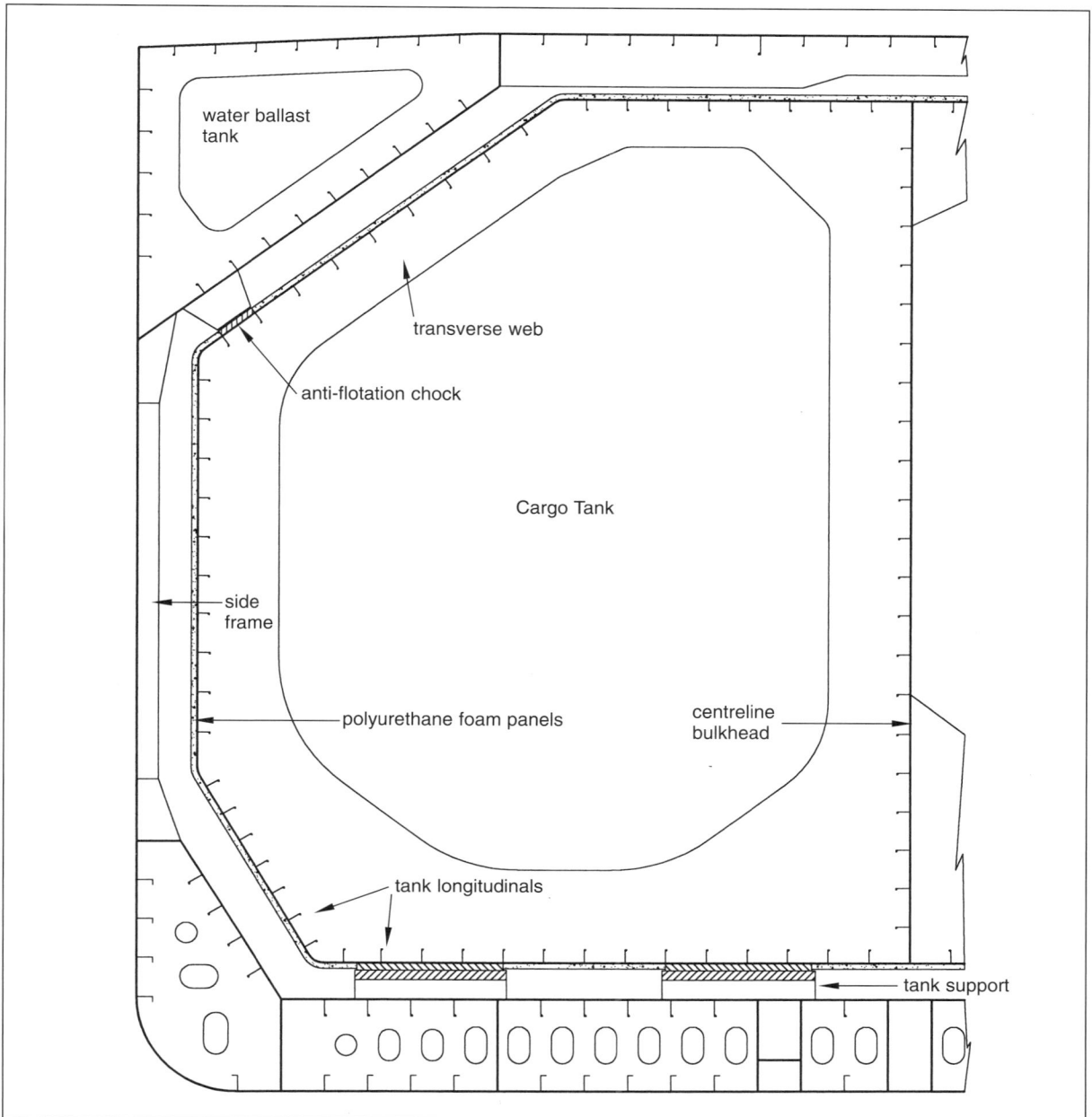

Figure 18-2 Midship Section of *Garinda* showing Cargo Tank and Supports

Plate 18-1 *Galconda* Thyssen Nordseewerke

Plate 18-2 *Garala* Thyssen Nordseewerke

[1] Hansa, *54,000 m³ LPG/NH₃ Carrier, Garinda,* 114, 1977.
[2] Rabson, Stephen, and O'Donoghue, Kevin, *P&O, A Fleet History*, World Ship Society, January 1989.

Chapter 19

Large and Small from Italy

The conversion of small coasters in the early 1950s, to supply LPG to the islands of Sardinia and Sicily, was the pioneering beginning of the Italian experience in transporting LPG by sea.[1] In 1956, the first LPG newbuilding, 585 m³ *Agipgas Seconda*, was delivered from the M & B Benetti shipyard, Viareggio, and many similar small fully pressurised LPG carriers were to follow from various Italian yards.[2, 3] Italian shipbuilders waited until 1977 before delivering a fully refrigerated LPG carrier. However, Italcantieri, Genoa, did build three 41,000 m³ LNG carriers with aluminium prismatic tanks in 1969/1970; *Esso Brega*, *Esso Portovenere* and *Esso Liguria*.

Luigi Lagrange

Principle Particulars	
Length o.a.	191.95 m
Length b.p.	176.00 m
Breadth	26.00 m
Depth	16.85 m
Draught	11.48 m
LPG Capacity	31,311 m³
Engine	Fiat A900.6
Power	17,400 hp/12,798 kW
Service speed	19 knots

Nuovi Cantieri Apuania SpA., Marina di Carrara, constructed two 31,000 m³ LPG/NH₃ carriers for two different owners during 1977 and 1978. The first, 31,311 m³ *Luigi Lagrange* was delivered to Societa di Navigazione Carbocoke SpA., in November 1977 and had dual classification with American Bureau of Shipping and Registro Italiano Navale.

The ship was arranged with raked transom stern, aft machinery and accommodation spaces, poop, main and forecastle decks, four cargo tanks and a bulbous bow. The ship was designed for the carriage of LPG, NH_3 and could also load a full cargo of vinyl chloride monomer, at a minimum temperature of -48°C, a maximum pressure of 0.30 kg/cm² and a maximum specific gravity of 0.972. For change of grades, three 80 m³ pressurised tanks were fitted on the main deck forward.

The gas handling plant consisting of three units was engineered and supplied by Liquid Gas Equipment Ltd., of Edinburgh and was housed on the main deck above No. 3 cargo tank. The ship was affectionately referred to by the Scottish engineers as *Big Luigi*. A cargo control room was located in the accommodation spaces below the bridge deck. Two 325 m³/hr Svanehøj deep-well pumps were fitted in each cargo tank with a similar size booster pump fitted on the deck.

A pipe tunnel was fitted at either side of the double bottom under the cargo tanks. The author crawled though this tunnel a few years back as part of a longevity inspection. Access from the forward ends of the pipe tunnels is relatively comfortable but in moving aft, the number of pipes in the tunnels increases towards the machinery spaces and the final right angle turn needs a trim figure to squeeze past the piping flanges. Did the naval architect or piping engineer responsible for the layout ever crawl through this tight space? Because their calculations did not seem to include a pasta factor, to take into account the effects of the usually splendid culinary delights found on an Italian manned ship.

The second ship, 31,243 m³ *Lord Kelvin*, had the same hull dimensions and cargo tank arrangement as *Luigi Lagrange* but was powered by an H Cegielski-Sulzer 6RND90 diesel engine, rated at 17,500 hp (12,871 kW). Classed with Lloyd's Register of Shipping, *Lord Kelvin* was delivered to Ocean Gas Transport Ltd., on 24 May 1978 and was placed under the management of Holder Brothers & Co. Ltd.

Plate 19-1   Nuovi Cantieri Apuania   Lloyd's Register of Shipping

Plate 19-2   *Lord Kelvin*   Lloyd's Register of Shipping

Capo Levante

Principle Particulars	
Length o.a.	76.51 m
Length b.p.	75.27 m
Breadth	9.71 m
Depth	4.12 m
Draught	2.95 m
LPG Capacity	1,350 m^3
Engines (2)	Deutz SBA 16 M 816
Power	1,632 hp/1,200 kW
Service speed	8.5 knots

The world's smallest purpose built fully refrigerated LPG carrier with cargo carried at just above atmospheric pressure was 1,350 m^3 Capo Levante, completed at the CLEMNA shipyard, La Spezia, in October 1979. Delivered to Compagnia di Navigazione Cossira SpA., and classed with Registro Italiano Navale, the ship had two prismatic cargo tanks designed for a minimum temperature of -48°C, a maximum pressure of 0.7 kg/cm^2 and a maximum specific gravity of 0.97. The ship was designed for the carriage of anhydrous ammonia, butane, butadiene, propane, propylene and VCM.[4]

The ship was constructed for Italian coastal and river trading on a long term time charter for Montedison. The primary trade was loading refrigerated anhydrous ammonia at Ravenna, entering the Adriatic Sea at Porto Corsini, and sailing northwards into the River Po or into the Torricelli Channel via Porto Marghera, near Venice. The vessel also traded with NH$_3$ between Augusta, Sicily and Crotone on the Italian mainland.

The vessel dimensions and air draught were chosen to suit the Torricelli Channel and to pass under river bridges. By fitting prismatic cargo tanks the maximum cargo capacity could be obtained within these tight parameters. Relatively large side and double bottom water ballast tanks were fitted to have the same draught in the loaded or ballast conditions. With the restricted air draught, the masts, aerials, ventilators and radar scanners were hinged in order to pass under the river bridges. In addition, the small wheelhouse could be hydraulically lowered into a recess on the main deck. With a draught of less than three metres a twin rudder arrangement was adopted with two Kort propellers.

The gas handling reliquefaction plants, designed in co-operation with Technigaz, France, were manufactured and supplied by Termomeccanica, La Spezia, and were fitted below the main deck between the two cargo tanks. The reliquefaction plants included two Sulzer K80-2A compressors, two condensers, two separators and a liquid receiver. Two 1,000 m^3/hr Hibon vapour blowers were fitted.

Two 85 m^3/hr hydraulic Eureka pumps were fitted in each cargo tank and the tanks were insulated with 80 mm of polyurethane foam. A 170 m^3/hr hydraulic Eureka booster pump and a cargo heater were also fitted.

For deep sea trading, Cantiere Rosetti of Ravenna modified Capo Levante, and in May 1995 the ship was redelivered to owners Lorion Compagnia di Navigazione Srl. The main deck was strengthened in way of the cargo tanks, the height of the forecastle was increased and an aft deckhouse was fitted. After the rebuilding, cargoes carried included anhydrous ammonia from Augusta to Cagliari, Sardinia and propylene from Augusta to Brindisi.

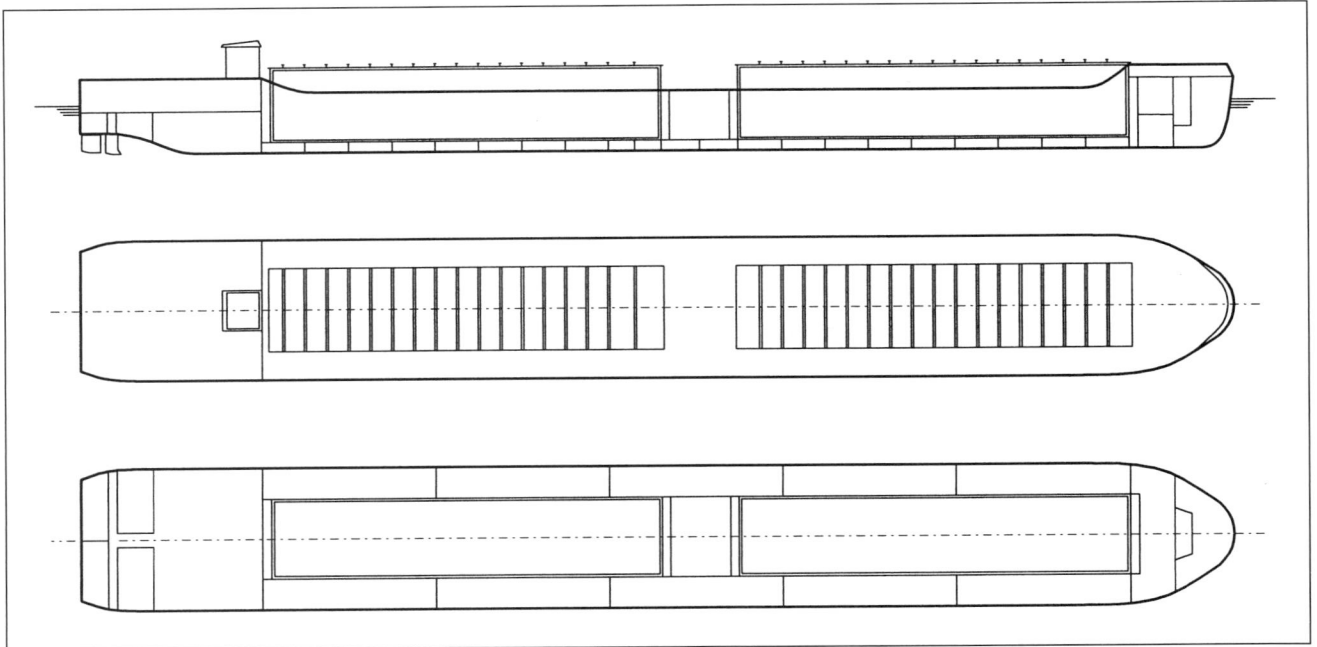

Figure 19-1 Outline Arrangement of *Capo Levante* for River and Coastal Trading

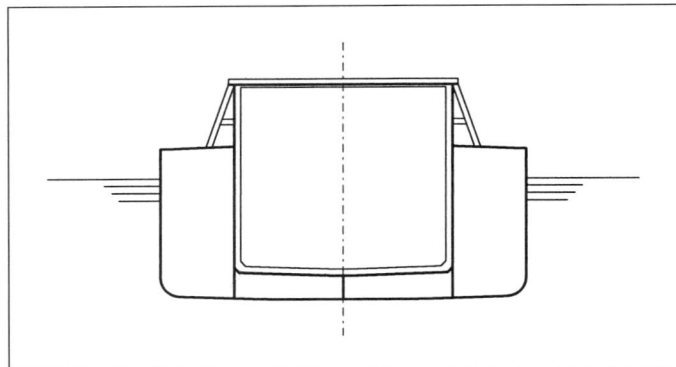

Figure 19-2 Midship Section of *Capo Levante*

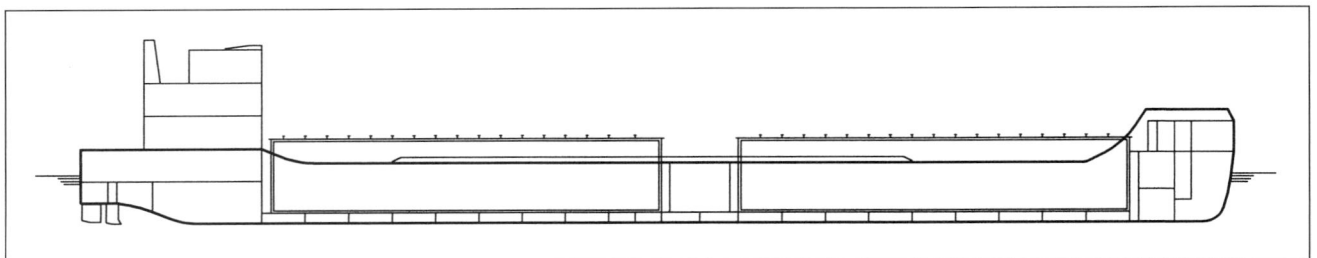

Figure 19-3 Profile of *Capo Levante* after Conversion for Deep Sea Trading

Plate 19-3   *Capo Levante* for river and coastal trading   EGM

Plate 19-4   *Capo Levante* after conversion for deep sea trading   EGM

Mossovet

Principle Particulars	
Length o.a.	234.98 m
Length b.p.	222.00 m
Breadth	35.80 m
Depth	22.80 m
Draught	12.20 m
LPG Capacity	76,506 m³
Engine	Bryansk-MAN B&W 9K80GF
Power	23,400 hp/17,211 kW
Service speed	16.5 knots

With consecutive hull numbers, 289, 290 and 291, Cantiere Navale Breda SpA., Venice, delivered three fully refrigerated LPG carriers to the USSR Black Sea Shipping Company during 1979 and 1980. Technigaz, France, were the design consultants and two different sizes of gas carriers were produced, two at 76,506 m³ and one at 37,829 m³. The first vessel constructed was 76,506 m³ *Mossovet*, which was delivered to the owners on 21 September 1979. The ship was dual classed with Det Norske Veritas and the USSR Register of Shipping for the carriage of anhydrous ammonia, butane, butadiene, propane and propylene.

The ship was arranged with a raked transom stern, aft machinery and accommodation spaces, flush main deck, four prismatic cargo tanks and a bulbous bow. The cargo tanks were insulated with 100 mm of polyurethane foam covered with galvanised steel sheets.

The three reliquefaction plants, supplied by Termomeccanica of La Spezia, Italy, were housed on the main deck forward of the cargo manifolds, with a cargo control room above the reliquefaction house. Two 650 m³/hr deep-well pumps were fitted in each cargo tank.

The second of the larger ships, *Lensovet*, was delivered in June 1980.

Smolnyy

Principle Particulars	
Length o.a.	197.42 m
Length b.p.	184.50 m
Breadth	29.00 m
Depth	17.85 m
Draught	10.10 m
LPG Capacity	37,829 m³
Engine	Bryansk-MAN B&W 9K80GF
Power	23,400 hp/17,211 kW
Service speed	16 knots

The third gas ship from Breda, 37,829 m³ *Smolnyy*, for USSR Black Sea Shipping Company, was delivered on 30 December 1980. Many features of the earlier built ships were utilised on the smaller ship, including a four cargo tank arrangement and three reliquefaction plants. The main deck of the smaller ship was protected by a forecastle deck and VCM was added to the cargo list. Two 320 m³/hr deep-well pumps were fitted in each cargo tank.

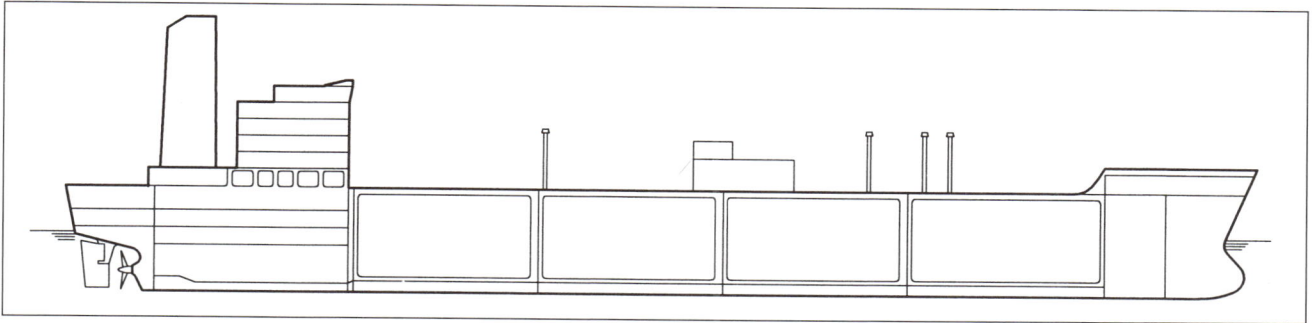

Figure 19-4 Profile of *Smolnyy*

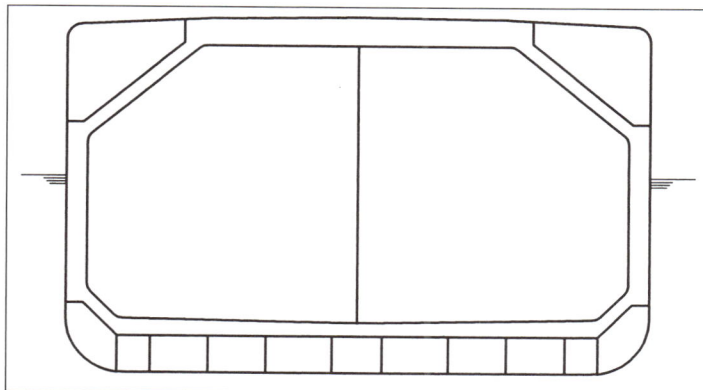

Figure 19-5 Midship Section of *Smolnyy*

Solaro

Principle Particulars	
Length o.a.	180.40 m
Length b.p.	169.00 m
Breadth	29.00 m
Depth	17.90 m
Draught	12.50 m
LPG Capacity	37,314 m³
Engine	GMT-Sulzer 5RTA62U
Power	15,092 hp/11,100 kW
Service speed	15.9 knots

With a gap of some 16 years, the next fully refrigerated LPG carrier to be delivered from an Italian shipbuilder was 37,314 m³ *Solaro*. Ordered by Carbofin SpA., the ship's hull dimensions and cargo capacity were close to the earlier built *Smolnyy* from Breda. The builders were Sestri Cantiere Navale SpA., Genoa, part of the Fincantieri Group, and the keel was laid on 1 April 1995, with a launching on 21 December 1995 and a delivery on 30 April 1996.[5, 6]

Classed with Registro Italiano Navale for the carriage of anhydrous ammonia, butane, butadiene, butylene, propane, propylene and VCM, the cargo tanks were designed for a minimum temperature of -48°C, a maximum pressure of 0.245 kg/cm² and a maximum specific gravity of 0.97. The ship was arranged with transom stern with free-fall lifeboat, aft machinery and accommodation, four cargo tanks, forecastle and a bulbous bow. A reliquefaction house was located on the main deck aft of the cargo manifolds. 110 m³ and 220 m³ change of grade tanks were fitted on the main deck, just aft of the forecastle.

The cargo tanks and cargo handling equipment were designed and supplied by Noell-LGA Gastechnik GmbH. The cargo tanks were not constructed in the shipyard and were transported to Genoa by barge with the insulation work completed. The tanks were insulated with a 170 mm layer of polyurethane foam covered with galvanised steel sheeting, for protection and to serve as a vapour barrier. Two 350 m³/hr Svanehøj deep-well cargo pumps were fitted in each tank and two Svanehøj 350 m³/hr booster pumps were fitted on deck. Three reliquefaction plants were fitted and cargo handling equipment included two gas/air blowers, an inert gas plant and a nitrogen generator.

Solaro entered service under a long term charter to Norwegian industrial group Norske Hydro.

[1] Hautefeuille, Roland, with Clayton, Richard, *Gas Pioneers*, Paris, 1998.
[2] Shipbuilding & Shipping Record, *An Italian Tanker for Carrying Liquefied Gas*, 13 December 1956.
[3] Pattofatto, G., *The Experience of Registro Italiano Navale with Gas Carriers*, Gastech 90, Amsterdam.
[4] Termomeccanica, *Marine Field*, brochure 5/MF.
[5] LGA Marine Consulting GmbH brochure, *Fully Refrigerated Gas Carrier*.
[6] Fincantieri Cantieri Navali Italiani SpA. brochure, *37,000 m³ LPG Carrier.*

Chapter 20

Boelwerf's Entrepreneurial Audacity

Generally, yards starting out in the gas ship building industry of the early 1970s, began cautiously and gradually increased their expertise with gas ships over the years, moving from building small and medium size LPG carriers before considering working on larger LNG carriers. The Belgian shipbuilders, Boelwerf, at Temse, near Antwerp, in a bold move, reached an agreement in 1972 to build a 130,000 m³ LNG carrier for Compagnie Maritime Belge (CMB), based on a speedily arranged co-operation with Chantiers de France-Dunkerque.[1] Quite a decision considering that at the time the yard had never built a gas ship, had no experience with steam turbine propulsion and had no suitable dock for the newbuilding. A building dock measuring 560m x 55m was constructed at Temse in 1975. The LNG carrier *Methania* with Gaz Transport membrane cargo tanks was the first ship to be built in the new dock. The vessel was delivered in October 1978, to load Algerian LNG for transportation to Montoir, France and Zeebrugge on behalf of Belgium's Distrigaz.

This initial entrepreneurial decision of the owners of the river Scheldt shipyard to enter the gas ship business was to result in the yard delivering twelve LPG and ethylene carriers between 1980 and 1994, including ten fully refrigerated LPG carriers.

Cantarell

Principle Particulars	
Length o.a.	215.70 m
Length b.p.	204.00 m
Breadth	32.25 m
Depth	19.00 m
Draught	12.02 m
LPG Capacity	57,000 m³
Engine	Sulzer 6RND90M
Power	20,100 hp/14,784 kW
Service speed	17 knots

Originally built to the shipyard's own account, Boelwerf delivered its first fully refrigerated LPG carrier as one of a pair, for Petroleos Mexicanos SA (PEMEX) in 1980.[2] The first ship, launched as *Petrogas II* on 22 September 1979, was delivered to the Mexican owners as *Cantarell* on 30 May 1980, and the second ship, launched as *Petrogas III* on 19 April 1980, was delivered on 17 October 1980 as *Ahkatun*. Marine Services GmbH of Hamburg assisted the shipyard with design, plan approval and building supervision. The ships were classed with Lloyd's Register of Shipping for the carriage of anhydrous ammonia, butane, propane and propylene at a minimum temperature of -50°C, a maximum pressure of 0.25 kg/cm² and a maximum specific gravity of 0.682.

Based on a Panamax beam, the ships were arranged with a transom stern, flush main deck, aft machinery and living quarters, four cargo tanks and a bulbous bow. A reliquefaction house, with an athwartships cargo control room above, was arranged on the main deck, aft of the cargo manifolds. Four cascade type reliquefaction plants were fitted with R22 as the refrigerant. A pair of units were rated at 326,000 kcal/hr in propane service, with a tank insulation thickness of 100 mm. The cargo tank domes were at the mid-length of the cargo tanks and each tank was fitted with two 400 m³/hr J C Carter electric submerged cargo pumps. Two 300 m³/hr Svanehøj booster pumps were fitted on the main deck. Azobé hardwood was used for the tank supports.

The shipyard developed its own Boelwerf Insulation System (BIS) for the cargo tanks, which consisted of handy sized prefabricated polyurethane panels covered with aluminium sheets.[3] The panels were secured to the cargo tanks by welded stainless steel studs covered by a cylindrical polyurethane plug. The gaps of about 10 mm left between the panels, to allow for thermal movement, were filled with soft foam or low density polyurethane and sealed with self-adhesive bituminous tape. The insulation panels were not glued to the cargo tanks and could be easily removed in service for inspection or repairs.

A third ship, *Eupen*, with the same hull dimensions and cargo tanks arrangement, was launched on 15 April 1983 and delivered to Exmar on 27 August 1983. The main propulsion unit was a Sulzer 6RLA90 diesel, rated at 21,600 hp (15,897 kW), for a service speed of 16.2 knots. Three cascade reliquefaction units were fitted, with a pair of units rated at 440,000 kcal/hr in propane service, with a tank insulation thickness of 120 mm. Two Thune Eureka deep-well pumps were fitted in each cargo tank. Compared to the PEMEX ships, the cargo control room location was changed to be above the starboard reliquefaction house.

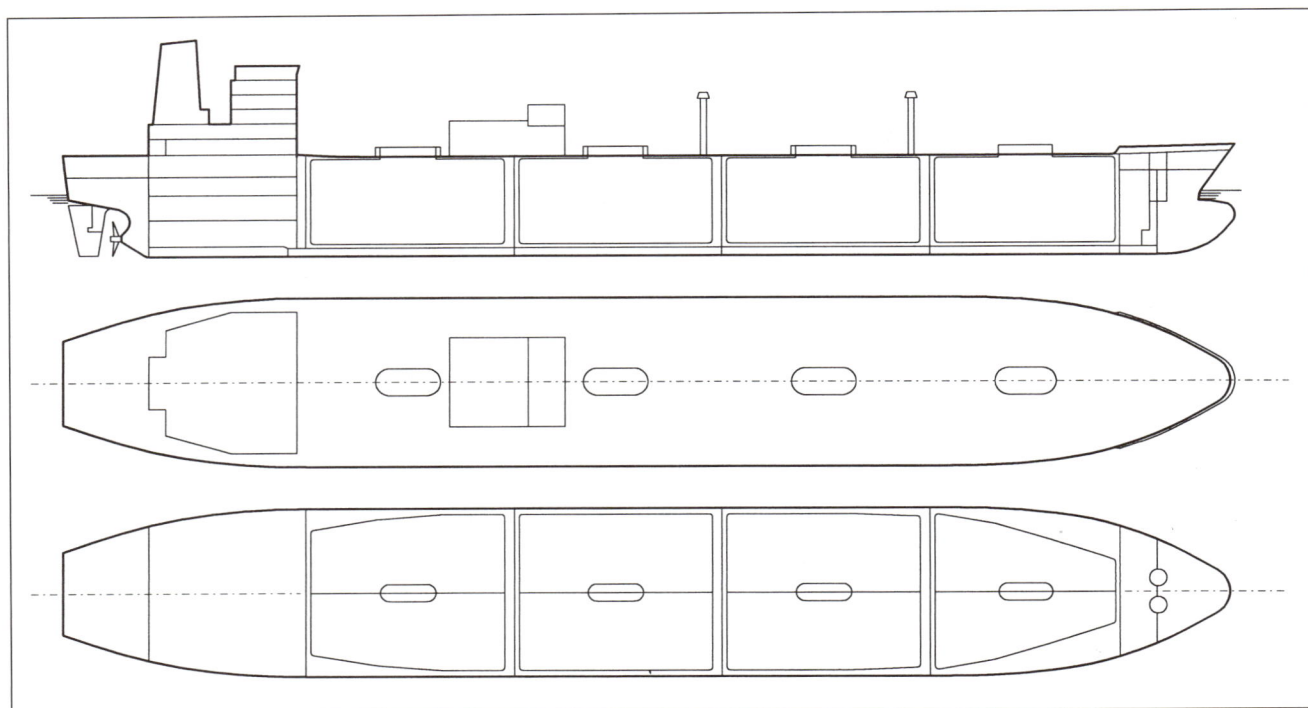

Figure 20-1 Outline Arrangement of *Cantarell*

Plate 20-1   *Eupen*   Boelwerf

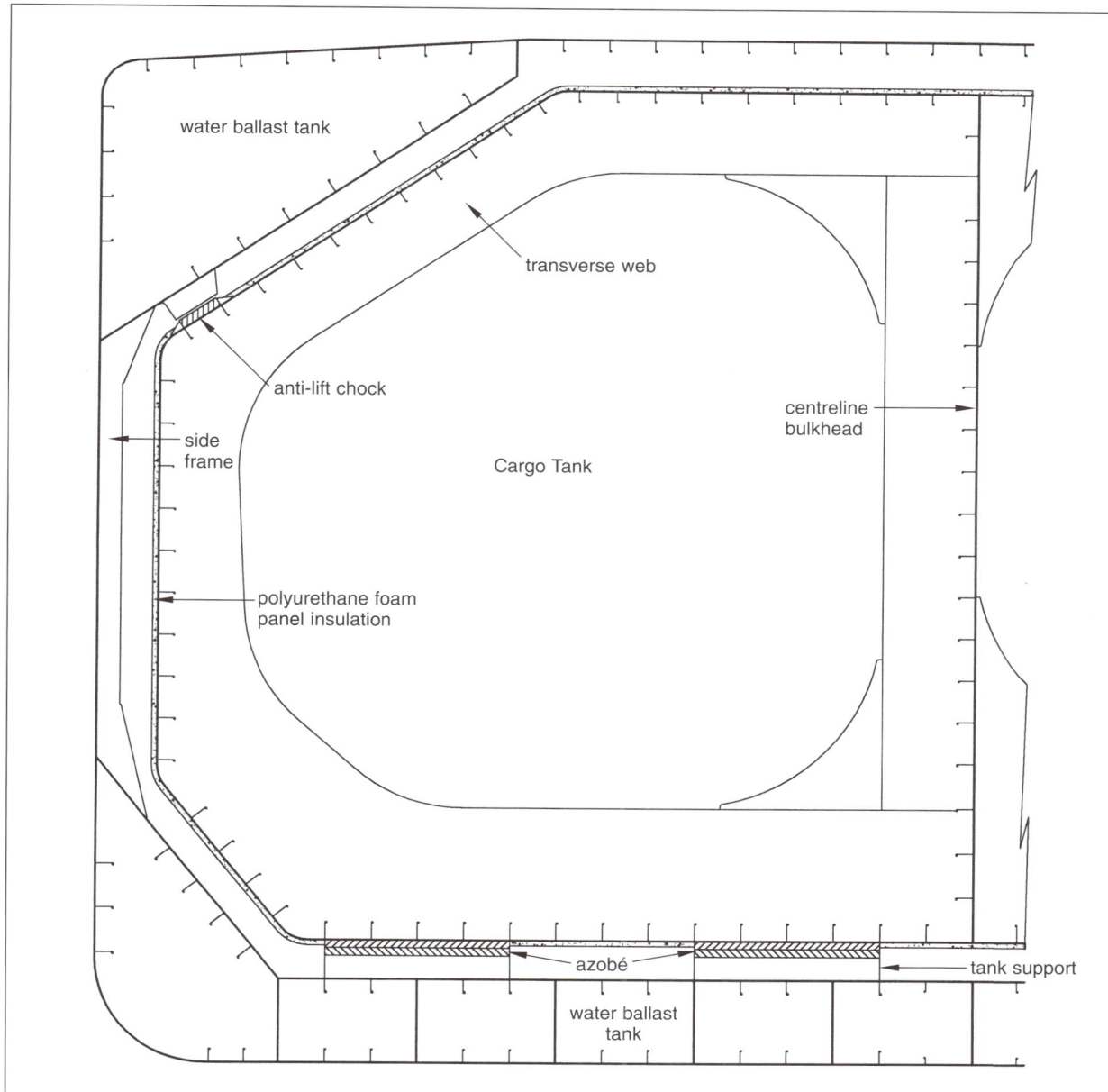

Figure 20-2 Midship Section of *Cantarell* showing Cargo Tank and Supports

Plate 20-2   *Cantarell*   Boelwerf

15 June 1985 – Pajaritos Phoenix

Five European built fully refrigerated LPG carriers were in the Pajaritos natural lagoon near Coatzacoalcos, Mexico, when a gas spill incident on *Ahkatun* put ships, crews and fire protection systems to the test.[4][5] The gas carriers were all berthed at the oil and gas terminals owned by PEMEX and Fertimex.

A few minutes after midday on Saturday 15 June 1985, the crew boat/tug *Pemex 383* was engulfed in a gas cloud from an LPG spillage on board *Ahkatun*, when a flexible hose broke during loading operations at berth No. 2 West. *Ahkatun* had already loaded approximately 25,000 tonnes of LPG. An explosion occurred on Pemex 383, followed by a fire, which quickly spread back to *Ahkatun* and with the wind's help reached at Berth No. 1 West, the 22,246 m³ *Nuevo Laredo*, formerly La Ciotat built *Sydfonn*. At least two workers on the crew boat were killed and many more were injured.

Covered in flames, *Ahkatun*, like a phoenix, was moved away from the berth to outside the port. The vessel moved under power, initially without tug assistance, after the mooring lines were released, cut or parted. As the ship left the berth, a loading hose was observed hanging loose from the cargo manifold and spitting flames. The on board fire was extinguished within one hour, and *Ahkatun* was later towed the short distance along the Coatzacoalcos River and out into the Gulf of Mexico.

Nuevo Laredo, which was ready to load anhydrous ammonia, suffered extensive fire damage to the living quarters, because when the flames reached the ship, the air conditioning system was under repair and most of the accommodation windows were open. The entire length of the starboard side was also damaged from heat and flames.

At Berth No. 1 East, the fire spread to Moss Værft built 19,462 m³ *Mundogas Rio*, but fortunately the ship was sheltered from the main fire by *Nuevo Laredo*. Damage to the ship was kept to a superficial level by an alert crew, who closed all openings and operated the water spray and water curtain fire protection systems.

The nearest ship upwind of *Ahkatun*, on Berth No. 3 West, was the 26,300 tons deadweight chemical carrier *Lake Anne*, which was loading pentane, but was not troubled by the fire and was able to move to a safer anchorage.

During the fire incident, minor damage was caused to Hawthorn Leslie built 11,750 m³ *Mariano Escobedo*, which was under repair at Berth No. 7 West. As the gas carrier was leaving the berth, a collision occurred with the tug *Gulf Tide* which was coming alongside to assist. The port side shell plating, over three strakes, was damaged and the internals in way of No. 3 cargo tank were set in.

The fifth gas ship at Pajaritos, CNIM built 53,400 m³ *Reynosa*, was in ballast, well away from the fire at Berth No. 9 West, and remained in the port.

With most of the Pajaritos LPG cargo still on board, repairs were carried out on *Ahkatun* to make the ship fit for a voyage to the west coast of Mexico. On 1 July, *Ahkatun* departed from Coatzacoalcos, passed the Panama Canal for the Pacific on 6 July and arrived at Guaymas on 15 July for discharge.

Plate 20-3   *Ahkatun*   PEMEX

Plate 20-4   *Ahkatun* leaving Pajaritos in ballast   PEMEX

Isomeria

Principle Particulars	
Length o.a.	210.00 m
Length b.p.	203.00 m
Breadth	31.40 m
Depth	21.45 m
Draught	12.48 m
LPG Capacity	59,725 m^3
Engine	Harland-MAN B&W 6K90GF
Power	20,500 hp/15,078 kW
Service speed	17 knots

During the building period of the Pemex 57,000 m³ LPG carriers, the Belgian yard was also involved in supplying the Boelwerf Insulation System (BIS) for two 59,725 m³ LPG carriers being built at Harland & Wolff, Belfast. Similar to their Temse counterparts, the Belfast yard had also started with an LNG carrier order before moving onto LPG carrier construction. In May 1964, 27,400 m³ *Methane Progress* was delivered from Harland & Wolff and like the Belgian built *Methania*, was to ship LNG from Algeria to Europe.

The two LPG carriers from Harland & Wolff were owned by North Sea Marine Leasing Company, a consortium of British banks, and were to be operated by Shell Tankers (UK) Ltd., primarily for the export of North Sea LPG from Braefoot Bay, on Scotland's Firth of Forth, to the USA.[6] The first of the pair, *Isomeria* was floated out on 21 March 1981 and delivered on 30 April 1982. The second ship, *Isocardia* was floated out on 23 January 1982 and delivered on 29 October 1982. With a cargo capacity of 59,725 m³, the ships are the largest LPG carriers to have been built in the United Kingdom.

The ships were classed with Lloyd's Register of Shipping for the carriage of butane and propane at a minimum temperature of -48°C, a maximum pressure of 0.25 kg/cm² and a maximum specific gravity of 0.61. The ships were arranged with an upright transom stern, aft machinery and accommodation spaces, flush main deck, five cargo tanks and a bulbous bow. For a planned trade to Boston, Massachusetts, USA, the height of the funnel was kept low in order to allow the ship to pass under the bridge on the approach to the USA terminal. Events changed and the trade to Boston did not materialise. A semi-tunnel stern was fitted and model tank tests predicted an improvement in speed by up to ¼ knot.

Technigaz, Paris, were the design consultants for the cargo tanks and cargo handling systems.

A reliquefaction house was located on the main deck above Nos. 4 and 5 cargo tanks. Four Kværner Kulde reliquefaction plants were fitted, based on a cascade system, with R22 as the refrigerant. Each unit had a capacity of 160,000 kcal/hr in propane service. Two 450 m³/hr J C Carter electric submerged pumps were fitted in each cargo tank. The cargo tank polyurethane panels of the Boelwerf Insulation System (BIS) ranged in thickness between 127 mm and 152 mm. Ekki hardwood and Philadelphia Resins epoxy liquid were used for the cargo tank supports. The cargo control room was in the accommodation spaces aft of the wheelhouse.

An emergency stern cargo discharge system was fitted. For the first time on a Shell ship, glass reinforced plastic (GRP) pipes were fitted in the straight sections of the water ballast systems in the double bottom tanks, with bends and T-pieces made of steel and coated with coal tar epoxy.

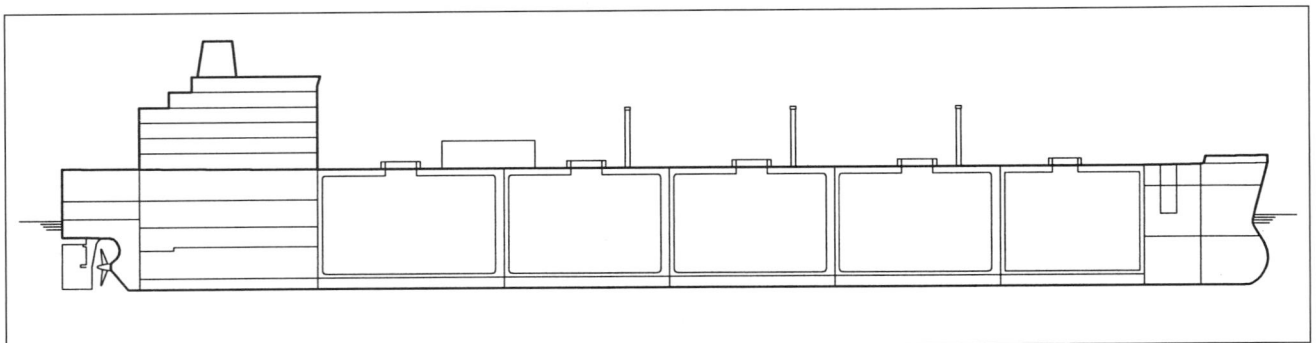

Figure 20-3 Profile of *Isomeria*

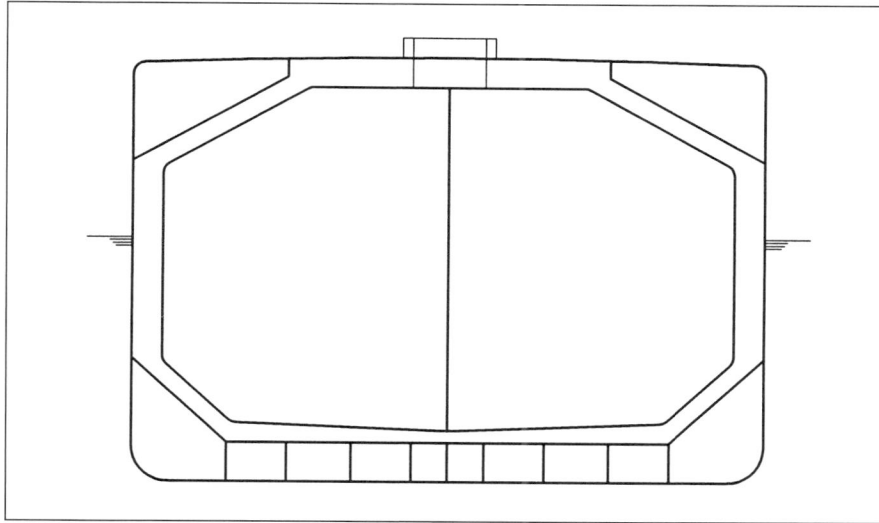

Figure 20-4 Midship Section of *Isomeria*

Plate 20-5   *Isomeria* on sea trials   Harland and Wolff

Tielrode

Principle Particulars	
Length o.a.	155.40 m
Length b.p.	147.00 m
Breadth	26.50 m
Depth	16.20 m
Draught	11.74 m
LPG Capacity	25,000 m³
Engine	Cockerill, Sulzer 6RLB66
Power	11,850 hp/8,716 kW
Service speed	16.2 knots

In a similar manner to the 57,000 m³ *Cantarell*, a smaller 25,000 m³ LPG/NH₃/VCM carrier was built in-house at Boelwerf. Confusingly, like *Cantarell*, the ship was also launched as *Petrogas II*, on 12 August 1983, to be delivered on 14 December of the same year to Exmar as *Tielrode*. Marine Services GmbH again provided design assistance to the yard. The ship was classed with Lloyds Register of Shipping for the carriage of anhydrous ammonia, LPG, butadiene, butylene, propylene, VCM, naphtha and several other products, at a minimum temperature of -50°C, a maximum pressure of 0.25 kg/cm³ and a maximum specific gravity of 0.972.[7]

The ship was arranged with an upright transom stern, aft machinery and accommodation, main deck, three cargo tanks, forecastle and a bulbous bow. A reliquefaction house with cargo control room above was located forward of the cargo manifolds. Three reliquefaction plants were fitted. Two 300 m³/hr Svanehøj deep-well pumps were mounted on domes at the aft part of each tank. The Boelwerf Insulation System (BIS) was again used with an insulation thickness of 120 mm. *Tielrode* was delivered without any deck tanks for change of grades, but provision was made for a future retrofit.

A second similar ship, *Gent*, was launched at Temse on 2 August 1985 and delivered to Exmar on 26 November 1985. Two 300 m³/hr Svanehøj booster pumps were fitted on the main deck. *Gent* was delivered with two 80m² change of grade tanks on the main deck above the forward cargo tank. In service, it was found that one tank was sufficient, and the redundant tank from *Gent* was retrofitted on the port main deck of *Tielrode* at Zeebrugge, when the ship was loading VCM.

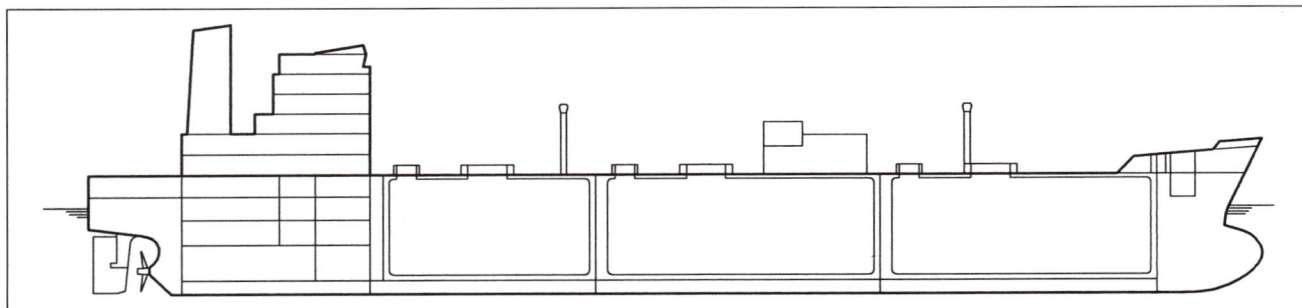

Figure 20-5 Profile of *Tielrode*

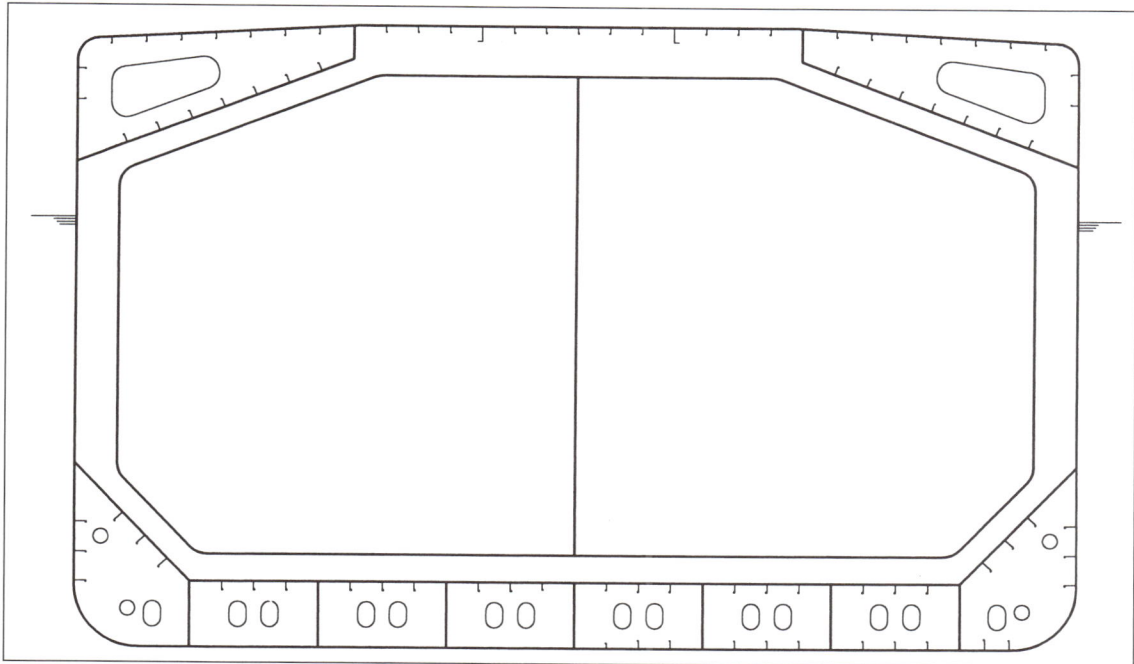

Figure 20-6 Midship Section of *Tielrode*

Plate 20-6   *Tielrode*   Boelwerf

Cheshire

Principle Particulars	
Length o.a.	165.66 m
Length b.p.	157.26 m
Breadth	26.50 m
Depth	16.20 m
Draught	11.74 m
LPG Capacity	28,000 m^3
Engine	Winterthur-Sulzer 6RLB66
Power	13,051 hp/9,600 kW
Service speed	16.2

In November 1987, Gasdam, a joint venture of Esdam and Exmar, associated companies within the Almabo-Boelwerf Group, ordered three 28,000 m³ gas carriers from Boelwerf. The design was a stretched version of 25,000 m³ *Tielrode*, with the same depth and breadth but with the length increased by 10.26m. The first vessel of the series was sold on to Bibby Line Ltd. of Liverpool and was delivered on 12 June 1989 as *Cheshire*. Two 300 m³/hr Svanehøj booster pumps were fitted on the main deck. Two change of grade tanks were fitted on the main deck above the aft cargo tank with capacities of 80 m³ and 250 m³. The ship could load a full cargo of VCM.

The second ship of the series was built to the joint account of Norwegian owner Christian Haaland and Exmar and was delivered on 23 October 1989 as *Nyhall*. The main propulsion unit was changed to a MAN B&W 6L60MC diesel, from Kværner Kinkaid, Greenock, and rated at 14,195 hp (10,440 kW) for a service speed of 16.2 knots.

The third ship of the series, *Chaconia*, was delivered to Exmar on 26 April 1990. Cockerill-Sambre supplied the MAN B&W 6L60MC main engine.

Plate 20-7   *Cheshire*   Boelwerf

Sombeke

Principle Particulars	
Length o.a.	165.66 m
Length b.p.	157.26 m
Breadth	26.50 m
Depth	18.60 m
Draught	11.72 m
LPG Capacity	33,619 m³
Engine	Cockerill-MAN B&W 6L60MC
Power	14,195 hp/10,441 kW
Service speed	16.2

In March 1987, Exmar ordered from Boelwerf a slightly larger vessel than the 28,000 m³ series. The length and breadth of *Cheshire* were retained and a 2.4 m increase in depth, produced a cargo capacity of 33,619 m³. *Sombeke* was basically similar to the 28,000 m³ series, except that VCM could only be loaded to 82.4% capacity. For change of grades, a 250 m³ and two 80 m³ deck tanks were fitted. *Sombeke* was delivered on 5 November 1990.

Plate 20-8   *Sombeke*   Boelwerf

Flanders Harmony

Principle Particulars	
Length o.a.	227.60 m
Length b.p.	217.00 m
Breadth	36.00 m
Depth	22.60 m
Draught	13.66 m
LPG Capacity	85,826 m³
Engine	Sulzer 5RTA72
Power	18,625 hp/12,330 kW
Service speed	16.5 knots

The largest and final fully refrigerated LPG carrier, as hull No. 1539, was completed in difficult times for the yard, with Boelwerf having filed for bankruptcy in the Belgian courts in 1992. Workers had occupied the yard and ship to prevent the sea trials, in the hope of forcing private shareholders to invest billions of Belgian francs to save the yard. The Belgian Government had promised a large subsidy for the construction, provided that the vessel could be considered as a prototype. A commission examined whether any of the design features were original, but concluded that the vessel was not a prototype, and consequently the subsidy was not paid. With no promise of new financial support, Boelwerf decided to file for bankruptcy, for a second time, after the first attempt was turned down. *Flanders Harmony* was delivered to Exmar on 17 December 1992.

Like all fully refrigerated LPG carriers built at Temse, the ship was constructed under the classification of Lloyd's Register of Shipping. The vessel was arranged with an upright transom stern, a stern free-fall lifeboat, aft machinery spaces and accommodation, four cargo tanks and a bulbous bow. The ship was designed to carry anhydrous ammonia, butane, butadiene, naphtha, propane and propylene, at a minimum temperature of -50°C, a maximum pressure of 0.24 kg/cm² and a maximum specific gravity of 0.71. Cargo handling equipment included three reliquefaction plants, eight 500 m³/hr deep-well pumps, two 560 m³/hr booster pumps and a combined cargo heater and vaporiser. The Boelwerf Insulation System (BIS) was installed and an inert gas plant was fitted.[8]

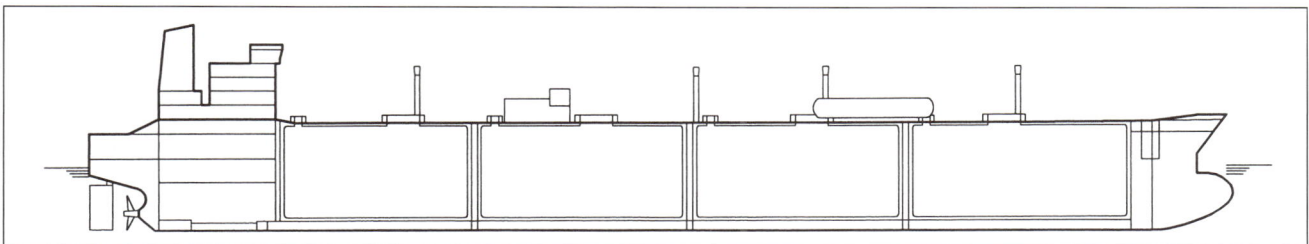

Figure 20-7 Profile of *Flanders Harmony*

1   Personal correspondence from Pieter Van Robaeys of Viamar NV to the author, 18 June 2001.
2   Boelwerf brochure, *LPG Carriers*, July 1977.
3   Boelwerf brochure, *Boelwerf Insulation System designed for LPG carriers*, October 1981.
4   Lloyd's List Casualty Reports, *Vessels and Berths, Pajaritos Lagoon, Mexico*, June/December 1985.
5   Hazardous Cargo Bulletin, *Problems at Pajaritos*, July/August 1985.
6   The Motor Ship, *Isomeria: a 58,950 m³ LPG tanker for Shell from Harland & Wolff*, May 1982.
7   Boelwerf brochure, *LPG-NH₃-VCM Carriers 25,000 m³*, October 1985.
8   Boelwerf brochure, *85,000 m³ LPG, NH₃, Naphtha Carrier*, September 1993.

Chapter 21

French Connection for NKK

In 1971, the Nippon Kokan K.K. (NKK Corporation) became licensed to build LNG carriers based on the Technigaz membrane technology. Some time later, a technical agreement was also made for Technigaz to provide assistance to the shipyard for the design and construction of LPG carriers. A strong bond was established between NKK and Technigaz in the 1970s, and co-operation continues up to the present day. In 1993, the first of the successful series of small LNG carriers using the Technigaz Mark III cargo containment system, the 18,900 m³ *Aman Bintulu*, was delivered from the Tsu shipyard of NKK.[1]

Benny Queen

Principle Particulars	
Length o.a.	224.50 m
Length b.p.	214.00 m
Breadth	32.20 m
Depth	22.00 m
Draught	10.98 m
LPG Capacity	70,792 m³
Engine	Mitsui B&W 7L67GFCA
Power	15,200 hp/11,179 kW
Service speed	15.4 knots

The fruits of the LPG agreement resulted in 70,792 m³ *Benny Queen* being delivered from the NKK Tsu works, to Japanese owners Showa Line Ltd., on 29 November 1981.[2][3] The design was based on the Panamax beam of 32.20 m. The ship was classed with Nippon Kaiji Kyokai as a Liquefied Gas Carrier for butane and propane, with the tanks designed for a minimum temperature of -46°C and a maximum pressure of 0.25 kg/cm². The ship was arranged with an upright transom stern with lower aft deck, aft machinery and living quarters, main deck, four cargo tanks and a bulbous bow.

The direct four reliquefaction plants were housed on deck above the forward end of No. 4 cargo tank. The cargo control room was located in the aft accommodation, as on most Technigaz designed ships. Mid-length cargo tank domes were fitted to accommodate the two 500 m³/hr J C Carter electric submerged pumps installed in each cargo tank. A void space steam eductor was fitted on the main deck. The cargo tanks were insulated with 120 mm of polyurethane foam, covered with galvanised steel sheets. An emergency stern cargo discharge system was also fitted.

A second, similar ship, *Tatsuta Maru*, was delivered from the Tsu yard to Nippon Yusen Kaisha (NYK Line) on 29 March 1982.

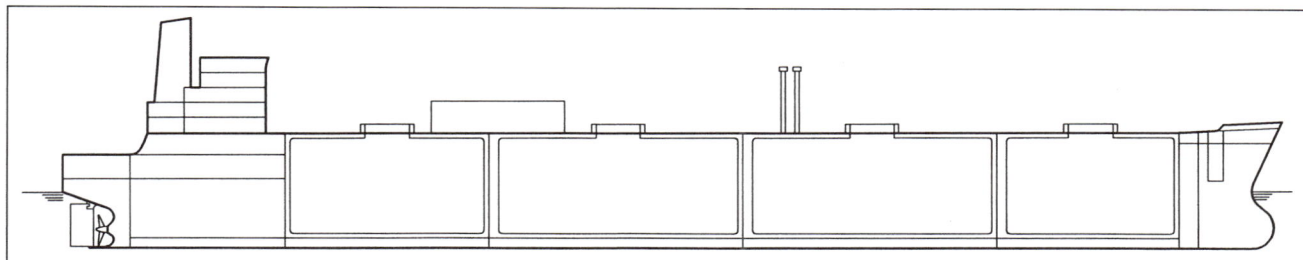

Figure 21-1 Profile of *Benny Queen*

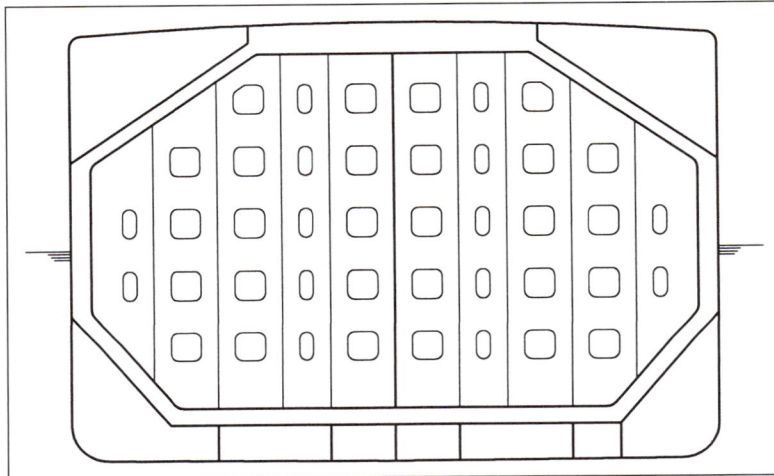

Figure 21-2 Midship Section of *Benny Queen* showing Cargo Tank Swash Bulkhead

Plate 21-1   *Benny Queen*   NKK

Plate 21-2   Void space steam eductor on *Benny Queen*

Plate 21-3   Operating void space steam eductor working on *Benny Queen*

Berge Commander

Principle Particulars	
Length o.a.	223.99 m
Length b.p.	212.00 m
Breadth	36.00 m
Depth	21.80 m
Draught	12.42 m
LPG Capacity	78,542 m³
Engine	Diesel United-Sulzer 7RTA62
Power	17,780 hp/13,077 kW
Service speed	16.75 knots

With Technigaz again acting as design consultants, the Tsu shipyard won an order for four multi-purpose fully refrigerated gas carriers from Bergesen dy A/S. The first of the series, 78,542 m³ *Berge Commander*, was launched on 17 October 1990 and delivered to the Norwegian owners on 26 March 1991. Compared to *Benny Queen*, which was designed for butane and propane trading, the main changes on the Bergesen ships were that the beam was increased to 36 metres and a wider range of cargoes were carried. The ship was classed with Det Norske Veritas as a Tanker for Liquefied Gas, and was also able to carry naphtha. The cargoes carried included anhydrous ammonia, butane, butadiene, butylene, naphtha, propane and propylene, with tanks designed for a minimum temperature of -50°C, a maximum pressure of 0.275 kg/cm² and a maximum specific gravity of 0.685.[4][5]

The ship's layout was similar to that of *Benny Queen*, with four cargo tanks. For the wider range of cargoes carried, two 560 m³/hr Kværner Eureka centrifugal deep-well pumps were fitted on domes at the aft end of each cargo tank. Two 300 m³/hr Kværner Eureka horizontal booster pumps and a cargo heater were also fitted. The four reliquefaction units were supplied by Nissin Refrigeration, with each including a Sulzer compressor and a sea water cooled condenser and rated at 190,000 kcal/hr in propane service. Propulsion efficiency was improved, with a semi-balanced rudder incorporating a NKK SURF (Swept-back Up-thrusting Rudder Fin).

The second ship of the series, *Berge Captain*, was launched on 26 April 1991 and delivered on 31 October 1991. *Berge Clipper* was launched on 25 October 1991 and delivered on 31 March 1992. The final ship of the quartet, *Berge Challenger*, was launched on 26 June 1992 and delivered on 26 November 1992.[6]

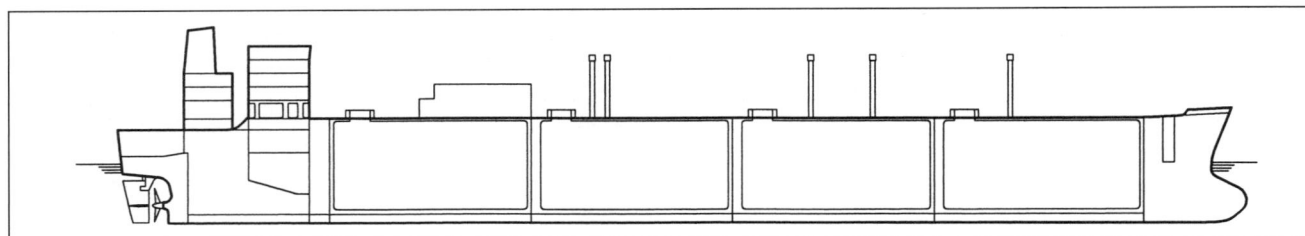

Figure 21-3 Profile of *Berge Commander*

On 1 October 2002, the shipbuilding operations of NKK Corporation and Hitachi Zosen Corporation were merged to form Universal Shipbuilding Corporation.

[1] SEA-Japan, *NKK to build its first LNG carrier*, No. 224, 1991.
[2] Shipbuilding & Marine Engineering in Japan JSEA, *Benny Queen, LPG Carrier*, 1982.
[3] NKK brochure, *NKK LPG Carrier*, November 1990.
[4] The Motor Ship, *Japan Delivers First Large LPG/ammonia Carrier*, September 1991.
[5] NKK brochure, *NKK LPG Carrier*, October 1994.
[6] Significant Ships of 1992, *Berge Clipper: Multi-purpose Gas Carrier*, Royal Institution of Naval Architects, London, February 1993.

Chapter 22

Scottish Roots for Hyundai Plants

The Ulsan shipyard of Hyundai Heavy Industries delivered their first gas carrier, the fully pressurised 4,000 m³ *Korea Gas*, in December 1986, to domestic owners. When looking at the pioneering work in European and Japanese shipyards, Hyundai was a comparative latecomer into the gas ship building business. However, in subsequent years the yard has become one of the driving forces in the unprecedented and rapid progress in South Korea with gas ship design and construction. Over forty gas ships have been delivered from Ulsan, with cylindrical, bi-lobe, prismatic and spherical tanks for LPG, NH₃, VCM, ethylene and LNG carriers. Capacities have ranged from 4,000 m³ LPG carriers to 137,000 m³ LNG carriers.

Jane Maersk

Principle Particulars	
Length o.a.	185.00 m
Length b.p.	173.40 m
Breadth	27.40 m
Depth	18.00 m
Draught	12.52 m
LPG Capacity	35,559 m³
Engine	Hyundai-MAN B&W 6S60MC
Power	15,300 hp/11,253 kW
Service speed	17.3 knots

The first fully refrigerated LPG carrier to be constructed at Ulsan was launched on 23 September 1990 and delivered on 28 November 1990, as 35,559 m³ *Jane Maersk*. The ship was one of a series of four ordered by A P Møller.[1][2][3] The ship was classed with Lloyd's Register of Shipping as a Liquefied Gas Carrier with tanks designed for a minimum temperature of -50°C, a maximum pressure of 0.28 kg/cm² and a maximum specific gravity of 0.97. Cargoes carried included anhydrous ammonia, butadiene, butane, butylene, propane, propylene and VCM.

The ship was arranged with an upright transom stern, stern thruster, aft machinery spaces and accommodation deck house, main deck, four cargo tanks, forecastle, bow thruster and a bulbous bow. A reliquefaction house was located forward of the cargo manifolds and a pressurised tank for change of grade was fitted on the main deck forward. The cargo tanks and secondary barrier were constructed with fine grain carbon manganese steel. The tanks were insulated with 120 mm of polyurethane foam with a protective covering. The insulation system was supplied by KangRin-Kaefer.

The gas handling plant and equipment were designed and supplied by Scottish engineering company Liquid Gas Equipment Ltd (LGE), of Loanhead, Edinburgh, who had worked closely with Hyundai for a number of years. Prior to the construction of the A P Møller ships, LGE had supplied gas handling equipment to all of the gas ships built at Ulsan. These early contributions by LGE helped to cement the foundations on which Hyundai were to build on, and from there they went from strength to strength in the gas shipbuilding business.

Eight Svanehøj vertical centrifugal deep-well pumps, (two per tank) and a Svanehøj booster pump were fitted, each rated at 350 m³/hr. Three cascade reliquefaction plants were fitted, with each plant including a Sulzer-Burckhardt labyrinth compressor, a Mycom R22 screw compressor, a seawater cooled condenser and a Aerzen vapour blower. Each plant was rated at 345,000 Kcal/hr in propane service.

The second ship of the series, *Jessie Maersk*, was floated out on 19 January 1991 and delivered on 20 March 1991. *Jakob Maersk* was floated out on 31 March 1991 and delivered on 24 May 1991. The final ship of the quartet, *Jesper Maersk*, was floated out on 1 June 1991 and delivered on 23 July 1991.

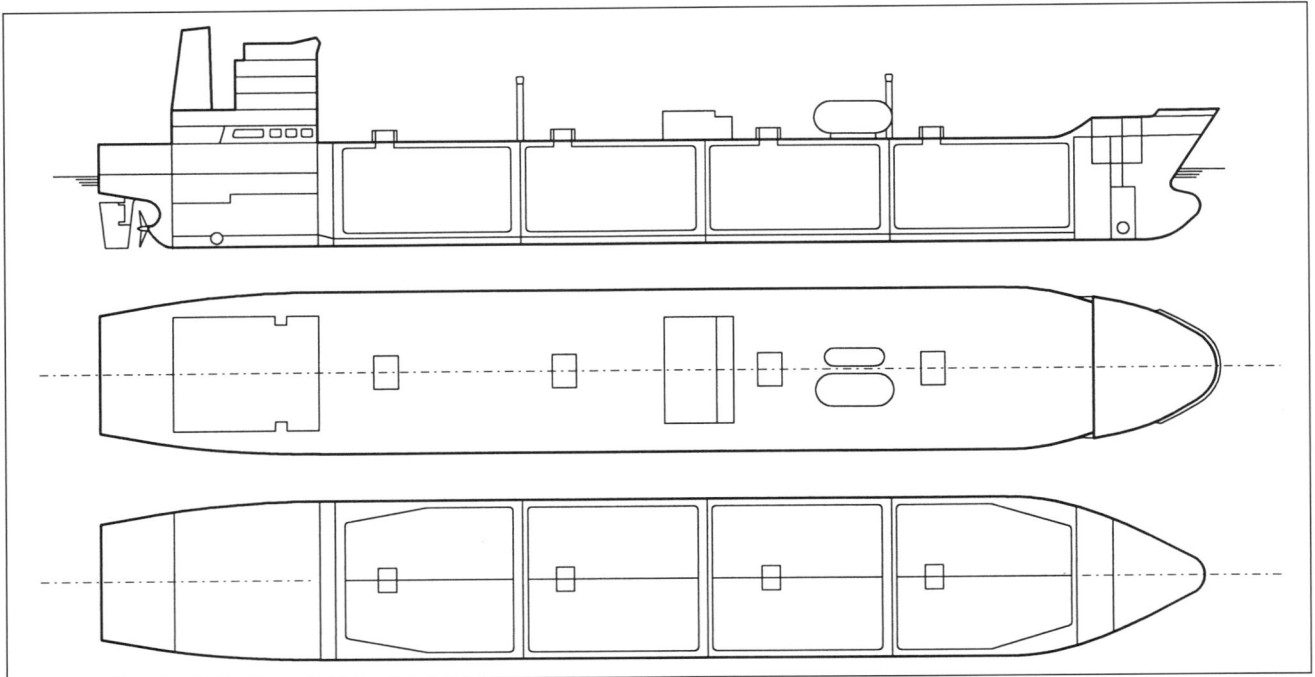

Figure 22-1 Outline Arrangement of *Jane Maersk*

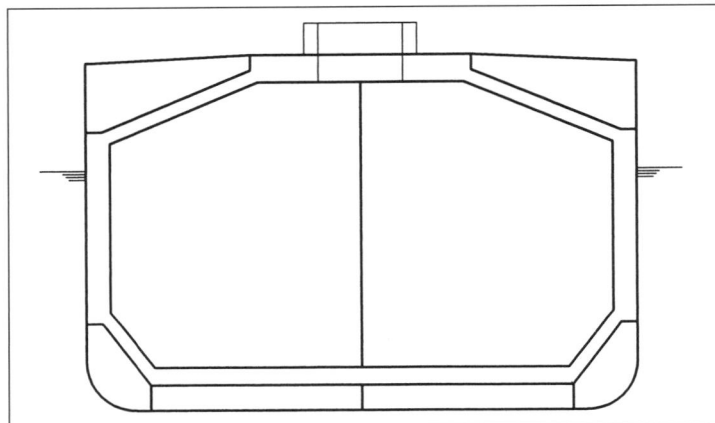

Figure 22-2 Midship Section of *Jane Maersk*

Plate 22-1   *Jane Maersk* under construction showing the bottom supports and keys for Nos. 1 & 2 cargo tanks   Hyundai/Archives of The Motor Ship

Plate 22-2   *Jane Maersk* under construction showing the forward end of No. 3 cargo tank   Hyundai/Archives of The Motor Ship

Plate 22-3   *Jane Maersk* on sea trials   Hyundai/Archives
of The Motor Ship

Nanga Parbat

Principle Particulars	
Length o.a.	160.00 m
Length b.p.	153.50 m
Breadth	25.90 m
Depth	15.40 m
Draught	8.31 m
LPG Capacity	22,500 m³
Engine	Hyundai-MAN B&W 6S50MC
Power	9,500 hp/6,987 kW
Service speed	15.3 knots

As well as delivering three A P Møller ships in 1991, Hyundai also delivered three 22,500 m³ fully refrigerated LPG carriers to Indian interests. The first two ships, *Nanga Parbat* and *Annapurna*, both named after 8,000 m Himalayan peaks, were for the Shipping Corporation of India. *Nanga Parbat* was floated out on 18 November 1990 and delivered on 30 January 1991. Dual classed with Lloyd's Register of Shipping and the Indian Register of Shipping, the vessel was designed to trade with anhydrous ammonia, butadiene, butane, butylene, propane and propylene cargoes. The fine grain carbon manganese steel cargo tanks were designed for a minimum temperature of -50°C, a maximum pressure of 0.28 kg/cm² and a maximum specific gravity of 0.7.

The ship was arranged with an upright transom stern, aft machinery spaces and superstructure, flush main deck with forward breakwater, three cargo tanks and a bulbous bow. As with the *Jane Maersk* series, the gas handling plant and equipment were supplied by Liquid Gas Equipment Ltd. The reliquefaction house was located aft of the manifolds and two 530 m³/hr Svanehøj vertical centrifugal deep-well pumps were fitted in each cargo tank, with two similar sized booster pumps fitted on the main deck.

The second ship for the Shipping Corporation of India, *Annapurna*, was floated out on 19 January 1991 and delivered on 3 April 1991.[4] The third ship for Indian owners, *Spic Diamond*, left the building dock on 30 March 1991 and was delivered to Southern Petrochemical Industries Company (SPIC) on 28 August 1991.

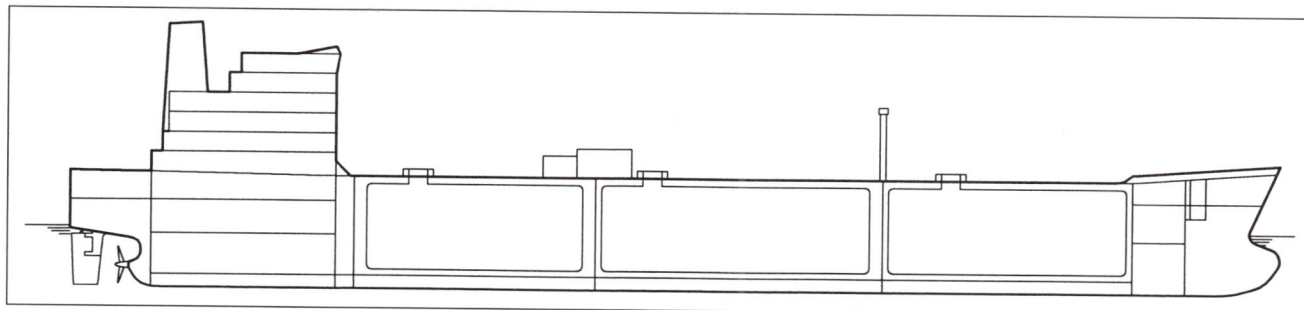

Figure 22-3 Profile of *Nanga Parbat*

Baltic Flame

Principle Particulars	
Length o.a.	219.89 m
Length b.p.	210.00 m
Breadth	34.20 m
Depth	22.50 m
Draught	13.40 m
LPG Capacity	76,643 m³
Engine	Hyundai-MAN B&W 5S70MC
Power	17,450 hp/12,834 kW
Service speed	16.5 knots

Hyundai completed a single 76,643 m³ LPG carrier, *Baltic Flame*, in 1992, for Mellitus Shipping Line under the management of Singapore's Tanker Pacific Management Ltd.[5] The ship was floated out of the Ulsan building dock on 10 June 1992 and was handed over to the owners on 30 November 1992. Classed with Lloyd's Register of Shipping as a LPG/NH$_3$ carrier, the ship was also able to load naphtha. The cargo tanks were designed for a minimum temperature of -48°C, a maximum pressure of 0.25 kg/cm² and a maximum specific gravity of 0.73.

The ship was arranged with an upright transom stern, lower aft deck, aft machinery and living quarters, main deck, four cargo tanks and a bulbous bow. A reliquefaction house was located forward of the cargo manifolds. Kværner Moss designed and supplied the cargo handling equipment, including the direct reliquefaction plants, 550 m³/hr Eureka centrifugal deep-well cargo pumps and an inert gas system.

The cargo tanks and secondary barrier were constructed with fine grain carbon manganese steel. Cargo tank supports incorporated both azobé hardwood and OBO-festholz laminated compressed beech wood. The tanks were insulated with 120 mm thick prefabricated polyurethane rigid foam panels, laminated with galvanised steel cladding, which was all supplied by KangRin-Kaefer. Each insulation panel was fastened to the cargo tank flat surface by a single stud-welded steel bolt and galvanised steel washer.

Plate 22-4   *Baltic Flame*   Hyundai

Lancashire

Principle Particulars	
Length o.a.	174.00 m
Length b.p.	165.00 m
Breadth	28.00 m
Depth	17.80 m
Draught	9.50 m
LPG Capacity	35,000 m³
Engine	Hyundai-MAN B&W 7S50MC
Power	13,580 hp/9,988 kW
Service speed	16.7 knots

United Kingdom shipowners Bibby Line Ltd., placed an order in South Korea for the first time, with a contract for a multi-purpose LPG carrier from HHI. The order was placed in August 2000, and 35,000 m³ *Lancashire* was delivered on 15 November 2002. Classed with Lloyd's Register of Shipping, the ship had three prismatic cargo tanks and two pressurised deck tanks. Cargoes which could be carried include anhydrous ammonia, butane, butadiene, dimethlyene, ethyl chloride, naphtha, propane, propylene and VCM. The gas handling systems were designed and supplied by Liquid Gas Equipment of Edinburgh.

In February 2002 HHI received an order for a 35,000 m³ LPG carrier from Japanese shipping company Mitsui OSK Lines. The vessel is scheduled to be delivered in the second half of 2003.

Hellas Nautilus

Principle Particulars	
Length o.a.	225.00 m
Length b.p.	215.00 m
Breadth	36.60 m
Depth	22.00 m
Draught	12.55 m
LPG Capacity	82,000 m³
Engine	Hyundai-MAN B&W 6S60MC-C
Power	15,300 hp/11,253 kW
Service speed	16.8 knots

The largest LPG carriers to be built in Ulsan were ordered for Greek clients of Consolidated Marine Management. With a capacity of 82,000 m³ and designed for LPG and anhydrous ammonia cargoes, *Hellas Nautilus* was delivered on 3 July 2003 and *Hellas Argosy* was delivered later in 2003.

A third 82,000 m³ vessel, *Kodeijisan* was delivered in 2003, to Japanese owner Shinwa Shipping.

In 2003, a 60,000 m³ LPG carrier was order from HHI by a Norwegian owner, for delivery in the fourth quarter of 2004.

---

[1] The Motor Ship, *Jane Maersk, First of a Series of Four Gas Carriers for A P Møller*, February 1991.
[2] Hazardous Cargo Bulletin, *Eye on Next Century*, September 1991.
[3] Significant Ships of 1991, *Jakob Maersk: an LPG Tanker for A P Møller*, Royal Institution of Naval Architects, London, February 1992.
[4] Significant Ships of 1991, *Annapurna: a Hyundai-built Gas Tanker for India*, Royal Institution of Naval Architects, London, February 1992.
[5] Significant Ships of 1992, *Baltic Flame: a Hyundai-built Gas Tanker*, Royal Institution of Naval Architects, London, February 1993.

Chapter 23

Pioneering French Connections at Daewoo

The foundations of the South Korean Okpo shipyard of Daewoo Shipbuilding & Marine Engineering Co. Ltd., (DSME), were laid on 26 September 1978. License agreements were made with Technigaz in 1981 and with Gaz Transport in 1990. Although the yard entered the gas ship building business even later than Hyundai in Ulsan, DSME has rapidly embraced both LNG and LPG gas ship technology. The yard's first gas carrier, the 130,600 m³ Gaz Transport membrane LNG carrier *Hanjin Pyeongtaek* was delivered to Hanjin Shipping Co. Ltd., on 30 September 1995. Since then the yard has made remarkable progress in series production and building of the components and ships based on the LNG containment system, with perlite filled plywood boxes and invar membrane strips. DSME have built, and have on order, over twenty 135,000 m³, 138,000 m³ and 140,500 m³ membrane LNG carriers.

Anne-Laure

Principle Particulars	
Length o.a.	224.50 m
Length b.p.	213.00 m
Breadth	36.00 m
Depth	22.30 m
Draught	11.70 m
LPG Capacity	78,680 m³
Engine	HSD-Sulzer 7RTA62U-B
Power	21,770 hp/16,012 kW
Service speed	17.6 knots

The first fully refrigerated LPG carrier to be constructed at DSME, 78,680 m³ *Anne-Laure,* was ordered on 5 May 1998, launched on 1 March 2000 and delivered on 30 June 2000. The ship was ordered by Geogas Shipping SA, Geneva, Switzerland. The vessel was classed with Bureau Veritas as a Liquefied Petroleum Gas Carrier with tanks designed for a minimum temperature of -48°C, a maximum pressure of 0.25 kg/cm² and a maximum specific gravity of 0.61. Cargoes carried included butane, propane and LPG mix.[1]

The ship was arranged with an upright transom stern with a lower aft deck, aft machinery spaces, separate engine casings, accommodation deck house, main deck, four prismatic cargo tanks and a bulbous bow. A reliquefaction house was located on the main deck above No. 4 cargo tank. The cargo tanks and secondary barrier were constructed with fine grain carbon manganese steel. The tanks were insulated with 40 kg/m³ density polyurethane foam panels covered with 0.5 mm galvanised steel sheets.

The gas handling systems were designed and supplied by Kværner Ships Equipment (KSE).[2] The reliquefaction plant, based on direct condensation, consisted of four skid-mounted units each with a Burckhardt Compression 3K 140-3A compressor and a sea water cooled cargo condenser. Two 550 m³/hr Eureka three-stage deep-well pumps were fitted in each cargo tank and two 550 m³/hr Eureka single stage booster pumps were fitted on the main deck. Other gas related equipment fitted included a shell and tube combined cargo heater and vaporiser, a 7,000 m³/hr inert gas generator and a 50 m³/hr nitrogen generator.

DSME currently have on order for Geogas Shipping SA a second similar sized vessel, building as Hull No. 2304.

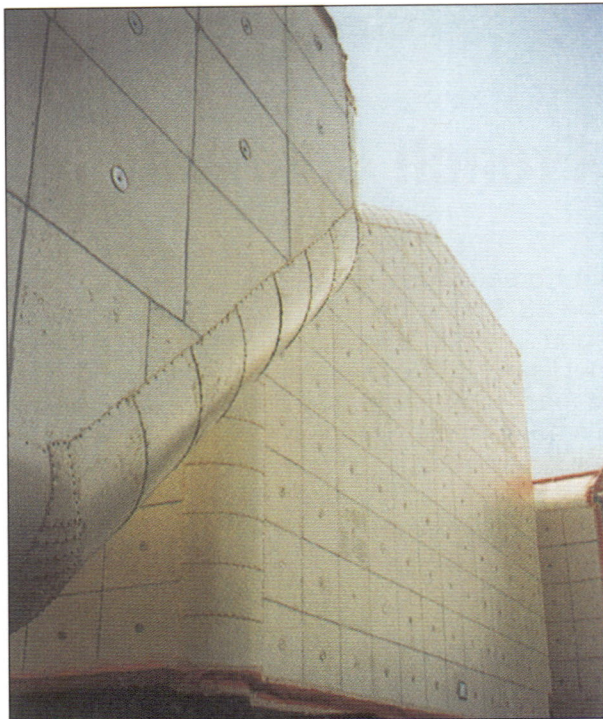

Plate 23-1   Insulated cargo tanks for *Anne-Laure*   KangRin-Kaefer

Plate 23-2   Positioning of cargo tank for *Anne-Laure*   KangRin-Kaefer

Plate 23-3   *Anne-Laure*   DSME

René

Principle Particulars	
Length o.a.	178.00 m
Length b.p.	170.00 m
Breadth	28.00 m
Depth	17.70 m
Draught	10.20 m
LPG Capacity	35,125 m³
Engine	MAN B&W 7S50MC
Power	13,580 hp/9,988 kW
Service speed	16.5 knots

Following on from *Anne-Laure*, the Swiss based Geogas Shipping SA ordered a smaller multi-purpose fully refrigerated LPG carrier from DSME. The keel was laid in November 2001 and 35,125 m³ *René* was delivered on 15 November 2002. Classed with Bureau Veritas, the vessel was designed to trade with anhydrous ammonia, butadiene, butane, butylene, propane, propylene and VCM cargoes. The fine grain carbon manganese steel cargo tanks were designed for a minimum temperature of -50°C, a maximum pressure of 0.25 kg/cm² and a maximum specific gravity of 0.97.

The ship was arranged with an upright transom stern, aft machinery spaces and living quarters, main deck, three cargo tanks, forecastle and a bulbous bow. A reliquefaction house was fitted on the main deck forward of the cargo manifolds. Nos. 1 and 3 cargo tanks were divided into port and starboard, whereas No. 2 cargo tank had no liquid tight centreline bulkhead. Two change of grade pressure tanks were fitted on the main deck above No. 1 cargo tank with capacities of 280 m³ port and 105 m³ starboard.

The gas handling plant and equipment were designed and supplied by Hamworthy KSE. Three direct reliquefaction plants were fitted, each with a 248 kW Burckhardt Compression 2K 160-2F oil free compressor and a sea water cooled cargo condenser. Two 400 m³/hr vertical centrifugal deep-well pumps were fitted in each cargo tank and similar sized horizontal booster pumps were fitted on the main deck. Other gas related equipment fitted included a shell and tube combined cargo heater and vaporiser, a 3,000 m³/hr inert gas generator and a 50 m³/hr nitrogen generator.

René Boudet played a major role in the development of LPG shipboard refrigeration, as described in Chapter 2. How fitting that this modern, sophisticated multi-purpose LPG carrier has been named *René* after the gas pioneer. The international LPG trading company Geogas was founded by René Boudet in 1979. He is now a director with the business, which since 1986, has been headed by his son Jacques. One of the key factors which has resulted in the success of today's gas shipping business is the continuous involvement of the major participants. The proud Boudet family connections are a prime example. The 1958 converted 1,012 m³ *Löex*, which cast doubt over the efficiency of pressurised cargo tanks, was named after the Boudet family estate in Savoie, France.

Earlier in 1962, 171 m³ *Agipgas Prima* was renamed *Jacques*. Three of the current Geogas LPG carrier fleet have the names of Jacques Boudet's daughters. 3,000 m³ *Lady Eline* was renamed *Philippine* in 1995, 17,900 m³ *Kelvin* was renamed *Victoire* in 1996, and *Anne-Laure* joined the fleet from DSME in 2002.

Plate 23-4   Deep-well pumps on *René*   Hamworthy KSE

Plate 23-5 Compressor room on *René* Hamworthy KSE

Plate 23-6 Cargo heater/booster pump skid for *René* Hamworthy KSE

Plate 23-7   Nyborg fan on *René*   Hamworthy KSE

Plate 23-8   *René* at sea   Geogas Shipping

Plate 23-9   Main deck looking forward on *René*   Geogas Shipping

In 2003, DSME won orders for five 38,000 m³ LPG carriers from three European owners. The newbuildings' Hull numbers are 2305 – 2309. Bergesen dy ASA and A P Møller each ordered two ships with Exmar taking a single ship. The ships, to join the Exmar-managed pool for medium sized FRLPG carriers, are scheduled for delivery during 2005 and 2006.

---

[1] Daewoo Shipbuilding & Marine Engineering Co. Ltd. brochure, *LPG Carrier Anne-Laure*, 2000.
[2] Lloyd's List, *KSE Gas Systems in Daewoo LPG Carrier*, 17 November 1998.

Chapter 24

STX Shipbuilding Company
Wins Order from Qatar Shipping Company

Since its foundation in 1962, the Busan Shipyard in South Korea has completed an impressive range of medium sized ships between 30,000 – 80,000 tonnes deadweight. Ships built include product, oil and chemical tankers, bulk carriers and containerships. Renamed STX Shipbuilding Company Ltd. in January 2002, the yard won its first gas ship order for a 23,000 m³ fully refrigerated LPG carrier for the Qatar Shipping Company (QSC) in April 2002. The option to build a second similar vessel was taken up in October 2002.

QSC Newbuildings

Principle Particulars	
Length o.a.	164.80 m
Length b.p.	155.30 m
Breadth	26.20 m
Depth	15.30 m
Draught	8.20 m
LPG Capacity	23,000 m³
Engine	MAN B&W 6S50MC-C Mk VII
Power	12,900 hp/9,488 kW
Service speed	16.5 knots

The Qatar Shipping Company currently have two 23,000 m³ fully refrigerated LPG carriers on order from STX Shipbuilding. The first, Hull No. 1112 is due for delivery in May 2004 and the second, Hull No. 1135 is due for delivery in December of the same year. The ships will be chartered to Qatar Fertiliser Company (QAFCO) to primarily carry anhydrous ammonia. The ships are designed as IMO type 2G vessels for the carriage of LPG, NH_3 and VCM in three independent prismatic cargo tanks. The ships are under construction to Det Norske Veritas classification.

Hull No. 1112 was launched as *Almarona* on 6 February 2004.

Plate 24-1   *Almarona* after launching   Qatar Shipping

Chapter 25

New Fully Refrigerated LPG Carrier Design Concept – *Ptarmigan*

This concluding chapter provides a good opportunity to examine where we are today and what the future holds for fully refrigerated LPG carrier design. The overall hull design and cargo tank construction of today's FRLPG carrier have changed little in the four decades which have passed since *Bridgestone Maru* was delivered from Nagasaki in 1961. What has changed is the gas handling and monitoring equipment. For example, direct reliquefaction has replaced cascade type reliquefaction, computer accuracy has improved the monitoring and custody transfer systems, and radar ullage systems have replaced the traditional float and wire ullage systems. Cargo tank supports, cargo tank and piping insulation techniques and cargo pump designs have evolved and improved with laminated compressed wood replacing azobé hardwood for example, panel insulation replacing on-site foam applications and the use of pre-insulated pipework.

Currently, the majority of fully refrigerated LPG carriers are built in Japan and South Korea. In the early days, European and Japanese yards were the driving forces in the development of gas ship technology. Although the shipbuilders have changed, with many pioneering European yards no longer in existence, the early connections are still there, influencing ship design and the specialist cargo handling equipment.

Take the numerous French connections, where a trace can be followed from René Boudet, Gazocéan and Technigaz to Bureau Veritas, La Ciotat, Shell, Compagnie Worms, CNIM, NKK and *René* built for Geogas at DSME. Early developments in Japan connect Mitsubishi, Bridgestone, Nippon Kaiji Kyokai, Conch, Shell, Kawasaki and *Kasmet*. The starting point in Sweden with Kockums, leads on to Phillips, Stal Refrigeration, Alfa Laval and even the Malmö gantry crane is now used by Hyundai in Ulsan. Germany's A G Weser provides early involvement for near neighbours Kaefer and for Marine Service GmbH and Esso. In Britain, the first FRLPG carrier was built at Hawthorn Leslie, and links can be found with Lloyd's Register of Shipping, George Gibson, Liquid Gas Equipment, Gazocéan, PEMEX, Bibby, Gastech, IMO, SIGTTO and Hyundai.

Moss Værft in Norway is the beginning of a steady line of influence within the industry, from this shipbuilding yard to Kværner, Det Norske Veritas, Mundogas, Moss Maritime, Havtor, Leif Höegh, Wärtsilä, Gdynia, Bergesen and Hamworthy KSE. In Belgium, shipbuilders Boelwerf can be connected with PEMEX, Harland & Wolff, Bibby and Exmar.

Land locked Switzerland's Burckhardt Compression still produce everyone's favourite LPG oil-free labyrinth compressor. An important continuous contribution has also been made by American submerged pump manufacturers J C Carter. Norsk Hydro's commitment to ammonia trading connects Verolme, IHI, Marine Transport Lines, Grace Lines, Hitachi and STX Shipbuilding.

These are some of the most obvious links, but the more you look, the more associations can be found within the gas shipbuilding industry world-wide. Long may this co-operation continue.

What about current designs for fully refrigerated LPG carriers. From Gdynia to Nagasaki, Genoa to Ulsan, all shipyards are offering basically the same design to ship owners. This design, with upper and lower wing water ballast tanks has become the industry's standard. Is this design so good that it cannot be improved?

I would like to close with a suggestion for a new concept for fully refrigerated LPG carriers. I have called the concept *Ptarmigan*. The ptarmigan is a bird native to cold regions of the northern hemisphere. Like a FRLPG carrier, it is equipped to adapt to changes in temperature. This remarkable bird has brown plumage in the warm summer and white plumage during the cold snowy winter months.

Ptarmigan

Principle Particulars	
Length o.a.	206.50 m
Length b.p.	195.00 m
Breadth	32.20 m
Depth	22.00 m
Draught	12.50 m
LPG Capacity	60,000 m³
Engine(s)	As required
Power	15,636 hp/11,500 kW
Service speed	16 knots

Ask any surveyor, superintendent, master, ship broker, manager or owner what the weak point of the fully refrigerated LPG carrier is, and the answer will invariably be the water ballast tanks. Water leaking from the periphery of the upper and lower wing water ballast tanks into the void space is a common problem to be faced when maintaining older LPG carriers. This water ingress into the void spaces causes damage to the insulation and in some instances has caused the cargo tank to float with resulting damage to the overhead main deck. Surveyors carrying out pre-purchase inspections of older gas ships will also examine the fore peak water ballast tank as another potential weak spot due to wastage and corrosion.

The new concept, *Ptarmigan*, has no upper and lower wing water ballast tanks and the fore peak is a dry space. On the *Ptarmigan* Panamax design, the distance from the keel to the inner bottom is increased to 3500 mm so that only the double bottom tanks are used for water ballast. A duct keel, which can be easily walked through, is arranged in the double bottom. A double side hull, extending from the inner bottom to the main deck, is incorporated in the design. The inner hull forms part of the secondary barrier and the construction offers greatly increased protection for the cargo tank from collision damage. I have always considered that the collision resistance of the fully refrigerated LPG carrier with the side hull forming part of the secondary barrier, could be improved.[1]

When considering collision risk, the greater the distance from the cargo tank to the side hull, the less chance there is of the cargo tank being ruptured. The distance of the cargo tank side to the side hull is 2100 mm on the 60,000 m³ *Ptarmigan* Panamax LPG carrier. The double side hull is a dry space.

The boundaries of the void spaces form the secondary barrier and have been arranged with all boundary stiffeners outside the void spaces. This is achieved by fitting transverse cofferdams between each cargo tank. Like the double side hull, each cofferdam is a dry space. This provides clear access to the void space for inspection and maintenance. On the conventional LPG carrier with a single transverse bulkhead fitted between each cargo tank large scantlings are required for the vertical webs of the transverse bulkheads, which reduces the space available for the cargo tank.

Fitting a transverse cofferdam between each of the cargo tanks reduces the overall length of the void spaces. The void space boundaries are constructed with few internal stiffeners. The cofferdam is of simple construction with horizontal stringers fitted in line with the side stringers in the inner hull.

Some of the design advantages of the *Ptarmigan* concept, are as follows;

- there is no change in capital cost over the conventional fully refrigerated LPG carrier.

- the overall ship dimensions are not increased.

- upper and lower wing water ballast tanks are eliminated.

- the fore peak is a dry space.

- more of the secondary barrier is constructed with flat plates.

- the cargo tank construction is simplified.

- the lower cargo tank square corners add to the cargo tank volume and this arrangement reduces the overall dimensions of the cargo tanks.

- the construction of the double side hull is simple with transverse plate webs, horizontal plate stringers and longitudinal stiffeners.

- the height of the inner bottom provides a comfortable space to work in for inspection and maintenance.

- the duct keel can be comfortably walked through.

- horizontal side stringers offer greater resistance to collision damage than side frames.

- unobstructed access is provided in the void spaces.

- access is provided through the inner side hull to the double bottom tanks without the need to provide low temperature steel access trunks within the void space.

- the side hull is mild steel and compared with a side hull constructed with low temperature steel, is easier to patch or repair in the event of minor damage from the knocks and bumps of general trading.

- the secondary barrier which is intended to contain any envisaged leakage of liquid cargo for a period of fifteen days is protected from external impact.

- the inner side hull is extended forward and aft to provide protection for the bunker tanks.

- any size fully refrigerated LPG carrier with independent prismatic cargo tanks can be considered.

From personal experience I also think that twin screw LPG carriers are another challenge for the future. On a number of occasions I have been on board gas ships when the ship lost its main propulsion, but fortunately the ships were well away from the shore at the time and weather conditions were favourable. The current industry buzz word on safety is *redundancy* and twin screw propulsion is an area that should not be overlooked.

I hope this publication provides a useful background to the world-wide development of the fully refrigerated LPG carrier, as well as offering challenging food for thought on possibilities of changes and improvements for the future.

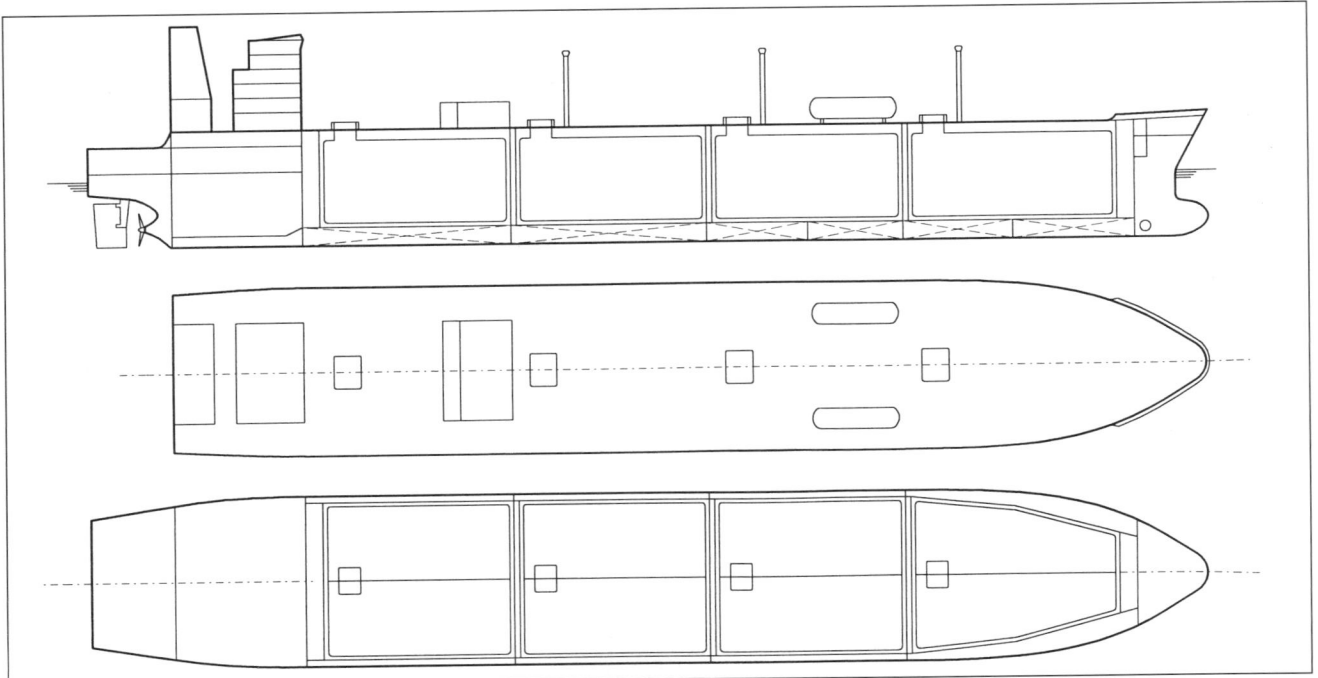

Figure 25-1 Outline Arrangement of a 60,000 m³ Panamax *Ptarmigan* FRLPG Carrier

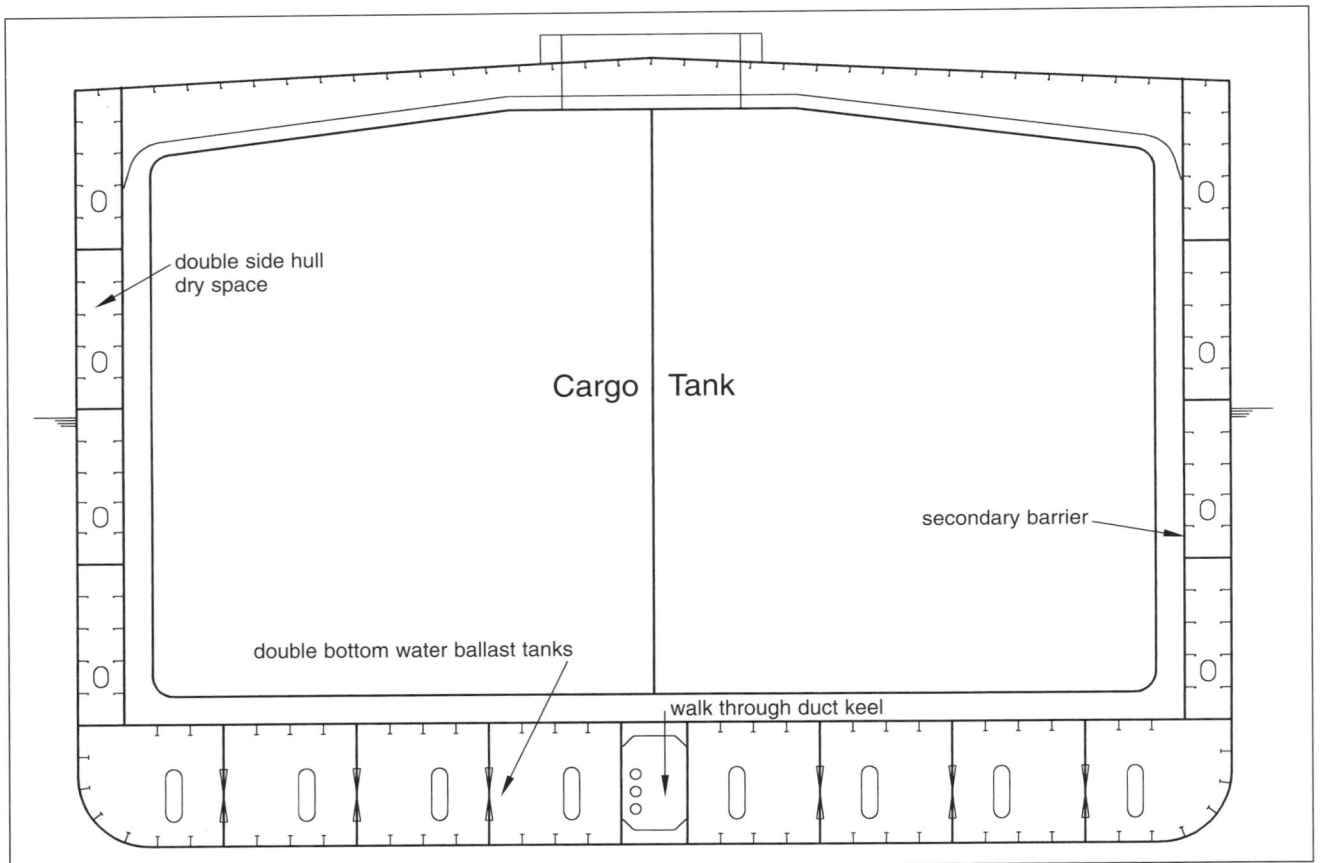

double side hull
dry space

Cargo | Tank

secondary barrier

double bottom water ballast tanks

walk through duct keel

Figure 25-2 Midship Section of a 60,000 m³ Panamax *Ptarmigan* FRLPG Carrier

¹ Harris, F. S., *Time for a Collision Resistant LPG Carrier Fleet,* Gastech 85, Nice.

Appendix I

Fully Refrigerated LPG Carriers Delivery Chronology

Delivery Date	Original Name	Shipbuilders	Hull No	Capacity m³	Current Name
Aug 1961	Iridina	La Ciotat, La Ciotat	conversion	10,808	Iridina
31 Oct 1961	Gohshu Maru	Mitsui, Tamano	658	11,300	Contovello
31 Jan 1962	Bridgestone Maru	Mitsubishi, Yokohama	845	28,837	Sea Petro
5 Mar 1962	Nisseki Maru	Hitachi, Innoshima	143 conversion	9,470	Beava
28 Sep 1962	Esso Centro America	A G Weser, Bremen	conversion	5,748	Gas Venture
Oct 1963	Toyosu Maru	Hitachi, Innoshima	conversion	13,145	Toyosu
28 May 1964	Paul Endacott	Kockums, Malmö	486	25,102	Petrogas I
6 Jun 1964	William R Grace	Verolme, Rotterdam	676	12,975	Amelina
5 Nov 1964	Bridgestone Maru II	Mitsubishi, Yokohama	856	36,008	Isavana
28 Dec 1964	Joseph P Grace	Verolme, Rotterdam	677	12,975	Savonetta
Sep 1965	Quentin	Grangemouth Dockyard	conversion	679	Quentin
25 Oct 1965	Joyama Maru	IHI, Nagoya	226	46,548	Joyama Maru
25 Nov 1965	Havgas	Moss Værft, Moss	150	11,071	Joule
14 May 1966	Bridgestone Maru No 3	IHI, Nagoya	235	47,124	Gaz Supplier
26 Jul 1966	Yuyo Maru No 10	Hitachi, Innoshima	4088	47,424	Yuyo Maru No 10
12 Oct 1966	Yamahide Maru	Mitsubishi, Yokohama	888	38,161	Bo Bengtsson
20 Oct 1966	Clerk-Maxwell	Hawthorn Leslie, Hebburn	759	11,750	Clerk-Maxwell
1 Nov 1966	Havfrost	Moss Værft, Moss	154	11,396	Gaz Channel
28 Mar 1967	Isfonn	La Ciotat, La Ciotat	235	18,790	Excel
21 Jun 1967	Petroquimico I	Hawthorn Leslie, Hebburn	764	3,499	Macuiltepetl
22 Jul 1967	Capella	La Ciotat, La Ciotat	240	14,268	Qeshm Gas
25 Aug 1967	Tatsuno Maru	Mitsubishi, Yokohama	889	50,542	Al-Hada 2
29 Sep 1967	Arquimedes	La Ciotat, La Ciotat	249	14,258	Pythagore
29 Sep 1967	M P Grace	IHI, Nagoya	244	19,450	Calina
30 Sep 1967	Kazutama Maru	Hitachi, Innoshima	4163	51,824	Kazutama Maru
Oct 1967	Aeolos	CNIM, La Seyne	1374	14,805	Asia Rainbow
11 Dec 1967	Mariano Escobedo	Hawthorn Leslie, Hebburn	763	11,474	Mariano Escobedo
Dec 1967	Aeolos II	CNIM, La Seyne	1375	14,465	Galileo
14 Feb 1968	Alexander Hamilton	Euskalduña, Bilbao	203	11,188	Aegis Diligence
8 Aug 1968	Kristian Birkeland	La Ciotat, La Ciotat	247	22,246	Mundogas Europe
16 Aug 1968	Gas Lion	Scotts', Greenock	771	11,843	Gas Pilot
27 Aug 1968	Roland	HDW, Kiel	1191	18,282	Andesgas
Aug 1968	Antilla Cape	A G Weser, Bremen	1366	29,540	Egypt Gas
6 Sep 1968	Wiltshire	Hawthorn Leslie, Hebburn	766	15,495	Zallaq
15 Oct 1968	Nyhavn	Moss Værft, Moss	160	19,450	Gaz Master
21 Jan 1969	Phillips Arkansas	Kockums, Malmö	519	26,505	Gaz Kandla
Jan 1969	Hypolite-Worms	CNIM, La Seyne	1376	29,866	Ile de la Réunion

Delivery Date	Original Name	Shipbuilders	Hull No	Capacity m³	Current Name
1 Apr 1969	Marine Eagle	Newport News	conversion	12,854	Marine Eagle
14 Apr 1969	Butanueve	Astilleros Cadiz	111	14,233	Kapitan Luca
20 May 1969	Gay-Lussac	La Ciotat, La Ciotat	261	40,232	Gaz Fountain
31 Jul 1969	Cypress	La Ciotat, La Ciotat	255	22,240	Mundogas Atlantic
13 Sep 1969	Bridgestone Maru No 5	Kawasaki, Kobe	1130	72,344	Bridgestone Maru No 5
22 Dec 1969	Gas Master	La Ciotat, La Ciotat	260	21,794	Cronos
24 Aug 1970	Kanayama Maru	Mitsubishi, Yokohama	908	70,238	Kanayma Maru
31 Aug 1970	Izumisan Maru	Mitsui, Tamano	866	60,990	Izumisan Maru
29 Dec 1970	Havis	Moss Værft, Moss	163	15,285	Nelina
4 Jan 1971	Faraday	Swan Hunter, Hebburn	12	31,215	Faraday
30 Apr 1971	World Bridgestone	Kawasaki, Kobe	1137	74,477	Sea Stone
10 Aug 1971	Cavendish	La Ciotat, La Ciotat	267	40,213	Gaz Supplier
27 Aug 1971	Yusho Maru	Hitachi, Innoshima	4308	73,211	Yusho
Aug 1971	Puerto Rican	Bethlehem Steel, Sparrows Point	4633	14,000	Puerto Rican
12 Oct 1971	Höegh Multina	Moss Rosenberg Værft, Stavanger	194	52,647	Havgast
16 Dec 1971	World Rainbow	Mitsubishi, Yokohama	924	70,247	Gaz Coral
28 Feb 1972	Gazana	Cammell Laird, Birkenhead	1341	29,791	Havjarl
9 Mar 1972	Lincolnshire	Swan Hunter, Hebburn	34	30,724	Lincolnshire
17 Jul 1972	Garmula	Moss Rosenberg Værft, Stavanger	195	52,647	OGC America
2 Feb 1973	Esso Fuji	Hitachi, Innoshima	4320	100,213	Esso Fuji
15 Feb 1973	Ogden Bridgestone	Kawasaki, Kobe	1171	74,578	Yuan Xing
2 Mar 1973	Gambada	Cammell Laird, Birkenhead	1342	29,791	Hesiod
18 Jun 1973	Antilla Bay	CNIM, La Seyne	1396	53,400	Havmann
Oct 1973	Dorsetown	CNIM, La Seyne	1397	53,400	Hesperus
24 Jan 1974	Hampshire	France Dunkerque	285	52,647	Hermes
28 Feb 1974	Amvrosios	Mitsubishi, Yokohama	946	70,131	Amvrosios
5 Jun 1974	Dovertown	CNIM, La Seyne	1398	53,400	Havprins
24 Jun 1974	Tokuho Maru	Mitsui, Tamano	952	61,203	Rainbow Gas
13 Aug 1974	Pine Queen	Mitsubishi, Yokohama	944	70,139	Gaz Med
10 Sep 1974	Sun River	Kawasaki, Kobe	1189	75,958	Sunny Gas
18 Oct 1974	Palace Tokyo	Hitachi, Innoshima	4408	100,181	Palace Tokyo
25 Nov 1974	Devonshire	France Dunkerque	286	52,647	Maharshi Vishwamitra
7 Feb 1975	Nektar	Mitsubishi, Yokahama	945	70,162	Nektar
4 Jul 1975	Nyhammer	La Ciotat, La Ciotat	296	66,341	OGC Energy
30 Sep 1975	Ogden General	Mitsubishi, Yokohama	954	70,358	Gaz Marmara
21 Oct 1975	Garbeta	Moss Værft, Moss	181	22,764	Maharshi Vyas
30 Mar 1976	Gandara	Swan Hunter, Hebburn	83	22,711	Maharshi Vasishth
3 Jun 1976	World Concord	Kawasaki, Kobe	1223	80,026	Gaz Concord
31 Aug 1976	Pioneer Louise	Mitsubishi, Yokohama	955	77,373	Louise
28 Dec 1976	World Creation	Kawasaki, Kobe	1224	80,026	Gaz Creation
31 Dec 1976	Höegh Swallow	Gdynia	B550/01	75,650	Gaz Poem
26 Jan 1977	Gas Gemini	Mitsubishi, Yokohama	956	77,961	Gas Gemini
31 Mar 1977	Garinda	Thyssen Nord, Emden	459	54,226	Hekabe
28 Jun 1977	World Vigour	Kawasaki, Kobe	1241	79,963	Gaz Suez
30 Jun 1977	Höegh Swift	Gdynia	B550/02	75,650	Evangelina 1

Delivery Date	Original Name	Shipbuilders	Hull No	Capacity m³	Current Name
6 Jul 1977	Monge	La Ciotat, La Ciotat	312	71,304	Berge Troll
27 Jul 1977	Esso Westernport	La Ciotat, La Ciotat	311	100,988	Gaz Imperial
30 Sep 1977	Staffordshire	France Dunkerque	297	74,537	Yuan Da
Nov 1977	Luigi Lagrange	Apuania SpA., Marina di Carrara	105	31,311	Luigi Lagrange
16 Dec 1977	Razi	La Ciotat, La Ciotat	313	70,914	Andean Gas
29 Dec 1977	Northern Arrow	Gdynia	B551/01	75,650	Berge Arrow
1 Feb 1978	Gas Diana	Mitsubishi, Yokohama	957	77,986	Gas Bauhinia
30 Mar 1978	Gas Al-Kuwait	La Ciotat, La Ciotat	314	72,121	Gas Beauty
31 Mar 1978	Galpara	Thyssen Nord, Emden	460	54,104	Havdrott
24 May 1978	Lord Kelvin	Apuania SpA, Marina di Carrara	108	31,243	Jag Vayu
5 Jun 1978	Sydfonn	La Ciotat, La Ciotat	318	22,182	Clipper Sun
30 Jun 1978	Northern Eagle 1	Gdynia	B551/02	75,650	Berge Eagle
18 Sep 1978	Gas Rising Sun	Wärtsilä, Perno	1229	75,680	Gas Rising Sun
29 Sep 1978	Galconda	Thyssen Nord, Emden	461	54,104	Havkong
21 Oct 1978	Centum	Moss Rosenberg Værft, Stavanger	204	52,647	Havglimt
30 Nov 1978	Höegh Sword	Gdynia	B550/03	75,650	Berge Sword
Dec 1978	Berge Sisu	Wärtsilä, Perno	1230	75,680	Berge Sisu
1978	Cornucopia	Todd Pacific, San Pedro	116	31,704	Cornucopia
2 Apr 1979	Gas Al-Burgan	La Ciotat, La Ciotat	315	72,121	Gas Al-Burgan
Apr 1979	Berge Sisar	Wärtsilä, Perno	1231	75,680	Berge Sisar
2 May 1979	Garala	Thyssen Nord, Emden	462	54,104	Hemina
28 May 1979	Yuyo Maru	Hitachi, Innoshima	4558	83,070	Yuyo
May 1979	Al Berry	l'Atlantique, St Nazaire I	26	76,929	Al Berry
Aug 1979	Monterrey	CNIM, La Seyne	1417	53,400	Steven N
Aug 1979	Reynosa	CNIM, La Seyne	1416	53,400	Clipper Lady
5 Sep 1979	Gas Al-Ahmadi	La Ciotat, La Ciotat	316	72,121	Gas Al-Ahmadi
21 Sep 1979	Mossovet	Breda, Venice	289	76,506	Gaz Progress
Sep 1979	Berge Saga	Wärtsilä, Perno	1232	75,680	Berge Saga
Sep 1979	Capo Levante	Clemna, La Spezia	22	1,350	Capo Levante
Dec 1979	Al Bida	l'Atlantique, St Nazaire	J 26	76,929	Al Bida
10 Mar 1980	Gas Al-Minagish	La Ciotat, La Ciotat	317	72,121	Gas Al-Minagish
31 Mar 1980	Gas Libra	Mitsubishi, Yokohama	958	77,327	Gas Aguila
Mar 1980	Golar Frost	Wärtsilä, Perno	1233	75,680	Berge Spirit
30 May 1980	Cantarell	Boelwerf, Temse	1500	57,590	Harriette N
Jun 1980	Lensovet	Breda, Venice	290	76,475	Gaz Atlantic
17 Sep 1980	Hektor	Moss Rosenburg Værft, Moss	194	24,048	José Colomo
17 Oct 1980	Ahkatun	Boelwerf, Temse	1501	57,000	Hugo N
15 Nov 1980	Genkai Maru	IHI, Aioi	2701	80,311	Genkai Maru
30 Dec 1980	Smolnyy	Breda, Venice	291	37,348	Havrim
Oct 1981	Berge Sund	Wärtsilä, Perno	1234	75,680	Berge Sund
25 Nov 1981	Iwakuni Maru	Hitachi, Innoshima	4666	8,082	Northern Lights I
29 Nov 1981	Benny Queen	NKK, Tsu	72	70,792	La Forge
2 Feb 1982	Tenryu Maru	Mitsubishi, Nagasaki	1876	77,290	Gaz Unity
29 Mar 1982	Tatsuta Maru	NKK, Tsu	75	70,792	Gas Meridian
1 Apr 1982	Berge Fister	Moss Rosenberg Værft, Stavanger	210	30,455	Herakles

Delivery Date	Original Name	Shipbuilders	Hull No	Capacity m³	Current Name
30 Apr 1982	Isomeria	Harland & Wolff, Belfast	1711	59,725	Isomeria
21 May 1982	Nichizan Maru	Mitsubishi, Nagasaki	1887	43,671	Libin
May 1982	Berge Strand	Wärtsilä, Perno	1235	75,684	Berge Strand
21 Jun 1982	Hektor	Frederikstad, Frederikstad	440	24,048	Hektor
29 Oct 1982	Isocardia	Harland & Wolff, Belfast	1712	59,725	Gaz Horizon
25 Feb 1983	Co-op Sunshine	Hitachi, Innoshima	4689	83,127	G Pioneer
30 Mar 1983	Clean River	Kawasaki, Kobe	1344	76,313	Clean River
Mar 1983	Floreal	NorMed, La Ciotat	328	85,662	Berge Frost
22 Jun 1983	Hebris	Frederikstad, Frederikstad	442	24,048	Hebris
27 Aug 1983	Eupen	Boelwerf, Temse	1509	57,000	Nejma
31 Aug 1983	Concordia Fjord	Moss Rosenburg Værft, Moss	200	24,054	Mahashi Dattatreya
14 Dec 1983	Tielrode	Boelwerf, Temse	1510	25,000	Oscar Viking
26 Apr 1984	Berge Rachel	La Ciotat, La Ciotat	331	81,600	Berge Rachel
29 Jun 1984	Hermion	Moss Rosenburg Værft, Moss	201	24,036	Hermion
25 Oct 1984	Toyosu Maru	IHI, Aioi	2865	39,113	Gaz Baraka
18 Mar 1985	Berge Racine	La Ciotat, La Ciotat	332	81,600	Berge Racine
21 Jun 1985	Koho Maru	IHI, Aioi	2922	80,681	Iris Gas
2 Jul 1985	Hourai Maru	Hitachi, Innoshima	4752	77,755	Hourai Maru
26 Nov 1985	Gent	Boelwerf, Temse	1519	24,663	Gent
6 Jan 1986	Berge Ragnhild	La Ciotat, La Ciotat	333	81,600	Berge Ragnhild
31 Jan 1986	Joyama Maru	Mitsubishi, Nagasaki	1957	82,513	Joyama
25 Mar 1987	Co-op Sunrise	Hitachi, Innoshima	4826	77,550	Berge Kobe
12 Jun 1989	Cheshire	Boelwerf, Temse	1529	28,000	Cheshire
21 Sep 1989	Nichiyuh Maru	Mitsubishi, Nagasaki	2023	78,507	Nichiyuh Maru
23 Oct 1989	Nyhall	Boelwerf, Temse	1530	27,473	Courcheville
19 Jan 1990	Kelvin	IHI, Kure	2983	17,900	Victoire
26 Apr 1990	Chaconia	Boelwerf, Temse	1532	28,150	Chaconia
19 Jun 1990	Sunny Hope	Mitsubishi, Nagasaki	2034	78,489	Sunny Hope
4 Jul 1990	Pacific Harmony	Kawasaki, Sakaide	1417	75,208	Pacific Harmony
20 Sep 1990	Gohshu	Mitsubishi, Nagasaki	2026	71,913	Gohshu
5 Nov 1990	Sombeke	Boelwerf, Temse	1533	33,619	Australgas
28 Nov 1990	Jane Maersk	Hyundai, Ulsan	668	35,559	Jane Maersk
13 Dec 1990	Gas Leo	Mitsubishi, Nagasaki	2028	78,484	Gas Leo
19 Dec 1990	Gas Roman	Mitsubishi, Nagasaki	2039	78,478	Gaz Energy
21 Dec 1990	Crystal Mermaid	Kawasaki, Sakaide	1420	75,203	Crystal Mermaid
30 Jan 1991	Nanga Parbat	Hyundai, Ulsan	681	22,500	Nanga Parbat
28 Feb 1991	Sunway	Mitsubishi, Nagasaki	2037	78,476	Sunway
20 Mar 1991	Jessie Maersk	Hyundai, Ulsan	669	35,559	Jessie Maersk
26 Mar 1991	Berge Commander	NKK, Tsu	123	78,542	Berge Commander
3 Apr 1991	Annapurna	Hyundai, Ulsan	682	22,478	Annapurna
5 Apr 1991	Helice	Kværner Govan	301	57,179	Helice
13 Jun 1991	Gas Aries	Mitsubishi, Nagasaki	2029	78,488	Gas Aries
24 Jun 1991	Jakob Maersk	Hyundai, Ulsan	670	35,559	Jakob Maersk
Jun 1991	Havfrost	Kværner Govan	302	57,179	Havfrost
23 Jul 1991	Jesper Maersk	Hyundai, Ulsan	730	35,559	Jesper Maersk

Delivery Date	Original Name	Shipbuilders	Hull No	Capacity m³	Current Name
23 Jul 1991	Tsugaru Gloria	Kawasaki, Kobe	1422	75,203	Berge Flanders
28 Aug 1991	Spic Diamond	Hyundai, Ulsan	700	22,478	Gaz Diamond
31 Oct 1991	Berge Captain	NKK, Tsu	124	78,542	Berge Captain
27 Nov 1991	Pacific Century	Mitsubishi, Nagasaki	2049	78,482	Pacific Century
26 Feb 1992	Noto Gloria	Kawasaki, Kobe	1429	75,203	Noto Gloria
17 Mar 1992	Sunny Green	Mitsubishi, Nagasaki	2056	78,507	Sunny Green
27 Mar 1992	Inger	Mitsubishi, Nagasaki	2053	78,488	N'Kossa II
31 Mar 1992	Berge Clipper	NKK, Tsu	129	78,542	Berge Clipper
29 Jul 1992	Helios	Kværner Govan	303	57,179	Helios
25 Sep 1992	Aries Duo	Kawasaki, Kobe	1425	75,203	Benny Princess
30 Oct 1992	Baltic Flame	Hyundai, Ulsan	750	76,643	Nordanger
26 Nov 1992	Berge Challenger	NKK, Tsu	131	78,542	Berge Challenger
10 Dec 1992	Gas Miracle	Mitsubishi, Nagasaki	2070	78,488	Gas Miracle
17 Dec 1992	Flanders Harmony	Boelwerf, Temse	1539	85,826	Flanders Harmony
25 Mar 1993	Musashi Gloria	Kawasaki, Kobe	1431	75,178	Musashi Gloria
27 Jan 1993	Energy Orpheus	Mitsubishi, Nagasaki	2069	78,488	Energy Orpheus
23 Feb 1993	Co-op Akebono	Kawasaki, Sakaide	1430	75,211	Co-op Akebono
25 Mar 1993	Gas Al-Mutlaa	Mitsubishi, Nagasaki	2057	78,488	Gas Al-Mutlaa
29 Jun 1993	Gas Al-Gurain	Mitsubishi, Nagasaki	2058	78,475	Gas Al-Gurain
8 Jul 1993	Hedda	Kawasaki, Kobe	1433	34,765	Hedda
22 Jul 1993	Oval Nova	Mitsubishi, Nagasaki	2060	78,469	Oval Nova
27 Dec 1993	Havis	Kværner Govan	304	57,179	Havis
25 Mar 1994	J A Sunshine	Kawasaki, Kobe	1437	75,386	J A Sunshine
29 Mar 1994	Helga	Kawasaki, Kobe	1434	34,765	Helga
12 Sep 1995	Eeklo	Kawasaki, Kobe	1448	37,520	Eeklo
22 Nov 1995	G Leader	Mitsubishi, Nagasaki	2103	78,479	G Leader
21 Dec 1995	Gas Scorpio	Mitsubishi, Nagasaki	2092	78,462	Gas Scorpio
10 Jan 1996	Elversele	Kawasaki, Kobe	1449	37,510	Elversele
31 Jan 1996	Gas Vision	Mitsubishi, Nagasaki	2104	78,502	Gas Vision
30 Apr 1996	Solaro	Fincantieri, Sestri	5962	37,314	Solaro
29 May 1996	Flanders Tenacity	Kawasaki, Sakaide	1456	84,269	Flanders Tenacity
19 Jul 1996	Lavender Passage	Mitsubishi, Nagasaki	2107	78,451	Lavender Passage
28 Nov 1996	Antwerpen Venture	Hitachi, Ariake	4889	39,270	Touraine
28 Jan 1997	Toyosu Maru	Mitsubishi, Nagasaki	2108	78,462	Toyosu Maru
31 Mar 1997	Agri Viking	Hitachi, Ariake	4903	18,152	Agri Viking
9 May 1997	Brugge Venture	Mitsubishi, Nagasaki	2113	35,418	Brugge Venture
30 Jul 1997	Gas Columbia	Mitsubishi, Nagasaki	2115	35,420	Gas Columbia
1 Oct 1997	Euro Viking	Hitachi, Ariake	4904	18,159	Euro Viking
25 Nov 1997	Oxfordshire	Mitsubishi, Nagasaki	2119	34,948	Oxfordshire
28 Nov 1997	Fountain River	Kawasaki, Sakaide	1469	79,527	Fountain River
29 Oct 1998	Carli Bay	Mitsubishi, Nagasaki	2146	25,302	Carli Bay
8 Feb 1999	Yuhsho	Mitsubishi, Nagasaki	2149	78,498	Yuhsho
31 Mar 1999	Eupen	Mitsubishi, Nagasaki	2147	38,961	Eupen
29 Nov 1999	Great Tribune	Mitsubishi, Nagasaki	2153	78,498	Great Tribune
30 Nov 1999	Reggane	Kawasaki, Sakaide	1487	84,350	Reggane

Delivery Date	Original Name	Shipbuilders	Hull No	Capacity m³	Current Name
30 Jun 2000	Anne-Laure	Daewoo, Okpo	2301	78,680	Anne-Laure
30 Jun 2000	Gas Diana	Mitsubishi, Nagasaki	2161	78,888	Gas Diana
28 Sep 2000	Berge Danuta	Gdynia	8185/1	78,550	Berge Danuta
4 Oct 2000	Djanet	Kawasaki, Sakaide	1492	84,310	Djanet
31 Oct 2000	Sunny Joy	Mitsubishi, Nagasaki	2150	78,874	Sunny Joy
29 Dec 2000	Berge Denise	Gdynia	8185/2	78,500	Berge Denise
31 Jan 2001	Linden Pride	Mitsubishi, Nagasaki	2164	78,874	Linden Pride
19 Mar 2001	Ocean Orchid	Kawasaki, Sakaide	1500	79,538	Ocean Orchid
29 Jun 2001	Gas Taurus	Mitsubishi, Nagasaki	2166	78,921	Gas Taurus
29 Aug 2001	Formosagas Apollo	Kawasaki, Sakaide	1497	84,300	Formosagas Apollo
28 Sep 2001	Dynamic Vision	Kawasaki, Sakaide	1510	82,200	Dynamic Vision
28 Dec 2001	Formosagas Bright	Kawasaki, Sakaide	1498	84,300	Formosagas Bright
15 Jan 2002	Yuhsan	Mitsubishi, Nagasaki	2174	78,929	Yuhsan
27 Jan 2003	Althea Gas	Kawasaki, Sakaide	1515	82,200	Althea Gas
27 Sep 2002	Dynamic Energy	Kawasaki, Sakaide	1511	82,200	Dynamic Energy
31 Oct 2002	Grace River	Kawasaki, Sakaide	1519	79,000	Grace River
15 Nov 2002	Lancashire	Hyundai, Ulsan	1414	35,000	Lancashire
15 Nov 2002	René	Daewoo, Okpo	2303	35,125	René
2002	Gaz Millennium	Hyundai, Ulsan	1367	22,500	Gaz Millennium
28 Feb 2003	Lycaste Peace	Mitsubishi, Nagasaki	2178	78,000	Lycaste Peace
26 Mar 2003	Clipper Star	Kawasaki, Sakaide	1522	59,200	Clipper Star
30 Jun 2003	Crystal Marine	Kawasaki, Sakaide	1518	80,138	Crystal Marine
30 Jun 2003	Gas Capricorn	Mitsubishi, Nagasaki	2179	78,934	Gas Capricorn
3 Jul 2003	Hellas Nautilus	Hyundai, Ulsan	1422	82,000	Hellas Nautilus
30 Sep 2003	Berge Nice	Kawasaki, Sakaide	1523	59,343	Berge Nice
2003	Hellas Argosy	Hyundai, Ulsan	1423	82,000	Hellas Argosy
2003	Gas Oriental	Hyundai, Ulsan	1430	35,000	Gas Oriental
2003	Kodaijisan	Hyundai, Ulsan	1436	82,000	Kodaijisan

Appendix 2

Fully Refrigerated LPG Carriers
Original Names

Original Name	Current Name	Capacity m³	Delivery year	Status
Aeolos	Asia Rainbow	14,805	1967	Broken up 1993
Aeolos II	Galileo	14,465	1967	Broken up 1984
Agri Viking	Agri Viking	18,152	1997	Trading
Ahkatun	Hugo N	57,000	1980	Trading
Al Berry	Al Berry	76,929	1979	Trading
Al Bida	Al Bida	76,929	1979	Trading
Alexander Hamilton	Aegis Diligence	11,188	1968	Broken up 1976
Althea Gas	Althea Gas	82,200	2003	Trading
Amvrosios	Amvrosios	70,131	1974	Broken up 1986
Annapurna	Annapurna	22,478	1991	Trading
Anne-Laure	Anne-Laure	78,680	2000	Trading
Antilla Bay	Havmann	53,400	1973	Broken up 2004
Antilla Cape	Egypt Gas	29,540	1968	Broken up 2003
Antwerpen Venture	Touraine	39,270	1996	Trading
Aries Duo	Benny Princess	75,203	1992	Trading
Arquimedes	Pythagore	14,258	1967	Broken up 1985
Baltic Flame	Nordanger	76,643	1992	Trading
Benny Queen	La Forge	70,792	1981	Trading
Berge Captain	Berge Captain	78,542	1991	Trading
Berge Challenger	Berge Challenger	78,542	1992	Trading
Berge Clipper	Berge Clipper	78,542	1992	Trading
Berge Commander	Berge Commander	78,542	1991	Trading
Berge Danuta	Berge Danuta	78,550	2000	Trading
Berge Denise	Berge Denise	78,500	2000	Trading
Berge Fister	Herakles	30,455	1982	Trading
Berge Nice	Berge Nice	59,343	2003	Trading
Berge Rachel	Berge Rachel	81,600	1984	Trading
Berge Racine	Berge Racine	81,600	1985	Trading
Berge Ragnhild	Berge Ragnhild	81,600	1986	Trading
Berge Saga	Berge Saga	75,680	1979	Trading
Berge Sisar	Berge Sisar	75,680	1979	Trading
Berge Sisu	Berge Sisu	75,680	1978	Trading
Berge Strand	Berge Strand	75,680	1982	Trading
Berge Sund	Berge Sund	75,680	1981	Trading
Bridgestone Maru	Sea Petro	28,837	1962	Broken up 1987
Bridgestone Maru II	Isavana	36,008	1964	Broken up 1984

Original Name	Current Name	Capacity m³	Delivery year	Status
Bridgestone Maru No 3	Gaz Supplier	47,124	1966	Broken up 1993
Bridgestone Maru No 5	Bridgestone Maru No 5	72,344	1969	Broken up 1985
Brugge Venture	Brugge Venture	35,418	1997	Trading
Butanueve	Kapitan Luca	14,233	1969	Broken up 1996
Cantarell	Harriette N	57,590	1980	Trading
Capella	Qeshm Gas	14,268	1967	Broken up 1999
Capo Levante	Capo Levante	1,350	1979	Trading
Carli Bay	Carli Bay	25,302	1998	Trading
Cavendish	Gaz Supplier	40,213	1971	Broken up 2002
Centum	Havglimt	52,647	1978	Trading
Chaconia	Chaconia	28,150	1990	Trading
Cheshire	Cheshire	28,000	1989	Trading
Clean River	Clean River	76,313	1983	Trading
Clerk-Maxwell	Clerk-Maxwell	11,750	1966	Broken up 1986
Clipper Star	Clipper Star	59,200	2003	Trading
Co-op Akebono	Co-op Akebono	75,211	1993	Trading
Co-op Sunrise	Berge Kobe	77,550	1987	Trading
Co-op Sunshine	G Pioneer	83,127	1983	Trading
Concordia Fjord	Mahashi Dattatreya	24,054	1983	Trading
Cornucopia	Cornucopia	31,704	1978	Broken up 2002
Crystal Marine	Crystal Marine	80,138	2003	Trading
Crystal Mermaid	Crystal Mermaid	75,203	1990	Trading
Cypress	Mundogas Atlantic	22,240	1969	Broken up 2001
Devonshire	Maharshi Vishwamitra	52,647	1974	Trading
Djanet	Djanet	84,310	2000	Trading
Dorsetown	Hesperus	53,400	1973	Broken up 2003
Dovertown	Havprins	53,400	1974	Trading
Dynamic Energy	Dynamic Energy	82,200	2002	Trading
Dynamic Vision	Dynamic Vision	82,200	2001	Trading
Eeklo	Eeklo	37,520	1995	Trading
Elversele	Elversele	37,510	1996	Trading
Energy Orpheus	Energy Orpheus	78,488	1993	Trading
Esso Centro America	Gas Venture	5,748	1962	Broken up 1993
Esso Fuji	Esso Fuji	100,213	1973	Broken up 1987
Esso Westernport	Gaz Imperial	100,988	1977	Trading
Eupen	Eupen	38,961	1999	Trading
Eupen	Nejma	57,000	1983	Trading
Euro Viking	Euro Viking	18,159	1997	Trading
Faraday	Faraday	31,215	1971	Broken up 1994
Flanders Harmony	Flanders Harmony	85,826	1992	Trading
Flanders Tenacity	Flanders Tenacity	84,269	1996	Trading
Floreal	Berge Frost	85,662	1983	Trading
Formosagas Apollo	Formosagas Apollo	84,300	2001	Trading
Formosagas Bright	Formosagas Bright	84,300	2001	Trading

Original Name	Current Name	Capacity m³	Delivery year	Status
Fountain River	Fountain River	79,527	1997	Trading
G Leader	G Leader	78,479	1995	Trading
Galconda	Havkong	54,104	1978	Trading
Galpara	Havdrott	54,104	1978	Trading
Gambada	Hesiod	29,791	1973	Broken up 2003
Gandara	Maharshi Vasishth	22,711	1976	Trading
Garala	Hemina	54,104	1979	Trading
Garbeta	Maharshi Vyas	22,764	1975	Trading
Garinda	Hekabe	54,226	1978	Trading
Garmula	OGC America	52,647	1972	Broken up 2002
Gas Al-Ahmadi	Gas Al-Ahmadi	72,121	1979	Trading
Gas Al-Burgan	Gas Al-Burgan	72,121	1979	Trading
Gas Al-Gurain	Gas Al-Gurain	78,475	1993	Trading
Gas Al-Kuwait	Gas Beauty	72,121	1978	Trading
Gas Al-Minagish	Gas Al-Minagish	72,121	1980	Trading
Gas Al-Mutlaa	Gas Al-Mutlaa	78,488	1993	Trading
Gas Aries	Gas Aries	78,488	1991	Trading
Gas Capricorn	Gas Capricorn	78,934	2003	Trading
Gas Columbia	Gas Columbia	35,420	1997	Trading
Gas Diana	Gas Diana	78,888	2000	Trading
Gas Diana	Gas Bauhinia	77,986	1978	Trading
Gas Gemini	Gaz Gemini	77,961	1977	Trading
Gas Leo	Gas Leo	78,484	1990	Trading
Gas Libra	Gas Aguila	77,327	1980	Trading
Gas Lion	Gas Pilot	11,843	1968	Broken up 1986
Gas Master	Cronos	21,794	1969	Broken up 1999
Gas Miracle	Gas Miracle	78,488	1992	Trading
Gas Oriental	Gas Oriental	35,000	2003	Trading
Gas Rising Sun	Gas Rising Sun	75,680	1978	Broken up 2003
Gas Roman	Gaz Energy	78,478	1990	Trading
Gas Scorpio	Gas Scorpio	78,462	1995	Trading
Gas Taurus	Gas Taurus	78,921	2001	Trading
Gas Vision	Gas Vision	78,502	1996	Trading
Gay-Lussac	Gaz Fountain	40,232	1969	Broken up 1985
Gaz Millennium	Gaz Millennium	22,500	2002	Trading
Gazana	Havjarl	29,791	1972	Broken up 2002
Genkai Maru	Genkai Maru	80,311	1980	Trading
Gent	Gent	24,663	1985	Trading
Gohshu	Gohshu	71,913	1990	Trading
Gohshu Maru	Contovello	11,300	1961	Broken up 1982
Golar Frost	Berge Spirit	75,680	1980	Trading
Grace River	Grace River	79,000	2002	Trading
Great Tribune	Great Tribune	78,498	1999	Trading
Hampshire	Hermes	52,647	1974	Broken up 2002

Original Name	Current Name	Capacity m³	Delivery year	Status
Havfrost	Gaz Channel	11,396	1966	Broken up 1996
Havfrost	Havfrost	57,179	1991	Trading
Havgas	Joule	11,071	1965	Broken up 1984
Havis	Havis	57,179	1993	Trading
Havis	Nelina	15,285	1970	Broken up 1994
Hebris	Hebris	24,048	1983	Trading
Hedda	Hedda	34,765	1993	Trading
Hektor	José Colomo	24,048	1980	Trading
Hektor	Hektor	24,048	1982	Trading
Helga	Helga	34,765	1994	Trading
Helice	Helice	57,179	1991	Trading
Helios	Helios	57,179	1992	Trading
Hellas Argosy	Hellas Argosy	82,000	2003	Trading
Hellas Nautilus	Hellas Nautilus	82,000	2003	Trading
Hermion	Hermion	24,036	1984	Trading
Höegh Multina	Havgast	52,647	1971	Broken up 2001
Höegh Swallow	Gaz Poem	75,650	1976	Broken up 2003
Höegh Swift	Evangelina 1	75,650	1977	Trading
Höegh Sword	Berge Sword	75,650	1978	Trading
Hourai Maru	Hourai Maru	77,755	1985	Trading
Hypolite-Worms	Ile de la Réunion	29,866	1969	Converted to Ro-Ro
Inger	N'Kossa II	78,488	1992	FSO
Iridina	Iridina	10,808	1961	Broken up 1969
Isfonn	Excel	18,790	1967	Broken up 1997
Isocardia	Gaz Horizon	59,725	1982	Trading
Isomeria	Isomeria	59,725	1982	Trading
Iwakuni Maru	Northern Lights I	8,082	1981	Trading
Izumisan Maru	Izumisan Maru	60,990	1970	Broken up 1986
J A Sunshine	J A Sunshine	75,386	1994	Trading
Jakob Maersk	Jakob Maersk	35,559	1991	Trading
Jane Maersk	Jane Maersk	35,559	1990	Trading
Jesper Maersk	Jesper Maersk	35,559	1991	Trading
Jessie Maersk	Jessie Maersk	35,559	1991	Trading
Joseph P Grace	Savonetta	12,975	1964	Broken up 1998
Joyama Maru	Joyama	82,513	1986	Trading
Joyama Maru	Joyama Maru	46,548	1965	Broken up 1985
Kanayama Maru	Kanayma Maru	70,238	1970	Broken up 1985
Kazutama Maru	Kazutama Maru	51,824	1967	Broken up 1983
Kelvin	Victoire	17,900	1990	Trading
Kodaijisan	Kodaijisan	82,000	2003	Trading
Koho Maru	Iris Gas	80,681	1985	Trading
Kristian Birkeland	Mundogas Europe	22,246	1968	Broken up 2000
Lancashire	Lancashire	35,000	2002	Trading
Lavender Passage	Lavender Passage	78,451	1996	Trading

Original Name	Current Name	Capacity m³	Delivery year	Status
Lensovet	Gaz Atlantic	76,475	1980	Trading
Lincolnshire	Lincolnshire	30,724	1972	Broken up 2002
Linden Pride	Linden Pride	78,874	2001	Trading
Lord Kelvin	Jag Vayu	31,243	1978	Trading
Luigi Lagrange	Luigi Lagrange	31,311	1977	Trading
Lycaste Peace	Lycaste Peace	78,000	2003	Trading
M P Grace	Calina	19,450	1967	Broken up 1999
Mariano Escobedo	Mariano Escobedo	11,474	1967	Trading
Marine Eagle	Marine Eagle	12,854	1969	Broken up 1985
Monge	Berge Troll	71,304	1977	Trading
Monterrey	Steven N	53,400	1979	Trading
Mossovet	Gaz Progress	76,506	1979	Trading
Mundogas Rio	Gaz Hudson	19,462	1967	Broken up 2002
Musashi Gloria	Musashi Gloria	75,178	1993	Trading
Nanga Parbat	Nanga Parbat	22,500	1991	Trading
Nektar	Nektar	70,162	1975	Broken up 1998
Nichiyuh Maru	Nichiyuh Maru	78,507	1989	Trading
Nichizan Maru	Libin	43,671	1982	Trading
Nisseki Maru	Beava	9,470	1962	Broken up 1974
Northern Arrow	Berge Arrow	75,650	1977	Trading
Northern Eagle 1	Berge Eagle	75,650	1978	Trading
Noto Gloria	Noto Gloria	75,203	1992	Trading
Nyhall	Courcheville	27,473	1989	Trading
Nyhammer	OGC Energy	66,341	1975	Broken up 2002.
Nyhavn	Gaz Master	19,450	1968	Trading
Ocean Orchid	Ocean Orchid	79,538	2001	Trading
Ogden Bridgestone	Yuan Xing	74,578	1973	Broken up 2002
Ogden General	Gaz Marmara	70,358	1975	Broken up 2003
Oval Nova	Oval Nova	78,469	1993	Trading
Oxfordshire	Oxfordshire	34,948	1997	Trading
Pacific Century	Pacific Century	78,482	1991	Trading
Pacific Harmony	Pacific Harmony	75,208	1990	Trading
Palace Tokyo	Palace Tokyo	100,181	1974	Broken up 1986
Paul Endacott	Petrogas I	25,102	1964	Broken up 1986
Petroquimico I	Macuiltepetl	3,499	1967	Broken up 1996
Phillips Arkansas	Gaz Kandla	26,505	1969	Broken up 2001
Pine Queen	Gaz Med	70,139	1974	Trading
Pioneer Louise	Louise	77,373	1976	Trading
Puerto Rican	Puerto Rican	14,000	1971	Constructive total loss 1986
Quentin	Quentin	679	1965	Broken up 1976
Razi	Andean Gas	70,914	1977	Trading
Reggane	Reggane	84,350	1999	Trading
René	René	35,125	2002	Trading
Reynosa	Clipper Lady	53,400	1979	Trading

Original Name	Current Name	Capacity m³	Delivery year	Status
Roland	Andesgas	18,282	1968	Broken up 1998
Smolnyy	Havrim	37,348	1980	Trading
Solaro	Solaro	37,314	1996	Trading
Sombeke	Australgas	33,619	1990	Trading
Spic Diamond	Gaz Diamond	22,478	1991	Trading
Staffordshire	Yuan Da	74,537	1977	Broken up 2003
Sun River	Sunny Gas	75,958	1974	Trading
Sunny Green	Sunny Green	78,507	1992	Trading
Sunny Hope	Sunny Hope	78,489	1990	Trading
Sunny Joy	Sunny Joy	78,874	2000	Trading
Sunway	Sunway	78,476	1991	Trading
Sydfonn	Clipper Sun	22,182	1978	Trading
Tatsuno Maru	Al-Hada 2	50,542	1967	Broken up 1985
Tatsuta Maru	Gaz Meridian	70,792	1982	Trading
Tenryu Maru	Gaz Unity	77,290	1982	Trading
Tielrode	Oscar Viking	25,000	1983	Trading
Tokuho Maru	Rainbow Gas	61,203	1974	Broken up 2003
Toyosu Maru	Toyosu Maru	78,462	1997	Trading
Toyosu Maru	Toyosu	13,145	1963	Broken up 1985
Toyosu Maru	Gaz Baraka	39,113	1984	Trading
Tsugaru Gloria	Berge Flanders	75,203	1991	Trading
William R Grace	Amelina	12,975	1964	Broken up 1999
Wiltshire	Zallaq	15,495	1968	Broken up 1998
World Bridgestone	Sea Stone	74,477	1971	Broken up 2003
World Concord	Gaz Concord	80,026	1976	Trading
World Creation	Gaz Creation	80,026	1976	Trading
World Rainbow	Gaz Coral	70,247	1971	Broken up 2003
World Vigour	Gaz Suez	79,963	1977	Trading
Yamahide Maru	Bo Bengtsson	38,161	1966	Broken up 1985
Yuhsan	Yuhsan	78,929	2002	Trading
Yuhsho	Yuhsho	78,498	1999	Trading
Yusho Maru	Yusho	73,211	1971	Broken up 1985
Yuyo Maru	Yuyo	83,070	1979	Trading
Yuyo Maru No 10	Yuyo Maru No 10	47,424	1966	Destroyed after fire 1974

Appendix 3

Fully Refrigerated LPG Carriers Current Names

Current Name	Original Name	Capacity m³	Delivery year	Status
Aegis Diligence	Alexander Hamilton	11,188	1968	Broken up 1976
Agri Viking	Agri Viking	18,152	1997	Trading
Al Berry	Al Berry	76,929	1979	Trading
Al Bida	Al Bida	76,929	1979	Trading
Al-Hada 2	Tatsuno Maru	50,542	1967	Broken up 1985
Amelina	William R Grace	12,975	1964	Broken up 1999
Amvrosios	Amvrosios	70,131	1974	Broken up 1986
Andean Gas	Razi	70,914	1977	Trading
Andesgas	Roland	18,282	1968	Broken up 1998
Annapurna	Annapurna	22,478	1991	Trading
Anne-Laure	Anne-Laure	78,680	2000	Trading
Asia Rainbow	Aeolos	14,805	1967	Broken up 1993
Australgas	Sombeke	33,619	1990	Trading
Beava	Nisseki Maru	9,470	1962	Broken up 1974
Benny Princess	Aries Duo	75,203	1992	Trading
Berge Arrow	Northern Arrow	75,650	1977	Trading
Berge Captain	Berge Captain	78,542	1991	Trading
Berge Challenger	Berge Challenger	78,542	1992	Trading
Berge Clipper	Berge Clipper	78,542	1992	Trading
Berge Commander	Berge Commander	78,542	1991	Trading
Berge Danuta	Berge Danuta	78,550	2000	Trading
Berge Denise	Berge Denise	78,500	2000	Trading
Berge Eagle	Northern Eagle 1	75,650	1978	Trading
Berge Flanders	Tsugaru Gloria	75,203	1991	Trading
Berge Frost	Floreal	85,662	1983	Trading
Berge Kobe	Co-op Sunrise	77,550	1987	Trading
Berge Nice	Berge Nice	59,343	2003	Trading
Berge Rachel	Berge Rachel	81,600	1984	Trading
Berge Racine	Berge Racine	81,600	1985	Trading
Berge Ragnhild	Berge Ragnhild	81,600	1986	Trading
Berge Saga	Berge Saga	75,680	1979	Trading
Berge Sisar	Berge Sisar	75,680	1979	Trading
Berge Sisu	Berge Sisu	75,680	1978	Trading
Berge Spirit	Golar Frost	75,680	1980	Trading
Berge Strand	Berge Strand	75,680	1982	Trading
Berge Sund	Berge Sund	75,680	1981	Trading

Current Name	Original Name	Capacity m³	Delivery year	Status
Berge Sword	Höegh Sword	75,650	1978	Trading
Berge Troll	Monge	71,304	1977	Trading
Bo Bengtsson	Yamahide Maru	38,161	1966	Broken up 1985
Bridgestone Maru No 5	Bridgestone Maru No 5	72,344	1969	Broken up 1985
Brugge Venture	Brugge Venture	35,418	1997	Trading
Calina	M P Grace	19,450	1967	Broken up 1999
Capo Levante	Capo Levante	1,350	1979	Trading
Carli Bay	Carli Bay	25,302	1998	Trading
Chaconia	Chaconia	28,150	1990	Trading
Cheshire	Cheshire	28,000	1989	Trading
Clean River	Clean River	76,313	1983	Trading
Clerk-Maxwell	Clerk-Maxwell	11,750	1966	Broken up 1986
Clipper Lady	Reynosa	53,400	1979	Trading
Clipper Star	Clipper Star	59,200	2003	Trading
Clipper Sun	Sydfonn	22,182	1978	Trading
Co-op Akebono	Co-op Akebono	75,211	1993	Trading
Contovello	Gohshu Maru	11,300	1961	Broken up 1982
Cornucopia	Cornucopia	31,704	1978	Broken up 2002
Courcheville	Nyhall	27,473	1989	Trading
Cronos	Gas Master	21,794	1969	Broken up 1999
Crystal Marine	Crystal Marine	80,138	2003	Trading
Crystal Mermaid	Crystal Mermaid	75,203	1990	Trading
Djanet	Djanet	84,310	2000	Trading
Dynamic Energy	Dynamic Energy	82,200	2002	Trading
Dynamic Vision	Dynamic Vision	82,200	2001	Trading
Eeklo	Eeklo	37,520	1995	Trading
Egypt Gas	Antilla Cape	29,540	1968	Broken up 2003
Elversele	Elversele	37,510	1996	Trading
Energy Orpheus	Energy Orpheus	78,488	1993	Trading
Esso Fuji	Esso Fuji	100,213	1973	Broken up 1987
Eupen	Eupen	38,961	1999	Trading
Euro Viking	Euro Viking	18,159	1997	Trading
Evangelina 1	Höegh Swift	75,650	1977	Trading
Excel	Isfonn	18,790	1967	Broken up 1997
Faraday	Faraday	31,215	1971	Broken up 1994
Flanders Harmony	Flanders Harmony	85,826	1992	Trading
Flanders Tenacity	Flanders Tenacity	84,269	1996	Trading
Formosagas Apollo	Formosagas Apollo	84,300	2001	Trading
Formosagas Bright	Formosagas Bright	84,300	2001	Trading
Fountain River	Fountain River	79,527	1997	Trading
G Leader	G Leader	78,479	1995	Trading
G Pioneer	Co-op Sunshine	83,127	1983	Trading
Galileo	Aeolos II	14,465	1967	Broken up 1984
Gas Aguila	Gas Libra	77,327	1980	Trading

Current Name	Original Name	Capacity m³	Delivery year	Status
Gas Al-Ahmadi	Gas Al-Ahmadi	72,121	1979	Trading
Gas Al-Burgan	Gas Al-Burgan	72,121	1979	Trading
Gas Al-Gurain	Gas Al-Gurain	78,475	1993	Trading
Gas Al-Minagish	Gas Al-Minagish	72,121	1980	Trading
Gas Al-Mutlaa	Gas Al-Mutlaa	78,488	1993	Trading
Gas Aries	Gas Aries	78,488	1991	Trading
Gas Bauhinia	Gas Diana	77,986	1978	Trading
Gas Beauty	Gas Al-Kuwait	72,121	1978	Trading
Gas Capricorn	Gas Capricorn	78,934	2003	Trading
Gas Columbia	Gas Columbia	35,420	1997	Trading
Gas Diana	Gas Diana	78,888	2000	Trading
Gas Leo	Gas Leo	78,484	1990	Trading
Gas Miracle	Gas Miracle	78,488	1992	Trading
Gas Oriental	Gas Oriental	35,000	2003	Trading
Gas Pilot	Gas Lion	11,843	1968	Broken up 1986
Gas Rising Sun	Gas Rising Sun	75,680	1978	Broken up 2003
Gas Scorpio	Gas Scorpio	78,462	1995	Trading
Gas Taurus	Gas Taurus	78,921	2001	Trading
Gas Venture	Esso Centro America	5,748	1962	Broken up 1993
Gas Vision	Gas Vision	78,502	1996	Trading
Gaz Atlantic	Lensovet	76,475	1980	Trading
Gaz Baraka	Toyosu Maru	39,113	1984	Trading
Gaz Channel	Havfrost	11,396	1966	Broken up 1996
Gaz Concord	World Concord	80,026	1976	Trading
Gaz Coral	World Rainbow	70,247	1971	Broken up 2003
Gaz Creation	World Creation	80,026	1976	Trading
Gaz Diamond	Spic Diamond	22,478	1991	Trading
Gaz Energy	Gas Roman	78,478	1990	Trading
Gaz Fountain	Gay-Lussac	40,232	1969	Broken up 1985
Gaz Gemini	Gaz Gemini	77,961	1977	Trading
Gaz Horizon	Isocardia	59,725	1982	Trading
Gaz Hudson	Mundogas Rio	19,462	1967	Broken up 2002
Gaz Imperial	Esso Westernport	100,988	1977	Trading
Gaz Kandla	Phillips Arkansas	26,505	1969	Broken up 2001
Gaz Marmara	Ogden General	70,358	1975	Broken up 2003
Gaz Master	Nyhavn	19,450	1968	Trading
Gaz Med	Pine Queen	70,139	1974	Trading
Gaz Meridian	Tatsuta Maru	70,792	1982	Trading
Gaz Millennium	Gaz Millennium	22,500	2002	Trading
Gaz Poem	Höegh Swallow	75,650	1976	Broken up 2003
Gaz Progress	Mossovet	76,506	1979	Trading
Gaz Suez	World Vigour	79,963	1977	Trading
Gaz Supplier	Bridgestone Maru No 3	47,124	1966	Broken up 1993
Gaz Supplier	Cavendish	40,213	1971	Broken up 2002

Current Name	Original Name	Capacity m³	Delivery year	Status
Gaz Unity	Tenryu Maru	77,290	1982	Trading
Genkai Maru	Genkai Maru	80,311	1980	Trading
Gent	Gent	24,663	1985	Trading
Gohshu	Gohshu	71,913	1990	Trading
Grace River	Grace River	79,000	2002	Trading
Great Tribune	Great Tribune	78,498	1999	Trading
Harriette N	Cantarell	57,590	1980	Trading
Havdrott	Galpara	54,104	1978	Trading
Havfrost	Havfrost	57,179	1991	Trading
Havgast	Höegh Multina	52,647	1971	Broken up 2001
Havglimt	Centum	52,647	1978	Trading
Havis	Havis	57,179	1993	Trading
Havjarl	Gazana	29,791	1972	Broken up 2002
Havkong	Galconda	54,104	1978	Trading
Havmann	Antilla Bay	53,400	1973	Broken up 2004
Havprins	Dovertown	53,400	1974	Trading
Havrim	Smolnyy	37,348	1980	Trading
Hebris	Hebris	24,048	1983	Trading
Hedda	Hedda	34,765	1993	Trading
Hekabe	Garinda	54,226	1978	Trading
Hektor	Hektor	24,048	1982	Trading
Helga	Helga	34,765	1994	Trading
Helice	Helice	57,179	1991	Trading
Helios	Helios	57,179	1992	Trading
Hellas Argosy	Hellas Argosy	82,000	2003	Trading
Hellas Nautilus	Hellas Nautilus	82,000	2003	Trading
Hemina	Garala	54,104	1979	Trading
Herakles	Berge Fister	30,455	1982	Trading
Hermes	Hampshire	52,647	1974	Broken up 2002
Hermion	Hermion	24,036	1984	Trading
Hesiod	Gambada	29,791	1973	Broken up 2003
Hesperus	Dorsetown	53,400	1973	Broken up 2003
Hourai Maru	Hourai Maru	77,755	1985	Trading
Hugo N	Ahkatun	57,000	1980	Trading
Ile de la Réunion	Hypolite-Worms	29,866	1969	Converted to Ro-Ro
Iridina	Iridina	10,808	1961	Broken up 1969
Iris Gas	Koho Maru	80,681	1985	Trading
Isavana	Bridgestone Maru II	36,008	1964	Broken up 1984
Isomeria	Isomeria	59,725	1982	Trading
Izumisan Maru	Izumisan Maru	60,990	1970	Broken up 1986
J A Sunshine	J A Sunshine	75,386	1994	Trading
Jag Vayu	Lord Kelvin	31,243	1978	Trading
Jakob Maersk	Jakob Maersk	35,559	1991	Trading
Jane Maersk	Jane Maersk	35,559	1990	Trading

Current Name	Original Name	Capacity m³	Delivery year	Status
Jesper Maersk	Jesper Maersk	35,559	1991	Trading
Jessie Maersk	Jessie Maersk	35,559	1991	Trading
José Colomo	Hektor	24,048	1980	Trading
Joule	Havgas	11,071	1965	Broken up 1984
Joyama	Joyama Maru	82,513	1986	Trading
Joyama Maru	Joyama Maru	46,548	1965	Broken up 1985
Kanayma Maru	Kanayama Maru	70,238	1970	Broken up 1985
Kapitan Luca	Butanueve	14,233	1969	Broken up 1996
Kazutama Maru	Kazutama Maru	51,824	1967	Broken up 1983
Kodaijisan	Kodaijisan	82,000	2003	Trading
La Forge	Benny Queen	70,792	1981	Trading
Lancashire	Lancashire	35,000	2002	Trading
Lavender Passage	Lavender Passage	78,451	1996	Trading
Libin	Nichizan Maru	43,671	1982	Trading
Lincolnshire	Lincolnshire	30,724	1972	Broken up 2002
Linden Pride	Linden Pride	78,874	2001	Trading
Louise	Pioneer Louise	77,373	1976	Trading
Luigi Lagrange	Luigi Lagrange	31,311	1977	Trading
Lycaste Peace	Lycaste Peace	78,000	2003	Trading
Macuiltepetl	Petroquimico I	3,499	1967	Broken up 1996
Mahashi Dattatreya	Concordia Fjord	24,054	1983	Trading
Maharshi Vasishth	Gandara	22,711	1976	Trading
Maharshi Vishwamitra	Devonshire	52,647	1974	Trading
Maharshi Vyas	Garbeta	22,764	1975	Trading
Mariano Escobedo	Mariano Escobedo	11,474	1967	Trading
Marine Eagle	Marine Eagle	12,854	1969	Broken up 1985
Mundogas Atlantic	Cypress	22,240	1969	Broken up 2001
Mundogas Europe	Kristian Birkeland	22,246	1968	Broken up 2000
Musashi Gloria	Musashi Gloria	75,178	1993	Trading
N'Kossa II	Inger	78,488	1992	FSO
Nanga Parbat	Nanga Parbat	22,500	1991	Trading
Nejma	Eupen	57,000	1983	Trading
Nektar	Nektar	70,162	1975	Broken up 1998
Nelina	Havis	15,285	1970	Broken up 1994
Nichiyuh Maru	Nichiyuh Maru	78,507	1989	Trading
Nordanger	Baltic Flame	76,643	1992	Trading
Northern Lights I	Iwakuni Maru	8,082	1981	Trading
Noto Gloria	Noto Gloria	75,203	1992	Trading
Ocean Orchid	Ocean Orchid	79,538	2001	Trading
OGC America	Garmula	52,647	1972	Broken up 2002
OGC Energy	Nyhammer	66,341	1975	Broken up 2002
Oscar Viking	Tielrode	25,000	1983	Trading
Oval Nova	Oval Nova	78,469	1993	Trading
Oxfordshire	Oxfordshire	34,948	1997	Trading

Current Name	Original Name	Capacity m³	Delivery year	Status
Pacific Century	Pacific Century	78,482	1991	Trading
Pacific Harmony	Pacific Harmony	75,208	1990	Trading
Palace Tokyo	Palace Tokyo	100,181	1974	Broken up 1986
Petrogas I	Paul Endacott	25,102	1964	Broken up 1986
Puerto Rican	Puerto Rican	14,000	1971	Constructive total loss 1986
Pythagore	Arquimedes	14,258	1967	Broken up 1985
Qeshm Gas	Capella	14,268	1967	Broken up 1999
Quentin	Quentin	679	1965	Broken up 1976
Rainbow Gas	Tokuho Maru	61,203	1974	Broken up 2003
Reggane	Reggane	84,350	1999	Trading
René	René	35,125	2002	Trading
Savonetta	Joseph P Grace	12,975	1964	Broken up 1998
Sea Petro	Bridgestone Maru	28,837	1962	Broken up 1987
Sea Stone	World Bridgestone	74,477	1971	Broken up 2003
Solaro	Solaro	37,314	1996	Trading
Steven N	Monterrey	53,400	1979	Trading
Sunny Gas	Sun River	75,958	1974	Trading
Sunny Green	Sunny Green	78,507	1992	Trading
Sunny Hope	Sunny Hope	78,489	1990	Trading
Sunny Joy	Sunny Joy	78,874	2000	Trading
Sunway	Sunway	78,476	1991	Trading
Touraine	Antwerpen Venture	39,270	1996	Trading
Toyosu	Toyosu Maru	13,145	1963	Broken up 1985
Toyosu Maru	Toyosu Maru	78,462	1997	Trading
Victoire	Kelvin	17,900	1990	Trading
Yuan Da	Staffordshire	74,537	1977	Broken up 2003
Yuan Xing	Ogden Bridgestone	74,578	1973	Broken up 2002
Yuhsan	Yuhsan	78,929	2002	Trading
Yuhsho	Yuhsho	78,498	1999	Trading
Yusho	Yusho Maru	73,211	1971	Broken up 1985
Yuyo	Yuyo Maru	83,070	1979	Trading
Yuyo Maru No 10	Yuyo Maru No 10	47,424	1966	Destroyed after fire 1974
Zallaq	Wiltshire	15,495	1968	Broken up 1998

Appendix 4

Fully Refrigerated LPG Carriers Capacity

Original Name	Capacity m³	Shipbuilders	Delivery year	Current Name
Quentin	679	Grangemouth Dockyard	1965	Quentin
Capo Levante	1,350	Clemna, La Spezia	1979	Capo Levante
Petroquimico I	3,499	Hawthorn Leslie, Hebburn	1967	Macuiltepetl
Esso Centro America	5,748	A G Weser, Bremen	1962	Gas Venture
Iwakuni Maru	8,082	Hitachi, Innoshima	1981	Northern Lights I
Nisseki Maru	9,470	Hitachi, Innoshima	1962	Beava
Iridina	10,808	La Ciotat, La Ciotat	1961	Iridina
Havgas	11,071	Moss Værft, Moss	1965	Joule
Alexander Hamilton	11,188	Euskalduña, Bilbao	1968	Aegis Diligence
Gohshu Maru	11,300	Mitsui, Tamano	1961	Contovello
Havfrost	11,396	Moss Værft, Moss	1966	Gaz Channel
Mariano Escobedo	11,474	Hawthorn Leslie, Hebburn	1967	Mariano Escobedo
Clerk-Maxwell	11,750	Hawthorn Leslie, Hebburn	1966	Clerk-Maxwell
Gas Lion	11,843	Scotts', Greenock	1968	Gas Pilot
Marine Eagle	12,854	Newport News	1969	Marine Eagle
William R Grace	12,975	Verolme, Rotterdam	1964	Amelina
Joseph P Grace	12,975	Verolme, Rotterdam	1964	Savonetta
Toyosu Maru	13,145	Hitachi, Innoshima	1963	Toyosu
Puerto Rican	14,000	Bethlehem Steel, Sparrows Point	1971	Puerto Rican
Butanueve	14,233	Astilleros Cadiz	1969	Kapitan Luca
Arquimedes	14,258	La Ciotat, La Ciotat	1967	Pythagore
Capella	14,268	La Ciotat, La Ciotat	1967	Qeshm Gas
Aeolos II	14,465	CNIM, La Seyne	1967	Galileo
Aeolos	14,805	CNIM, La Seyne	1967	Asia Rainbow
Havis	15,285	Moss Værft, Moss	1970	Nelina
Wiltshire	15,495	Hawthorn Leslie, Hebburn	1968	Zallaq
Kelvin	17,900	IHI, Kure	1990	Victoire
Agri Viking	18,152	Hitachi, Ariake	1997	Agri Viking
Euro Viking	18,159	Hitachi, Ariake	1997	Euro Viking
Roland	18,282	HDW, Kiel	1968	Andesgas
Isfonn	18,790	La Ciotat, La Ciotat	1967	Excel
M P Grace	19,450	IHI, Nagoya	1967	Calina
Nyhavn	19,450	Moss Værft, Moss	1968	Gaz Master
Mundogas Rio	19,462	Moss Værft, Moss	1967	Gaz Hudson
Gas Master	21,794	La Ciotat, La Ciotat	1969	Cronos
Sydfonn	22,182	La Ciotat, La Ciotat	1978	Clipper Sun

Original Name	Capacity m³	Shipbuilders	Delivery year	Current Name
Cypress	22,240	La Ciotat, La Ciotat	1969	Mundogas Atlantic
Kristian Birkeland	22,246	La Ciotat, La Ciotat	1968	Mundogas Europe
Annapurna	22,478	Hyundai, Ulsan	1991	Annapurna
Spic Diamond	22,478	Hyundai, Ulsan	1991	Gaz Diamond
Nanga Parbat	22,500	Hyundai, Ulsan	1991	Nanga Parbat
Gaz Millennium	22,500	Hyundai, Ulsan	2002	Gaz Millennium
Gandara	22,711	Swan Hunter, Hebburn	1976	Maharshi Vasishth
Garbeta	22,764	Moss Værft, Moss	1975	Maharshi Vyas
Hermion	24,048	Moss Rosenberg Værft, Moss	1984	Hermion
Hektor	24,048	Moss Rosenburg Værft, Moss	1980	José Colomo
Hebris	24,048	Frederikstad, Frederikstad	1983	Hebris
Hektor	24,048	Frederikstad, Frederikstad	1982	Hektor
Concordia Fjord	24,054	Moss Rosenburg Værft, Moss	1983	Mahashi Dattatreya
Gent	24,663	Boelwerf, Temse	1985	Gent
Tielrode	25,000	Boelwerf, Temse	1983	Oscar Viking
Paul Endacott	25,102	Kockums, Malmö	1964	Petrogas I
Carli Bay	25,302	Mitsubishi, Nagasaki	1998	Carli Bay
Phillips Arkansas	26,505	Kockums, Malmö	1969	Gaz Kandla
Nyhall	27,473	Boelwerf, Temse	1989	Courcheville
Cheshire	28,000	Boelwerf, Temse	1989	Cheshire
Chaconia	28,150	Boelwerf, Temse	1990	Chaconia
Bridgestone Maru	28,837	Mitsubishi, Yokohama	1962	Sea Petro
Antilla Cape	29,540	A G Weser, Bremen	1968	Egypt Gas
Gazana	29,791	Cammell Laird, Birkenhead	1972	Havjarl
Gambada	29,791	Cammell Laird, Birkenhead	1973	Hesiod
Hypolite-Worms	29,866	CNIM, La Seyne	1969	Ile de la Réunion
Berge Fister	30,455	Moss Rosenberg Værft, Stavanger	1982	Herakles
Lincolnshire	30,724	Swan Hunter, Hebburn	1972	Lincolnshire
Faraday	31,215	Swan Hunter, Hebburn	1971	Faraday
Lord Kelvin	31,243	Apuania SpA, Marine di Carrara	1978	Jag Vayu
Luigi Lagrange	31,311	Apuania SpA., Marina di Carrara	1977	Luigi Lagrange
Cornucopia	31,704	Todd Pacific, San Pedro	1978	Cornucopia
Sombeke	33,619	Boelwerf, Temse	1990	Australgas
Hedda	34,765	Kawasaki, Kobe	1993	Hedda
Helga	34,765	Kawasaki, Kobe	1994	Helga
Oxfordshire	34,948	Mitsubishi, Nagasaki	1997	Oxfordshire
Lancashire	35,000	Hyundai, Ulsan	2002	Lancashire
Gas Oriental	35,000	Hyundai, Ulsan	2003	Gas Oriental
René	35,125	Daewoo, Okpo	2002	René
Brugge Venture	35,418	Mitsubishi, Nagasaki	1997	Brugge Venture
Gas Columbia	35,420	Mitsubishi, Nagasaki	1997	Gas Columbia
Jakob Maersk	35,559	Hyundai, Ulsan	1991	Jakob Maersk
Jessie Maersk	35,559	Hyundai, Ulsan	1991	Jessie Maersk
Jane Maersk	35,559	Hyundai, Ulsan	1990	Jane Maersk
Jesper Maersk	35,559	Hyundai, Ulsan	1991	Jesper Maersk

Original Name	Capacity m³	Shipbuilders	Delivery year	Current Name
Bridgestone Maru II	36,008	Mitsubishi, Yokohama	1964	Isavana
Solaro	37,314	Fincantieri, Sestri	1996	Solaro
Smolnyy	37,348	Breda, Venice	1980	Havrim
Elversele	37,510	Kawasaki, Kobe	1996	Elversele
Eeklo	37,520	Kawasaki, Kobe	1995	Eeklo
Yamahide Maru	38,161	Mitsubishi, Yokohama	1966	Bo Bengtsson
Eupen	38,961	Mitsubishi, Nagasaki	1999	Eupen
Toyosu Maru	39,113	IHI, Aioi	1984	Gaz Baraka
Antwerpen Venture	39,270	Hitachi, Ariake	1996	Touraine
Cavendish	40,213	La Ciotat, La Ciotat	1971	Gaz Supplier
Gay-Lussac	40,232	La Ciotat, La Ciotat	1969	Gaz Fountain
Nichizan Maru	43,671	Mitsubishi, Nagasaki	1982	Libin
Joyama Maru	46,548	IHI, Nagoya	1965	Joyama Maru
Bridgestone Maru No 3	47,124	IHI, Nagoya	1966	Gaz Supplier
Yuyo Maru No 10	47,424	Hitachi, Innoshima	1966	Yuyo Maru No 10
Tatsuno Maru	50,542	Mitsubishi, Yokohama	1967	Al-Hada 2
Kazutama Maru	51,824	Hitachi, Innoshima	1967	Kazutama Maru
Devonshire	52,647	France Dunkerque	1974	Maharshi Vishwamitra
Garmula	52,647	Moss Rosenberg Værft, Stavanger	1972	OGC America
Höegh Multina	52,647	Moss Rosenberg Værft, Stavanger	1971	Havgast
Centum	52,647	Moss Rosenberg Værft, Stavanger	1978	Havglimt
Hampshire	52,647	France Dunkerque	1974	Hermes
Dorsetown	53,400	CNIM, La Seyne	1973	Hesperus
Reynosa	53,400	CNIM, La Seyne	1979	Clipper Lady
Dovertown	53,400	CNIM, La Seyne	1974	Havprins
Monterrey	53,400	CNIM, La Seyne	1979	Steven N
Antilla Bay	53,400	CNIM, La Seyne	1973	Havmann
Galpara	54,104	Thyssen Nord, Emden	1978	Havdrott
Galconda	54,104	Thyssen Nord, Emden	1978	Havkong
Garala	54,104	Thyssen Nord, Emden	1979	Hemina
Garinda	54,226	Thyssen Nord, Emden	1978	Hekabe
Ahkatun	57,000	Boelwerf, Temse	1980	Hugo N
Eupen	57,000	Boelwerf, Temse	1983	Nejma
Helice	57,179	Kværner Govan	1991	Helice
Havfrost	57,179	Kværner Govan	1991	Havfrost
Havis	57,179	Kværner Govan	1993	Havis
Helios	57,179	Kværner Govan	1992	Helios
Cantarell	57,590	Boelwerf, Temse	1980	Harriette N
Clipper Star	59,200	Kawasaki, Sakaide	2003	Clipper Star
Berge Nice	59,343	Kawasaki, Sakaide	2003	Berge Nice
Isocardia	59,725	Harland & Wolff, Belfast	1982	Gaz Horizon
Isomeria	59,725	Harland & Wolff, Belfast	1982	Isomeria
Izumisan Maru	60,990	Mitsui, Tamano	1970	Izumisan Maru
Tokuho Maru	61,203	Mitsui, Tamano	1974	Rainbow Gas

Original Name	Capacity m³	Shipbuilders	Delivery year	Current Name
Nyhammer	66,341	La Ciotat, La Ciotat	1975	OGC Energy
Amvrosios	70,131	Mitsubishi, Yokohama	1974	Amvrosios
Pine Queen	70,139	Mitsubishi, Yokohama	1974	Gaz Med
Nektar	70,162	Mitsubishi, Yokohama	1975	Nektar
Kanayama Maru	70,238	Mitsubishi, Yokohama	1970	Kanayma Maru
World Rainbow	70,247	Mitsubishi, Yokohama	1971	Gaz Coral
Ogden General	70,358	Mitsubishi, Yokohama	1975	Gaz Marmara
Benny Queen	70,792	NKK, Tsu	1981	La Forge
Tatsuta Maru	70,792	NKK, Tsu	1982	Gaz Meridian
Razi	70,914	La Ciotat, La Ciotat	1977	Andean Gas
Monge	71,304	La Ciotat, La Ciotat	1977	Berge Troll
Gohshu	71,913	Mitsubishi, Nagasaki	1990	Gohshu
Gas Al-Minagish	72,121	La Ciotat, La Ciotat	1980	Gas Al-Minagish
Gas Al-Burgan	72,121	La Ciotat, La Ciotat	1979	Gas Al-Burgan
Gas Al-Kuwait	72,121	La Ciotat, La Ciotat	1978	Gas Beauty
Gas Al-Ahmadi	72,121	La Ciotat, La Ciotat	1979	Gas Al-Ahmadi
Bridgestone Maru No 5	72,344	Kawasaki, Kobe	1969	Bridgestone Maru No 5
Yusho Maru	73,211	Hitachi, Innoshima	1971	Yusho
World Bridgestone	74,477	Kawasaki, Kobe	1971	Sea Stone
Staffordshire	74,537	France Dunkerque	1977	Yuan Da
Ogden Bridgestone	74,578	Kawasaki, Kobe	1973	Yuan Xing
Musashi Gloria	75,178	Kawasaki, Kobe	1993	Musashi Gloria
Noto Gloria	75,203	Kawasaki, Kobe	1992	Noto Gloria
Crystal Mermaid	75,203	Kawasaki, Sakaide	1990	Crystal Mermaid
Tsugaru Gloria	75,203	Kawasaki, Kobe	1991	Berge Flanders
Aries Duo	75,203	Kawasaki, Kobe	1992	Benny Princess
Pacific Harmony	75,208	Kawasaki, Sakaide	1990	Pacific Harmony
Co-op Akebono	75,211	Kawasaki, Sakaide	1993	Co-op Akebono
J A Sunshine	75,386	Kawasaki, Kobe	1994	J A Sunshine
Höegh Sword	75,650	Gdynia	1978	Berge Sword
Höegh Swift	75,650	Gdynia	1977	Evangelina 1
Northern Arrow	75,650	Gdynia	1977	Berge Arrow
Höegh Swallow	75,650	Gdynia	1976	Gaz Poem
Northern Eagle 1	75,650	Gdynia	1978	Berge Eagle
Golar Frost	75,680	Wärtsilä, Perno	1980	Berge Spirit
Berge Strand	75,680	Wärtsilä, Perno	1982	Berge Strand
Berge Sisu	75,680	Wärtsilä, Perno	1978	Berge Sisu
Gas Rising Sun	75,680	Wärtsilä, Perno	1978	Gas Rising Sun
Berge Saga	75,680	Wärtsilä, Perno	1979	Berge Saga
Berge Sund	75,680	Wärtsilä, Perno	1981	Berge Sund
Berge Sisar	75,680	Wärtsilä, Perno	1979	Berge Sisar
Sun River	75,958	Kawasaki, Kobe	1974	Sunny Gas
Clean River	76,313	Kawasaki, Kobe	1983	Clean River
Lensovet	76,475	Breda, Venice	1980	Gaz Atlantic

Original Name	Capacity m³	Shipbuilders	Delivery year	Current Name
Mossovet	76,506	Breda, Venice	1979	Gaz Progress
Baltic Flame	76,643	Hyundai, Ulsan	1992	Nordanger
Al Bida	76,929	l'Atlantique, St Nazaire	1979	Al Bida
Al Berry	76,929	l'Atlantique, St Nazaire	1979	Al Berry
Tenryu Maru	77,290	Mitsubishi, Nagasaki	1982	Gaz Unity
Gas Libra	77,327	Mitsubishi, Yokohama	1980	Gas Aguila
Pioneer Louise	77,373	Mitsubishi, Yokohama	1976	Louise
Co-op Sunrise	77,550	Hitachi, Innoshima	1987	Berge Kobe
Hourai Maru	77,755	Hitachi, Innoshima	1985	Hourai Maru
Gas Gemini	77,961	Mitsubishi, Yokohama	1977	Gaz Gemini
Gas Diana	77,986	Mitsubishi, Yokohama	1978	Gas Bauhinia
Lycaste Peace	78,000	Mitsubishi, Nagasaki	2003	Lycaste Peace
Lavender Passage	78,451	Mitsubishi, Nagasaki	1996	Lavender Passage
Toyosu Maru	78,462	Mitsubishi, Nagasaki	1997	Toyosu Maru
Gas Scorpio	78,462	Mitsubishi, Nagasaki	1995	Gas Scorpio
Oval Nova	78,469	Mitsubishi, Nagasaki	1993	Oval Nova
Gas Al-Gurain	78,475	Mitsubishi, Nagasaki	1993	Gas Al-Gurain
Sunway	78,476	Mitsubishi, Nagasaki	1991	Sunway
Gas Roman	78,478	Mitsubishi, Nagasaki	1990	Gaz Energy
G Leader	78,479	Mitsubishi, Nagasaki	1995	G Leader
Pacific Century	78,482	Mitsubishi, Nagasaki	1991	Pacific Century
Gas Leo	78,484	Mitsubishi, Nagasaki	1990	Gas Leo
Energy Orpheus	78,488	Mitsubishi, Nagasaki	1993	Energy Orpheus
Gas Al-Mutlaa	78,488	Mitsubishi, Nagasaki	1993	Gas Al-Mutlaa
Gas Miracle	78,488	Mitsubishi, Nagasaki	1992	Gas Miracle
Inger	78,488	Mitsubishi, Nagasaki	1992	N'Kossa II
Gas Aries	78,488	Mitsubishi, Nagasaki	1991	Gas Aries
Sunny Hope	78,489	Mitsubishi, Nagasaki	1990	Sunny Hope
Yuhsho	78,498	Mitsubishi, Nagasaki	1999	Yuhsho
Great Tribune	78,498	Mitsubishi, Nagasaki	1999	Great Tribune
Berge Denise	78,500	Gdynia	2000	Berge Denise
Gas Vision	78,502	Mitsubishi, Nagasaki	1996	Gas Vision
Nichiyuh Maru	78,507	Mitsubishi, Nagasaki	1989	Nichiyuh Maru
Sunny Green	78,507	Mitsubishi, Nagasaki	1992	Sunny Green
Berge Challenger	78,542	NKK, Tsu	1992	Berge Challenger
Berge Captain	78,542	NKK, Tsu	1991	Berge Captain
Berge Clipper	78,542	NKK, Tsu	1992	Berge Clipper
Berge Commander	78,542	NKK, Tsu	1991	Berge Commander
Berge Danuta	78,550	Gdynia	2000	Berge Danuta
Anne-Laure	78,680	Daewoo, Okpo	2000	Anne-Laure
Linden Pride	78,874	Mitsubishi, Nagasaki	2001	Linden Pride
Sunny Joy	78,874	Mitsubishi, Nagasaki	2000	Sunny Joy
Gas Diana	78,888	Mitsubishi, Nagasaki	2000	Gas Diana
Gas Taurus	78,921	Mitsubishi, Nagasaki	2001	Gas Taurus

Original Name	Capacity m³	Shipbuilders	Delivery year	Current Name
Yuhsan	78,929	Mitsubishi, Nagasaki	2002	Yuhsan
Gas Capricorn	78,934	Mitsubishi, Nagasaki	2003	Gas Capricorn
Grace River	79,000	Kawasaki, Sakaide	2002	Grace River
Fountain River	79,527	Kawasaki, Sakaide	1997	Fountain River
Ocean Orchid	79,538	Kawasaki, Sakaide	2001	Ocean Orchid
World Vigour	79,963	Kawasaki, Kobe	1977	Gaz Suez
World Creation	80,026	Kawasaki, Kobe	1976	Gaz Creation
World Concord	80,026	Kawasaki, Kobe	1976	Gaz Concord
Crystal Marine	80,138	Kawasaki, Sakaide	2003	Crystal Marine
Genkai Maru	80,311	IHI, Aioi	1980	Genkai Maru
Koho Maru	80,681	IHI, Aioi	1985	Iris Gas
Berge Ragnhild	81,600	La Ciotat, La Ciotat	1986	Berge Ragnhild
Berge Racine	81,600	La Ciotat, La Ciotat	1985	Berge Racine
Berge Rachel	81,600	La Ciotat, La Ciotat	1984	Berge Rachel
Hellas Nautilus	82,000	Hyundai, Ulsan	2003	Hellas Nautilus
Hellas Argosy	82,000	Hyundai, Ulsan	2003	Hellas Argosy
Kodaijisan	82,000	Hyundai, Ulsan	2003	Kodaijisan
Dynamic Energy	82,200	Kawasaki, Sakaide	2002	Dynamic Energy
Dynamic Vision	82,200	Kawasaki, Sakaide	2001	Dynamic Vision
Althea Gas	82,200	Kawasaki, Sakaide	2003	Althea Gas
Joyama Maru	82,513	Mitsubishi, Nagasaki	1986	Joyama
Yuyo Maru	83,070	Hitachi, Innoshima	1979	Yuyo
Co-op Sunshine	83,127	Hitachi, Innoshima	1983	G Pioneer
Flanders Tenacity	84,269	Kawasaki, Sakaide	1996	Flanders Tenacity
Formosagas Bright	84,300	Kawasaki, Sakaide	2001	Formosagas Bright
Formosagas Apollo	84,300	Kawasaki, Sakaide	2001	Formosagas Apollo
Djanet	84,310	Kawasaki, Sakaide	2000	Djanet
Reggane	84,350	Kawasaki, Sakaide	1999	Reggane
Floreal	85,662	NorMed, La Ciotat	1983	Berge Frost
Flanders Harmony	85,826	Boelwerf, Temse	1992	Flanders Harmony
Palace Tokyo	100,181	Hitachi, Innoshima	1974	Palace Tokyo
Esso Fuji	100,213	Hitachi, Innoshima	1973	Esso Fuji
Esso Westernport	100,988	La Ciotat, La Ciotat	1977	Gaz Imperial

Fully Refrigerated LPG Carriers
Lead Ship Dimensions

Capacity m³	Original Name	Shipbuilders	Sisters	Loa m	Lbp m	Breadth m	Depth m	Draught m	Coefficient Cc	Tank Shape
679	Quentin	Grangemouth Dockyard	None	52.95	49.70	8.54	4.22	3.44	0.379	Trunk
1,350	Capo Levante	Clemna, La Spezia	None	76.51	75.27	9.71	4.12	2.95	0.448	Trunk
3,499	Petroquimico I	Hawthorn Leslie, Hebburn	None	73.02	71.34	14.63	6.40	4.50	0.523	Double Hull – Barge
5,748	Esso Centro America	A G Weser, Bremen	None	116.50	111.56	14.69	9.99	6.07	0.297	Conversion
8,082	Iwakuni Maru	Hitachi, Innoshima	None	109.88	104.00	20.00	11.90	5.90	0.326	Standard – Type B
9,470	Nisseki Maru	Hitachi, Innoshima	None	183.54	177.42	22.86	14.40	9.75	0.162	Conversion – Oil/LPG
10,808	Iridina	La Ciotat, La Ciotat	None	169.38	161.54	21.11	11.89	9.04	0.267	Conversion – Membrane
11,071	Havgas	Moss Værft, Moss	1 of 2	141.00	130.00	19.20	12.00	9.52	0.370	Double Hull + Ins – Trunk
11,188	Alexander Hamilton	Euskalduña, Bilbao	None	143.92	132.44	19.60	11.30	7.67	0.372	Double Hull – Trunk
11,300	Gohshu Maru	Mitsui, Tamano	None	221.44	212.00	30.40	15.17	11.84	0.116	Oil/LPG
11,750	Clerk-Maxwell	Hawthorn Leslie, Hebburn	1 of 3	140.70	131.07	19.21	11.89	8.25	0.393	Single Hull – Trunk
12,854	Marine Eagle	Newport News	None	187.42	178.52	24.39	14.41	10.33	0.351	Conversion – Methanol
12,975	William R Grace	Verolme, Rotterdam	1 of 2	156.45	142.65	21.18	12.50	7.53	0.343	Inner Side Hull
13,145	Toyosu Maru	Hitachi, Innoshima	None	178.57	177.25	22.86	14.41	9.95	0.225	Conversion – Oil/LPG
14,000	Puerto Rican	Bethlehem Steel, Sparrows Point	None	201.27	192.72	27.46	13.92	11.17	0.190	Chemical/LPG
14,233	Butanueve	Astilleros Cadiz	None	153.20	139.80	21.26	12.35	8.52	0.388	Double Hull – Trunk
14,268	Capella	La Ciotat, La Ciotat	1 of 2	150.61	141.00	21.70	13.30	7.88	0.350	Double Hull – Perlite
14,805	Aeolos	CNIM, La Seyne	1 of 2	154.50	144.00	23.00	12.80	7.70	0.352	Double Hull – Perlite
15,285	Havis	Moss Værft, Moss	None	146.75	136.30	21.75	13.50	10.61	0.382	Double Hull
15,495	Wiltshire	Hawthorn Leslie, Hebburn	None	151.73	141.74	21.34	12.50	8.23	0.410	Top Wing
17,900	Kelvin	IHI, Kure	None	146.09	137.00	23.00	14.70	8.55	0.378	Top Wing
18,152	Agri Viking	Hitachi, Ariake	1 of 2	153.92	147.00	24.60	13.10	9.37	0.383	Standard

Capacity m³	Original Name	Shipbuilders	Sisters	Loa m	Lbp m	Breadth m	Depth m	Draught m	Coefficient Cc	Tank Shape
18,282	Roland	HDW, Kiel	None	166.18	152.30	22.60	14.00	9.22	0.379	Double Hull + Ins – Trunk
18,790	Isfonn	La Ciotat, La Ciotat	None	177.00	165.00	24.40	13.70	7.72	0.340	Double Hull + Ins
19,450	M P Grace	IHI, Nagoya	None	162.84	154.00	23.31	14.35	8.40	0.367	Double Hull – Top Wing
19,462	Mundogas Rio	Moss Værft, Moss	1 of 2	162.55	150.00	22.50	14.50	9.52	0.398	Double Hull
22,246	Kristian Birkeland	La Ciotat, La Ciotat	1 of 3	171.00	160.92	24.40	15.50	9.03	0.366	Double Hull – Perlite
22,500	Nanga Parbat	Hyundai, Ulsan	1 of 3	160.00	153.50	25.90	15.40	8.31	0.375	Standard
22,500	Gaz Millennium	Hyundai, Ulsan	None	154.00	147.00	25.50	16.00	8.70	0.375	Standard
22,711	Gandara	Swan Hunter, Hebburn	None	160.51	152.00	24.00	16.20	9.82	0.384	Standard
22,764	Garbeta	Moss Værft, Moss	None	165.00	155.00	23.00	15.50	10.32	0.412	Standard
24,048	Hektor	Moss Rosenburg Værft, Moss	1 of 5	157.79	149.00	24.40	16.00	10.78	0.413	Standard
25,000	Tielrode	Boelwerf, Temse	1 of 2	155.40	147.00	26.50	16.20	11.74	0.388	Standard
25,102	Paul Endacott	Kockums, Malmö	None	180.53	166.70	25.00	14.70	10.62	0.406	Double Hull + Ins – Trunk
25,302	Carli Bay	Mitsubishi, Nagasaki	None	155.00	148.00	25.80	16.30	10.20	0.398	Standard
26,505	Phillips Arkansas	Kockums, Malmö	None	184.79	172.52	25.50	16.10	9.70	0.367	Standard
28,000	Cheshire	Boelwerf, Temse	1 of 3	165.66	157.26	26.50	16.20	11.74	0.406	Standard
28,837	Bridgestone Maru	Mitsubishi, Yokohama	None	183.71	175.00	25.00	16.70	9.30	0.395	Double Hull
29,540	Antilla Cape	A G Weser, Bremen	None	173.84	164.00	25.80	17.10	10.22	0.408	Standard
29,791	Gazana	Cammell Laird, Birkenhead	1 of 2	178.00	165.00	26.00	17.00	10.02	0.408	Standard
29,866	Hypolite-Worms	CNIM, La Seyne	None	177.90	165.00	24.50	15.50	10.42	0.475	Membrane
30,455	Berge Fister	Moss Rosenberg Værft, Stavanger	None	158.25	149.75	27.60	18.20	13.61	0.404	Standard
30,724	Lincolnshire	Swan Hunter, Hebburn	None	187.05	178.50	26.80	15.40	9.78	0.417	Standard
31,215	Faraday	Swan Hunter, Hebburn	None	187.05	178.31	26.83	15.40	9.75	0.424	Standard
31,311	Luigi Lagrange	Apuania SpA., Marina di Carrara	1 of 2	191.95	176.00	26.00	16.85	11.48	0.406	Standard
31,704	Cornucopia	Todd Pacific, San Pedro	None	191.40	179.84	27.44	16.39	9.47	0.392	Conversion – Double Hull – Perlite
33,619	Sombeke	Boelwerf, Temse	None	165.66	157.26	26.50	18.60	11.72	0.434	Standard
34,765	Hedda	Kawasaki, Kobe	1 of 2	170.00	160.00	27.36	18.20	12.57	0.436	Standard
34,948	Oxfordshire	Mitsubishi, Nagasaki	None	169.90	162.00	27.40	18.20	11.13	0.433	Standard
35,000	Lancashire	Hyundai, Ulsan	1 of 2	174.00	165.00	28.00	17.80	9.50	0.426	Standard
35,125	René	Daewoo, Okpo	None	178.00	170.00	28.00	17.70	10.20	0.417	Standard
35,418	Brugge Venture	Mitsubishi, Nagasaki	1 of 3	169.90	162.00	27.40	18.20	11.11	0.430	Standard

Capacity m³	Original Name	Shipbuilders	Sisters	Loa m	Lbp m	Breadth m	Depth m	Draught m	Coefficient Cc	Tank Shape
35,420	Gas Columbia	Mitsubishi, Nagasaki	None	170.00	162.00	27.40	18.20	11.13	0.438	Standard
35,559	Jane Maersk	Hyundai, Ulsan	1 of 4	185.00	173.40	27.40	18.00	12.52	0.416	Standard
36,008	Bridgestone Maru II	Mitsubishi, Yokohama	None	187.49	178.00	27.50	18.30	10.50	0.402	Top Wing
37,314	Solaro	Fincantieri, Sestri	None	180.40	169.00	29.00	17.90	12.50	0.425	Standard
37,348	Smolnyy	Breda, Venice	None	197.42	184.50	29.00	17.85	10.10	0.391	Standard
37,520	Eeklo	Kawasaki, Kobe	1 of 2	179.00	169.00	27.36	18.20	11.60	0.446	Standard
38,161	Yamahide Maru	Mitsubishi, Yokohama	None	187.49	178.25	27.50	18.30	10.50	0.441	Double Hull
38,961	Eupen	Mitsubishi, Nagasaki	None	179.92	172.00	27.40	18.20	10.00	0.445	Standard
39,113	Toyosu Maru	IHI, Aioi	None	176.70	169.00	30.00	17.60	9.20	0.438	Top Wing
39,270	Antwerpen Venture	Hitachi, Ariake	None	195.93	186.00	29.40	17.00	10.07	0.414	Standard
40,232	Gay-Lussac	La Ciotat, La Ciotat	1 of 2	194.13	182.00	29.00	18.90	9.91	0.397	Double Hull – Perlite
43,671	Nichizan Maru	Mitsubishi, Nagasaki	None	192.00	182.00	30.80	18.90	9.80	0.412	Standard
46,548	Joyama Maru	IHI, Nagoya	None	198.04	190.00	29.00	19.40	11.03	0.433	Top Wing
47,124	Bridgestone Maru No 3	IHI, Nagoya	None	187.50	180.00	29.00	18.00	10.52	0.293	Intergral & Top Wing
47,424	Yuyo Maru No 10	Hitachi, Innoshima	None	227.10	215.00	35.80	20.75	12.00	0.297	Oil/LPG
50,542	Tatsuno Maru	Mitsubishi, Yokohama	None	202.12	190.00	30.00	19.90	11.81	0.447	Top Wing
51,824	Kazutama Maru	Hitachi, Innoshima	None	199.95	188.00	31.40	21.00	11.63	0.418	Standard
52,647	Höegh Multina	Moss Rosenberg Værft, Stavanger	1 of 3	207.08	196.00	31.40	18.60	11.32	0.460	Standard
52,648	Hampshire	France Dunkerque	1 of 2	207.02	196.00	31.40	18.60	11.28	0.459	Standard
53,400	Antilla Bay	CNIM, La Seyne	1 of 5	216.52	203.00	32.25	18.40	11.02	0.443	Standard
54,226	Garinda	Thyssen Nord, Emden	1 of 4	219.69	208.00	28.50	20.00	11.80	0.456	Standard
57,179	Helice	Kvaerner Govan	1 of 4	205.00	193.60	32.20	20.00	13.02	0.459	Standard
57,590	Cantarell	Boelwerf, Temse	1 of 3	215.70	204.00	32.25	19.00	12.02	0.456	Standard
59,200	Clipper Star	Kawasaki, Sakaide	1 of 5	205.00	195.00	32.20	20.20	10.50	0.467	Standard
59,725	Isomeria	Harland & Wolff, Belfast	1 of 2	210.00	203.00	31.40	21.45	12.48	0.436	Standard
60,990	Izumisan Maru	Mitsui, Tamano	1 of 2	215.07	203.00	32.00	21.50	11.03	0.437	Standard
66,341	Nyhammer	La Ciotat, La Ciotat	None	230.89	215.00	32.20	21.50	12.60	0.448	Double Hull – Perlite
70,238	Kanayama Maru	Mitsubishi, Yokohama	1 of 6	223.96	213.00	34.60	21.40	11.93	0.445	Standard
70,792	Benny Queen	NKK, Tsu	1 of 2	224.50	214.00	32.20	22.00	10.98	0.466	Standard
71,304	Monge	La Ciotat, La Ciotat	1 of 2	213.65	216.19	34.80	22.30	13.55	0.425	Double Hull – Perlite

Capacity m³	Original Name	Shipbuilders	Sisters	Loa m	Lbp m	Breadth m	Depth m	Draught m	Coefficient Cc	Tank Shape
71,913	Gohshu	Mitsubishi, Nagasaki	None	217.40	206.40	36.60	20.40	11.03	0.467	Standard
72,121	Gas Al-Kuwait	La Ciotat, La Ciotat	1 of 4	231.10	216.18	34.80	22.30	12.71	0.430	Double Hull – Perlite
72,344	Bridgestone Maru No 5	Kawasaki, Kobe	1 of 3	210.50	200.00	32.50	21.80	12.20	0.511	Semi-membrane & Intergral
73,211	Yusho Maru	Hitachi, Innoshima	None	227.00	215.00	34.80	23.20	11.51	0.422	Standard
74,537	Staffordshire	France Dunkerque	None	226.30	215.00	34.20	21.60	13.03	0.468	Standard
75,208	Pacific Harmony	Kawasaki, Sakaide	1 of 8	224.05	212.00	36.00	20.70	11.02	0.557	Standard
75,650	Höegh Swallow	Gdynia	1 of 5	229.30	217.00	32.20	22.50	12.92	0.481	Standard
75,680	Gas Rising Sun	Wärtsilä, Perno	1 of 7	224.75	213.00	34.20	21.60	13.02	0.481	Standard
75,958	Sun River	Kawasaki, Kobe	None	224.00	213.00	32.50	21.80	11.93	0.503	Semi-membrane & Intergral
76,313	Clean River	Kawasaki, Kobe	None	214.99	204.02	34.00	23.02	12.03	0.478	Semi-membrane & Intergral
76,506	Mossovet	Breda, Venice	1 of 2	234.98	222.00	35.80	22.80	12.20	0.422	Standard
76,643	Baltic Flame	Hyundai, Ulsan	None	219.89	210.00	34.20	22.50	13.40	0.474	Standard
76,929	Al Berry	l'Atlantique, St Nazaire	1 of 2	228.86	216.00	36.50	22.25	13.52	0.439	Double Hull – Perlite
77,290	Tenryu Maru	Mitsubishi, Nagasaki	None	228.00	217.00	36.60	21.45	10.98	0.453	Standard
77,327	Gas Libra	Mitsubishi, Yokohama	None	228.00	216.00	36.60	21.45	11.50	0.455	Standard
77,373	Pioneer Louise	Mitsubishi, Yokohama	1 of 3	229.00	215.80	36.60	21.45	11.60	0.448	Internal Insulation later Standard
77,550	Co-op Sunrise	Hitachi, Innoshima	None	219.74	210.01	38.41	21.01	11.02	0.458	Standard
77,755	Hourai Maru	Hitachi, Innoshima	None	219.74	210.00	38.40	21.00	11.02	0.516	Standard
78,507	Nichiyuh Maru	Mitsubishi, Nagasaki	1 of 30	230.00	219.00	36.60	20.40	10.83	0.480	Standard
78,542	Berge Commander	NKK, Tsu	1 of 4	223.99	212.00	36.00	21.80	12.42	0.472	Standard
78,550	Berge Danuta	Gdynia	1 of 2	225.57	218.58	36.40	22.00	11.25	0.449	Standard
78,680	Anne-Laure	Daewoo, Okpo	None	224.50	213.00	36.00	22.30	11.72	0.460	Standard
79,527	Fountain River	Kawasaki, Sakaide	1 of 3	230.00	219.70	36.00	20.70	10.77	0.486	Standard
80,026	World Concord	Kawasaki, Kobe	1 of 3	224.00	213.00	32.50	21.80	12.53	0.530	Semi-membrane & Intergral
80,138	Crystal Marine	Kawasaki, Sakaide	None	227.50	222.00	37.20	21.00	11.20	0.462	Standard
80,311	Genkai Maru	IHI, Aioi	None	224.00	212.00	36.00	22.30	11.40	0.471	Top Wing – Type B
80,681	Koho Maru	IHI, Aioi	None	221.50	209.00	36.00	22.60	11.60	0.474	Top Wing
81,600	Berge Rachel	La Ciotat, La Ciotat	1 of 3	228.60	216.00	35.50	22.80	13.68	0.467	Double Hull – Perlite
82,000	Hellas Nautilus	Hyundai, Ulsan	1 of 3	225.00	215.00	36.60	22.00	12.55	0.474	Standard
82,200	Dynamic Vision	Kawasaki, Sakaide	1 of 3	227.00	216.00	36.00	21.90	11.60	0.483	Standard

Capacity m³	Original Name	Shipbuilders	Sisters	Loa m	Lbp m	Breadth m	Depth m	Draught m	Coefficient Cc	Tank Shape
82,513	Joyama Maru	Mitsubishi, Nagasaki	None	225.00	214.00	36.00	22.30	11.33	0.480	Standard
83,070	Yuyo Maru	Hitachi, Innoshima	None	228.00	216.00	35.40	22.60	11.75	0.481	Semi-membrane & Intergral
83,127	Co-op Sunshine	Hitachi, Innoshima	None	220.00	210.00	38.40	22.80	11.30	0.454	Standard Type B & Integral
84,269	Flanders Tenacity	Kawasaki, Sakaide	1 of 3	230.00	219.70	36.00	21.90	11.60	0.487	Standard
84,300	Formosagas Apollo	Kawasaki, Sakaide	1 of 2	230.00	219.70	36.00	21.90	11.62	0.487	Standard
84,350	Reggane	Kawasaki, Sakaide	1 of 2	230.00	219.70	36.00	21.90	11.62	0.487	Standard
85,662	Floreal	NorMed, La Ciotat	None	249.80	237.00	35.50	22.90	12.85	0.444	Double Hull – Perlite
85,826	Flanders Harmony	Boelwerf, Temse	None	227.60	217.00	36.00	22.60	13.60	0.481	Standard
100,213	Esso Fuji	Hitachi, Innoshima	1 of 2	246.13	234.00	39.90	25.50	12.70	0.421	Standard
100,988	Esso Westernport	La Ciotat, La Ciotat	None	255.45	231.27	35.50	23.45	12.60	0.524	Double Hull – Perlite

Appendix 6

Fully Refrigerated LPG Carriers Shipbuilders

Hull No	Capacity m³	Original Name	Delivery year	Current Name
A G Weser, Bremen, Germany				
conversion	5,748	Esso Centro America	1962	Gas Venture
1366	29,540	Antilla Cape	1968	Egypt Gas
Apuania SpA, Marine di Carrara, Italy				
105	31,311	Luigi Lagrange	1977	Luigi Lagrange
108	31,243	Lord Kelvin	1978	Jag Vayu
Astilleros Cadiz, Spain				
111	14,233	Butanueve	1969	Kapitan Luca
l'Atlantique, St Nazaire, France				
I 26	76,929	Al Berry	1979	Al Berry
J 26	76,929	Al Bida	1979	Al Bida
Bethlehem Steel, Sparrows Point, USA				
4633	14,000	Puerto Rican	1971	Puerto Rican
Boelwerf, Temse, Belgium				
1500	57,590	Cantarell	1980	Harriette N
1501	57,000	Ahkatun	1980	Hugo N
1509	57,000	Eupen	1983	Nejma
1510	25,000	Tielrode	1983	Oscar Viking
1519	24,663	Gent	1985	Gent
1529	28,000	Cheshire	1989	Cheshire
1530	27,473	Nyhall	1989	Courcheville
1532	28,150	Chaconia	1990	Chaconia
1533	33,619	Sombeke	1990	Australgas
1539	85,826	Flanders Harmony	1992	Flanders Harmony
Breda, Venice, Italy				
289	76,506	Mossovet	1979	Gaz Progress
290	76,475	Lensovet	1980	Gaz Atlantic
291	37,348	Smolnyy	1980	Havrim
Cammell Laird, Birkenhead, United Kingdom				
1341	29,791	Gazana	1972	Havjarl
1342	29,791	Gambada	1973	Hesiod

Hull No	Capacity m³	Original Name	Delivery year	Current Name
La Ciotat, La Ciotat, France				
conversion	10,808	Iridina	1961	Iridina
235	18,790	Isfonn	1967	Excel
240	14,268	Capella	1967	Qeshm Gas
247	22,246	Kristian Birkeland	1968	Mundogas Europe
249	14,258	Arquimedes	1967	Pythagore
255	22,240	Cypress	1969	Mundogas Atlantic
260	21,794	Gas Master	1969	Cronos
261	40,232	Gay-Lussac	1969	Gaz Fountain
267	40,213	Cavendish	1971	Gaz Supplier
296	66,341	Nyhammer	1975	OGC Energy
311	100,988	Esso Westernport	1977	Gaz Imperial
312	71,304	Monge	1977	Berge Troll
313	70,914	Razi	1977	Andean Gas
314	72,121	Gas Al-Kuwait	1978	Gas Beauty
315	72,121	Gas Al-Burgan	1979	Gas Al-Burgan
316	72,121	Gas Al-Ahmadi	1979	Gas Al-Ahmadi
317	72,121	Gas Al-Minagish	1980	Gas Al-Minagish
318	22,182	Sydfonn	1978	Clipper Sun
328	85,662	Floreal	1983	Berge Frost
331	81,600	Berge Rachel	1984	Berge Rachel
332	81,600	Berge Racine	1985	Berge Racine
333	81,600	Berge Ragnhild	1986	Berge Ragnhild
Clemna, La Spezia, Italy				
22	1,350	Capo Levante	1979	Capo Levante
CNIM, La Seyne, France				
1374	14,805	Aeolos	1967	Asia Rainbow
1375	14,465	Aeolos II	1967	Galileo
1376	29,866	Hypolite-Worms	1969	Ile de la Réunion
1396	53,400	Antilla Bay	1973	Havmann
1397	53,400	Dorsetown	1973	Hesperus
1398	53,400	Dovertown	1974	Havprins
1416	53,400	Reynosa	1979	Clipper Lady
1417	53,400	Monterrey	1979	Steven N
Daewoo, Okpo, South Korea				
2301	78,680	Anne-Laure	2000	Anne-Laure
2303	35,125	René	2002	René
Euskalduña, Bilbao, Spain				
203	11,188	Alexander Hamilton	1968	Aegis Diligence
Fincantieri. Sestri, Italy				
5962	37,314	Solaro	1996	Solaro

Hull No	Capacity m³	Original Name	Delivery year	Current Name
France Dunkerque, France				
285	52,647	Hampshire	1974	Hermes
286	52,647	Devonshire	1974	Maharshi Vishwamitra
297	74,537	Staffordshire	1977	Yuan Da
Frederikstad, Frederikstad, Norway				
440	24,048	Hektor	1982	Hektor
442	24,048	Hebris	1983	Hebris
Gdynia, Poland				
B550/01	75,650	Höegh Swallow	1976	Gaz Poem
B550/02	75,650	Höegh Swift	1977	Evangelina 1
B551/01	75,650	Northern Arrow	1977	Berge Arrow
B550/03	75,650	Höegh Sword	1978	Berge Sword
B551/02	75,650	Northern Eagle 1	1978	Berge Eagle
8185/1	78,550	Berge Danuta	2000	Berge Danuta
8185/2	78,500	Berge Denise	2000	Berge Denise
Grangemouth Dockyard, United Kingdom				
conversion	679	Quentin	1965	Quentin
Harland & Wolff, Belfast, United Kingdom				
1711	59,725	Isomeria	1982	Isomeria
1712	59,725	Isocardia	1982	Gaz Horizon
Hawthorn Leslie, Hebburn, United Kingdom				
759	11,750	Clerk-Maxwell	1966	Clerk-Maxwell
763	11,474	Mariano Escobedo	1967	Mariano Escobedo
764	3,499	Petroquimico I	1967	Macuiltepetl
766	15,495	Wiltshire	1968	Zallaq
HDW, Kiel, Germany				
1191	18,282	Roland	1968	Andesgas
Hitachi, Ariake, Japan				
4889	39,270	Antwerpen Venture	1996	Touraine
4903	18,152	Agri Viking	1997	Agri Viking
4904	18,159	Euro Viking	1997	Euro Viking

Hull No	Capacity m³	Original Name	Delivery year	Current Name
Hitachi, Innoshima, Japan				
143 conversion	9,470	Nisseki Maru	1962	Beava
conversion	13,145	Toyosu Maru	1963	Toyosu
conversion	13,145	Toyosu Maru	1963	Toyosu
4088	47,424	Yuyo Maru No 10	1966	Yuyo Maru No 10
4163	51,824	Kazutama Maru	1967	Kazutama Maru
4308	73,211	Yusho Maru	1971	Yusho
4320	100,213	Esso Fuji	1973	Esso Fuji
4408	100,181	Palace Tokyo	1974	Palace Tokyo
4666	8,082	Iwakuni Maru	1981	Northern Lights I
4689	83,127	Co-op Sunshine	1983	G. Pioneer
4752	77,755	Hourai Maru	1985	Hourai Maru
4826	77,550	Co-op Sunrise	1987	Berge Kobe
Hyundai, Ulsan, South Korea				
668	35,559	Jane Maersk	1990	Jane Maersk
669	35,559	Jessie Maersk	1991	Jessie Maersk
670	35,559	Jakob Maersk	1991	Jakob Maersk
681	22,500	Nanga Parbat	1991	Nanga Parbat
682	22,478	Annapurna	1991	Annapurna
700	22,478	Spic Diamond	1991	Gaz Diamond
730	35,559	Jesper Maersk	1991	Jesper Maersk
750	76,643	Baltic Flame	1992	Nordanger
1367	22,500	Gaz Millennium	2002	Gaz Millennium
1414	35,000	Lancashire	2002	Lancashire
1422	82,000	Hellas Nautilus	2003	Hellas Nautilus
1423	82,000	Hellas Argosy	2003	Hellas Argosy
1430	35,000	Gas Oriental	2003	Gas Oriental
1436	82,000	Kodaijisan	2003	Kodaijisan
IHI, Aioi, Japan				
2701	80,311	Genkai Maru	1980	Genkai Maru
2865	39,113	Toyosu Maru	1984	Gaz Baraka
2922	80,681	Koho Maru	1985	Iris Gas
IHI, Kure, Japan				
2983	17,900	Kelvin	1990	Victoire
IHI, Nagoya, Japan				
226	46,548	Joyama Maru	1965	Joyama Maru
235	47,124	Bridgestone Maru No 3	1966	Gaz Supplier
244	19,450	M P Grace	1967	Calina

Hull No	Capacity m³	Original Name	Delivery year	Current Name
Kawasaki, Kobe, Japan				
1130	72,344	Bridgestone Maru No 5	1969	Bridgestone Maru No 5
1137	74,477	World Bridgestone	1971	Sea Stone
1171	74,578	Ogden Bridgestone	1973	Yuan Xing
1189	75,958	Sun River	1974	Sunny Gas
1223	80,026	World Concord	1976	Gaz Concord
1224	80,026	World Creation	1976	Gaz Creation
1241	79,963	World Vigour	1977	Gaz Suez
1344	76,313	Clean River	1983	Clean River
1422	75,203	Tsugaru Gloria	1991	Berge Flanders
1425	75,203	Aries Duo	1992	Benny Princess
1429	75,203	Noto Gloria	1992	Noto Gloria
1431	75,178	Musashi Gloria	1993	Musashi Gloria
1433	34,765	Hedda	1993	Hedda
1434	34,765	Helga	1994	Helga
1437	75,386	J A Sunshine	1994	J A Sunshine
1448	37,520	Eeklo	1995	Eeklo
1449	37,510	Elversele	1996	Elversele
Kawasaki, Sakaide, Japan				
1417	75,208	Pacific Harmony	1990	Pacific Harmony
1420	75,203	Crystal Mermaid	1990	Crystal Mermaid
1430	75,211	Co-op Akebono	1993	Co-op Akebono
1456	84,269	Flanders Tenacity	1996	Flanders Tenacity
1469	79,527	Fountain River	1997	Fountain River
1487	84,350	Reggane	1999	Reggane
1492	84,310	Djanet	2000	Djanet
1497	84,300	Formosagas Apollo	2001	Formosagas Apollo
1498	84,300	Formosagas Bright	2001	Formosagas Bright
1500	79,538	Ocean Orchid	2001	Ocean Orchid
1510	82,200	Dynamic Vision	2001	Dynamic Vision
1511	82,200	Dynamic Energy	2002	Dynamic Energy
1515	82,200	Althea Gas	2003	Althea Gas
1518	80,138	Crystal Marine	2003	Ctystal Marine
1519	79,000	Grace River	2002	Grace River
1522	59,200	Clipper Star	2003	Clipper Star
1523	59,200	Crystal Marine	2003	Crystal Marine
1530	59,200	To be named	2003	
1531	59,200	To be named	2003	
1543	59,200	To be named	2004	
1546	59,200	To be named	2004	
1547	59,200	To be named	2004	
1548	59,200	To be named	2004	
Kockums, Malmö, Sweden				
486	25,102	Paul Endacott	1964	Petrogas I
519	26,505	Phillips Arkansas	1969	Gaz Kandla

Hull No	Capacity m³	Original Name	Delivery year	Current Name
Kværner Govan, Govan, United Kingdom				
301	57,179	Helice	1991	Helice
302	57,179	Havfrost	1991	Havfrost
303	57,179	Helios	1992	Helios
304	57,179	Havis	1993	Havis
Mitsubishi, Nagasaki, Japan				
1876	77,290	Tenryu Maru	1982	Gaz Unity
1887	43,671	Nichizan Maru	1982	Libin
1957	82,513	Joyama Maru	1986	Joyama
2023	78,507	Nichiyuh Maru	1989	Nichiyuh Maru
2026	71,913	Gohshu	1990	Gohshu
2028	78,484	Gas Leo	1990	Gas Leo
2034	78,489	Sunny Hope	1990	Sunny Hope
2039	78,478	Gas Roman	1990	Gaz Energy
2029	78,488	Gas Aries	1991	Gas Aries
2037	78,476	Sunway	1991	Sunway
2049	78,482	Pacific Century	1991	Pacific Century
2053	78,488	Inger	1992	N'Kossa II
2056	78,507	Sunny Green	1992	Sunny Green
2070	78,488	Gas Miracle	1992	Gas Miracle
2057	78,488	Gas Al-Mutlaa	1993	Gas Al-Mutlaa
2058	78,475	Gas Al-Gurain	1993	Gas Al-Gurain
2060	78,469	Oval Nova	1993	Oval Nova
2069	78,488	Energy Orpheus	1993	Energy Orpheus
2092	78,462	Gas Scorpio	1995	Gas Scorpio
2103	78,479	G Leader	1995	G Leader
2104	78,502	Gas Vision	1996	Gas Vision
2107	78,451	Lavender Passage	1996	Lavender Passage
2108	78,462	Toyosu Maru	1997	Toyosu Maru
2113	35,418	Brugge Venture	1997	Brugge Venture
2115	35,420	Gas Columbia	1997	Gas Columbia
2119	34,948	Oxfordshire	1997	Oxfordshire
2146	25,302	Carli Bay	1998	Carli Bay
2147	38,961	Eupen	1999	Eupen
2147	78,498	Yuhsho	1999	Yuhsho
2153	78,498	Great Tribune	1999	Great Tribune
2150	78,874	Sunny Joy	2000	Sunny Joy
2161	78,888	Gas Diana	2000	Gas Diana
2164	78,874	Linden Pride	2001	Linden Pride
2166	78,921	Gas Taurus	2001	Gas Taurus
2174	78,929	Yuhsan	2002	Yuhsan
2178	78,000	Lycaste Peace	2003	Lycaste Peace
2179	78,000	Gas Capricorn	2003	Gas Capricorn
2182	78,000	To be named	2003	
2188	78,000	To be named	2004	

Hull No	Capacity m³	Original Name	Delivery year	Current Name
Mitsubishi, Yokohama, Japan				
845	28,837	Bridgestone Maru	1962	Sea Petro
856	36,008	Bridgestone Maru II	1964	Isavana
888	38,161	Yamahide Maru	1966	Bo Bengtsson
889	50,542	Tatsuno Maru	1967	Al-Hada 2
908	70,238	Kanayama Maru	1970	Kanayma Maru
924	70,247	World Rainbow	1971	Gaz Coral
944	70,139	Pine Queen	1974	Gaz Med
946	70,131	Amvrosios	1974	Amvrosios
945	70,162	Nektar	1975	Nektar
954	70,358	Ogden General	1975	Gaz Marmara
955	77,373	Pioneer Louise	1976	Louise
956	77,961	Gas Gemini	1977	Gaz Gemini
957	77,986	Gas Diana	1978	Gas Bauhinia
958	77,327	Gas Libra	1980	Gas Aguila
Mitsui, Tamano, Japan				
658	11,300	Gohshu Maru	1961	Contovello
866	60,990	Izumisan Maru	1970	Izumisan Maru
952	61,203	Tokuho Maru	1974	Rainbow Gas
Moss Rosenberg Værft, Stavanger, Norway				
194	52,647	Höegh Multina	1971	Havgast
195	52,647	Garmula	1972	OGC America
204	52,647	Centum	1978	Havglimt
210	30,455	Berge Fister	1982	Herakles
Moss Rosenberg, Moss, Norway				
201	24,048	Hermion	1984	Hermion
194	24,048	Hektor	1980	José Colomo
200	24,054	Concordia Fjord	1983	Mahashi Dattatreya
Moss Værft, Moss, Norway				
150	11,071	Havgas	1965	Joule
154	11,396	Havfrost	1966	Gaz Channel
155	19,462	Mundogas Rio	1967	Gaz Hudson
160	19,450	Nyhavn	1968	Gaz Master
163	15,285	Havis	1970	Nelina
181	22,764	Garbeta	1975	Maharshi Vyas
Newport News, USA				
conversion	12,854	Marine Eagle	1969	Marine Eagle

Hull No	Capacity m³	Original Name	Delivery year	Current Name
NKK, Tsu, Japan				
72	70,792	Benny Queen	1981	La Forge
75	70,792	Tatsuta Maru	1982	Gaz Meridian
123	78,542	Berge Commander	1991	Berge Commander
124	78,542	Berge Captain	1991	Berge Captain
129	78,542	Berge Clipper	1992	Berge Clipper
131	78,542	Berge Challenger	1992	Berge Challenger
238	82,000	To be named	2004	
Scotts', Greenock, United Kingdom				
771	11,843	Gas Lion	1968	Gas Pilot
Swan Hunter, Hebburn, United Kingdom				
12	31,215	Faraday	1971	Faraday
34	30,724	Lincolnshire	1972	Lincolnshire
83	22,711	Gandara	1976	Maharshi Vasishth
Thyssen Nord, Emden, Germany				
459	54,226	Garinda	1978	Hekabe
460	54,104	Galpara	1978	Havdrott
461	54,104	Galconda	1978	Havkong
462	54,104	Garala	1979	Hemina
Todd Pacific, San Pedro, USA				
116	31,704	Cornucopia	1978	Cornucopia
Verolme, Rotterdam, Netherlands				
676	12,975	William R Grace	1964	Amelina
677	12,975	Joseph P Grace	1964	Savonetta
Wärtsilä, Perno, Finland				
1229	75,680	Gas Rising Sun	1978	Gas Rising Sun
1230	75,680	Berge Sisu	1978	Berge Sisu
1231	75,680	Berge Sisar	1979	Berge Sisar
1232	75,680	Berge Saga	1979	Berge Saga
1233	75,680	Golar Frost	1980	Berge Spirit
1234	75,680	Berge Sund	1981	Berge Sund
1235	75,680	Berge Strand	1982	Berge Strand

Fully Refrigerated LPG Carriers Previous Names

Previous Name	Current Name	Previous Name	Current Name
Abdoun Gas	Egypt Gas	Clyde River	Cronos
Aeolos	Asia Rainbow	Concordia Fjord	Mahashi Dattatreya
Aeolos II	Galileo	Contank Bridgestone	Sea Petro
African Rainbow	Qeshm Gas	Co-op Sunrise	Berge Kobe
Ahkatun	Hugo N	Co-op Sunshine	G. Pioneer
Alex Gas	Egypt Gas	Cypress	Mundogas Atlantic
Alexander Hamilton	Aegis Diligence	Danian Gas	Gaz Kandla
Amy Multina	Gaz Kandla	Darwin	Andean Gas
Antilla Bay	Havmann	David Gas	Gaz Kandla
Antilla Cape	Egypt Gas	Devonshire	Maharshi Vishwamitra
Antwerpen Venture	Touraine	Discaria	Mundogas Atlantic
APCC Gas	Egypt Gas	Discaria Harvest	Mundogas Atlantic
Aries Duo	Benny Princess	Dorsetown	Hesperus
Arquimedes	Pythagore	Dovertown	Havprins
Atlante	Hesperus	Esso Centro America	Gas Venture
Baleares	Hesperus	Esso Parkersburg	Marine Eagle
Baltic Flame	Nordanger	Esso Venezuela	Gas Venture
Benny Queen	La Forge	Esso Westernport	Gaz Imperial
Berge Fister	Herakles	Eupen	Nejma
Blue Ocean	Gaz Poem	Excalibur	Berge Sword
Blue Star	Qeshm Gas	Extol	Berge Troll
Bridgestone Maru	Sea Petro	Fernvalley	Mundogas Atlantic
Bridgestone Maru II	Isavana	Fernwind	Mundogas Europe
Bridgestone Maru No 3	Gaz Supplier	Fernwood	Cronos
Bridgestone Multina	Sea Petro	Floreal	Berge Frost
Butanaval	Kapitan Luca	Flanders Gloria	Berge Flanders
Butanueve	Kapitan Luca	Galconda	Havkong
Caltex Lisbon	Toyosu	Galpara	Havdrott
Cantarell	Harriette N	Gambada	Hesiod
Capella	Qeshm Gas	Gambhira	Kapitan Luca
Capo Ovest	Asia Rainbow	Gandara	Maharshi Vasishth
Cassie Hill	Petrogas I	Garala	Hemina
Cavendish	Gaz Supplier	Garbeta	Maharshi Vyas
Censor	Havmann	Garinda	Hekabe
Centum	Havglimt	Garmula	OGC America
Cerons	Galileo	Gas Al-Kuwait	Gas Beauty

Previous Name	Current Name	Previous Name	Current Name
Gas Al-Kuwait I	Gas Beauty	Isfonn	Excel
Gas Diana	Gas Bauhinia	Isle Hope	Northern Lights I
Gas Enterprise	Andean Gas	Isocardia	Gaz Horizon
Gas Gemini	Gaz Gemini	Iwakuni Maru	Northern Lights I
Gas Gloria	Egypt Gas	Joseph P Grace	Savonetta
Gas King	Gas Al-Burgan	Joyama Maru	Joyama
Gas Libra	Gas Aguila	Katrisa	Andesgas
Gas Lion	Gas Pilot	Kelvin	Victoire
Gas Master	Cronos	Koho Maru	Iris Gas
Gas Poem	Gaz Poem	Kristian Birkeland	Mundogas Europe
Gas Prime	G Pioneer	Lensovet	Gaz Atlantic
Gas Prince	Gas Al-Minagish	Lilac Princess	Gaz Meridian
Gas Princess	Gas Al-Ahmadi	Lily Pacific	Gaz Unity
Gas Queen	Gas Beauty	Lonia Prima	Asia Rainbow
Gas Roman	Gaz Energy	Lord Kelvin	Jag Vayu
Gay-Lussac	Gaz Fountain	Luigi Casale	Qeshm Gas
Gaz Med	Mahashi Dattatreya	Lulligas	Kapitan Luca
Gazana	Havjarl	M P Grace	Calina
General	Gaz Marmara	Mandrill	Havprins
Gloria	Berge Flanders	Mariotte	Asia Rainbow
Gohshu Maru	Contovello	Mondebello	Gas Venture
Golar Frost	Berge Spirit	Monge	Berge Troll
Grand Rextar	Isavana	Monomer Venture	Gas Venture
Great Crane	Contovello	Monterrey	Steven N
Hampshire	Hermes	Mossovet	Gaz Progress
Havfrost	Gaz Channel	Mundogas America	OGC America
Havfrost	Havgast	Mundogas Energy	OGC Energy
Havgas	Joule	Mundogas Orinoco	Yuan Xing
Havis	Nelina	Mundogas Pacific	Cronos
Havpil	Kapitan Luca	Mundogas Rio	Gaz Hudson
Hektor	José Colomo	Murray River	Mundogas Europe
Helikon	Maharshi Vasishth	Nichizan Maru	Libin
Helios	Jag Vayu	Nisseki Maru	Beava
Hemera	Maharshi Vishwamitra	Noble Sky	Gaz Master
Herdis	Jag Vayu	Nopal Tellus	Andesgas
Hermod	Maharshi Vyas	Nordic Rainbow	Qeshm Gas
Höegh Multina	Havgast	Norfolk Multina	Petrogas I
Höegh Skean	Havgast	Northern Arrow	Berge Arrow
Höegh Swallow	Gaz Poem	Northern Eagle 1	Berge Eagle
Höegh Swift	Evangelina 1	Nuevo Laredo	Clipper Sun
Höegh Sword	Berge Sword	Nyhall	Courcheville
Hudson River	Gaz Hudson	Nyhammer	OGC Energy
Hypolite-Worms	Ile de la Réunion	Nyhavn	Gaz Master
Inger	N'Kossa II	Nyholm	Mahashi Dattatreya
Inger Maersk	N'Kossa II	Ocean Frost	Gaz Channel

Previous Name	Current Name	Previous Name	Current Name
Ogden Bridgestone	Yuan Xing	Stena Oceanica	Havprins
Ogden General	Gaz Marmara	Sunset	Toyosu
Orinoco Gas	Yuan Xing	Sun River	Sunny Gas
Oscar Gas	Oscar Viking	Sydfonn	Clipper Sun
Parkersburg	Marine Eagle	Tarauca	Gas Venture
Paul Endacott	Petrogas I	Tatsuno Maru	Al-Hada 2
Pearl River	Mundogas Atlantic	Tatsuta	Gaz Meridian
Petrogas II	Nejma	Tatsuta Maru	Gaz Meridian
Petrologas 2	Evangelina 1	Tenryu Maru	Gaz Unity
Petron Gasul	Sea Petro	Tielrode	Oscar Viking
Petroquimico I	Macuiltepetl	Tokuho Maru	Rainbow Gas
Phillips Arkansas	Gaz Kandla	Toyosu	Gaz Baraka
Pine Queen	Gaz Med	Toyosu Maru	Gaz Baraka
Pioneer Louise	Louise	Toyosu Maru	Toyosu
PNOC Petron Gasul	Sea Petro	Trina Multina	Andesgas
Providence Multina	Hesperus	Tsugaru Gloria	Berge Flanders
Razi	Andean Gas	Westernport	Gaz Imperial
Reliance Gas	Gaz Kandla	William R Grace	Amelina
Reynosa	Clipper Lady	Wiltshire	Zallaq
Ribagorça	Gaz Supplier	World Bridgestone	Sea Stone
Roland	Andesgas	World Concord	Gaz Concord
Sandrina	Hesperus	World Creation	Gaz Creation
Shanta Samett	Mundogas Atlantic	World Rainbow	Gaz Coral
Sheldon Gas	Excel	World Sky	Sea Stone
Sister Katingo	Cornucopia	World Vigour	Gaz Suez
Smolnyy	Havrim	Yamahide Maru	Bo Bengtsson
Sombeke	Australgas	Yusho Maru	Yusho
Spic Diamond	Gaz Diamond	Yuyo Maru	Yuyo
Staffordshire	Yuan Da	Zeebrugge	Mahashi Dattatreya
Star River I	Sunny Gas	Zenon	Galileo

Appendix 8

Fully Refrigerated LPG Carriers Name Changes

Aeolos 1968, Mariotte 1976, Capo Ovest 1982, Lonia Prima 1988, Asia Rainbow

Aeolos II 1968, Cerons 1971, Zenon 1974, Galileo

Ahkatun 1999, Hugo N

Alexander Hamilton 1973, Aegis Diligence

Antilla Bay 1987, Censor 1987, Havmann

Antilla Cape 1983, Gas Gloria 1997, APCC Gas 1997, Abdoun Gas 1998, Alex Gas 2003, Egypt Gas

Antwerpen Venture 1997, Touraine

Aries Duo 1996, Benny Princess

Arquimedes 1975, Pythagore

Baltic Flame 2001, Nordanger

Benny Queen 1996, La Forge

Berge Fister 1988, Herakles

Bridgestone Maru 1971, Bridgestone Multina 1978, Contank Bridgestone 1979, PNOC Petron Gasul 1982, Petron Gasul 1983, Sea Petro

Bridgestone Maru II 1974, Grand Rextar 1981, Isavana

Bridgestone Maru No 3 1981, Ribagorça 1989, Gaz Supplier

Butanueve 1971, Butanaval 1973, Gambhira 1986, Havpil 1991, Lulligas 1994, Kapitan Luca

Cantarell 2000, Harriette N

Capella 1973, Luigi Casale 1987, Blue Star 1989, African Rainbow 1989, Nordic Rainbow 1997, Qeshm Gas

Cavendish 1995, Gaz Supplier

Centum 1987, Havglimt

Co-op Sunrise 2003, Berge Kobe

Co-op Sunshine 1994, Gas Prime 2001, G Pioneer

Concordia Fjord 1990, Nyholm 1996, Zeebrugge 1996, Gaz Med 1996, Zeebrugge 2002, Mahashi Dattatreya

Cypress 1973, Fernvalley 1979, Discaria 1985, Discaria Harvest 1987, Shanta Samett 1989, Pearl River 1993, Mundogas Atlantic

Devonshire 1989, Hemera 1998, Maharshi Vishwamitra

Dorsetown 1973, Providence Multina 1979, Atlante 1980, Sandrina 1985, Baleares 1987, Hesperus

Esso Westernport 1994, Westernport 1997, Gaz Imperial

Eupen 1984, Petrogas II 1986, Eupen 1995, Nejma

Floreal 1991, Berge Frost

Fort Cornwallis 1946, Esso Parkersburg 1956, Parkersburg 1968, Marine Eagle

Galconda 1987, Havkong

Galpara 1987, Havdrott

Gambada 1986, Hesiod

Gandara 1986, Helikon 1996, Maharshi Vasishth

Garala 1987, Hemina

Garbeta 1987, Hermod 1996, Maharshi Vyas

Garinda 1986, Hekabe

Garmula 1979, Mundogas America 1998, OGC America

Gas Al-Ahmadi 1987, Gas Princess 1989, Gas Al-Ahmadi

Gas Al-Burgan 1987, Gas King 1989, Gas Al-Burgan

Gas Al-Kuwait 1 1978, Gas Al-Kuwait 1987, Gas Queen 1989, Gas Al-Kuwait 2003, Gas Beauty

Gas Al-Minagish 1987, Gas Prince 1989, Gas Al-Minagish

Gas Diana 1989, Gas Bauhinia

Gas Gemini 2003, Gas Gemini

Gas Libra 2001, Gas Aguila

Gas Lion 1980, Gas Pilot

Gas Master 1974, Fernwood 1979, Mundogas Pacific 1990, Clyde River 1996, Cronos

Gas Roman 2003, Gaz Energy

Gay-Lussac 1981, Gaz Fountain

Gazana 1987, Havjarl

Gohshu Maru 1973, Great Crane 1980, Contovello

Golar Frost 1989, Berge Spirit

Hampshire 1989, Hermes

Havfrost 1981, Ocean Frost 1982, Gaz Channel

Havgas 1974, Joule

Havis 1991, Nelina

Hektor 1981, José Colomo

Höegh Multina 1977, Höegh Skean 1986, Havfrost 1987, Havgast

Höegh Swallow 1979, Blue Ocean 1988, Gas Poem 1995, Gaz Poem

Höegh Swift 1982, Petrolagas 2 2003, Evangelina 1

Höegh Sword 1986, Excalibur 1988, Berge Sword

Hypolite-Worms 1974, Ile de la Réunion

Inger 1992, Inger Maersk 1996, N'Kossa II

Isfonn 1983, Sheldon Gas 1987, Excel

Isocardia 99, Gaz Horizon

Iwakuni Maru 1995, Isle Hope 1996, Northern Lights I

Joseph P Grace 1987, Savonetta

Joyama Maru 1995, Joyama

Kelvin 1996, Victoire

Koho Maru 1995, Iris Gas

Kristian Birkeland 1975, Fernwind 1979, Mundogas Europe 1991, Murray River 1993, Mundogas Europe

Lensovet 1992, Gaz Atlantic

Lord Kelvin 1987, Helios 1991, Herdis 1997, Jag Vayu

M P Grace 1992, Calina

Malmros Multina 1979, Mandrill 1980, Stena Oceanica 1988, Havprins

Monge 1987, Extol 1988, Berge Troll

Monterry 1999, Steven N

Mossovet 1992, Gaz Progress

Mundogas Rio 1989, Hudson River 1995, Gaz Hudson

Nichizan Maru 1998, Libin

Nisseki Maru 1969, Beava

Northern Arrow 1984, Berge Arrow

Northern Eagle 1 1984, Berge Eagle

Nyhall 1996, Courcheville

Nyhammer 1994, Mundogas Energy 1997, OGC Energy

Nyhaven 1986, Noble Sky 1989, Nyhavn 1993, Gaz Master

Ogden Bridgestone 1985, Orinoco Gas 1988, Mundogas Orinoco 1998, Yuan Xing

Ogden General 1986, General 1997, Gaz Marmara

Paul Endacott 1973, Norfolk Multina 1978, Cassie Hill 1978, Petrogas I

Petroquimico I 1989, Macuiltepetl

Phillips Arkansas 1971, Amy Multina 1977, Reliance Gas 1983, Danian Gas 1983, David Gas 1998, Gaz Kandla

Pine Queen 1999, Gaz Med

Pioneer Louise 2003, Louise

Razi 1980, Gas Enterprise 1992, Darwin 2001, Andean Gas

Reynosa 1999, Clipper Lady

Roland 1974, Trina Multina 1977, Katrisa 1982, Nopal Tellus 1983, Andesgas

Sister Katingo 1978, Cornucopia

Smolnyy 1994, Havrim

Sombeke 2002, Australgas

Spic Diamond 2000, Gaz Diamond

Staffordshire 1998, Yuan Da

Sun River 1997, Star River I 1998, Sunny Gas

Sunset 1952, Caltex Lisbon 1963, Toyosu Maru 1977, Toyosu

Sydfonn 1979, Nuevo Laredo 2000, Clipper Sun

Tarauca 1945, Mondebello 1947, Esso Venezuela 1962, Esso Centro America 1969, Monomer Venture 1984, Gas Venture

Tatsuno Maru 1982, Al-Hada 2

Tatsuta Maru 1985, Tatsuta 1993, Lilac Princess 2003, Gaz Meridian

Tenryu Maru 1988, Lily Pacific 2003, Gaz Unity

Tielrode 1990, Oscar Gas 1996, Oscar Viking

Tokuho Maru 1984, Rainbow Gas

Toyosu Maru 1994, Toyosu 1996, Gaz Baraka

Tsugaru Gloria 1996, Gloria 1997, Flanders Gloria 2003, Berge Flanders

William R Grace 1992, Amelina

Wiltshire 1994, Zallaq

World Bridgestone 1985, World Sky 1999, Sea Stone

World Concord 1993, Gaz Concord

World Creation 1996, Gaz Creation

World Rainbow 2000, Gaz Coral

World Vigour 1995, Gaz Suez

Yamahide Maru 1982, Bo Bengtsson

Yusho Maru 1978, Yusho

Yuyo Maru 1990, Yuyo

Index